Adobe® Flex® 3.0 For Dummies®

Keyboard Shortcuts

Flex Builder includes a number of keyboard shortcuts that can let you use some powerful (yet often unknown) features and speed up repetitive tasks. You use the shortcut keys in this table while editing source code; some commands are context sensitive and perform tasks on selected text.

Command	Key Combo	What It Does
Code Assist	Ctrl+spacebar	Displays code-completion hints and helps you quickly write entire lines of code by typing only a few letters
Organize Imports	Ctrl+Shift+O (Windows) ⌘+Shift+O (Mac)	Organizes the import statements at the top of any ActionScript file
Context-Sensitive Help	F1 (Windows) ⌘+Shift+/ (Mac)	Opens Flex Help topics related to the ActionScript or MXML code you highlighted
Quick Outline	Ctrl+O	Opens an in-place outline view of the class you're editing
Go to Documentation	Shift+F2	Opens the API documentation for any selected class in the Flex framework
Go to Line	Ctrl+L (Windows) ⌘+L (Mac)	Opens a dialog box to let you jump to any specific line of code
Open Resource	Ctrl+Shift+R (Windows) ⌘+Shift+R (Mac)	Lets you quickly jump to any file located within your workspace
Open Type	Ctrl+Shift+T (Windows) ⌘+Shift+T (Mac)	Lets you quickly find any class by name (similar to the Open Resource shortcut)
Find Declarations	Ctrl+G (Windows) ⌘+G (Mac)	Launches a search for all references to the variable, function, or class type you select within your workspace
Debug Last Launched	Ctrl+F11 (Windows) ⌘+F11 (Mac)	Runs the last launched Flex application in Debug mode
Run Last Launched	Ctrl+Shift+F11 (Windows) ⌘+Shift+F11 (Mac)	Runs the last Flex application in Debug mode
Show All Shortcut Keys	Ctrl+Shift+L (Windows) ⌘+Shift+L (Mac)	Displays a complete list of all available shortcut keys (in case this list isn't enough for you)

Adobe® Flex® 3.0 For Dummies®

Cheat Sheet

Quick Links

- **LiveDocs:** `http://livedocs.adobe.com/flex/3`

  The official Flex documentation from Adobe, known as *LiveDocs*, includes API documentation and comprehensive Help documentation.

- **ActionScript 3 Language Reference:** `http://livedocs.adobe.com/flex/3/langref/index.html`

  The ActionScript 3 Language Reference contains full documentation of every class in the Flex 3 framework. This complete documentation covers every class and property that you can use on all Flex framework components.

- **Flex Bug Database:** `http://bugs.adobe.com/flex`

  The Flex open-source bug database is a searchable list of all known bugs in all Flex products, including the Flex SDK and Flex Builder IDE. As a Flex developer, you can submit bugs directly to the bug database to the Flex team at Adobe.

- **Flex Developer Center:** `www.adobe.com/devnet/flex`

  Adobe Flex DevNet contains articles and tutorials to guide you through the learning process. It also contains the user-generated Flex Cookbook.

- **Flex Showcase:** `http://flex.org/showcase`

  The Flex.org showcase contains hundreds of sample Flex applications. Use the showcase to get inspiration or to find impressive examples to "sell" to your boss the decision to choose Flex.

- **Flex Builder Trial download:** `www.adobe.com/go/flex_trial`

  You can download a fully functional, free trial version of Flex Builder and use it to make working Flex applications for 30 days. The only limitation during the trial period is that the chart components display a watermark.

- **Flex Builder, free for students and educators:** `www.flexregistration.com`

  The full version of Flex Builder is free for all students and faculty members at educational institutions. Visit the registration Web site to submit proof of eligibility to receive your free Flex Builder license.

For Dummies: Bestselling Book Series for Beginners

Adobe® Flex® 3.0 FOR DUMMIES®

by Doug McCune and Deepa Subramaniam

WILEY

Wiley Publishing, Inc.

Adobe® Flex® 3.0 For Dummies®

Published by
Wiley Publishing, Inc.
111 River Street
Hoboken, NJ 07030-5774

www.wiley.com

Copyright © 2008 by Wiley Publishing, Inc., Indianapolis, Indiana

Published by Wiley Publishing, Inc., Indianapolis, Indiana

Published simultaneously in Canada

For general information on our other products and services, please contact our Customer Care Department within the U.S. at 800-762-2974, outside the U.S. at 317-572-3993, or fax 317-572-4002.

For technical support, please visit www.wiley.com/techsupport.

Wiley also publishes its books in a variety of electronic formats. Some content that appears in print may not be available in electronic books.

Library of Congress Control Number: 2008932381

ISBN: 978-0-470-27792-8

Manufactured in the United States of America

10 9 8 7 6 5 4 3 2 1

WILEY

About the Authors

Doug McCune is a passionate Flex developer, consultant, and community contributor. He has been developing Flex applications since 2004 and is currently a Principal Software Engineer at Universal Mind. Doug received a Bachelor of Arts degree in Science, Technology, and Society from Stanford University. Doug is active in the Flex open-source community and maintains a blog of his thoughts, code samples, and tutorials at www.dougmccune.com. He co-founded FlexLib, a leading resource for open-source Flex components created by community developers. Doug also enjoys speaking at Flex and Flash conferences — he has spoken at 360|Flex and Flash on the Beach.

Deepa Subramaniam is a Computer Scientist working on the Flex Framework team at Adobe. She joined Macromedia/Adobe in 2003, straight out of University of California, Berkeley where she received her Bachelor of Arts degree in Computer Science (Go Bears!). Deepa joined the early efforts that culminated in Flex 1.0 and has been working on Flex ever since. She might be described as one of the most enthusiastic Flex team members and is thrilled to be working with such bright engineers on such a cool product. Deepa is an active member of the Flex community, often speaking at large Flex and RIA conferences like Adobe MAX and 360|Flex. You can learn more about Deepa at her Web site, which includes her popular Flex blog, at www.iamdeepa.com.

Dedication

We dedicate this book to Doc, for always keeping us on the clock and in good spirits.

Authors' Acknowledgments

We would like to thank Katie Feltman, Kim Darosett, and everyone else at Wiley who made this book happen. Thank you for believing in us and pushing us to the finish line. We also want to thank Darron Schall for his superb technical editing of the book. And finally, we would like to thank everyone at Adobe, especially the Flex and Flex Builder teams, for encouraging us and offering technical support whenever we needed it. You guys are just awesome.

Doug's Acknowledgments

I would like to thank the loving and beautiful Jocelyn Sze — your patience and support during this process have been invaluable. You are my favorite. I also want to thank my father. As I write this, he is in the middle of the ocean sailing single-handedly across the Atlantic. Thank you, Dad, for never ceasing to inspire.

Deepa's Acknowledgments

This book would not have been possible without the love and encouragement of my amazing parents, S.N.P (Sam) and Amirtham Subramaniam, as well as my rocking sister, Suguna. They never waver with their loving support, and for this, I am ever thankful. Much love Amma, Appa, and Goons! A big thank you also goes to my extended group of friends who have listened to me chatter away about this book, Flex, and my life in general. Your friendship means so much to me.

Publisher's Acknowledgments

We're proud of this book; please send us your comments through our online registration form located at www.dummies.com/register/.

Some of the people who helped bring this book to market include the following:

Acquisitions and Editorial, and Media Development

Project Editor: Kim Darosett

Senior Acquisitions Editor: Katie Feltman

Copy Editor: Becky Whitney

Technical Editor: Darron Schall

Editorial Manager: Leah Cameron

Media Development Project Manager: Laura Moss-Hollister

Media Development Assistant Project Manager: Jenny Swisher

Media Development Assistant Producers: Angela Denny, Josh Frank, Shawn Patrick, and Kit Malone

Editorial Assistant: Amanda Foxworth

Sr. Editorial Assistant: Cherie Case

Cartoons: Rich Tennant (www.the5thwave.com)

Composition Services

Project Coordinator: Erin Smith

Layout and Graphics: Ana Carrillo, Nikki Gately, Laura Pence, Christin Swinford, Christine Williams

Proofreaders: Melissa Bronnenberg, Christine Sabooni

Indexer: Potomac Indexing, LLC

Publishing and Editorial for Technology Dummies

    Richard Swadley, Vice President and Executive Group Publisher

    Andy Cummings, Vice President and Publisher

    Mary Bednarek, Executive Acquisitions Director

    Mary C. Corder, Editorial Director

Publishing for Consumer Dummies

    Diane Graves Steele, Vice President and Publisher

Composition Services

    Gerry Fahey, Vice President of Production Services

    Debbie Stailey, Director of Composition Services

Contents at a Glance

Table of Contents

Introduction

*T*here has never been a better time to be a software developer. Web-based applications have come a long way since the early 1990s. You can now create applications that provide amazingly rich experiences, all of which can be delivered through a simple Web browser to any computer in the world. Rich Internet Applications (RIAs) aren't just a passing fad; they signal the emergence of a new breed of powerful, immersive applications that will lead the evolution of the Web.

Flex is on the forefront of this movement. And, the fact that you took the first step by picking up this book means that you're part of this exciting time. RIA developers are making applications that people didn't think were possible. With Flex, you can create full enterprise-scale Web applications that have as much interactivity as the best desktop applications. Flex enables some exciting possibilities. We hope that this book exposes this powerful technology to a much wider audience and lowers the barrier for new developers.

Flex lets you leverage the power of the Adobe Flash technology to make large applications. And, because Flash is deployed on nearly all Internet-connected computers, you're developing for a near-ubiquitous platform without ever having to worry about browser differences and incompatibilities. The move to Flex from other Web technologies means that you can focus on creating impressive applications rather than debug in three different browsers. And, because Flex is based on Flash, you can instantly add video and other rich media to your applications.

So, if you're ready to step up your game and start making the next generation of Web applications, crack open this book and get started. Welcome to Flex!

About This Book

Most books about Flex are massive and assume that the reader has been programming since age 12. *Adobe Flex 3.0 For Dummies,* on the other hand, has been written specifically for the beginning Flex developer. If you have heard about Flex, but aren't quite sure what all the buzz is about, this book is for you. We hope that our enthusiasm is contagious because we truly believe that Flex is the most exciting program a software developer can use.

Foolish Assumptions

Adobe Flex 3.0 For Dummies is an introductory book, so we don't assume that you already know how to use Flex, although we hope that you know enough about it to realize that it's something you want to use. Part I of this book covers some general programming concepts that you need for developing Flex applications; however, we don't cover the most basic programming topics. If you have experience in writing code in another language, such as JavaScript, Java, or C++, you shouldn't have any trouble because we introduce ActionScript (which is the language you use for Flex). We do assume that you've written code in another programming language. If you come from a background in using Flash and ActionScript 2, be sure to brush up on the first few chapters to make the transition to ActionScript 3. (After you do, you'll never go back.)

We also assume that you have a cursory understanding of HTML. Although Flex doesn't use HTML, some of the markup language used in Flex applications is similar to HTML, and we draw analogies between the two.

Conventions Used in This Book

When we mention new terms, we write them in *italics,* followed by explanations of the terms. Also, we include a lot of sample code in this book because we figure that one of the best ways to find out how to write code is to see it. The code in this book appears in a special font, as shown here:

```
text="Hello World"
```

How This Book Is Organized

Adobe Flex 3.0 For Dummies is organized into six main parts, which contain a total of 20 chapters. Don't feel that you need to read these parts in sequential order; you can jump around as much as you like, and each part is meant to stand on its own. The beginning of the book introduces Flex and some general programming concepts that are useful if you haven't done much object-oriented programming. Depending on your background, you may want to start by jumping straight to the meat of the Flex framework in Part III, or start at the beginning with an overview of ActionScript and MXML in Part I. Part V is the only part that covers more advanced topics and probably requires that you read some of the earlier content before tackling it.

Part I: Introducing Flex

In Part I, we introduce Flex and the technology that you use to create jaw-dropping RIAs. Chapter 1 describes the evolution of Web technologies and how Flex stacks up against some competing technologies. Without overloading you with complex details, we help you jump right into building your first Flex application in Chapter 2. Then, in Chapter 3, we back up a bit and explain some important object-oriented programming principles.

Part II: Using Flex Builder (The Flex IDE)

Part II is all about the tool you use to create Flex applications: Flex Builder. Chapter 4 gives you an overview of Flex Builder, and then we divide the content to highlight developer-focused features (Chapter 5) and designer-focused features (Chapter 6).

Part III: The Flex Framework and Charting Components

Flex contains a large and powerful toolset of components that you use to create applications. In Part III, we dive head first into the Flex framework and show examples of using all the different components. The chapters in this part are fairly self-contained, although later chapters might reference components that we cover earlier. Each chapter covers a set of related components, and at the end of each chapter, a larger example ties together all the components covered in the chapter.

Part IV: Working with Data in Flex

Flex applications are only as good as the data that drives them. Chapter 12 covers data binding, which is one key piece that makes Flex development so powerful. Chapter 13 dives into data collections, and Chapter 14 explains how to pull data from other sources on the Web.

Part V: Exploring Advanced Flex Topics

The first four parts cover the bulk of Flex, but in this part we dive into a few selected topics that are more complex than the other parts. In Chapter 15, we explore the inner workings of the Flex "manager" classes, such as PopUpManager and SystemManager. Chapter 16 delves into component architecture and touches on custom component development. Chapters 17 and 18 cover elements that give your applications a bit more kick, such as transitions, skins, and styling.

Part VI: The Part of Tens

The Part of Tens consists of a few fun lists that let you continue finding out about Flex after you finish this book. Chapter 19 has a list of ten open-source projects that you can freely use in any of your Flex projects. (Haven't you been dying to play with a 3D engine?) Chapter 20 lists ten resources that are essential bookmarks for all Flex developers.

Companion Web site

We write quite a bit of code in this book, but don't worry: You don't have to retype it all by hand. Most of the code that you see here is provided on this book's companion Web site:

```
www.dummies.com/go/adobeflexfd
```

You can download the code and then copy and paste it directly into your Flex projects.

Additionally, a bonus chapter titled "Optimizing Your Flex Applications" is available for downloading from the companion Web site. This chapter gives you some optimization tips to help streamline your Flex application's performance.

Icons Used in This Book

As you're reading, you'll notice a few funny-looking icons on the edge of the page. Here's what each of these icons means:

The Tip icon points out some information that we think is especially important or interesting. It's often something that might not be obvious but that saves you time and makes Flex development even easier.

This icon marks certain nuggets of information that we think are extra important to remember. This information is good to drill into your head because we're sure that it will come up repeatedly in your Flex development.

Sometimes we throw in some extra details that aren't essential but can give you a broader understanding of what's going on behind the scenes. This information often includes details about the inner workings of Flex.

 We all make mistakes, and we use this icon to warn you of potential mistakes (ones we've already made!).

Where to Go from Here

If you're brand-new to Flex, the first few chapters provide an overview of the core concepts that become important building blocks. If you already have experience in programming (with ActionScript or a language such as JavaScript), you can probably jump past a chapter or two in Part I. Every chapter in *Adobe Flex 3.0 For Dummies* is meant to stand on its own, so feel free to jump around as you like and find information in the order that interests you the most.

Part I
Introducing Flex

The 5th Wave   By Rich Tennant

"It's a horse racing Web application. It analyzes my betting history and makes suggestions. Right now it's suggesting I try betting on football."

In this part . . .

We agree with you: Flex can be overwhelming in the beginning. Part I eases you into the world of Flex by introducing the core concepts and providing a bit of context so that you understand how Flex fits in with other, related technologies. Chapter 1 talks about the evolution of Flex and compares Flex with other software products — and then explains why Flex comes out on top, of course! After getting to know Flex a bit, you jump right in with Chapter 2 and start building an application. Then in Chapter 3, we back up and explain some of the key programming concepts that you use in Flex development. If you're already familiar with Flex or object-oriented programming (OOP), you can probably jump straight to Part II. But if you haven't been exposed to OOP principles, take a little time to review these chapters.

Chapter 1

Getting to Know Flex

In This Chapter

▶ Understanding what Rich Internet Applications (RIAs) are

▶ Comparing Flex to other RIA technologies: Flash, AJAX, and Silverlight

▶ Taking Flex applications offline by using Adobe Integrated Runtime (AIR)

Adobe Flex is an application development platform that you can use to build Rich Internet Applications (RIAs). Flex applications are Web-based, but they provide immersive levels of interactivity and rich media experiences that make them seem more like computer desktop programs than traditional Web applications. Flex is the ideal technology to use when you want to create complex data visualization, performance dashboards, multimedia experiences, and countless other interactive applications. RIAs are raising the bar for Web applications, and Flex is leading the way. In this chapter, we discuss what Flex is, what it isn't, and how it compares to other technologies.

Using Flex to Develop Rich Internet Applications

The computer world has come a long way from static HyperText Markup Language (HTML) Web pages. Over the past two decades, rich online experiences have gradually evolved into RIAs. Flex is on the forefront of technology that allows you to create such engaging Web-based applications, but it has taken nearly 20 years since the first HTML page was created to get to where we are now. (See the nearby sidebar for more on the journey from HTML to RIA.)

Understanding what an RIA is

The term *Rich Internet Application* (RIA) was coined in a Macromedia white-paper written in 2002 to describe a new model for application development that separated the back-end data services from a rich front-end client. One of the cornerstones of RIA development is the ability to asynchronously load data within the application. Simple HTML Web pages require a full page refresh to load new data. RIAs, on the other hand, load data *asynchronously,* which means they can load chunks of data without requiring page refreshes and they keep track of the application state in memory. Flex applications are *stateful clients*, which means they store data about the current state of the application, such as the content of a shopping cart, in memory in the client.

RIAs usually load data by using eXtensible Markup Language (XML). Asynchronously loading XML is an integral part of all RIA technologies (not only Flex). Version 4 of Flash, which was released in 1999, was the first version of Flash that let developers load external XML data into Flash applications.

Taking a look at the rise of Flex

Macromedia, which Adobe later acquired, introduced the first version of Flex in March of 2004. Initially, the first two major releases, Flex 1 and 1.5, were expensive server-based products. A license for Flex 1.5 cost about $15,000, and you had to deploy a server application that would compile your Flex applications and serve them to the user. These initial versions of Flex were based on Flash Player 7 and ActionScript 2, and the code editor was based on the Macromedia Dreamweaver editor.

The release of Flex 2 marked a dramatic shift in the product line. Flex 2 was no longer a server technology at all; instead, Flex was a completely client-side product. The cost dropped dramatically, and Adobe rewrote the entire Flex framework and the Integrated Development Environment (IDE) from the ground up. Flex 2 was based on Flash Player 9 and ActionScript 3, which brought serious performance gains.

Flex 3 added additional functionality to Flex Builder, such as refactoring and enhanced styling support, as well as new data visualization components in the Flex framework. Flex 3 also marked the official open-source release of the Flex SDK and Flex compiler. For more on the open-source aspect of Flex, visit `http://opensource.adobe.com`.

Defining Flex

Defining exactly what Flex is can be confusing because Flex actually includes a combination of different technologies. Flex is not a single software product, but instead includes the following four main pieces:

✔ **Languages:** ActionScript 3 and MXML

You use a combination of ActionScript, a scripting language, and MXML, a markup language, to create Flex applications. MXML is similar to HTML, so if you have experience creating HTML Web pages, then you should be able to figure out MXML pretty easily.

✔ **Component framework:** Flex SDK

The *Flex SDK* (also known as the *Flex framework*) is a set of user interface components, such as lists, buttons, and charts, that you use to build Flex applications. The Flex SDK (with the exception of the charting package) is free and open source.

✔ **Integrated Development Environment (IDE):** Flex Builder

You use Flex Builder to edit your code, compile your applications, debug your code, and profile performance. Flex Builder is an integrated development environment (IDE) sold by Adobe.

✔ **Cross-browser runtime:** Flash Player

You deploy Flex applications in a Web browser with the Flash Player plug-in. You can also deploy Flex applications as standalone desktop applications by using the Adobe Integrated Runtime (AIR).

From HTML to RIA

When programmers began tinkering with the Web, they used HTML to create Web pages that looked like actual pages of a book. These pages contained a bunch of text that someone wrote and published for the world to read. Those were the good old days of choppy animated images and heavy use of the `<blink>` tag, which was about as "rich" as the Internet got in the early '90s. Then, Web servers became more sophisticated and started serving up dynamic content, depending on what users were looking for or how they interacted with the Web site. For the first time, Web pages started turning into *Web applications.*

Server-side languages, such as Java, PHP, and ColdFusion, increased the capabilities of Web applications on the back-end. An e-commerce site could let you keep track of items in your shopping cart while you browsed the retailer's site, but each time you added an item, the full Web page would have to reload so that the number of items shown in your cart would stay updated. The state of the application was stored completely on the server, either in memory or in a database. Whenever the server wanted to show you something new, you were sent to a new static HTML page.

But then those static Web pages became animated when a small company called FutureWave Software released FutureSplash Animator, which was purchased by Macromedia and renamed to Flash in 1996. A whole new breed of silly animated movies and impressive visual effects appeared. The Flash platform brought a greater level of interactivity to the Web than ever before. Designers could create interactive visual experiences that went far beyond what was possible with simple HTML.

Flash 5 included the ActionScript programming language, which turned Flash into much more than a simple animation tool. Developers started creating complex Flash interactive experiences by combining the visual and programming capabilities to produce full-blown applications within a Web browser. The first RIAs were being created before the term RIA was widely used or understood. Then in 2004 Macromedia released the first version of Flex. Finally developers had a tool that was specifically for creating RIAs.

What's next?

Adobe is actively developing Flex 4, codenamed Gumbo. This version will focus on an improved workflow between developers and designers, and will likely include an improved component framework model to more gracefully separate the visual design of your Flex applications from the underlying code. Toward a similar goal, an additional product in the Flex product line (code-named Thermo) will focus specifically on allowing designers to create complex RIA user interfaces and interactions by using a visual editor, which will create Flex application code that the designer and developer can share.

Flex has been largely in a class of its own when it comes to RIA development platforms, but that reign is now being challenged because some serious competitors are entering the RIA market. Microsoft's Silverlight platform and Sun's JavaFX are two RIA development products aimed directly at taking on Flex. Over the next few years, the competition will get serious, which can only be a good thing for all the developers out there. RIA development is an exciting field; you've chosen wisely!

Comparing Flex to Flash, AJAX, and Silverlight

Because you bought this book, we assume you've decided that Flex is the right choice for your project. But, if you need to sell the decision to your boss, he or she will probably ask you how Flex compares to related technologies. The following sections summarize some of the key differences between Flex and a few other RIA technologies.

Flex versus Flash

Whenever Doug tries to explain what he does for a living, someone always asks whether Flex is Flash. This question quickly leads to a heated discussion about Flash advertisements, and he has to calm everyone down and explain that, fundamentally, Flex is a Flash-based technology, but no, he doesn't make those annoying ads — he makes applications. Flex is an application development framework and toolset that you can use to create RIAs. These applications are delivered over the Internet by using the Flash Player.

So, what's the difference between Flex and Flash? The following list identifies a few of the most important features that Flex offers that are not available in Flash:

- ✔ **The Flex framework:** Flash has its own component set that has some of the same functionality as the Flex SDK, but it does not provide as many components and does not include charting components, layout containers, and other framework features that are very useful for developing large applications.

- ✔ **MXML:** You can use MXML markup to create your Flex applications, but this markup language is not available in Flash. Flash does use the same ActionScript 3 scripting language, however.

- ✔ **A powerful Integrated Development Environment (IDE):** Flex Builder was designed specifically to build applications, as opposed to the Flash Authoring tool, which was originally designed to create animations. You can use both tools to create RIAs, but Flex Builder has features like code-hinting, a powerful debugger, and a profiler that make it a more powerful development tool.

You can use Flash, rather than Flex, to create RIAs, but you have to work in the Flash Authoring environment, which means you don't get the benefits of Flex Builder (such as code hinting), and you can't use the MXML markup language. You may find the Flash Authoring tool really helpful if you're creating animated movies. It uses the timeline metaphor when you create animations and includes drawing tools. Flex Builder, on the other hand, is designed for application development, not animation creation. Flex Builder doesn't include any drawing tools, and it has no timeline.

If you have to decide between Flex and Flash for a specific project, think about exactly what kind of project you're working on. Flex excels when you're creating large desktop-like applications, sharing work among a team of developers, or visualizing data with charts and graphs. For other kinds of projects that require complete control over the visual experience, such as games or advertisements, Flash might be a more appropriate choice.

Flex versus AJAX

Asynchronous JavaScript and XML (AJAX) is a technique that you can use to load data into HTML Web pages without refreshing the full page. Instead of sending a new HTML page to the user's Web browser for every change, AJAX applications send XML asynchronously and update relevant portions of the screen when needed. By using AJAX, you often end up with a much more responsive user interface and a more desktop-like application experience. Flex applications also asynchronously load XML data.

JavaScript and ActionScript are very similar languages; both are based on a language specification called *ECMAScript*, which is developed by Ecma International, a collective group of representatives from various technology companies (Adobe is a member). The ECMAScript specification has had few revisions. ECMAScript Edition 3 is the latest published edition, and Ecma is currently developing Edition 4. JavaScript is currently an implementation of ECMAScript Edition 3. The current version of JavaScript most closely resembles ActionScript 2, which also implemented ECMAScript Edition 3. Adobe released ActionScript 3 in 2006, which is based on the preliminary draft of ECMAScript Edition 4. After Ecma officially releases a new version of ECMAScript Edition 4 and Web browsers support an updated version of JavaScript, the JavaScript programming language should become more like ActionScript 3.

Because of the similarities between the ActionScript and JavaScript languages, and their similar approaches to asynchronously loading XML data, the fundamental benefits of Flex have to do with its underlying Flash Player technology. Here's a rundown of some of those benefits:

- ✔ **Multimedia capabilities:** Flash Player allows you to create a whole range of rich multimedia experiences that you simply can't achieve by using HTML and JavaScript. Flash has powerful graphics capabilities that can do complex drawing and image manipulation. In addition, Flash supports audio and video streaming, so many leading online video sites use it to play video on the Web.

- ✔ **Cross-browser support:** You can be sure that any Flex application you develop will look and behave the same way in all browsers on all platforms. Web browsers all have their own quirks and idiosyncrasies when it comes to how they render HTML and even how they run JavaScript. When you develop AJAX applications, you need to test your application in multiple Web browsers to make sure your application is compatible with them all. However, because Flex applications rely on the Flash Player, you can be assured that your application will look the same, pixel for pixel, and behave the same across all browsers.

Flex versus Silverlight

Microsoft's competitive RIA technology is Silverlight, a browser plug-in, like Adobe's Flash Player. Just like you have to install the Flash Player plug-in to run Flex applications, you need the Silverlight plug-in to run Silverlight applications. Because Silverlight is fairly new, the Silverlight plug-in isn't nearly as common as Flash Player. Silverlight will likely become more widely used in the future, but right now, the Flash Player plug-in has a strong advantage because of the large number of computers on which it is installed.

The first release of Silverlight 1.0 included the browser plug-in and focused on streaming video on the Web. This release certainly competed with Flash Player because it focused on some of the media features of Flash, but it didn't really threaten Flex's position because Silverlight 1.0 didn't contain a set of user interface controls that you could use to build RIAs. Silverlight 1.0 provided all the low-level graphics capabilities but none of the application framework pieces.

In early 2008, Microsoft released the first beta version of Silverlight 2.0 (originally named Silverlight 1.1), which included a set of UI controls, such as a DataGrid, CheckBox, and Slider. These new controls make Silverlight a closer competitor with Flex. The competition between Flex and Silverlight has just begun, and it's too early to draw any firm conclusions about how serious a competitor Silverlight will become.

Taking Flex to the Desktop with AIR

Adobe developed Adobe Integrated Runtime (AIR), previously code-named Apollo, to let you deploy Flex applications as computer desktop applications. By using AIR, you can create your own desktop applications that can run natively on Windows, Mac, and Linux operating systems. You can create AIR applications as Flex applications or AJAX applications, so if you know how to create Flex or AJAX applications, you can create desktop applications, too.

When deciding whether AIR is the right technology for your application, consider these three main features that AIR provides:

✔ **Local file-system access:** One of the main reasons for moving from a Web-based Flex application to a desktop AIR application is the integrated local file-system access that AIR offers. If you build a Flex-based AIR application, you get a few extra tools that don't come in the normal Flex framework. These tools let you read and write to the user's local file system.

✔ **Integrated Web browser:** The AIR runtime includes a built-in Web browser: the open-source WebKit browser. This Web browser allows you to load full HTML pages right into your application, something that you can't do in a Web-based Flex application. The AIR framework also lets you display PDF files within your application.

✔ **Embedded SQLite database:** AIR applications can access an embedded database for offline database access. So, you can build applications that can connect to a server database (like a typical Flex application can) or to an offline database if your application is only occasionally connected to the Internet.

Using the AIR-specific framework controls falls outside the scope of this book. If you're interested in finding out more about AIR, visit www.adobe. com/products/air.

Chapter 2

Building Your First Flex Application

*I*n an homage to software examples all over the world, in this chapter you use Flex Builder to write your first Flex application, the classic Hello World, which displays the words *Hello World* on the screen. While writing this application, you find out how to choose Flex user interface controls, construct an application in the Flex Builder tool, and launch and run the application so that it can be viewed in a browser window.

The focus of this chapter is to show you how to create a quick-and-dirty application so that you can see how the development tool and framework elements work together. The rest of this book describes Flex Builder (the Flex development tool) and the Flex framework in more detail. In later chapters, you find out more about how to construct and debug a Flex application, how to determine which elements are available when building your Flex applications, and how to wire them together.

Creating a Flex Project in Flex Builder

To write your Hello World Flex application, you use the best tool for writing, debugging, and running Flex applications: *Flex Builder.* You can use this integrated development environment to do the following:

✔ Write Flex applications with MXML and ActionScript code.

✔ Visually assemble Flex applications by placing controls on a visual design stage.

✔ Debug Flex code by using a visual debugger.

✔ Build and run your Flex application in a browser window or as a desktop application.

If you don't have Flex Builder already installed, you can download the free trial version from `www.adobe.com/go/flex/`. The trial version lets you build full Flex applications for 60 days before deciding if you want to purchase the product. Refer to Chapter 4 for more detailed instructions on downloading Flex Builder and a description of the different versions of Flex Builder.

To write the Hello World Flex application, you must first create a new project in Flex Builder. Follow these steps:

1. Open Flex Builder.

The first time you launch Flex Builder, the Flex start page opens, as shown in Figure 2-1. This page has all sorts of handy links and information to help get you started building Flex applications. To get up to speed quickly, check out the tutorials that are linked from the Flex start page.

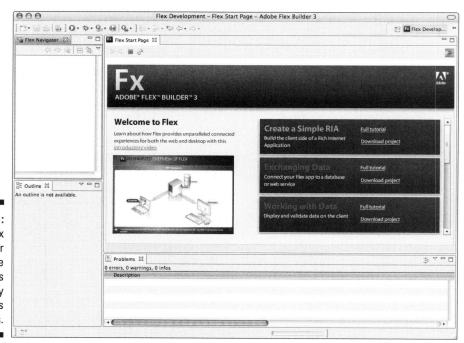

Figure 2-1:
The Flex Builder start page provides many handy tutorials and tips.

2. Choose File⇨New⇨Flex Project.

The New Project Wizard for creating Flex project types appears, as shown in Figure 2-2. The wizard walks you through the steps of creating the project.

Flex Builder organizes its Flex content within projects. You can create several different kinds of projects, depending on what kind of application you want to build. (To find out more about the different kinds of projects available and how to create them in Flex Builder, refer to Chapter 4.)

The most common and basic project type is a Flex project. You create this type of project to house your Hello World Flex application. After you've created a project, the other Flex Builder features — such as the code editor, visual debugger, and visual Design mode — are available for you to use.

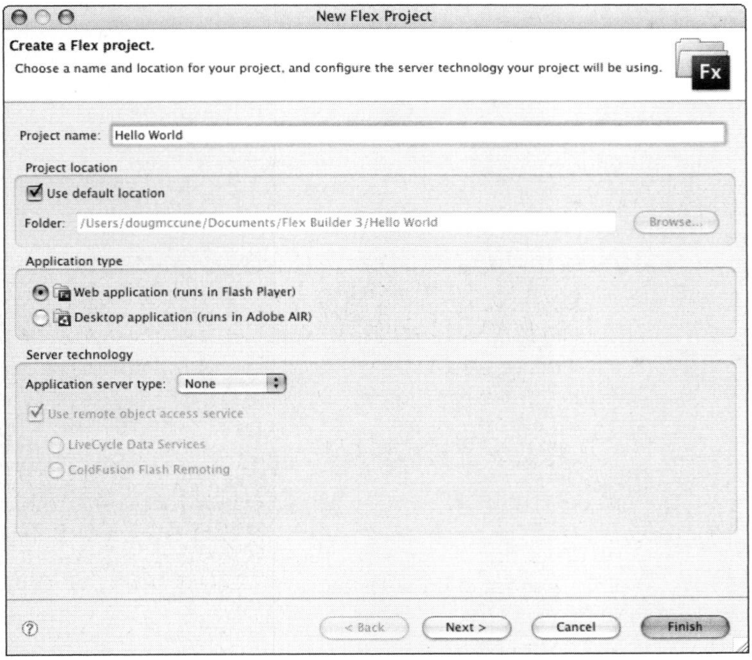

Figure 2-2:
The Flex Builder New Project Wizard walks you through creating a Flex project.

3. Enter a project name (for the sample application, enter Hello World**) and click Finish.**

For this simple Hello World example, accept the default entries that Flex Builder suggests. All you really want to do is name your Flex project. This name appears in Navigator view, which traditionally lives on the left side of Flex Builder in either Source mode or Design mode and lists all projects that exist in your workspace. A *workspace* is a location that houses all your projects.

A status bar appears at the bottom of the New Project Wizard, indicating that Flex Builder is creating all the necessary files on the file system to house your Hello World project. After the project is created, you see it in Navigator view on the left. A set of folders is created, and the root Flex application for that project opens in Source mode, as shown in Figure 2-3. By default, Flex Builder names the root application for a project main.mxml.

Source mode

Design mode

Navigator View

Figure 2-3: Your new Flex project appears in Navigator view, which lists all projects in the workspace.

Writing Code for Your Project

When you create your Flex project, you can start writing code. A simple Flex application, main.mxml, is also created, and Flex Builder opens the MXML application in Source mode (refer to Figure 2-3). This Flex Builder mode offers all the developer-related tools, such as code editors, the debugger, and refactoring options.

Deciphering the default code

After you create a project, Flex Builder writes the following chunk of code into main.mxml, by default:

```xml
<?xml version="1.0" encoding="utf-8"?>
<mx:Application xmlns:mx="http://www.adobe.com/2006/mxml"
          layout="absolute">

</mx:Application>
```

The code breaks down as follows:

- ✔ **XML declaration:** An XML declaration tag appears at the top of the application, identifying the document as an XML document.

- ✔ **Application MXML tag:** Below the XML declaration is the Application MXML tag, which is the root tag of any Flex application. The Application tag has some important jobs, such as expressing the namespace of the controls used in the application. By default, Flex Builder autogenerates code that fills in the mx namespace (xmlns:mx="http://www.adobe.com/2006/mxml"), which is the namespace where the Flex controls and containers live. You can see this namespace declaration directly in the Application tag.

- ✔ **Attribute declaration:** Following the namespace declaration on the Application tag is an attribute declaration. The layout attribute determines which type of visual layout the Application control invokes when positioning its children. By default, Flex Builder sets the layout property to the value absolute, which means that the child elements of the Application control are all positioned at explicit x and y locations within the document.

- ✔ **Closing Application tag:** Because all XML tags must be closed, Flex Builder adds the </mx:Application> closing tag to make the document valid.

Creating the Hello World application

You know that you want to create a Flex application that simply displays Hello World when it's run. The Flex framework has a variety of user interface controls that can be used to display information in a Flex application. (To find out more about all the available Flex user interface controls, refer to Part III of this book.) One simpler control that you can use is the Flex Label control. This display-only text control writes text to the screen. You can create a Flex Label control by using the <mx:Label /> MXML tag. The contents of the Label control (the text that it chooses to display) is set in the text attribute to a value that is a String object.

Follow these steps to use the Label control to display `Hello World` in your application:

1. **Write an `<mx:Label />` tag directly in the MXML code editor, which opens by default when you create a new Flex project.**

   Flex Builder's *code hinting* feature uses built-in intelligent heuristics to suggest different tags and attributes based on the characters you're typing. As you start typing an opening tag, <, Flex Builder makes component suggestions in a drop-down list. As you continue typing the `mx:` namespace prefix and the first letter of Label, `L`, Flex Builder narrows its suggestions to match the characters you type. After you type the `L`, Flex Builder suggests the Label component, as shown in Figure 2-4. You can press Enter to autofill the Flex Builder suggestion, or you can finish typing `<mx:Label />` on your own.

   Now that you have created a Label control in your Flex application, you need to tell it to display the words `Hello World`. This task is simple — a Label control uses the `text` attribute to specify the text it should display.

Figure 2-4:
The code hinting drop-down list gives you suggestions as you enter code in the code editor.

2. **Directly in the Label MXML tag, add the following code:**

   ```
   text="Hello World!"
   ```

   You may have noticed, as you add the `text` attribute to the Label tag, that Flex Builder suggests other attributes that can be set on a Flex Label control. Flex Builder provides not only tag-level code hinting but also attribute code hinting.

   So now you should have the following line of code within your Flex `Application` tag:

   ```
   <mx:Label text="Hello World!" />
   ```

   Flex Builder created the default Application tag with the `layout` property set to `absolute`, which means that all child components will be positioned based on their x and y properties. Because the Label control hasn't specified an explicit x, y position, the Application container places the Label control at its default position: 0,0. This position indicates that the Label control lives at the upper-left corner of the screen.

If you center the Label control within your application, you can create a more visually pleasing effect. You can easily use the built-in layout constraints, where user interface controls are constrained to the edges of their parent container. (To find out more about layout constraints, refer to Chapter 10.)

3. **To center the Label control, add one center constraint to the Label tag by using the `horizontalCenter` attribute and setting the value to 0. Add this code to the Label MXML tag:**

```
horizontalCenter="0"
```

The `horizontalCenter` constraint is set to a pixel value that determines the distance between the center of the control and the center of its parent container. Setting the Label's `horizontalCenter` attribute to a value of 0 perfectly centers the control in the center of the application.

When you're finished, your code should look like this (see Figure 2-5):

```
<mx:Label text="Hello World!" horizontalCenter="0" />
```

Voilà — you've written all the code for your simple Hello World Flex application.

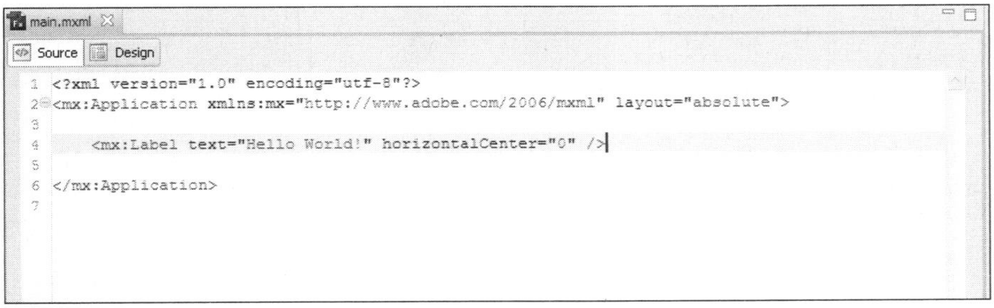

Figure 2-5: The finished code for your Hello World Flex application.

Viewing Your Application in Design Mode

In addition to offering Source mode, where application-specific code is written, Flex Builder offers Design mode. You can use Design mode to see how the application will look when it's run and to edit the application and its components visually. You can easily switch to Design mode by clicking the Design tab in the upper-left toolbar in Source mode (refer to Figure 2-3). (To find out more about Flex Builder Design mode and how to author and modify Flex applications and components visually, refer to Chapter 6.)

When you click the Design tab, Flex Builder changes to Design mode, shown in Figure 2-6. This view has a design stage that shows how the application's current state appears. Additionally, you can use the panels flanking the design stage to drag new Flex components to add to the design and to edit existing components. Whenever anything is done in Design mode that changes the state of the application (for example, dragging out a new component or changing a component property), the corresponding code is added or modified in Source mode. Everything done in Design mode results in generating or modifying the correct code in Source mode. Similarly, every change you make in Source mode gets represented in Design mode.

In Figure 2-6, you can see that the design stage shows a Flex Label component centered in the `Application` container. That's how your Hello World application will look in the browser when you run it.

Run button   Design stage

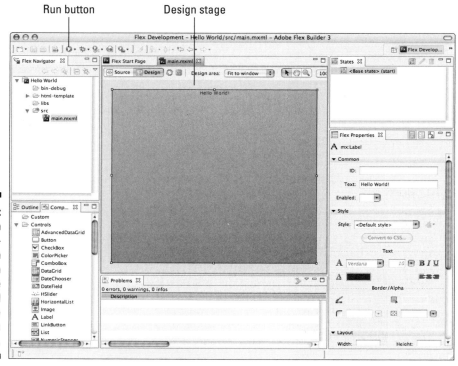

Figure 2-6:
Design
mode ren-
ders an
application
to indicate
what it will
look like
when you
run it.

Running the Application

Flex Builder is a one-stop tool for all your Flex development needs. Within Flex Builder, you can write, run, and debug applications. Before you can run a Flex project, however, you need to build it. *Building* a project means that you invoke a compiler — in this case, the Flex MXML compiler — to compile code and check for errors. If errors exist, you need to fix them and then build the project again. After the project is successfully built, you can run it and view your Flex application in a browser window.

When you launch a Flex application, you're building the application, checking for errors, and then running the application in a browser window. Flex Builder offers a variety of toolbars that have buttons for invoking different actions, such as running, debugging, or profiling an application. To launch your Hello World project, click the Run button on the main code toolbar (refer to Figure 2-6), which is available in either Source mode or Design mode. Flex then builds the application and launches it in a browser window. By default, Flex Builder launches the application in your computer's default Web browser.

If problems exist in your application code, you see them written out to Problems view, at the bottom of the code editor window. If no errors exist, your application is launched in the default browser window, and you should see your application running! The result of the Hello World program looks like Figure 2-7.

There you go. In just a few, simple steps, you built a simple Flex application in Source mode, viewed it in Design mode, and ran the application in a browser window.

Figure 2-7:
Running the
application
launches
a browser
window
showing
the finished
product.

Chapter 3

Flexing Your Muscle with MXML and ActionScript

In This Chapter

▶ Understanding MXML and ActionScript

▶ Developing object-oriented applications

▶ Using inheritance and interfaces

▶ Working with the event model

---

*F*lex applications are created by using a combination of the declarative markup language *MXML* and the scripting language *ActionScript*. You use both MXML and ActionScript, often together, to create your projects. If you're familiar with developing AJAX Web applications, try drawing an analogy between HTML and JavaScript. When you create AJAX applications, you use HTML as the declarative markup language to lay out the user interface elements of your application, and then you use JavaScript to add interactivity. MXML and ActionScript work much the same way, with MXML often serving to create the visual layout of your application and ActionScript adding powerful programming capabilities.

In this chapter, we provide an overview of MXML and ActionScript and explain the power and unique capabilities of each technology. To become a successful Flex developer, you should grasp some important general programming concepts, so we cover some object-oriented programming principles and discuss the event model that's used for communication among the different pieces of your application.

In this chapter, we make some assumptions about your programming knowledge. We assume that you have some experience in writing code in a programming language such as JavaScript, Java, C, C++, or Basic and that you have at least a cursory understanding of HTML or XML. Although you certainly don't need to be an expert programmer in any specific language, we don't cover all the small details of fundamental programming concepts. If tasks such as working with for loops, declaring variables, and invoking functions are foreign to you, you may need to spend some time reading about these fundamental concepts because a discussion of that information is outside the scope of this book.

Introducing MXML

MXML is a tag-based declarative markup language that you use to compose Flex applications. When you start a new Flex project, you begin with a new MXML file. As we explain in Chapter 2, every Flex application starts out as an MXML file with an empty `<mx:Application>` tag. MXML is contained in files that use the `.mxml` extension.

You create components by creating new MXML tags. The following tag creates a new Button component and sets the label that's displayed on the Button:

```
<mx:Button label="My Button" />
```

By adding that single line to your main application MXML file you have added an interactive Button. The Flex framework contains a number of different user interface controls that you can use in your applications, with the Button being one of the simplest ones. All the Flex framework controls can be added with MXML. Listing 3-1 creates a simple login form, shown in Figure 3-1.

Listing 3-1: A Simple Login Form

```
<?xml version="1.0" encoding="utf-8"?>
<mx:Application xmlns:mx="http://www.adobe.com/2006/mxml">
    <mx:Form>
        <mx:FormItem label="Username">
            <mx:TextInput id="username" />
        </mx:FormItem>
        <mx:FormItem label="Password">
            <mx:TextInput id="password"
              displayAsPassword="true" />
        </mx:FormItem>
        <mx:FormItem>
            <mx:Button label="Submit" />
        </mx:FormItem>
    </mx:Form>
</mx:Application>
```

Figure 3-1:
The login
form pro-
duced by
MXML
markup.

For now, don't worry about exactly what the Form or TextInput controls can do; we cover all the controls in later chapters. (We discuss Forms in Chapter 9 and text controls, such as TextInput, in Chapter 7). Notice how the MXML components are defined in Listing 3-1, however, because you use this general syntax throughout your Flex development.

Comparing MXML and HTML

If you're familiar with HTML, MXML probably doesn't look much different. But don't let the similarity of the syntax fool you; MXML is completely different from HTML. None of the normal HTML user interface components are present. There are some similar components, however, such as TextInput (which can be created with the `<mx:TextInput />` MXML tag). TextInput is similar to the `<input type="text" />` HTML tag. But even though some of the MXML tags might resemble HTML components, be aware that they are, in fact, different controls.

Nesting MXML containers

The Flex *containers* are a subset of the components in the Flex framework that are specifically designed to hold other controls. A few of the containers that you use in your applications are Canvas, HBox, VBox, and Panel. You can define these containers in MXML and add child components by nesting MXML tags. The following example creates a horizontal box container that holds two Button controls (shown at the top of Figure 3-2):

```
<mx:HBox>
    <mx:Button label="Button 1" />
    <mx:Button label="Button 2" />
</mx:HBox>
```

Because the two `<mx:Button />` tags are placed between the opening HBox tag (`<mx:HBox>`) and the closing HBox tag (`</mx:HBox>`), they are added to the HBox, which lays them out horizontally. You can nest MXML tags within each other multiple levels deep, to produce complex layouts. The following code creates a Panel container that contains an HBox, which contains the two Buttons (as shown at the bottom of Figure 3-2):

```
<mx:Panel width="200" height="200">
    <mx:HBox>
        <mx:Button label="Button 1" />
        <mx:Button label="Button 2" />
    </mx:HBox>
</mx:Panel>
```

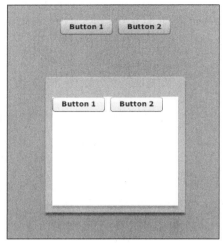

Figure 3-2:
Using
nested
containers
to lay out
Flex
controls.

Notice how the opening and closing tags for the Panel and the HBox have to completely surround their contents. Make sure that you always properly nest your MXML tags, or else your code doesn't compile. The following is an *incorrect* example of nesting that generates an error:

```
<mx:Panel width="200" height="200">
   <mx:HBox>
      <mx:Button label="Button 1" />
      <mx:Button label="Button 2" />
   </mx:Panel>
</mx:HBox>
```

If you tried to run the above code the compiler would tell you that you haven't properly closed the HBox tag.

Refer to Chapter 10 for detailed coverage of the Flex containers.

Introducing ActionScript

MXML can be great for creating layouts of user interface controls for your applications, but when you need more programmatic control, you use ActionScript. The syntax of ActionScript is close to that of JavaScript and Java (although JavaScript is definitely closest), so if you have experience with either of those languages, the syntax should be familiar.

Making the shift to ActionScript's object-oriented programming

ActionScript 3 is an object-oriented programming (OOP) language, which means, in general terms, that the fundamental structural unit of your application is an object. Objects expose specific functionality in the form of *properties* and *methods*, which you use to interact with the objects.

If you have programming experience in earlier versions of ActionScript (1 or 2), the shift to ActionScript 3 may feel daunting. ActionScript 3 forces you to follow stricter OOP syntax when writing code, and you'll notice throughout this book there is never a reference to _root or global variables. If you have a background in other object-oriented programming languages, such as Java or C++, you already have experience in writing OOP applications, and the shift to ActionScript 3 should be fairly painless.

Understanding objects and classes

At the heart of object-oriented programming is the object, which encapsulates functionality. When an object is *encapsulated,* it has certain capabilities that it exposes through properties and methods you can use, but it hides all other details about how it does what it does. A *class* is the definition of an object. An *object* is one particular instance of a class. Each ActionScript class is defined in its own ActionScript file (with the .as file extension).

To illustrate the concept of a class, think about an employee within an organization. An Employee class might contain the following *properties:*

- firstName
- lastName
- socialSecurityNumber
- salary

And, an Employee might have the following actions *(methods)* that it can perform:

- doTask
- takeBreak
- submitTimesheet
- complainAboutBoss

The preceding lists include four properties and four methods of the Employee class. The basic Employee ActionScript class might look like the code in Listing 3-2.

Listing 3-2: The Employee Class with Four Properties and Methods

```
package com.dummies
{
  public class Employee                                           →3
  {
    public function Employee()                                    →5
    {
       //in the constructor you can initialize the object
    }

    //define the public variables
    public var firstName:String;                                  →11
    public var lastName:String;
    public var socialSecurityNumber:String;
    public var salary:Number;

    //define the public methods
    public function doTask(task:Task):void {                      →17
       //do something to accomplish the task
    }

    public function takeBreak(minutes:Number):void {

    }

    public function submitTimesheet(timesheet:Timesheet):void {

    }

    public function complainAboutBoss():void {

    }
  }
}
```

Listing 3-2 defines the outline structure of your Employee class:

→ **3**   You name the class on Line 3, `public class Employee`, which defines the Employee class, and corresponds with the filename of the ActionScript file in your project. Because this class is named Employee, you have a file named `Employee.as` in your project.

→ **5**   The *constructor* is a special function that creates the object. When a new Employee is created by calling `new Employee();` this constructor (Lines 5–8) is called. In the constructor, you can do any kind of initial setup that your class needs.

→ **11** You define a few public properties in Lines 11–14. Other classes can use these properties to interact with the Employee class.

→ **17** You also create public methods that are used to interact with the Employee class (Lines 17–31). These methods define all the things an Employee can do.

Defining getters and setters

ActionScript has a special syntax to define *getters* and *setters* on a class, which are unique ways to combine the functionality of both a variable and a method. Although a getter or a setter looks like a normal variable to the outside world, when it's accessed, it runs a function. The easiest way to explain getters and setters is by describing the example in Listing 3-3.

Listing 3-3: Defining a Getting and Setter for `hourlyRate`

```
public class Employee
{
    public var salary:Number;

    public function get hourlyRate():Number {
        var hoursPerYear:Number = 40 * 50;
        return salary/hoursPerYear;
    }

    public function set hourlyRate(value:Number):void {
        this.salary = value * 40 * 50;
    }
}
```

Listing 3-3 defines a getter and setter for the `hourlyRate` property of the Employee class. The `hourlyRate` getter isn't a normal property, however, and is instead determined by the `salary` property. (In this example, we assume 40-hour workweeks and 50 workweeks in a year.)

You can access getters and setters just as you access normal properties of a class. The following code creates a new Employee, sets the salary to $100,000 (we're Flex developers, after all), and then uses the `hourlyRate` getter:

```
var employee:Employee = new Employee();
employee.salary = 100000;

var hourly:Number = employee.hourlyRate;
trace(hourlyRate);
```

Because you defined `hourlyRate` as a getter, you can access it the same way you access a normal property. But when you access the `hourlyRate` getter, the function you defined runs and performs the calculation.

Because setters work the same way, you can have specific code that runs whenever a certain property is set. In Listing 3-3, the setter for `hourlyRate` calculates the yearly salary for that rate and sets the `salary` property.

Learning to love the black box

An important concept in object-oriented programming is that every object is a black box, which exposes specific functionality but doesn't let you peer behind the curtain to see the details of the implementation. When you program in an object-oriented language, you don't need to worry about how a certain class does what it does; all you need to know is which methods and properties you can use. To illustrate this point, we apply the theoretical OOP principle to a real-life example.

If you're like most folks, you have no idea how a microwave oven heats food. You know that seemingly magical invisible rays fly around, but that's about the extent of your understanding. But you know how you're supposed to *use* a microwave oven: You place food inside it, enter on a keypad the length of time you want the food to cook, and then press the Start button — and the food is then heated. To you, the microwave is a "black" box. Here's a simple OOP example that illustrates this concept:

```
var microwave:Microwave = new Microwave();
microwave.addFood(food);
microwave.time = 1.5;
microwave.warmUp();
```

Within the `warmUp` method, any number of behind-the-scenes events can be happening. For all you know, a thousand gerbils running on treadmills generate an electric current that heats your food. But all you care about are the exposed properties and methods of the Microwave class. You know that you can call the `addFood()` method and pass in something for it to warm up. And, you know that you can set the `time` property, which determines how hot the Microwave makes the food. Then you call `warmUp()`, and you can assume that the Microwave will fulfill its side of the bargain and warm your food. You don't need to know anything about molecular physics to get all those tasks to work. All these pieces, such as the `time` property and the `warmUp()` method, define the *interface* that you use to interact with the Microwave class. The interface is the collection of public properties and methods that a class exposes to the developer.

Object-oriented programming is all about using the exposed interfaces defined by classes and not having to worry about how they do what they do. One outstanding benefit of this approach is that you can completely change the underlying implementation without affecting the rest of your application. As long as the exposed methods and variables stay the same, all the behind-the-scenes implementation details can change.

Recognizing that packages are where classes live

Classes are located in *packages,* which serve as a way to organize the ActionScript files in your project and to locate the classes within your code. The package of a class is the list of strings separated by periods that precede the class names. All Flex framework classes exist within the mx package, which means that the full package name of every class in the Flex framework resembles mx.subPackage.Class. For example, the full package structure of the Button class is mx.controls.Button. This example shows that the Button class lives in the controls package within the mx package.

When you create your own, custom ActionScript classes, you should use packages to organize your code. Picking a package structure involves organizing your ActionScript files into a series of folders that match the package structure you want to use. You must also ensure that the package definition at the top of your ActionScript class matches the folder structure. The first line in any of your ActionScript classes defines the package for the class by using the package keyword followed by the full package name.

You can pick any package-naming structure you want, although a standard that's often used is the *reverse* domain name syntax. It uses domain names to uniquely identify packages, but in reverse order. If you take a look at the first line in Listing 3-2, you see the use of the com.dummies package for the Employee class:

```
package com.dummies
{
```

In this line, the Employee.as source file is placed in the com/dummies/ directory within your project, as shown in Figure 3-3. You can use any package-naming scheme that you like; however, it is a common practice to group related classes together under the same package. As you work with the different components within the Flex framework, notice how they are grouped in logical packages, such as mx.controls and mx.containers.

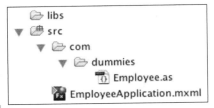

Figure 3-3:
Package
structure
corresponds
with folder
structure.

The package-naming convention you use is arbitrary, and if you choose to use the reverse domain style, it doesn't mean that it needs to map to a real URL. The `com.dummies` package was used in the example, but that doesn't have any true relationship to the dummies.com domain name.

Inheritance: Extending a class

An ActionScript class can *extend* another class, which means that it inherits all the functionality of the class it's extending. The class can then add functionality in addition to what was contained in the base class. In the Employee example in the previous section, you can split the Employee class into two classes. First and foremost, an Employee is a Person, which has certain properties, such as `firstName` and `lastName`. The following listing contains a simple Person class:

```
package com.dummies
{
    public class Person
    {
        public var firstName:String;
        public var lastName:String;
    }
}
```

Now that you have a Person class that contains the `firstName` and `lastName` properties, you can make the Employee class extend Person, and you can remove the `firstName` and `lastName` properties from Employee because they're contained in Person. Here's a portion of the new Employee class:

```
package com.dummies
{
    public class Employee extends Person
    {
        public var socialSecurityNumber:String;
        public var salary:Number;
        ...
```

Now that you have the base Person class, you can make other classes that also extend Person. For example, you can make a Boss class that defines the specific functionality of a Boss. The Boss class is shown in Listing 3-4.

Listing 3-4: The Boss Class Extends Person

```
package com.dummies
{
   public class Boss extends Person
   {
      public var employees:Array;

      public function giveRaise(employee:Employee, percent:Number):void {
         employee.salary = employee.salary + (employee.salary * percent);
      }

      public function giveRaiseToAll(percent:Number):void {
         for(var i:int=0; i<employees.length; i++) {
            giveRaise(employee, percent);
         }
      }
   }
}
```

Because Boss also extends Person, you don't have to create the `firstName` or `lastName` properties; it inherits those properties just like the Employee class does. But the Boss class contains all elements specific to a Boss. In this example, a Boss has a list of employees and can give raises (which, in an ideal world, the boss would do).

Understanding interfaces

An *interface,* which is a special kind of ActionScript file, is similar to a class but doesn't define any specific implementation details. An interface defines a list of methods, but unlike a class, the interface doesn't have any code to define how the method works. Instead, classes are supposed to *implement* the interface, which means that the class must include all methods defined in the interface. The following code snippet defines a simple interface named IPayee that has a single function named `receiveMoney`:

```
package com.dummies
{
   public interface IPayee
   {
      function receiveMoney(amount:Number):void;
   }
}
```

The interface looks similar in structure to a class; however, notice in the third line the use of the word `interface` rather than the word `class`. The interface defines a function, although you can see the lack of a `public`, `private`, or `protected` keyword. A class that implements an interface must implement all functions defined in the interface as public functions. You can define only public methods within an interface, not properties. However, because getters and setters are methods, you can define those in an interface as well.

You can modify the Employee class to implement the IPayee interface. To do so, you need to add the `implements` keyword to the class definition, and you create a method named `receiveMoney`:

```
public class Employee extends Person implements IPayee
{
    public function receiveMoney(amount:Number):void {
        trace("I'm rich!");
    }
    ...
```

To understand the benefit of using interfaces, imagine which kinds of entities the Boss class you created might have to pay. Obviously, all employees need to get paid, but also, possibly, merchants, utility companies, and government tax boards, for example. In this context, each of these entities could be a completely different class, but they can all implement the IPayee interface, which indicates that each class can receive money. The Boss doesn't need to know about each different class that needs to be paid; instead, the Boss knows only about the IPayee interface, and can know how to interact with any class that implements that interface.

Exploring static methods and variables

If a method or variable has the `static` keyword before the method or variable name, it behaves differently from normal variables or methods of the class. Static methods and variables belong to the class itself, not to any particular instance of the class. When you call a static method, you're calling a method on a class, as opposed to a method on an object.

The code in Listing 3-5 creates the CustomMath class, which has two static functions: one for returning the sum of an array of numbers and another for returning the average.

After those static methods are defined in the CustomMath class, you can invoke them by calling `CustomMath.sum()` and `CustomMath.average()` — for example, `var avg:Number = CustomMath.average(3, 4, 5)`. You *never* create a new instance of the CustomMath class. This usage is wrong, for example: `var math:CustomMath = new CustomMath()`.

Listing 3-5: Creating a Class with Two Static Functions

```
package
{
    public class CustomMath
    {
        public static function sum(numbers:Array):Number {
            var sum:Number = 0;

            for(var i:int=0; i<numbers.length; i++) {
                sum += Number(numbers[i]);
            }

            return sum;
        }

        public static function average(numbers:Array):Number {
            return CustomMath.sum(numbers)/numbers.length;
        }
    }
}
```

A few main static methods and variables are built into the Flex framework that you will use. The following list describes a few of the most common ones you see while building Flex applications:

- ✔ `Application.application`: You can always access the main Application object that is the root of your Flex application by using the static variable `Application.application`.

- ✔ `Alert.show()`: The Alert class lets you display pop-up dialog windows by using the `Alert.show` static function. The following line pops up a window with the title `Error` and the message `Houston, we have a problem.`

  ```
  Alert.show("Houston, we have a problem.", "Error");
  ```

- ✔ `PopUpManager`: The PopUpManager class contains a set of static methods that let you work with your own, custom pop-up windows. The main methods you use are `addPopUp`, `removePopUp`, and `centerPopUp`.

- ✔ `Math`: The Math class has a whole series of static math functions, such as `min`, `max`, `sin`, and `cos`. For example, to compute the lesser of two numbers (defined as variables x and y), you can call

  ```
  var min:Number = Math.min(x, y);
  ```

- ✔ `System.setClipboard()`: You can set the text that's on the user's Clipboard by calling `System.setClipboard("text to set")`. Note that for security reasons, you cannot get text from the Clipboard; you can only set it.

Comparing ActionScript and JavaScript

ActionScript and JavaScript are similar languages, and both are based on the same language specification, ECMAScript. The main difference is that ActionScript is an implementation of a newer draft of the ECMAScript standard, Version 4. But because both JavaScript and ActionScript are based on the same base specification, the syntax you use is similar.

One big difference between the two languages involves the *strict-typing* of ActionScript 3, which supports compile-time type checking. When you declare a variable, you specify which type of variable it is — a String or Number or any custom class you might be using. The following line of code declares a variable named myDate that is a Date:

```
var myDate:Date = new Date(1982, 1, 16);
```

Because the myDate variable is declared as a Date object, if you try to assign any value that isn't a Date, the compiler catches it and notifies you. So, the following line generates a compile-time error:

```
myDate = 5; //won't work because 5 is a Number, not a Date
```

Having this type of compile-time type checking might not seem like a big deal, but it's invaluable for writing bug-free code. Without compile-time type checking, you can easily write code that makes mistakes that go uncaught. These types of errors would crop up eventually, but only at runtime when you're debugging your application. Compile-time type checking forces you to write clear, structured code that's less prone to errors.

Understanding the Relationship between ActionScript and MXML

Every MXML tag is actually ActionScript code behind the scenes. Each of the components in the Flex framework is written in ActionScript. When you compile a Flex application, the compiler translates all the MXML code into pure ActionScript code, which is the code that is then compiled and run. MXML is just a shortcut that makes certain tasks, such as laying out the pieces of the user interface in your application, much easier than having to code the comparable ActionScript by hand. But you should understand that anything you can do with MXML markup, you can also do with ActionScript. Depending on the task, some tasks are easier to do with MXML markup, and some are easier (or only possible) with ActionScript.

MXML helps most in two areas:

✔ **Application design:** MXML simplifies application design when you're composing the visual layout of your applications.

✔ **Data binding:** MXML lets you use data binding with a simple tag-based syntax. For more on data binding, see Chapter 12.

The following example illustrates how to simplify the layout of your application. Listing 3-6 creates a simple Flex application with a Panel container that contains an Image.

Listing 3-6: Using MXML to Create and Lay Out Your Application

```
<?xml version="1.0" encoding="utf-8"?>
<mx:Application xmlns:mx="http://www.adobe.com/2006/mxml">
   <mx:Panel title="My Panel" roundedBottomCorners="true" width="300"
             height="300">
      <mx:Image source="myImage.jpg" width="100%" height="100%" />
   </mx:Panel>
</mx:Application>
```

The entire sample application in Listing 3-6 consists of six lines of MXML code. You can create exactly the same application by using almost all ActionScript code, and it would look like the code in Listing 3-7.

Listing 3-7: Using Pure ActionScript to Create and Lay Out Your Application

```
<?xml version="1.0" encoding="utf-8"?>
<mx:Application xmlns:mx="http://www.adobe.com/2006/mxml"
   creationComplete="init()">
   <mx:Script>
      <![CDATA[
         import mx.controls.Image;
         import mx.containers.Panel;

         private function init():void {
            var panel:Panel = new Panel();
            panel.title = "My Panel";
            panel.width = 300;
            panel.height = 300;
            panel.setStyle("roundedBottomCorners", true);

            var image:Image = new Image();
            image.source = "myPicture.jpg";
            image.percentWidth = 100;
            image.percentHeight = 100;

            panel.addChild(image);
```

(continued)

Listing 3-7 *(continued)*

```
        this.addChild(panel);
      }
    ]]>
  </mx:Script>
</mx:Application>
```

This listing produces exactly the same application, but it needs four times as many lines of code, which highlights what makes MXML so useful.

Working with the Event Model

The Flex framework relies heavily on events as the preferred method of communication between components. An *event* is an announcement that something has happened. This "something" might be a mouse click or a notification that a file has finished downloading or anything else that a component wants to tell other components about. Events are a fundamental part of the Flex framework, and you must properly understand how the event model is supposed to work in Flex applications.

All components in the Flex framework define specific events that you can listen for. When something happens within a component that it wants to announce, such as a button click, the component *dispatches* an event. Dispatching an event is a way to announce that something has happened to all the other parts of your application.

The Button control is a good example for exploring the event model. The Button control primarily displays a button with some text and lets the user click it. An application that uses a Button control doesn't know anything about what happens when the user interacts with the Button. For instance, an application doesn't care how the Button draws itself when the mouse rolls over or off. All you need to pay attention to are the events that the Button dispatches. The most important event that a Button dispatches is probably the `click` event. When the Button is clicked, it dispatches a new event to announce that it was clicked. The Button is responsible only for making that announcement and doesn't care which other parts of your application, if any, are listening for the announcement.

Dispatching events is one-half of the event model. But because the components that dispatch events don't know anything about what's supposed to happen when these events occur, in order to make something *happen,* you need to have *event listeners* that listen for these events. In the case of the Button control, when the user clicks the control, it dispatches the `click` event, but the dispatching of that event doesn't do anything on its own. In your application, you attach a listener to the `click` event, which is a function that's run when the event fires. After you add a listener, the code within your listener method runs every time that particular event is dispatched.

The words *listener* and *handler* are often used interchangeably when talking about events. Adobe has a set of coding guidelines that define their best practices for writing ActionScript 3 code. These best practices recommend names for your event listener methods, such as `eventNameHandler`, which is the convention we use in this book. So, an event listener for a mouse-down event would be named `mouseDownHandler`. To review the best practices guidelines, visit `http://opensource.adobe.com/wiki/display/flexsdk/Coding+Conventions`.

Adding event listeners with MXML

The easiest way to add event listeners to Flex components is to add MXML attribute listeners. You add event listeners in a similar way as you define properties or styles in the MXML tag. But event listeners are different than properties and styles, because they define ActionScript code that's run when the event fires. You can add a listener to the click event of a Button control, like this:

```
<mx:Button label="My Button"
          click="clickHandler(event);"/>
```

The `click` and `label` are both MXML tags, but the `label` tag defines a property and the `click` tag defines an event listener. Event listeners defined inline in this way consist of ActionScript code that's executed when the event fires.

You don't have to point only to a function to handle the event; you can write ActionScript code directly in the MXML tag, if you want. For instance, the following example displays an Alert message by using ActionScript code directly in the click MXML tag:

```
<mx:Button label="My Button" click="mx.controls.Alert.
          show('You clicked!')" />
```

However, as a general practice, code is often much more readable and manageable if you always use functions defined outside the MXML tag as your event listeners.

Examining the structure of an event listener

The event listener defined in your ActionScript code should be a function that takes a single Event object parameter. Your functions generally look like this:

```
private function eventHandler(event:Event):void {
    //do your event handling stuff here
}
```

Notice that the `event` parameter is an Event object. Event handlers are always passed an Event object that has a few important properties. Most importantly, the Event object has a property named `target` that identifies the component that dispatched the event. Be aware also of a different property named `currentTarget`. The differences between `target` and `currentTarget` are discussed later in this chapter, when we cover event bubbling. For now, just know that you can use `target` to get a reference to the component that dispatched the event.

The following example displays two buttons, both of which use the same event listener for the `click` event. The event listener uses the `target` property to get a reference to the particular Button control that was clicked, and then displays an Alert pop-up message showing the label of the Button.

```
<mx:Script>
    <![CDATA[
        import mx.controls.Button;
        import mx.controls.Alert;

        private function clickHandler(event:Event):void {
            var button:Button = event.target as Button;
            Alert.show("You clicked: " + button.label);
        }
    ]]>
</mx:Script>

<mx:Button label="Button 1" click="clickHandler(event)" />
<mx:Button label="Button 2" click="clickHandler(event)" />
```

Notice that you have to *cast* the `event.target` property to the Button class, which is accomplished by specifying `event.target as Button`. You use the `as` operator to cast from one variable to another. When you cast a variable, you are usually assigning a variable that is a higher-level generic type to a more specific type. In this example, the `target` property of an Event is defined only as a generic ActionScript Object, so in the listener function, you cast it to the appropriate class, which is Button in this case. You know that the target property is actually a Button because the event handler was added on the `<mx:Button />` component. Explicitly casting it to a Button lets you access the Button-specific properties of the object, such as `label`.

Event is the base class for all events, but more specific classes also extend Event to provide more detailed information about particular kinds of events. For example, mouse interaction events use the MouseEvent class, which adds the `localX`, `localY`, `stageX`, and `stageY` properties that define the coordinates, relative to the component and the stage, of the mouse when the event was dispatched.

The example in Listing 3-8 adds a listener to the `change` event of a horizontal slider control. When the HSlider dispatches the change event, it dispatches a SliderEvent event, which has a few specific properties that tell you more about the interaction with the slider. In this example, you can access the `value` property of the event to get the latest slider value.

Listing 3-8: Adding a Listener to the Change Event of a Slider Control

```
<mx:Script>
    <![CDATA[
        import mx.controls.Alert;
        import mx.events.SliderEvent;

        private function changeHandler(event:SliderEvent):void {
            Alert.show("New value: " + event.value);
        }
    ]]>
</mx:Script>

<mx:HSlider change="changeHandler(event)" snapInterval="1" />
```

Many Flex components dispatch their own custom events, so they can indicate this type of detailed information. The documentation for each of the components in the Flex framework explains all the different events that each component dispatches. Giving you a comprehensive list of all events and event types is beyond the scope of this book, although in Part III, we touch on the common events for many of the framework controls.

Adding event listeners with ActionScript

You can also add event listeners with ActionScript rather than with MXML tags. All Flex components have a method named `addEventListener` that you can use. When you call `addEventListener`, you have to specify which event you're listening for and the handler function that runs when the event is dispatched. The example in Listing 3-9 creates ten Button controls when the application first loads and adds a click event listener to each one.

Listing 3-9: Adding an Event Listener with ActionScript

```xml
<?xml version="1.0" encoding="utf-8"?>
<mx:Application xmlns:mx="http://www.adobe.com/2006/mxml"
    creationComplete="createButtons()">
    <mx:Script>
        <![CDATA[
            import mx.controls.Alert;
            import mx.controls.Button;

            private function createButtons():void {
                for(var i:int=0; i<10; i++) {
                    var button:Button = new Button();
                    button.label = "Button " + (i+1);
                    button.addEventListener(MouseEvent.CLICK, clickHandler);
                    box.addChild(button);
                }
            }

            private function clickHandler(event:Event):void {
                var button:Button = event.currentTarget as Button;
                Alert.show("You clicked: " + button.label);
            }
        ]]>
    </mx:Script>

    <mx:HBox id="box" width="100%" />

</mx:Application>
```

When you add the click event listener with ActionScript, you use `MouseEvent.CLICK` as the event type. This static variable is defined by the MouseEvent class. The `MouseEvent.CLICK` variable translates to the string `click`. You can add the same listener by calling `addEventListener("click", clickHandler)`. However, when you add event listeners with ActionScript, you should always use the static variables instead, such as `MouseEvent.CLICK`. Using the static variables ensures that you don't have any accidental typos in your code, and your code benefits from proper compile-time checking. If you used a string to represent the event type, the compiler can't help look for potential problems. For example, you might type the following line:

```
button.addEventListener("rollover", rollOverHandler)
```

The proper event name, however, is `rollOver` (notice the capitalization difference). If you use `MouseEvent.ROLL_OVER` rather than the string, you can always be sure that you're using the correct event type. So, rather than `"rollOver"`, the proper way to add the event listener is

```
button.addEventListener(MouseEvent.ROLL_OVER,
        rollOverHandler)
```

One benefit of using ActionScript to add event listeners is that you can remove them by using the `removeEventListener` method. Only listeners that are added with the `addEventListener` method can be removed; you cannot remove event listeners that are added with inline MXML tags. If you later want to remove the click listener that you added on one of those buttons, you can add this line:

```
button.removeEventListener(MouseEvent.CLICK, clickHandler)
```

Understanding event propagation

When an event is dispatched by a component, it propagates up and down the hierarchy of components in your application. During the propagation of a single event, three phases make up the event life cycle: capture, target, and bubble. Event listeners can register and receive notification at any of these three phases:

✔ **Capture:** This phase is the first phase, but is rarely used. In the capture phase, the Event begins at the top-level parent component and works its way down the display list until it reaches the target component that dispatched the event. In the hierarchy shown in Figure 3-4, the Event begins in the capture phase at the Panel and then moves down to the Hbox and then down to the Button.

When you add an event listener, you have to specify whether the listener should listen in the capture phase. The third parameter in the `addEvent Listener` method is a Boolean value that determines whether the capture phase is used (it defaults to `false`). To add a listener to the Button control on the capture phase, you can use the following line of code:

```
button.addEventListener(MouseEvent.CLICK, clickHandler, true);.
```

For most event handling in your applications, you never need to use capture phase listeners. Unless you need extremely aggressive event handling for some reason, you can probably just stick to target and bubble phase listeners.

✔ **Target:** Because the Button control was the component that dispatched the event, after the event propagates down to the Button, it reaches the targeting phase. This phase is used only for event listeners that were added to the component that dispatched the event (when `event. target` and `event.currentTarget` are the same).

✔ **Bubble:** After reaching the targeting phase, the event then propagates back up the display list in the bubbling phase. In the example, the event hits the HBox and then the Panel while bubbling. The order of the bubble phase is the opposite of the capture phase.

Figure 3-4 shows the propagation of an event through the three phases as it travels down the display list and back up.

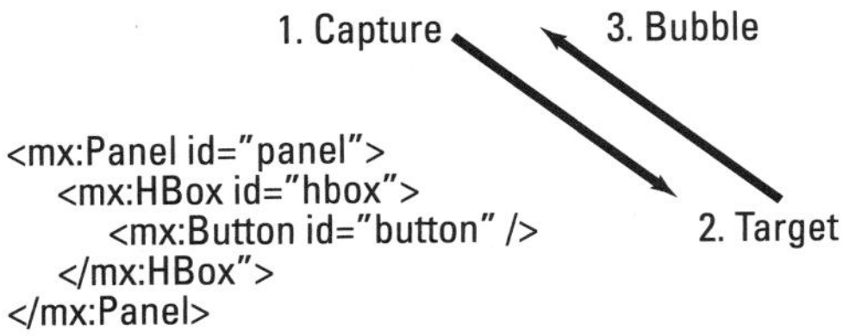

Figure 3-4:
The propagation of a single event through the capture, target, and bubble phases.

1. Capture   3. Bubble

```
<mx:Panel id="panel">
    <mx:HBox id="hbox">
        <mx:Button id="button" />
    </mx:HBox">
</mx:Panel>
```

2. Target

At any point in your event listeners, you can figure out which phase is active by inspecting the eventPhase property of the Event. The example in Listing 3-10 demonstrates the complete propagation of a single click event. The example adds click event listeners to the Panel, HBox, and Button. When the click event fires. the event listener uses trace() to output debugging information about the event.

Listing 3-10: An Example to Debug Event Propagation

```
<?xml version="1.0" encoding="utf-8"?>
<mx:Application xmlns:mx="http://www.adobe.com/2006/mxml"
    creationComplete="setupListeners()" name="app">
  <mx:Script>
    <![CDATA[
        private function setupListeners():void {
            panel.addEventListener(MouseEvent.CLICK, clickHandler);
            panel.addEventListener(MouseEvent.CLICK, clickHandler, true);

            hbox.addEventListener(MouseEvent.CLICK, clickHandler);
            hbox.addEventListener(MouseEvent.CLICK, clickHandler, true);

            button.addEventListener(MouseEvent.CLICK, clickHandler);
            button.addEventListener(MouseEvent.CLICK, clickHandler, true);
        }

        private function clickHandler(event:MouseEvent):void {
            trace("phase: " + event.eventPhase + " | target: " + event.target +
                " | currentTarget: " + event.currentTarget);
        }
    ]]>
  </mx:Script>

  <mx:Panel id="panel">
```

```
    <mx:HBox id="hbox">
        <mx:Button id="button" />
    </mx:HBox>
  </mx:Panel>

</mx:Application>
```

When you run the code in Listing 3-10 and click the button, you see the following debugging output:

```
phase: 1 | target: app.panel.hbox.button | currentTarget: app.panel
phase: 1 | target: app.panel.hbox.button | currentTarget: app.panel.hbox
phase: 2 | target: app.panel.hbox.button | currentTarget: app.panel.hbox.button
phase: 3 | target: app.panel.hbox.button | currentTarget: app.panel.hbox
phase: 3 | target: app.panel.hbox.button | currentTarget: app.panel
```

This chunk of code shows the complete propagation of a single click event. In the sample output, the event phases are displayed as the numbers 1, 2, or 3, which correspond with the capture, target, and bubble phases. The event begins in the capture phase at the top-level Panel container and then travels down the display list, still in the capture phase, to the HBox container. The event then reaches the Button control, and because the Button is the component that dispatched the event, the event is now in the target phase. (Notice that the `target` and `currentTarget` properties of the event are the same.) The event then travels back up the display list in the bubble phase, hitting the HBox first and then the top-level Panel container.

At any point in the event propagation cycle, you can call `stopPropagation()` or `stopImmediatePropagation()` on the event, which stops the event in its tracks. The `stopImmedaiteProgpagation()` event stops the event right away, and no other listeners that are registered for that event are called. If you call `stopPropagation()` instead, any other event listeners for that event on the same component are executed, but the event doesn't move any farther up or down the display list.

Listening for some common events

All components in the Flex framework dispatch a few useful events. The following list describes a few of the common events you might use in your applications:

✔ `show`, `hide`: Whenever a component's `visible` property is changed, either the `show` or `hide` event fires.

✔ `move`, `resize`: These events are dispatched when the component's location or dimensions are changed.

✔ initialize, creationComplete: These events indicate when a component starts and finishes the creation process (including the creation of child components). If you have some ActionScript code that needs to run after all the child components have been created, be sure to use the creationComplete event (see Listing 3-10).

✔ change: Many Flex components let the user change a selected value, such as the slider controls and the NumericStepper. Many of the controls in the framework will dispatch a change event to notify you that a change has occurred.

Part II
Using Flex Builder (The Flex IDE)

The 5th Wave   By Rich Tennant

YOU KIDDING!! TRUE INTERACTIVE CONTENT?! ME CAN'T WAIT, PULL LEVER, OPEN SCREEN!

In this part . . .

In this part, we explore Flex Builder, the development tool you use to create Flex applications. Take a look around and get comfortable because Flex Builder is your new home. We begin by stepping you through the process of setting up Flex projects, tweaking settings, and running applications. Then we divide up Chapters 5 and 6 to cover the designer-oriented and the developer-oriented aspects of the tool. Regardless of whether you consider yourself a designer, developer, or "devigner," both chapters provide valuable information for creating Flex applications.

Chapter 4

Flex Builder: The Best Flex Development Tool

▶ Installing Flex Builder

▶ Understanding the different Flex Builder perspectives

▶ Creating and configuring Flex projects in Flex Builder

▶ Importing and exporting Flex projects

▶ Using the Help options to access sample code and Flex documentation

This chapter gets you up to speed on installing and using Flex Builder, the best development tool for working with Flex applications. Flex Builder is based on the Eclipse IDE (Integrated Development Environment), and it has different perspectives that allow you to develop, debug, and profile Flex applications. In this chapter, you can find out how to install Flex Builder and use Flex Builder for all of your Flex development needs. We cover how to create different types of Flex projects based on the type of application you're building; organize your Flex projects; build, clean, and run your projects; and edit project settings.

This chapter also explains how to access the help materials, such as sample code and Flex documentation, that are included with your Flex Builder installation. After the details about how to set up and run a Flex project become second nature, you can develop your Flex projects with ease!

What's Flex Builder, and Why Should I Care?

Flex Builder is the best and easiest-to-use development tool for building, debugging, and profiling Flex applications and components. It offers features for developers and designers:

✔ **Developer-oriented features:** Include a very robust ActionScript, MXML, and CSS code editor; a visual debugger; a visual profiler that allows you to profile performance and memory use; code refactoring so that code name changes can percolate throughout your project and workspace; and many other tool capabilities.

✔ **Designer-oriented features:** Include a Design view that allows you to visually assemble and edit Flex applications and components; and a CSS Design view that lets you visually style Flex applications and components.

Chapter 5 of this book covers the developer-oriented features of Flex Builder, and Chapter 6 focuses on the designer-oriented features. Look over both of those chapters for more specific information.

Often, each release of Flex is accompanied with a new release of Flex Builder so that the two technologies stay in sync. When a new feature is added into the Flex framework, the corresponding tooling support is usually added to Flex Builder so that developers can use the new feature when they author their Flex applications.

Flex Builder is an Eclipse-based IDE (Integrated Development Environment). You may already be familiar with Eclipse if you use the Eclipse IDE to write Java-based applications. Because Flex Builder is built atop Eclipse, you can use all the special plug-ins built for Eclipse in your Flex Builder tool. For example, many source-code management plug-ins allow you to check files in and out of your source-code repository directly from your Eclipse environment. You can easily install these plug-ins on top of your Flex Builder installation because Flex Builder is based on Eclipse. If you want to find out more about Eclipse, check out *Eclipse For Dummies* by Barry Burd (Wiley).

Installing Flex Builder

You can install Flex Builder from the Flex product page at www.adobe.com/ go/flex_trial. You can install a 60-day trial version of Flex Builder and then at the end of the 60 days purchase the product for use permanently. To purchase Flex Builder directly, or at the conclusion of your trial, go to the online store at the Adobe Web site at www.adobe.com. Flex Builder is supported on the Windows and Macintosh platforms, and installers for both supported platforms are included on the trial download page as well as the Adobe online store.

From the trial download page, download the installer for the platform of your choice. You will notice that Flex Builder 3 Professional is the only download choice. This is one of the "flavors" of Flex Builder, and we discuss it in more detail in a minute. After you've downloaded the installer, run through it to install Flex Builder as well as all of the source code for the Flex framework onto your computer.

A Linux version of Flex Builder is in active development. At the time of publication, Flex Builder Linux is in a public alpha release, which you can find at Adobe's Labs site at `http://labs.adobe.com/technologies/flex/ flexbuilder_linux/`.

Flex Builder comes in two flavors for purchase (the trial download page lets you try out only Flex Builder Professional):

- **Flex Builder Standard:** This version includes the MXML, ActionScript, and CSS editors and the visual debugger.

- **Flex Builder Professional:** This version includes everything contained in the Standard version, as well as the advanced data visualization libraries, such as the Flex charting components, the memory and performance profiler, and the Flex automated testing harness. Chapters 5 and 6 in this book describe these features and capabilities in more detail.

The trial version of Flex Builder is Flex Builder Professional, which includes capabilities such as the advanced data visualization components and the memory and performance profiler. Adobe offers the Professional version so that you can use the trial version as a way to evaluate which version of Flex Builder you want to actually purchase, Standard or Professional.

In addition to Flex Builder Standard and Flex Builder Professional, Flex Builder has two configuration flavors:

- **Flex Builder Plug-In:** Use this configuration version if you already use the Eclipse tool and want to install Flex Builder as an Eclipse plug-in atop your existing Eclipse setup. For example, if you already use Eclipse to develop Java applications, you may want to install the Flex Builder plug-in into your existing Eclipse environment.

- **Flex Builder Stand-Alone:** This is a packaged installation of the Eclipse environment and Flex Builder functionality. This configuration is specifically for building and deploying Flex and ActionScript applications. The Stand-Alone configuration has a much easier to use interface than the Flex Builder Plug-In version, because it's targeted directly toward developing Flex and ActionScript applications. Users new to ActionScript and Flex development should work with this configuration. All the examples and images in this book use the Stand-Alone configuration of Flex Builder.

You have to make the configuration version choice when you install Flex Builder.

Taking a look at the Flex Builder perspectives

Flex Builder has a concept of *perspectives* in which a particular perspective consolidates the Flex Builder user interface to target a particular task. Flex Builder Standard has two perspectives — Debugging and Developing — and Flex Builder Professional includes a third perspective, Profiling. By using these perspectives, you can execute particular workflows or tasks more easily because each view targets a particular task. Figures 4-1 through 4-3 show the default user interface for the development, debugging, and profiling perspectives.

Flex Builder automatically changes the perspective when you do certain tasks. For example, when you create a new Flex project, the perspective automatically switches to the Flex Builder Development perspective. Similarly, when you set a breakpoint with the visual debugger and that breakpoint is hit, Flex Builder automatically switches to the Flex Builder Debugging perspective. To find out more about what a breakpoint is and how to use the visual debugger, jump over to Chapter 5, which discusses how to debug Flex applications.

Current perspective

Navigator view

Switch perspectives

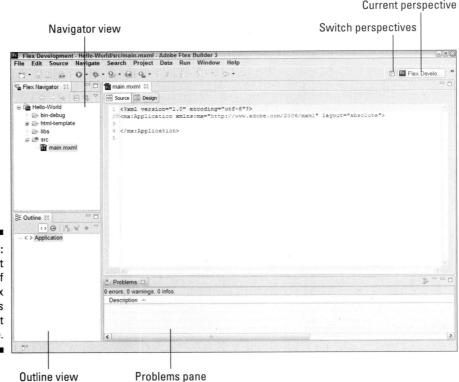

Figure 4-1:
The default view of Flex Builder's Development perspective.

Outline view

Problems pane

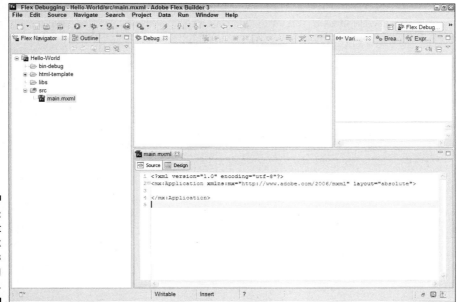

Figure 4-2:
The default view of Flex Builder's Debugging perspective.

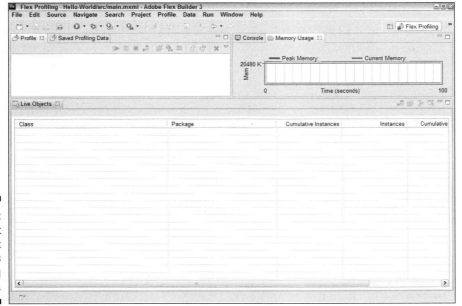

Figure 4-3:
The default view of Flex Builder's Profiling perspective.

By default, Flex Builder prompts you about switching Flex Builder perspectives when you start a task that requires a perspective change. For example, hitting a breakpoint causes Flex Builder to open a dialog box, prompting you that it would like to switch to the Debugging perspective. Normally, you want to click Yes because the perspective change, which focuses the user interface more toward the task at hand, makes executing your task easier. If you don't want this confirmation dialog box to appear each time, select the Remember My Decision check box before you click Yes.

You can always see what perspective you're currently in by looking at the upper-right corner of your Flex Builder window. A button identifies the current perspective (refer to Figure 4-1), and you can click that button to switch to another perspective.

You can also manually switch perspectives by using the top-level Flex Builder menus: Choose Window➪Perspective➪Flex Debugging *or* Flex Development *or* Flex Profiling to switch perspectives.

Customizing perspective views

When you change the view in a particular Flex Builder perspective, those changes become associated with that perspective; then when you switch back to that perspective later, those changes are reproduced. You can make many changes to the views in Flex Builder's user interface. You can resize views several ways:

- ✔ Minimize or maximize view by using the icons at the top of each view (refer to Figure 4-1).
- ✔ Use the double-headed arrow cursor that appears when you hover over a view's border. When the double-headed arrow appears, click and drag to resize that particular view.

When you modify and resize different perspectives, you may want to go back to the default view for that perspective. You can reset the current perspective back to its size and layout defaults by choosing Window➪Perspective➪Reset Perspective. When you reset the perspective, you lose all the modifications that you made to that perspective's views.

Similarly, you can drag and drop views into different locations by hovering over the view's label and then dragging. The cursor changes into a folder icon to indicate you're moving the view. Flex Builder gives visual cues about where that view will be relocated when you drop it. In the example in Figure 4-4, we dragged and dropped the Outline view so that it's now next to the Navigator view.

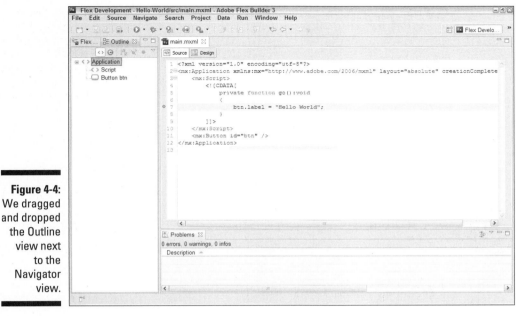

Figure 4-4:
We dragged
and dropped
the Outline
view next
to the
Navigator
view.

Creating Different Types of Projects in Flex Builder

Flex Builder groups all the MXML, ActionScript, and CSS code files, as well as assets and other folders, into projects. A *project* is basically all the resources that comprise your application or component. Flex Builder lets you create different types of projects. The three main types of projects are

- ✔ **Flex Project:** You create this type of project when writing Flex applications. This is the most common type.

- ✔ **ActionScript Project:** You create this type of project when you want to write an application that does not use the Flex framework but is instead an application written purely in ActionScript code.

- ✔ **Flex Library Project:** Create this type of project when you want to write custom code that you'll distribute to other developers or link into other Flex projects.

To create one of these types of projects, choose File➪New➪Flex Project *or* ActionScript Project *or* Flex Library Project. In the following sections, we discuss each type of project in more detail.

Flex Projects

Most often, you'll create Flex Projects, which is the type of project you create when you build most types of Flex applications. When you create a new Flex Project, you specify all the information that you need to configure and identify that project. Information such as the project name, what type of data back-end the project uses, how the project should be built, and whether you want to target the application you're building for the Web or a computer desktop. When you choose File➪New➪Flex Project, the New Flex Project Wizard appears, ready to walk you through setting up the Flex Project (see Figure 4-5). Just follow these steps:

1. **Specify the project name in the Project Name text field.**

   This name shows up in the Flex Navigator, which keeps track of all your projects.

2. **Choose the project location in the Project Location section.**

   Decide where you want all the source files, asset files, and ancillary information related to your project to live. Usually, you can just let Flex Builder use the default location.

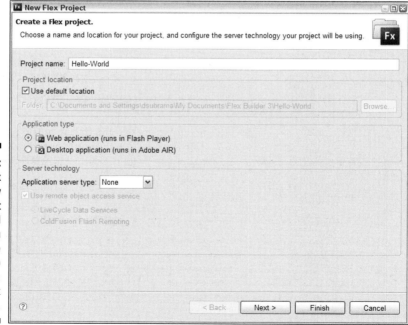

Figure 4-5:
The Flex Builder New Project Wizard walks you through the steps to create a new Flex project.

3. Select the application type in the Application Type section.

The application type determines whether you want to target the application that you're building for the Web or for the computer desktop. New in Flex 3 is the integration with Adobe AIR, a new technology that lets you use Flex technologies to build desktop applications. In Flex Builder 3, you can configure your Flex application to run as a Web application or as a desktop application. You can find out more about Adobe AIR at www.adobe.com/products/air.

You should make this choice based on which platform you are targeting. By default, Flex Builder creates Flex projects that are targeted for the Web. If you change this option, Flex Builder uses the new option the next time you create a Flex project.

4. Choose the data back-end for your Flex application in the Server technology section.

By default, the None server option is selected. This setting often suffices when you're building Flex applications that use the Flex RPC libraries, such as the WebService MXML tag or HTTPService MXML tag. By selecting the appropriate option from the Application Server Type drop-down list, you can also target an ASP.NET, J2EE, ColdFusion, or PHP back-end. You select the J2EE option when you build a Flex application that targets LiveCycle Data Services. LiveCycle Data Services is an Adobe technology that includes many of the high-end, enterprise level data features large projects desire. You can find out more about LiveCycle Data Services on the Adobe Web site.

5. Click Next.

The next step in the wizard for creating a new Flex project appears.

6. Specify the folder in which you want to place the output for your Flex application. Then click Next.

By default, the output is put in a folder called bin-debug at the root of your Flex project. You can almost always use this default but may choose to change the folder name to follow your own coding conventions.

After you click Next, the next step appears, in which you specify the build paths for your Flex application, as shown in Figure 4-6.

7. If needed, add additional source files to the build path.

Build paths specify the location of external source and library files. By default, all the controls and components that comprise the Flex framework are specified in the Library pane. So, right out of the box, a new Flex project is set up to build Flex applications. Most of the time, when you start building and creating Flex applications, you don't need to add any additional source files to the build path.

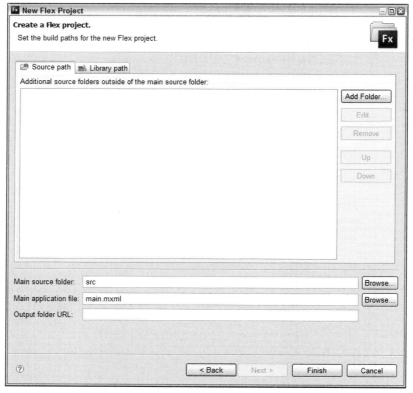

Figure 4-6:
The Flex Builder New Project Wizard prompts you for modifications to the build path.

8. **Click Finish to create a Flex project that has all the settings you've specified in the New Project Wizard.**

After you create the project, it appears in the Flex Builder Navigator view. You use the Navigator view to delete projects or modify the properties of existing Flex projects. The root MXML file for the new project opens automatically in Flex Builder once the project has been created, and this file is usually the entry point into your Flex application and where you begin your application development. For example, if you create a new project called HelloWorld, `HelloWorld.mxml` is the root MXML application for the project, and a skeleton MXML file opens in the MXML editor. *Voilà,* you're ready to go!

If the Flex project name has a space or hyphen in it, the root MXML file that is auto-created by Flex Builder is named main.mxml. If the project doesn't have a space or hyphen in it, Flex Builder names the root MXML file the same name as the project.

ActionScript Projects

ActionScript Projects are applications that don't use the Flex Framework (and thus MXML) and, instead, are built purely with ActionScript code and the libraries offered natively by the Flash Player. Because Flex Builder has a very powerful ActionScript code editor and debugger, Flex Builder is the perfect tool for building ActionScript-only applications.

To create a new ActionScript project, choose File⇨New⇨ActionScript. Then follow these steps to use the New ActionScript Project Wizard (shown in Figure 4-7) to create your project:

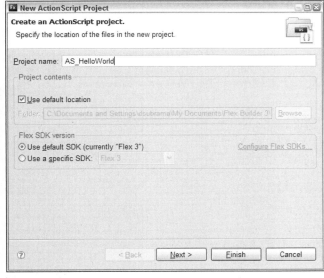

Figure 4-7:
The Flex
Builder New
Project
Wizard
walks you
through
creating
a new
ActionScript
project.

1. **Enter the name of your project in the Project Name text field.**

   This name appears in the Flex Navigator view representing your project.

2. **Specify the location for the project's code files, asset files, and all other source material in the Project Contents section.**

   Often, you can use the default location that Flex Builder chooses.

3. **Choose which version of the Flex framework the application should target in the Flex SDK Version section.**

   A new feature in Flex Builder 3 allows you to build a Flex or ActionScript application that targets a particular version of the Flex framework. We discuss this feature in more detail in the "Targeting different versions of the Flex Software Development Kit (SDK)" section, later in this chapter. By default, Flex Builder always creates a new application that targets the latest released version of the Flex framework. Certain prior versions of the Flex framework source code are shipped with Flex Builder, and your application can target these prior versions. Simply select the Use a Specific SDK radio button and select the desired version of the Flex framework in the version drop-down list.

4. Click the Next button.

Flex opens the Build Paths pane in the New ActionScript Project Wizard, shown in Figure 4-8.

5. If needed, add additional source files to the build path.

In this window, you can specify where external source files or libraries are located and include them into the source path of your application so that your application can access that code. Often, you can use the default settings because Flex Builder already adds the Flex Framework source code into the build path so that you can access all the classes and code in the various Flex Framework libraries.

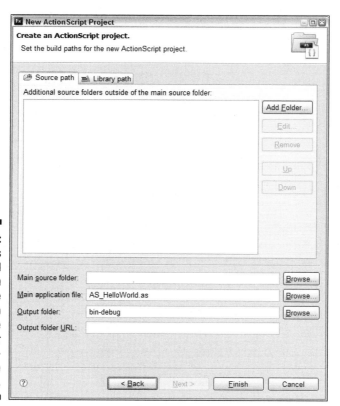

Figure 4-8:
In this wizard pane, you can edit the build path to include other source-code libraries.

6. Click Finish.

The new ActionScript project is created and appears in the Flex Navigator view. You use this entry in the Flex Navigator to edit the project's settings or delete the project.

After you create the project, the root ActionScript file opens in the ActionScript code editor automatically. This root ActionScript file is usually the entry point into your application, and it's the file that Flex Builder compiles when creating your application's output.

Flex Library Projects

The final type of project that you can create is a Flex Library Project. You use a Flex Library Project to create custom code libraries that you link into other Flex applications or distribute to other developers. A Flex Library Project produces *SWC files,* which are compressed files containing ActionScript and MXML code. Flex Library Projects are an advanced topic, and you can consult the Flex Builder documentation included with your Flex Builder installation for more information on configuring Flex Library projects. The "Accessing Flex Builder Help Materials" section, later in this chapter, describes how you can access Flex Builder documentation directly within Flex Builder.

Organizing and Editing Your Projects

You can organize the source files related to your project however you want, but Flex Builder automatically uses some organizational methods to help you maintain your project. By default, Flex Builder puts source files such as MXML, AS, and CSS files into the src folder in the project directory. The outputted SWF and HTML files that represent your application are put in the bin-debug folder that lives in the project directory.

You can create new folders for organizing your source files. Usually, you want to create these new folders as subdirectories to the src folder. For example, Flex application developers often create a folder called images or imgs to hold their visual assets, such as `.jpg`, `.gif` or `.png` files.

To create a new folder, follow these steps:

1. Locate the directory in the Flex Navigator view that you want the new folder to live in and then right-click that directory.

A context menu opens, containing options that let you modify the project properties and source files.

2. **Choose New➪Folder from the context menu.**

   The New Folder dialog box opens, as shown in Figure 4-9.

   When you choose New from the context menu, you can create other elements, in addition to folders. For example, you can create a new MXML application, MXML component, ActionScript class, or a plain file.

3. **Specify the name and location of the new folder**

   In Figure 4-9, we're creating a new folder to hold our application's images.

4. **Click Finish.**

Whenever you need to add any new document to your project, right-click the project and select the New option in the context menu or select which document you want to create from the top-level menu options (File➪New). The Flex Builder wizards walk you through naming and setting properties on these new documents.

Figure 4-9:
You can right-click projects in the Flex Navigator to create new files or folders.

Editing existing project settings

You can edit project properties such as build path and output folders on an existing project very easily by using the Flex Navigator. Simply right-click the project name in the Flex Navigator and select Properties from the context menu that appears. A Properties dialog box, similar to Figure 4-10, appears. Select a listing from the left pane to edit that particular property or setting.

For example, if you want to create a Flex application that's *accessibility enabled* — meaning a Flex application that an assistive screen reader can read — open the Properties dialog box (shown in Figure 4-10), select Flex Compiler, and select the Generate Accessible SWF File check box.

 If you tweak your project properties too much and want to go back to Flex Builder's project defaults, simply click the Restore Defaults button at the bottom of the project Properties dialog box. All the settings on that particular project restore back to their defaults.

 In addition to the Flex Navigator, you can use the top-level Flex Builder menus to open the project Properties dialog box. Simply select the project in the Flex Navigator view and choose File➪Properties.

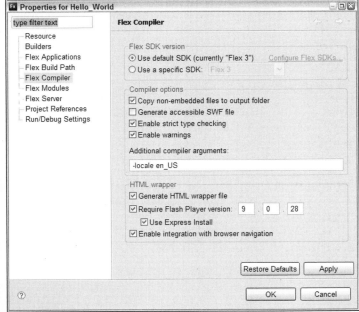

Figure 4-10: The Properties dialog box lets you edit the existing project's properties.

Deleting projects

To delete a project, right-click the project in the Flex Navigator view and select Delete from the context menu that appears. The Confirm Project Delete dialog box opens. You can choose one of the following options to delete the project:

✔ Delete the project from the Flex Navigator view and keep all the project's content. If you select this option, you can always import the project back into Flex Builder. To find out more about importing Flex Builder projects, check out the section "Importing and Exporting Existing Flex Builder Projects," later in this chapter.

✔ Delete the project, as well as all its contents, meaning any source files that comprise that project.

Be careful when choosing to delete all of a project's content because you can't restore it after deletion. By default, the Do Not Delete Contents option is selected.

Targeting different versions of the Flex Software Development Kit (SDK)

Flex Builder 3 includes a new feature that allows you to choose which version of the Flex SDK (Software Development Kit) you want your Flex or ActionScript project to target. The Flex SDK is basically all of the code libraries and the MXML compiler that is needed to create and compile a Flex application.

When new versions of the Flex SDK are released, Flex Builder installs the newest version as well as some prior versions of the Flex SDK during the installation process. That way, Flex Builder lets you target prior versions of the Flex SDK when you build your Flex application. By default, Flex Builder creates projects that target the latest version of Flex. You may choose to target an older Flex SDK, for example, when a new version of Flex Builder comes out and you import one of your pre-existing projects. For example, you may want to ensure that the old project targets the older version of the Flex framework if you don't want to update your project's source code to work with the newer version of the Flex SDK

You can set or edit the targeted SDK project property by following these steps:

1. **Right-click the project's name in the Flex Navigator and select Properties from the context menu that appears.**

   The Properties dialog box appears.

2. **In the left pane of the Properties dialog box, select the Flex Compiler option.**

In the Flex SDK Version section on the right side of the dialog box, the Use Default SDK option is selected, as shown earlier in Figure 4-10. That option also displays what the default SDK is (it's often the latest version of the Flex SDK like Flex 3).

3. **To choose which SDK version you want the project to target, select the Use a Specific SDK radio button. Then from the SDK drop-down list, select which Flex version you want to target.**

4. **Click OK to close the dialog box.**

Importing and Exporting Existing Flex Builder Projects

Flex Builder lets you import an existing project or export a project as an archive file. You may find this feature helpful in situations in which Flex projects are archived in a source control repository for sharing code among team members.

A *source control repository* (also known as revision control software) is a piece of software that allows for the management and organization of multiple versions of software between team members. CVS, Perforce, and SVN are all common types of source control repository software.

You can simply import projects from a source control repository that already have their project settings configured. This is because as you create a project and edit its properties, Flex Builder creates a file representing that project and its configuration and saves the file in the project directory. You can import the project directory into Flex Builder, and the project can be created and configured based on the information in that project file. If you're working on a team that has multiple developers working on the same projects, these project-importing capabilities can be very handy for quickly setting up complex projects. Similarly, you can use the export project options to export a project as a Zip file and then easily share the project with other developers who use Flex Builder.

Importing a project

The steps to import an existing project are very straightforward:

1. **Choose File⇨Import⇨Flex Project.**

    The Import Flex Project dialog box opens, as shown in Figure 4-11.

Decide whether you want to import the project from an existing archive file — that is, a Zip file — or from a folder on your file system that contains all the project source files and a file capturing the project configurations

2. **Click the Browse buttons for whichever option describes the project that you want to import and select the Zip file or folder that encompasses your project.**

3. **(Optional) To change the location where you want the files to be imported, un-check the Use Default Location option and, in the Folder text field, specify the location in your file system.**

4. **Click Finish to close the wizard.**

Figure 4-11:
Flex Builder's Import Wizard lets you import existing projects from an archive Zip file or existing source code on your file system.

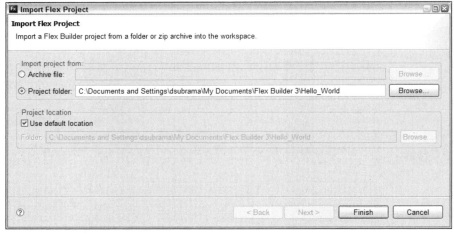

Exporting a project as an archive

Flex Builder offers a simple wizard that you can use to export an existing project into an archive (that is, a Zip) file. Just follow these steps:

1. **Select the project in the Flex Navigator view. Then, choose File⊅ Export⊅Flex Project Archive.**

   The Export Wizard appears, as shown in Figure 4-12.

2. **Select the project that you want to export from the Project drop-down list.**

3. **Use the Browse button to choose a location where you want to place your project's archive Zip file.**

   This Zip file contains all the source code and assets that comprise the Flex application.

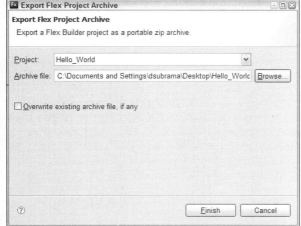

Figure 4-12:
Flex
Builder's
Export
Wizard lets
you export
your proj-
ect into an
archive
Zip file.

4. Click the Finish button.

Voilà, your project exports into a handy Zip file that you can send to other developers on your team!

Running and Releasing Your Projects

Flex Builder allows you to *build* your project — that is, compile the project into the appropriate end result — for use in a debugging session or for releasing to your end users. The most common build task is for you to enable the Build Automatically option, which means that the project is built continually, and Flex Builder reports errors in the current state of your project in the Problems view in real time. By default, the Build Automatically option is not set because this capability can take a long time, depending on the size of your project.

Building and cleaning your projects

To enable the Build Automatically option, choose Project➪Build Automatically from the menu bar. When you write code in your project with Build Automatically enabled, Flex Builder alerts you of errors, such as compilation errors, in the Flex Builder Problems view. For example, in Figure 4-13, the Problems view points out an error in which a component id is inaccurate.

If you are working on a small to medium-size project, feel free to enable the Build Automatically option. As you work, if you notice Flex Builder is taking too long to build and analyze the current state of your project, you can disable Build Automatically to gain a performance boost.

If you don't enable Build Automatically, you can build your applications by selecting the appropriate build options in the top-level Project menu. You can choose to build all your projects, a single project, or a set of projects.

Sometimes, you may want to clean your projects before building to ensure that all the changes have been analyzed and the prior build output is cleared. To clean your projects, choose Project⇨Clean. The Clean dialog box opens, in which you can choose to clean all the projects in your workspace or a specific project. Get into the habit of cleaning your projects so that you can ensure they stay in up-to-date shape.

Run

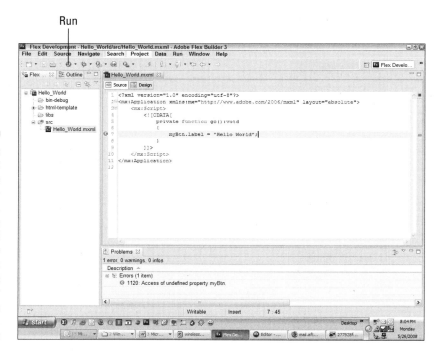

Figure 4-13:
When you enable Build Automatically, compilation and build problems appear in the Flex Builder Problems view.

Running your projects

To *run* your project — that is, to output the project into its runable form, such as loading a SWF application in a Web browser — click the Run icon, shown in Figure 4-13. Flex then compiles the project and opens the application in a browser window so that you can view it. If Flex encounters compilation problems, those problems appear in the Problems view, and you need to fix them before you can run the application.

To find out how to debug your application, refer to Chapter 5 for information on using Flex Builder's visual debugger.

Releasing your projects

After you develop your projects to satisfactory form, you need to get all the files built in a way that is appropriate for the application to be released to its end users. Flex Builder gives you the option to export a project into a release version, in which the project does not include any bloat-inducing materials, such as debug information.

To export a release version of your application by using the Export Release Build Wizard, follow these steps:

1. **Choose File⇨Export⇨Release Build.**

    The Export Release Build Wizard, shown in Figure 4-14, opens.

2. **From the Project drop-down list, select the project that you want to export, and from the Application drop-down list, select the root MXML or ActionScript file for that project.**

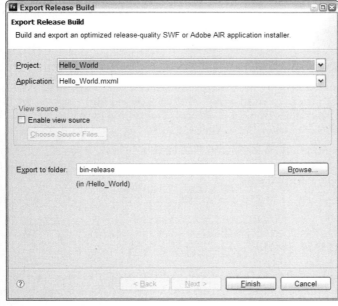

Figure 4-14:
Use the Export Release Build Wizard to create a release version of your project.

3. **(Optional) Check the Enable View Source check box if you want to build a release version of your application that allows users to right-click in your running application and view the source files and code (including ActionScript, MXML, and CSS files) that comprise your application.**

   By default, this option is unchecked, but if it's okay to introduce an element of *transparency* in your application (that is, let users see the code behind the running application), go ahead and select the Enable View Source option.

4. **In the last section of the dialog box, browse to a location in the file system where you want to write the release version files.**

5. **Click Finish.**

   You now have an export-worthy version of your project that you can upload to your production servers and share with the world!

Accessing Flex Builder Help Materials

Flex and Flex Builder documentation that you can use to understand features and quickly get help when you're working on your projects are built into Flex Builder. You can use most of these options through Flex Builder's top-level Help menu. Here are some of the options available on this menu:

- ✔ **Help Contents:** View help materials in a separate window.
- ✔ **Search:** Query the help documentation.
- ✔ **Report a Bug:** Access the public, online Flex bug-base, in which you can enter new bugs, and watch and vote on existing bugs in the Flex framework and Flex Builder products. The online Flex bug base is located at http://bugs.adobe.com/flex.
- ✔ **Flex Start Page:** Return to Flex Builder's start page, which has all sorts of useful information and a tutorial to get you up and running building simple Flex projects.

Chapter 5

Introducing Flex Builder for Developers

In This Chapter

▶ Understanding the composition of an MXML file

▶ Improving productivity with a few Flex Builder tricks

▶ Debugging and profiling your application

▶ Refactoring your code

*1*n this chapter, we cover the Flex Builder features that you will specifically use for writing code, debugging, and optimizing your applications. This chapter covers the nuts and bolts of how to build and run Flex applications; if you're interested in finding out how to make your applications look pretty, page ahead to Chapter 6.

This chapter starts off by breaking down the different parts of an MXML file and explaining how you can combine MXML code, ActionScript code, and style blocks together and make them all play nice. Then you discover a few Flex Builder tips that will make you glad you purchased Flex Builder. In the last few sections of this chapter, you find out about debugging and profiling with Flex Builder's built-in tools.

Anatomy of an MXML File

All Flex applications start as a single MXML file that contains a base `<mx:Application>` tag. As your project grows, you likely create multiple MXML or ActionScript files to separate pieces of your projects into their own files, but you always have a single MXML file that contains the Application tag. All MXML files can contain three main parts:

✔ MXML markup

✔ ActionScript code blocks

✔ CSS Script blocks

These three elements can be used interchangeably within a single file. The example in Listing 5-1 is a small Flex application that contains all three individual pieces.

Listing 5-1: A Typical MXML Application with MXML Markup and Style and Script Blocks

```
<?xml version="1.0" encoding="utf-8"?>
<mx:Application xmlns:mx="http://www.adobe.com/2006/mxml">

    <mx:Style>                                                      →4
        .redButton {
            fill-colors: #ff0000, #330000;
            fill-alphas: 1, 1;
            color: #FFFFFF;
            text-roll-over-color: #FFFF00;
        }
    </mx:Style>                                                     → 11

    <mx:Script>                                                     → 13
        <![CDATA[
            import mx.controls.Alert;

            private function clickHandler(event:Event):void {
                Alert.show("You clicked the Button");
            }
        ]]>
    </mx:Script>                                                    → 22

    <mx:Button click="clickHandler(event)"                          → 24
        styleName="redButton" label="Click Me" />                   → 25

</mx:Application>                                                    → 27
```

The following list takes a closer look at Listing 5-1:

→ **4** On Lines 4 through 11, you create an `<mx:Style>` block that contains a CSS style. In this example, you create a style named `redButton` that sets the `fill-colors` and `fill-alphas` styles, which create an opaque red gradient background fill. You also set the `color` and `text-rollover-color` styles, which affect the color of the text on the Button that will apply this style. (See the "Introducing the <mx:Style /> tag" section, later in this chapter, for more on CSS.)

→ **13** Lines 13–22 define a `<mx:Script>` block that contains an ActionScript function. Anything within the `<mx:Script>` block must be ActionScript code; you cannot mix and match ActionScript and MXML within the `<mx:Script>` block. In this example, you create a function that runs when the user clicks the Button defined in this Application.

→ **24**   After the `<mx:Script>` block, you add the rest of the MXML tags that create this Application. In this simple example, you add a single `<mx:Button>` that will create a clickable button with a label that says Click Me. You reference the ActionScript `clickHandler` function that you defined previously in the `<mx:Script>` block (Lines 13–22).

→ **25**   You set the `styleName` of this Button to `redButton`, which references the CSS style that you created in the `<mx:Style>` block (Lines 4–11). This gives the Button a red gradient background.

Including ActionScript with the <mx:Script /> tag

You can create simple Flex applications with just MXML, but to make an application *do* something, you need to write some ActionScript. The good news is that MXML and ActionScript can coexist in the same file, so you can use the full power of ActionScript with the declarative markup of MXML.

The `<mx:Script>` block in Listing 5-2 shows how to include ActionScript within MXML. The `<!CDATA[` part of the `<mx:Script>` block is required, but should get automatically inserted by Flex Builder when you type `<mx:Script>`. You can declare variables and methods within the `<mx:Script>` block, and then you can reference those variables and methods in your MXML component tags.

Listing 5-2: Combining ActionScript with MXML Markup

```
<?xml version="1.0" encoding="utf-8"?>
<mx:Application xmlns:mx="http://www.adobe.com/2006/mxml">
   <mx:Script>
      <![CDATA[
        [Bindable]
        private var myCounter:int = 0;

        private function incrementCounter():void {
           myCounter++;
        }

        private function decrementCounter():void {
           myCounter--;
        }

      ]]>
   </mx:Script>
```

(continued)

Listing 5-2 *(continued)*

```
    <mx:Button label="Increment"
        click="incrementCounter()" />
    <mx:Button label="Decrement"
        click="decrementCounter()" />

    <mx:Label text="Current value: {myCounter}" />

</mx:Application>
```

Listing 5-2 shows how to declare a variable — myCounter — in ActionScript that then gets referenced in MXML. In this example, you use *data binding* to populate the text property of the <mx:Label> component. Data binding is a powerful feature of MXML that allows you to reference ActionScript variables within MXML markup. The curly braces that you see around the myCounter variable in Listing 5-2 show data binding in action. At runtime, the contents of the text property will always be updated to include the latest value of myCounter whenever it changes. For an in-depth look at data binding, head over to Chapter 12.

This listing also shows how to invoke ActionScript functions in response to user interaction with components defined in MXML. You add a few <mx:Button> tags to your application and use the click event on the buttons to call the functions you defined in the <mx:Script> block.

Introducing the <mx:Style /> tag

Flex supports styling using Cascading Style Sheets (CSS), similar to how CSS is used in HTML pages. CSS lets you define sets of styles that will affect the visual look and feel of your application. You can define styles for specific components or use custom style names, and these styles will affect everything from border color to font size. However, you should note that CSS styling in Flex applications isn't the same as CSS styling in HTML. Flex supports only a subset of the full functionality of CSS, and the style names you may be familiar with in HTML CSS aren't the same. For example, CSS in HTML allows nested (cascading) styles, but nested styles aren't allowed in Flex. This means that Flex supports styling in a similar way as CSS, but without the cascading part. Think of the styling approach in Flex as similar to CSS, but not *real* CSS.

You can style your Flex applications in four ways:

   ✔ Use the <mx:Style> block within your Application file to define the styles.

   ✔ Use an external CSS file and point to that file by setting the source property of a <mx:Style> tag.

✔ Set styles on individual MXML tags for specific components.

✔ Set styles through ActionScript by calling the `setStyle(styleName, value)` method on a specific component.

Listing 5-1 uses the first method to create the red button style. For more detailed information about styling, refer to Chapter 18.

Developer Tips and Tricks

You don't technically need Flex Builder in order to create Flex applications. If you're inclined, you can download the free (and open source) Flex SDK, use a text editor to write your code, and compile the code with the command-line compiler. So why would you shell out the cash to purchase Flex Builder? A number of its features dramatically improve your productivity while building Flex applications. We cover two of the most important features, the Debugger and the Profiler, later in this chapter. This section focuses on a few other helpful features that Flex Builder provides.

Get the hint: Code hinting

Flex Builder provides code hinting while you type, and after you experience code hinting, you'll cry if you ever have to go back to an editor without it. *Code hinting,* or *content assistance,* shows a drop-down list of possible options to complete the line you're typing. This feature works while you're editing both MXML and ActionScript.

To understand the power of code hinting, create a new Flex application and add a simple button to your application by typing <mx:Button. After you type the first space after <mx:Button, you see a list of all available properties, styles, events, and effects that you use for the Button component. Figure 5-1 shows the code hinting overlay that appears. As you continue typing, the list is filtered to show only the items that begin with the characters you typed.

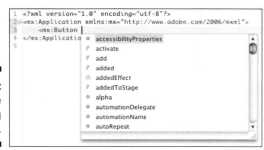

Figure 5-1:
The code hinting overlay.

At any point while you're typing, you can use the arrow keys to scroll through the applicable options. After you get the hang of using code hinting, you find that have to type only the first few letters of the properties you want and then quickly select the appropriate property from the list.

When you're editing an MXML tag, code hinting is automatically invoked when you type the space character. You can manually invoke code hinting at any time by pressing the key combination Ctrl+spacebar. We have become so dependent on code hinting that we inadvertently press Ctrl+spacebar on normal Web page forms, in the hope that code hinting will automatically complete the form for use. Learn to use the Ctrl+spacebar shortcut well, and it will become your best friend.

When you first use Flex, you may have difficulty keeping track of all the names of the properties available for each component. You can use the online Flex SDK documentation to look up a full list of properties, but often the fastest way is to invoke code hinting on an MXML tag and browse through the list. In fact, if you simply type the beginning of an MXML tag in your application by typing <, the full list of all components you can use in your application pop ups, which is useful before you memorize the names of the full Flex SDK component set (see Figure 5-2).

Figure 5-2: Using code hinting to browse all available components.

Code hinting also works when you edit ActionScript code. While editing ActionScript, you can use the same Ctrl+spacebar keyboard shortcut to manually invoke code hinting where it's available. As you type, you notice that code hinting is automatically displayed at various points — for example, whenever you type a period after a variable name to access properties of that variable.

Figure 5-3 shows the code hinting that appears in ActionScript as you type `button.s`, which lists all properties, styles, events, and effects available on the `button` variable that begin with the letter *s*.

Chapter 5: Introducing Flex Builder for Developers

Exploring the Flex SDK source code

You can use the Ctrl+click approach to jump to the source file of any class in the Flex SDK, not just to the source files you have created. If you Crl+click a class that's part of the Flex framework, Flex Builder loads the source for that particular class. This action lets you dive into the details of how the Adobe Flex team built the Flex SDK. Try not to get overwhelmed the first time: The source code for the Flex SDK is large and full of useful information, but you must have a fairly advanced knowledge of Flex to properly understand this resource. After you get a solid understanding of how Flex works, you can start digging into the internal workings of the framework by analyzing the source code of the framework itself. For now, just know that the code is available to you if you want to dig in and figure out how Adobe did something.

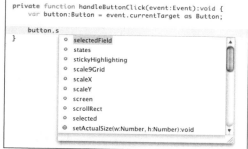

Figure 5-3:
Using code hinting while typing ActionScript code.

Going straight to the source code

Another powerful advantage of using Flex Builder is that you can jump into the source code for any MXML tag or ActionScript class you see in your application. If you move the mouse cursor over any MXML tag while holding down the Ctrl key (or the ⌘ key, if you're a Mac user), an underline appears under the class name of the MXML tag, as shown in Figure 5-4. Clicking this tag while holding down the Ctrl key opens the source file for that class, which can be useful when your application is divided into multiple MXML components and you reference one MXML file within another.

Figure 5-4:
Ctrl+Click to jump to the source file.

```
<mx:Application xmlns:mx="h
    xmlns:local="*">

    <local:MyComponent />

</mx:Application>
```

Using automatic builds

To run your Flex application, you need to build a compiled SWF file from the source MXML and ActionScript files. You have two build options:

- ✔ **Automatic:** You can turn automatic builds on or off by toggling the Project⇨Build Automatically menu item, shown in Figure 5-5. If automatic builds are turned on, each time you save changes to your source files, the compiler rebuilds your application.

- ✔ **Manual:** If you turn off automatic builds, you have to perform manual builds. The primary reason for disabling automatic builds is to improve the performance of Flex Builder. If you notice Flex Builder running sluggishly whenever you save a file, you might want to try turning off automatic builds. For more on building your project, see Chapter 4.

Figure 5-5:
The Project menu with its build options.

Organizing import statements

When you write ActionScript code, you need to have, at the top of your class, a block of *import statements* that let the compiler know which external classes you reference. Flex Builder is good at automatically adding the import statements to the top of your class, although if you aren't using the content assistance features fully, you may have to write some import statements by hand. At the top of your class, you see lines that look like this:

```
import mx.controls.Button;

import mx.managers.PopUpManager;
import mx.containers.Canvas;

import mx.collections.ArrayCollection;
import flash.events.Event;
import mx.controls.Alert;
```

These import statements tell the compiler where to find all the classes that you use somewhere in your code. As you write more and more code, the number of import statements grows. If you remove chunks of code and you no longer reference certain classes, extraneous import statements are left in your code. Luckily, Flex Builder can automatically organize your import statements, which removes any unused imports and orders your imports by package name and in alphabetical order.

Flex Builder can be set to always keep your import statements organized, or you can manually run the Organize Imports command whenever you like. The default Flex Builder installation has automatic import organization turned on. To modify the import organization properties, choose Window⇨Preferences⇨ Flex⇨Editors⇨ActionScript Code to open the Preferences panel, as shown in Figure 5-6.

Figure 5-6:
Flex Builder
import
organization
options.

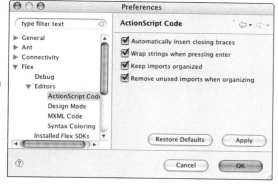

If Flex Builder is set to automatically organize your import statements, then it will reorganize the code in the previous example to produce the following lines:

```
import flash.events.Event;

import mx.collections.ArrayCollection;
import mx.containers.Canvas;
import mx.controls.Alert;
import mx.controls.Button;
import mx.managers.PopUpManager;
```

Notice that the import statements are now in alphabetical order based on the full package name, and an extra white space line is inserted between blocks of imports from different base packages. If you have Flex Builder set to not automatically organize your import statements and they seem cluttered and unorganized, try running the Organize Imports command manually by choosing Source⇨Organize Imports.

Import organization is available only if you're editing a pure ActionScript file. If you're editing an MXML file that contains an `<mx:Script>` block with ActionScript code, you have to manually organize your own import statements.

Squashing Bugs with the Visual Debugger

Debugging code is an integral part of writing software applications. Nobody writes bug-free code, so having a solid debugging tool to help track down those pesky bugs is a must. If you come from a Flash development background, you have probably had the unpleasant experience of writing ActionScript code in the Flash IDE and using millions of `trace()` statements throughout your code as the primary means of debugging. Thankfully, Flex Builder provides a full-fledged debugger that's essential for powerful application development.

Launching the debugging perspective

To begin debugging your application, run the debug version of the compiled SWF. To launch debugging, select your main application file, right-click, and choose Debug As➪Flex Application. This command switches Flex Builder from the Flex Development perspective to the Flex Debugging perspective, shown in Figure 5-7.

Using breakpoints to step through code

An essential debugging technique involves adding breakpoints to your code. *Breakpoints* are markers at specific lines in your source code that pause code execution. After a breakpoint is reached, you can step into the code, inspect variables, and step through the code line by line to understand exactly what's happening as the code executes.

You can add a breakpoint to your code in two ways:

- Place the cursor at the line you want in your code and choose Run➪Toggle Breakpoint from the Flex Builder menu.
- Double-click the line number of the line you want.

After a breakpoint is added, you see a round dot icon next to the line number, indicating that the breakpoint has been added (see Figure 5-8).

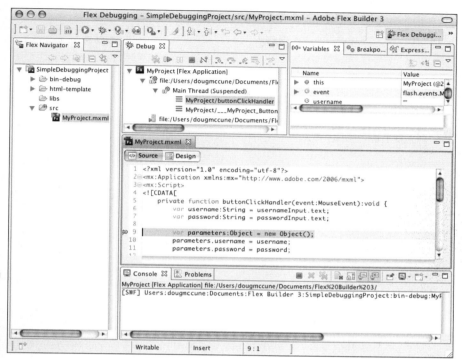

Figure 5-7:
The Flex
Debugging
perspective.

Figure 5-8:
A break-
point on
Line 9.

When you run the application in Debug mode, it pauses when it reaches a breakpoint, and at that point you can use the debug controls to step through the code. The debugging control bar is shown in Figure 5-9.

You can use the first few buttons on the toolbar shown in Figure 5-9 to control the debugging session by resuming code execution or terminating the debugging session. If you press the play button to resume code execution, the application continues to run until the next breakpoint is reached. The fairly self-explanatory stop button ends your debugging session.

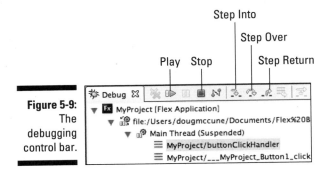

Step Into

Step Over

Play   Stop   Step Return

Figure 5-9:
The
debugging
control bar.

Use the three buttons with the arrow icons (refer to Figure 5-9) to step through your code line by line:

- ✔ **Step Into:** The first button in this set, the Step Into button, steps into any functions in the current line of code. If the debugger is paused on a line that contains calls to another function, which might be contained in a separate class, clicking the Step Into button loads that function (even if it is defined in a different class) and continues debugging.

- ✔ **Step Over:** Alternatively, you may want to stay in the function you're debugging and not jump around into each of the functions that are referenced. In this case, you can use the Step Over button to "step over" the function and continue debugging on the next line.

- ✔ **Step Return:** The third button, Step Return, jumps out of the current function and pauses the debugger wherever that function returns. You then jump to wherever that function was called and continue debugging from there.

Debugging a Flex application consists of stepping through much of the code line by line to identify the exact location of bugs. You will become quite familiar with setting breakpoints and stepping into, out of, and over your source code.

Inspecting variables

Stepping through lines of code on its own isn't incredibly useful, but inspecting the state of variables while debugging certainly is. During the debugging process, the Variables panel (shown in Figure 5-10) contains a list of all populated variables and their values.

The example in Figure 5-10 sets a breakpoint in `buttonClickHandler`, after the values for `username` and `password` have been assigned. You can then view the values in the Variables panel and ensure that they are in fact valid values before they get sent to the Web service later in the function.

Figure 5-10:
The
Variables
panel.

Name	Value
▶ ◉ this	MyProject (@2c4120a1)
▶ ◉ event	flash.events.MouseEvent (@1d7
◉ username	"dougmccune"
◉ password	"secretPassword"
◉ parameters	undefined

Profiling Your Application

Flex applications can produce stunning visual effects and load tremendous amounts of data, but an inherent danger accompanies that power. Flex applications also have the potential to consume massive amounts of memory and processing power on the user's computer. Building a large and impressive Flex application is a constant balancing act in which you have to always be aware of the cost, in terms of RAM use and CPU performance, for these rich experiences.

Of all the new features added to version 3 of Flex Builder, perhaps the most useful is the *Flex Profiler,* which lets you monitor your application's performance and dig in to identify bottlenecks and memory leaks. Writing high-performance, scalable Flex applications is no easy task, but the Flex Profiler takes much of the guesswork out of application optimization.

In this section, we give you an overview of using the Flex Profiler, for both memory management and performance profiling. For more detailed performance tips and further discussion of using the Flex Profiler, refer to the bonus chapter titled "Optimizing Your Flex Applications," available for downloading at www.dummies.com/go/adobeflexfd.

The Flex Profiler is available only if you purchased the Professional version of Flex Builder 3. In this section, we assume that you have purchased Flex Builder Pro. If you have the trial version of Flex Builder, you can test the features of the Profiler that we discuss here during your trial period.

Taking out the garbage: The Garbage Collector

Before we talk about profiling memory use, you must have a basic understanding of the Garbage Collector and the impact it has on the memory use of your Flex application. As your application runs, it generates objects in memory. Every time you create a new variable, you're creating an object that takes up an amount of space. If you create a new String or Number object, the amount of space for that individual object is fairly small. But if you create a new Image or BitmapData object, the size of that single object can be quite large. As all these objects accumulate in memory, the amount of RAM needed to run your application increases.

If the number of objects in memory continues rising, eventually your application becomes sluggish and unresponsive and might even lock up the user's computer. As your application runs, the *Garbage Collector* continuously monitors the memory use of your application and ensures that any objects you need stay in memory and that all unneeded objects are dumped. By dumping unneeded objects, the Garbage Collector frees up memory to keep your application running smoothly.

To determine which objects should stay in memory and which ones can be collected, the Garbage Collector checks all objects for references to the object in other parts of the application. If a reference to the object is found, the object cannot be garbage-collected because that would make it unavailable and the other part of your application that needs it would have a problem accessing it.

You can use a few tips and tricks to help ensure that you're freeing up references to objects that you want garbage-collected. See the bonus chapter ("Optimizing Your Flex Applications") for a discussion of some of these hints.

You cannot predict when the Garbage Collector will sweep through and collect the trash. How often it runs is determined by a variety of factors, including the memory limitations placed on Flash Player by the browser in which your application is running. The garbage-collection process might run more often in one browser than in another, or more often on one user's computer than on another. Because the Garbage Collector tries to run only when necessary, your Flex application eats up as much memory as it wants, to a certain point — when Flash Player decides that it's time for a little housecleaning.

Profiling memory use

When you're optimizing your Flex application, you should focus on two distinct areas: memory usage and CPU performance. *Profiling* memory use involves keeping track of all objects held in memory and identifying memory leaks. A *memory leak* occurs when an object that's no longer needed continues to be held in memory. In this section, we cover profiling memory usage, but for in-depth coverage of identifying and preventing memory leaks, refer to the bonus chapter.

If you want to initialize the Profiler, you launch your application in a slightly different way. You can either right-click a main application MXML file and choose Profile As➪Flex Application or choose Run➪Profile from the main Flex Builder menu, shown in Figure 5-11.

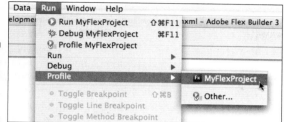

Figure 5-11:
Launching
the Flex
Profiler.

Before launching the profiling session, you can specify which profiling options you want to enable. The properties dialog box shown in Figure 5-12 lets you enable or disable different options for memory and performance profiling.

The Enable Memory Profiling check box controls whether the Profiler keeps track of memory statistics. If you deselect this box, you can still profile the performance of your application, but no memory details will be available. Within memory profiling, you have two configuration options:

- ✔ **Watch Live Memory Data box:** If you select this check box, a list of all objects in memory is displayed in real time as your application runs. Otherwise, you have to take a memory snapshot when you want to see the objects that are in memory.

- ✔ **Generate Object Allocation Stack Traces:** This check box controls whether the Flex Profiler keeps track of where in your source code each object in memory was created. If you select this check box, you can inspect each individual object and see exactly where the object was created, which can be helpful for tracking down memory leaks.

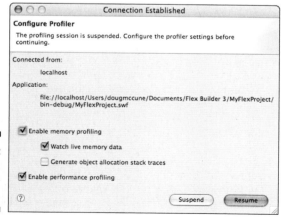

Figure 5-12:
Profiling
configura-
tion options.

The Watch Live Memory Data and Generate Object Allocation Stack Traces
options both provide useful information while profiling your application but
require significant resources on your computer. If you have a powerful computer, you can probably select both options; if you find the performance of the
Profiler to be an issue, however, try disabling them. You don't create a complete
picture without them, but sometimes the Flex Profiler can be a resource hog.

After you begin profiling your application, Flex Builder switches into the
Profiling perspective, as shown in Figure 5-13. The Profiling perspective is
divided into three main parts: the profiling session controls in the upper-left
area, the Memory Usage chart in the upper-right area, and the Live Objects
list along the bottom.

Profiling session controls   Memory Usage chart

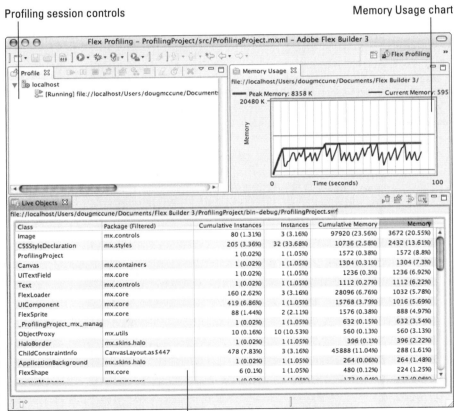

Figure 5-13:
The Flex
Profiling
perspective.

Live Objects list

Inspecting live objects

If you leave the Watch Live Memory Data check box selected in the Profiler's option panel, the Profiling perspective shows a list of all objects in memory as your application runs. This list can be sorted and filtered in real time and can help you inspect object creation and collection as it happens.

Figure 5-14 shows some sample output in the Live Objects panel. The list shows unique entries for each class and displays the number of instances and the amount of memory that was allocated.

Take Memory Snapshot

Filters

Class	Package (Filtered)	Cumulative Instances	Instances	Cumulative Memory	Memory
Image	mx.controls	92 (1.32%)	5 (4.95%)	112608 (23.7%)	6120 (28.87%)
CSSStyleDeclaration	mx.styles	229 (3.28%)	32 (31.68%)	11888 (2.5%)	2432 (11.47%)
FlexLoader	mx.core	184 (2.63%)	5 (4.95%)	32320 (6.8%)	1720 (8.11%)
ProfilingProject		1 (0.01%)	1 (0.99%)	1572 (0.33%)	1572 (7.42%)
Canvas	mx.containers	1 (0.01%)	1 (0.99%)	1304 (0.27%)	1304 (6.15%)
UITextField	mx.core	1 (0.01%)	1 (0.99%)	1236 (0.26%)	1236 (5.83%)
Text	mx.controls	1 (0.01%)	1 (0.99%)	1112 (0.23%)	1112 (5.25%)

Figure 5-14: Inspecting live objects in memory.

Here's a closer look at the individual columns in the Live Objects panel:

✓ **Class column and Package column:** The first two columns, Class and Package, identify the class so that you can track down exactly which objects you're looking at. By default, the Flex Profiler filters out the Flex and Flash packages (all classes under the `mx.*` or `flash.*` package structure). These default filters can be useful if you want to focus on custom classes, but sometimes you want to include the classes from the Flex framework to see how they're affecting memory usage. You can change the filters by clicking the Filters icon (refer to Figure 5-14).

In Figure 5-14, we removed the `mx.*.*` filter so that we can see the Flex classes that are taking up memory.

✓ **Cumulative Instances column and Instances column:** The next two columns, Cumulative Instances and Instances, tell you how many objects of a given class have been created:

  • *Cumulative Instances:* Refers to the total number of objects that have been created since the application started

  • *Instances:* Displays the number of instances that are live in memory

If the count in the Cumulative Instances column is higher than the count in the Instances column, you know that some of the objects that were created were garbage-collected.

If you compare the numbers in the Cumulative Instances column and the Instances column shown in Figure 5-14, you can see that the application created 92 total instances of the Image class and that only 5 remain in memory. The other 87 instances of the Image class, therefore, were garbage-collected.

✔ **Cumulative Memory column and Memory column:** The next two columns, Cumulative Memory and Memory, indicate how much total memory has been allocated for each class and how much memory each class is occupying. If you look at the corresponding numbers in Figure 5-14, you can see that the 92 instances of the Image class occupied a combined 112,608 bytes. The more important number in this view, however, is in the Memory column, which indicates that the 5 Image objects that remain in memory are occupying a total of 6,120 bytes. This number contributes to the total memory footprint of your application.

If your application is correctly freeing objects for garbage collection, the general trend you see is that the numbers in the Cumulative Instances and Cumulative Memory columns keep increasing while the values in the Instances and the Memory columns rise and fall, indicating that objects are being created and garbage-collected correctly. A common sign of a memory leak is if the numbers in the Incidents column and Memory column continue to increase but never decrease.

Taking memory snapshots

Inspecting live memory allocation in your application can be incredibly useful, but sometimes you want to compare the amount of memory used in your application at different stages. At any point while the Flex Profiler is running, you can take a memory snapshot, which captures the memory allocation data at the time you take the snapshot and saves it so that you can analyze it later. To take a snapshot, click the Take Memory Snapshot button, as shown in Figure 5-14.

When you take a memory snapshot, a new snapshot entry is added to the profiling session, as shown in Figure 5-15. You can select a snapshot by double-clicking the entry, which loads the snapshot details into a new panel.

Capture Performance Snapshot

Finding Loitering Objects

Figure 5-15:
Multiple
memory
snapshots.

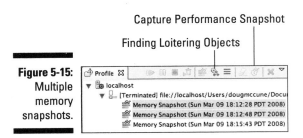

Each memory snapshot contains information that's similar to the information shown in the Live Objects panel, except that it contains only the information about the in-memory objects at that particular moment.

No loitering!

If you have two memory snapshots, you can compare them to find *loitering objects,* which have been left in memory and might indicate memory leaks. To view a list of loitering objects, you can select two memory snapshots in the list and compare them by clicking the Find Loitering Objects button (refer to Figure 5-15).

If you compare two memory snapshots and find an unexpected list of loitering objects that are taking up memory, it might be an indication of a memory leak in your application.

Because the Garbage Collector runs intermittently, a certain number of loitering objects remain in memory between garbage-collection cycles. So, finding a few loitering objects isn't a concrete indication of a memory leak — you may have just caught the Garbage Collector between cycles. While you are running the Flex Profiler, you can force the Garbage Collector to run by clicking the Run Garbage Collector button. (You cannot force the Garbage Collector to run unless you are using the Flex Profiler.)

To track down why loitering object cannot be garbage-collected, you can inspect the individual object instances and check the references to those objects.

Inspecting object references

When you view a list of objects in memory, either while inspecting a memory snapshot or a list of loitering objects, you can double-click a specific entry to view the object references for that class. When you double-click an entry, a new Object References panel loads, as shown in Figure 5-16.

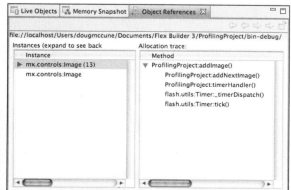

Figure 5-16:
The Object References panel.

In Figure 5-16, you're inspecting the references to Image objects. You can see two instances of the Image class listed in the left pane. In this list, you see not only the individual instances but also how many references to these objects are in the application. The listing shown in Figure 5-16 indicates that the first Image instance in the list has 13 references in the application. The second Image object, however, has no references, which indicates that it will be garbage-collected in the next pass of the Garbage Collector.

The right pane shows where in the code that particular object was created. Note that this information is available only if you turned on the Generate Object Allocation Stack Traces option when you launched the Flex Profiler. You can use this information to trace the sequence of steps that created a particular object.

If external references to an object exist, the Garbage Collector cannot collect that object. So, if you examine all references to loitering objects, you can determine which references are keeping the object from being collected.

A picture is worth a thousand words

The upper-right panel in the Profiler perspective is a live memory chart that shows the memory usage of your application during its lifetime (refer to Figure 5-13). You can gain a great deal of insight into your application's memory usage by checking image snapshots, but viewing the graph of memory allocation sometimes makes memory problems jump out at you.

Figure 5-17 shows a typical memory chart for an application. The application that generated this chart is a slide show application that loaded a series of images one after the other.

Figure 5-17:
A healthy memory-allocation chart.

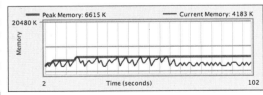

Looking at this chart, you can see the allocation of memory as new images are created, which is indicated by the increases in the chart. But you can also see the Garbage Collector doing its job and cleaning up the old images that are no longer needed. Notice that memory usage rises and falls but stays within an acceptable range. This application could run for hours on end, and its memory usage would remain fairly constant, even though it's continuously creating new Image objects.

You can compare the healthy memory chart shown in Figure 5-17 with the unhealthy one shown in Figure 5-18. This new chart reflects the same application, but references to old Image objects aren't removed from the main application, so the old Image objects are never garbage-collected.

Figure 5-18:
An
unhealthy
memory-
allocation
chart.

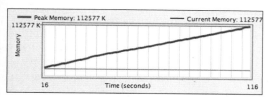

If you notice that certain interactions with your application cause the memory-allocation chart to rise and never fall back to previous levels, you may be noticing a memory leak in your application.

Profiling CPU performance

In addition to profiling the memory usage of your application, the Flex Profiler can profile the performance of your application and tell you which methods are taking the most time to execute. In terms of diagnosing a slow Flex application, memory usage and performance are the two contributing factors that can lead to a bad user experience. In earlier sections in this chapter, you find out how to use the Profiler to diagnose memory issues; in this section, we cover how to use the Profiler to find performance bottlenecks.

Taking a performance snapshot

When the Flex Profiler is running, you can take a performance snapshot by pressing the Capture Performance Profile button (refer to Figure 5-15).

This saved performance snapshot entry is added to the profiling session, just like the saved memory snapshots. You can double-click one of the performance snapshot entries to load a new Performance Profile panel with the details of that snapshot (see Figure 5-19).

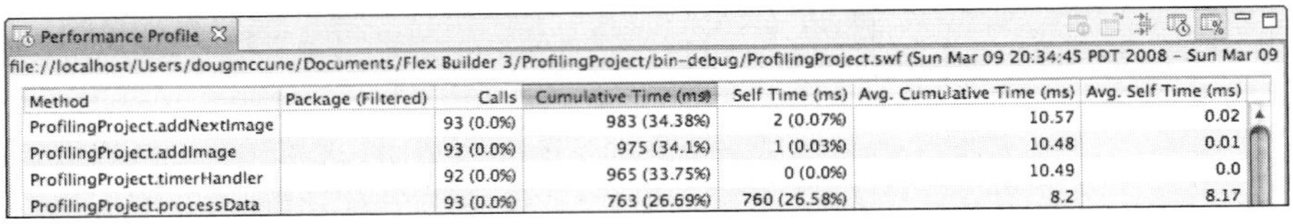

Figure 5-19:
The Perfor-
mance
Profile
panel.

The Performance Profile panel shows you individual functions and how much time, in milliseconds, each function took to complete. Just as cumulative and individual measures indicate memory usage, cumulative and individual measures gauge the performance of a function. Cumulative measures indicate the total length of time it took for the function, including any subfunctions within that function, to execute. The self-time measurements Self Time and Average Self Time report only the length of time that was spent executing within the function itself.

If you examine the results in Figure 5-19, you can see the addNextImage method took the longest cumulative time. But the processData function took the longest *self-time*. The reason is that the processData function gets called within the addNextImage function. So the cumulative time for addNextImage also includes the time taken by processData.

Digging into a method

To further clarify which methods take the longest to process, you can double-click a particular method to open the Method Statistics panel, shown in Figure 5-20.

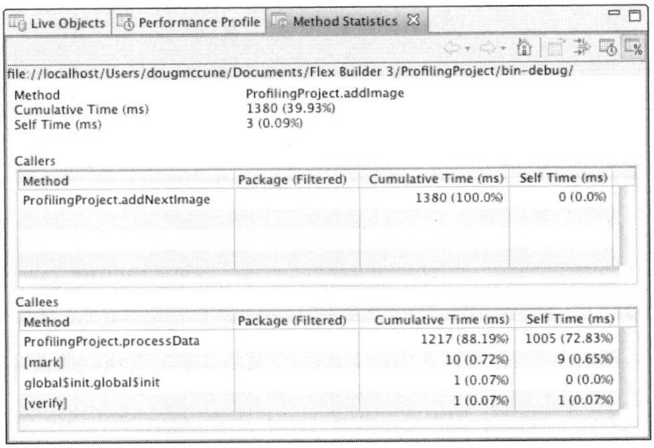

Figure 5-20:
Viewing
detailed
method
statistics.

Figure 5-20 shows the statistics for the custom method `addImage`. The top pane indicates which methods called it. In this case, you can see that the `addImage` method was called from the `addNextImage` method. You can also see all other methods within `addImage` that were called and how much time each one took. By viewing this breakdown, it becomes clear that the `processData` method is the piece that takes the most time. You can then identify exactly which pieces of code are taking the most time to process and head in the right direction when you want to optimize your code.

Refactoring Your Code

Refactoring is the process of reorganizing your code while preserving the functionality of that code. The term *refactoring* refers to the broad concept of moving things around to achieve better structure and encapsulation: changing the names of classes, moving methods from one class to another, or breaking a large class into two or more smaller classes, for example.

For a crash course in object-oriented programming methodology, refer to Chapter 3.

Changing class names

The simplest reason to refactor your code is if you want to change the name of a class. The simple act of renaming a file, however, can be far more difficult than it appears. To manually change the name of a class, you rename the file, and then you have to track down all references to the old class in your code and update them with the new name. Luckily, Flex Builder has built-in support for this kind of refactoring.

The following steps guide you through refactoring a class in your Flex project:

1. **In the Flex Builder, select the file in Flex Navigator view, right-click, and choose Rename, as shown in Figure 5-21.**

   Alternatively, you can choose File⇨Rename. Either approach loads the refactoring wizard to step you through the refactoring process.

2. **Enter the new name for the class in the Rename Class dialog box.**

   When you rename a class, enter the name of the class, not the full name of the file itself. If you're renaming a file named `CustomComponent.mxml`, for example, notice that the name that appears in the refactoring wizard reads `CustomComponent`, without the file extension. It's the name of the class. To rename it, you should enter a different name and still omit the file extension. In Figure 5-22, the new name is `MyNewlyNamedComponent`.

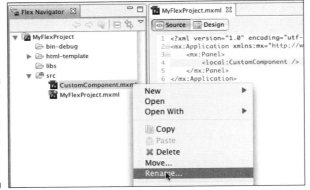

Figure 5-21:
Accessing
the Rename
menu item
to begin
refactoring.

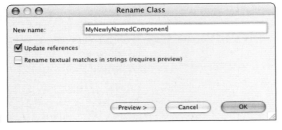

Figure 5-22:
Entering a
new class
name in the
refactoring
wizard.

If you deselect the Update References check box, Flex Builder doesn't refactor your code; it only renames the file. You then have to manually look through your code and change any references to the class.

If you select the Rename Textual Matches in Strings check box, Flex Builder performs a deeper text search in your source code and replaces any string references to the old filename. Be careful with this option, and make sure that you follow the next step and click the Preview button to double-check that Flex Builder is doing what you want.

3. **Click the Preview button to see Preview view, shown in Figure 5-23.**

    Preview view shows you each change in your source code that Flex Builder will perform. This way, you can double-check and verify that all the changes are appropriate. In Figure 5-23, you can see that this refactoring results in an updated reference to the CustomComponent class within the MyFlexProject application, as well as the moving (renaming) of the CustomComponent MXML file.

4. **Click OK to complete the refactoring.**

    Your code is now refactored and should still compile and run with the new class name.

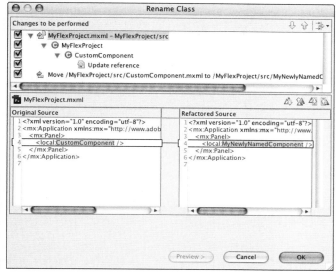

Figure 5-23:
Previewing the refactoring changes.

You can use the Rename refactoring method on both MXML and ActionScript class files. The preceding steps show you how to rename a custom MXML class, but the same process works for ActionScript classes as well.

Changing method and variable names

In addition to changing the names of classes, you can use the refactoring capabilities of Flex Builder to rename individual methods and variables within your classes. This process is similar to how you rename a class, although to invoke method or variable renaming, you need to select the method or variable name within your class, right-click, and choose the Rename menu item. Figure 5-24 shows how to invoke the refactoring wizard on the method named showStatusAlert in a custom class.

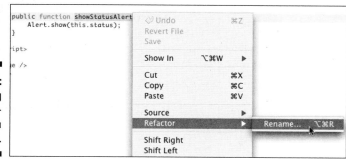

Figure 5-24:
Invoking refactoring on a method.

The same method of right-clicking and choosing the Rename menu item is used when renaming variables. After you invoke the refactoring wizard, either for method renaming or variable renaming, the steps are the same as they are for renaming a class.

Living with limitations

The refactoring support in Flex Builder 3 is limited to simple class and method renaming. However, when you refactor applications, you often change the package structure of classes as well, which means moving source files from one directory to another to better organize the class hierarchy. Flex Builder 3 doesn't support this kind of package-level refactoring. If you need to refactor your code more aggressively and move classes between packages, you have to do most of it manually.

As we discuss in Chapter 4, Flex Builder is based on the Eclipse IDE, a powerful editor that can be used to edit much more than Flex and ActionScript code. If you're familiar with using Eclipse for Java development, you will likely notice that the refactoring options in Flex Builder fall very short of the refactoring support for Java. You have to learn to live with this limitation until Adobe beefs up the refactoring capabilities in future versions of Flex Builder.

Chapter 6

Visually Designing Applications in Flex Builder

*F*lex Builder enables you to develop applications in either Source mode or Design mode. In this chapter, we focus on Design mode, which enables you to visually assemble Flex applications and components. In the other mode, Source mode, you can write code that can be visually rendered when switched into Design mode; see Chapter 5 for details about this mode.

This chapter gives you the lowdown on how to work in Design mode to create and visually customize Flex components; set properties, styles, and events on components in the design area; navigate the design area with fine control; create states for your Flex applications; and style components in detail.

Getting to Know Flex Builder Design Mode

Flex Builder has two modes for wiring up Flex components and applications:

✔ **Source mode** refers to the robust ActionScript editor, debugger, profiler, and other code-related features, such as code refactoring (where name changes in the code propagate throughout your project), that Flex Builder has to offer.

✔ **Design mode** is the Flex Builder mode that allows developers and designers to visually assemble applications and components. Design mode is the visual representation of the code that's created in Source mode; similarly, Source mode is updated with code when you create Flex content in Design mode.

To switch between Source mode and Design mode, you use the Source and Design buttons, which are located in the upper-left corner of the main pane of the Flex Builder window, as shown in Figure 6-1.

Figure 6-1:
Flex Builder in Source mode with the Source button selected.

To see Design mode, shown in Figure 6-2, just click the Design button. This list describes the various areas identified in the figure:

✔ **Design stage:** Featured in the default layout of Design mode (it's the area in the center), where components and containers appear and are modified.

✔ **Design toolbar:** Located above the design stage; used to pan and zoom in the design stage and to adjust the design area dimensions.

✔ **Flex Navigator view:** Lets you navigate your projects and their source files.

✔ **Components view:** Allows Flex components and custom components to be dragged to the stage.

✔ **Outline view:** Provides a visual outline of the hierarchy and contents of your Flex application in its current state.

✔ **States view:** Lets you partition your application into new states as well as edit already configured states. Using this view to create and edit states is often the preferred way to author states (preferred over hand-coding states in Source mode).

✔ **Properties inspector:** Contains a series of panels that allow the setting of properties and styles of the selected Flex item or set of items on the stage.

The rest of this chapter covers each of these elements of Design mode in more detail.

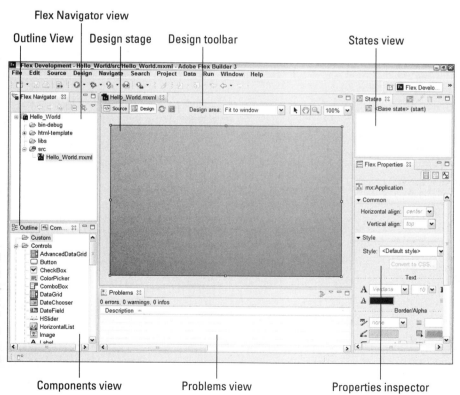

Flex Navigator view

Outline View   Design stage   Design toolbar   States view

Components view   Problems view   Properties inspector

Figure 6-2:
The default
view of Flex
Builder
Design
mode.

Navigating Through the Design Area

The size of the Flex Builder design area can be customized for your convenience. Some developers like to work in a fixed design area, whereas others don't mind scrolling around the design area to produce a more detailed view of the design stage.

You control the design area size and navigation capabilities by using the Design toolbar (shown in Figure 6-3). By default, the design editor size is set to Fit to Window, which means that it doesn't display scrollbars and instead adjusts its layout, if possible, to fit the design window size. This size is the most convenient one to work with. You can change the design editor size by using the design area drop-down list. Other options include preset fixed sizes, such as 1024 x 768 or 800 x 600, or you can enter your own sizing dimensions by choosing the Custom Size option.

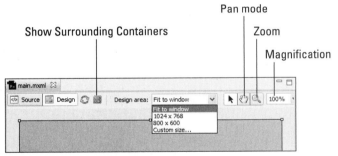

Figure 6-3:
You can control the dimensions of the design stage.

Pan mode
Show Surrounding Containers
Zoom
Magnification

If the size of your layout is larger than the design editor window, Flex creates scrollbars to preserve the layout.

In addition to adjusting the dimensions of the design area, Flex Builder offers a way to navigate the design area with great control, as discussed in the following sections.

Using Pan & Zoom

Flex Builder 3 added the useful and cool feature Pan & Zoom. You can use it to

- **Zoom into the design area:** Observe the fine-grain visual details of components on the design stage.
- **Zoom out of the design area:** See a bird's-eye view of the design stage.
- **Pan around the design stage:** Navigate quickly and efficiently.

Panning

To enter Pan mode, you click the Pan Mode button, in the upper-right bank of navigation buttons (refer to Figure 6-3). To enter Pan mode from the keyboard, press the H key after you have clicked on the design stage. In Pan mode, the cursor turns into a hand icon. To navigate in Pan mode, hold down the mouse button while moving in the application. You see that this type of navigation is much easier and faster than using the design area scrollbars, especially to navigate to hard-to-reach parts of the application when you zoom into the design area.

Zooming

Whenever you zoom in or out, the magnification percentage is displayed in the Magnification drop-down list. The list, which is the rightmost input field on the Design toolbar, is located in the upper-right area of the design stage. You can zoom in and out of the design area in a few different ways:

- ✔ Open the magnification drop-down list and select a specific zoom percentage.
- ✔ Choose Design⇨Zoom In or Design⇨Zoom Out.
- ✔ Right-click in the design area to open the design context menu, which has options to zoom in or out of the design stage or to set the magnification of the stage to preset values.
- ✔ To enter Zoom mode without using the menu options, press the Z key or click the Zoom button after you have clicked on the design stage, on the Design toolbar (refer to Figure 6-3).

When you enter Zoom mode, the cursor turns into a magnifying glass next to a + or – sign, depending on whether you're zooming in or out. To zoom in, press Ctrl+= (or ⌘+= on the Mac); to zoom out, press Ctrl+– (or ⌘+– on the Mac).

After you start using pan and zoom when working on the design stage, you can achieve greater fidelity when skinning and styling components. The reason is that you can zoom in to view more detail regarding the visual appearance of components on the design stage.

Showing surrounding containers

The Flex Builder design area has a neat feature that allows you to visualize the nesting and hierarchy of containers in your Flex applications. This feature can be useful when determining the layering of containers in your Flex application or when you want to quickly select a particular container instance from many nested containers.

To enable this feature and show nested containers, click the Show Surrounding Containers button on the Design toolbar (refer to Figure 6-3). When you click this button, the top-level container in the design stage is overlaid with a semitransparent film to differentiate it from other containers, as shown in Figure 6-4. As you click other containers in the application, they too are overlaid with a transparent film; additionally, each container is affixed with a label specifying its type and its `id` value if it's set. To exit this Nested Container mode, simply click the Show Surrounding Containers button again. To trigger Show Surrounding Containers by using a keyboard shortcut, simply press the F4 key on the keyboard after having clicked on the design stage.

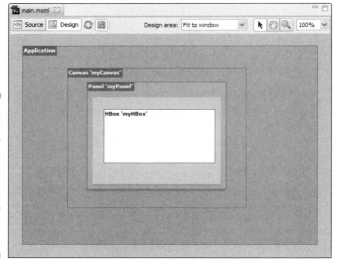

Figure 6-4:
Use the Show Surrounding Containers button to show the nesting of multiple containers.

Figure 6-4 shows a Canvas container with a Panel child container that has an HBox child container. In Show Surrounding Containers mode, notice how a transparent overlay is drawn over each container and each container is labeled with its type and `id` value.

Selecting Controls in the Design Area

The features in Flex Builder's Design mode are primarily driven by whichever components and controls are selected on the design stage. For example, the properties inspector shows the properties, styles, and events that can be set on the components selected on the design stage. Thus, you must understand how to select and deselect single and multiple components on the design stage:

✔ **Select a component:** On the design stage, click the component's visual representation on the design stage or select the component in Outline view. You can learn more about the Flex Builder Outline view in the "Viewing the Contents of Your Application in Outline View" section.

✔ **Select multiple components:** You can select multiple components on the design stage in several ways:

- Ctrl+click (or ⌘+click on the Mac) on each component you want to select.

- Click into the design stage with the mouse and draw a box that overlaps all components you want to select. Notice that an overlay is drawn that visualizes which components are selected by this action, as shown in Figure 6-5.

- Ctrl+click (or ⌘+click on the Mac) multiple components in the Flex Builder Outline view.

Selecting multiple components is useful when you want to reposition multiple controls simultaneously, delete a set of controls, or set common properties on multiple controls.

✔ **Select all components on the design stage:** Open the design menu by right-clicking the design stage (or ⌘+clicking it on the Mac) and choosing the Select All menu option. Similarly, you can type Ctrl+A (or ⌘+A on the Mac) to select all components on the design stage by using a keyboard shortcut.

✔ **Deselect a single component or multiple components:** Click in the background of any container in the design stage, click an unselected component on the design stage, or click in the gray margin surrounding the root component.

Figure 6-5:
Select
multiple
components
on the
design stage
by drawing a box
around them
with the
mouse.

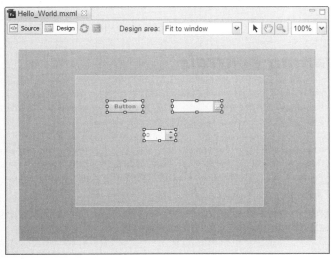

To delete a component or many components on the design stage, you simply select the components you want deleted and press the Delete key on the keyboard. Similarly, after having selected the components you want to delete, you can right-click (Ctrl+click on the Mac) the design stage to open the Design menu and then select Delete from the menu options, as shown in Figure 6-6.

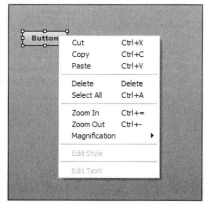

Figure 6-6:
Right-click the design stage to open the Design menu.

Controlling the Layout and Size of Controls in the Design Area

Flex Builder offers a plethora of features that allow you to control the layout and size of controls on the design stage. Knowing how to use these features can greatly improve your efficiency and ability to construct complex, pixel-perfect layouts.

Positioning controls

You can control the position of components on the design stage in quite a few ways. Be sure to note that the behavior of the parent container affects how child components are positioned on the design stage:

- ✔ In absolute positioning containers, such as Canvas, or containers that have the `layout` property that can be set to `absolute` (such as Panel, TitleWindow, or Application), child controls can be positioned at any `x` and `y` value.

- ✔ In relative layout containers, such as HBox and VBox, child controls can be positioned according to the layout rules of their parents.

See Chapter 10 for more on both types of containers.

You can drag and drop all controls on the design stage to reposition them on the design stage. Remember that you can also set position and size-related properties in the properties inspector and the controls on the design stage (as well as the code generated in Source mode) are then visually updated automatically. Often, when the visual designer gives you fixed positions for controls, it's easier to enter these values into the x and y input fields in the properties inspector to achieve pixel-perfect accuracy. Flex Builder's properties inspector is discussed in further detail in the "Configuring Controls with the Flex Builder Properties Inspector" section, later in this chapter.

To reposition a control that's already on the design stage, simply select the control and drag it. The cursor changes into a four-arrow cursor. As you drag the controls, you see only the outline of the controls being dragged, which results in a clearer view.

After you have repositioned controls that reside in an absolute positioning container, the properties inspector is updated to report the new x and y values for the controls.

When you reposition controls that reside in relative layout managers, such as HBox or VBox, you notice that as you drag around a control or a set of controls, you see a blue line indicating the new position of the control relative to the other child controls living in the container (see Figure 6-7). This visual cue indicates where the newly dropped control will be positioned.

Blue line

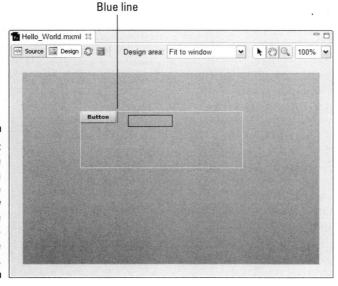

Figure 6-7:
A blue line is used as a visual cue to show where the new component will be inserted.

You can also nudge a set of controls with the arrow keys. It's an easy way to move a bank of components by just a few pixels in any direction. Simply select a set of components and use the arrow keys to move controls en masse to the right, left, top, or bottom.

Snapping controls relative to each other

As you drag controls around, or drag out new controls from Components view to the design stage in a container that has absolute positioning, blue lines appear at certain positions. Using this Flex Builder *snapping* feature, you can position controls relative to others in order to line them up vertically or horizontally.

The Flex Builder snapping feature is available only when you're repositioning controls that are in absolute positioning containers, such as Canvas, or Panel, TitleWindow, or Application, with the `layout` property set to `absolute`.

As you reposition controls, Flex Builder hints where snapping will occur. When the edges of repositioned controls line up with the edges of other sibling controls, a blue line appears to show the snapping position. This behavior is helpful for lining up components, especially text components, along a common baseline. Using snapping ensures that the components are aligned so that their text is in a single line. Figure 6-8 shows how three components — a Button, TextInput, and CheckBox — have been aligned according to their text by using snapping. Notice that when you drag a new component from Components view, the blue snapping lines indicate where to drop the control so that its text is aligned with the already aligned Button, TextInput, and CheckBox.

Snapping is turned on by default, but it can be turned off to clear the design stage of visual hints. To turn off Flex Builder's snapping behavior, choose Design➪Enable Snapping. To enable or disable snapping as a global preference in Flex Builder, choose Windows➪Preferences to open the preferences dialog box, navigate to Flex➪Editors➪Design Mode, and select or deselect the Enable Snapping check box.

Aligning controls

Flex Builder has built-in functionality to help manage the alignment of child controls in layout containers that support absolute positioning (Canvas, Application, Panel, and TitleWindow). One of the more robust ways to control alignment is to use a constraint-based layout by using the Constraints control in the properties inspector. To find out how to use this control, check out the section "Setting constraints visually with the Constraints Control," later in this chapter.

Blue snapping line

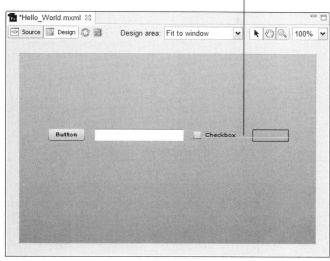

Figure 6-8:
The snapping feature shows where to drop the control for good alignment.

Additionally, Flex Builder allows the alignment of a set of controls alongside their left edges, right edges, centers, top edges, lower edges, or baselines by using Design menu options. First, select a set of controls that you want to align relative to each other. Next, open the top-level Design menu. Notice the options: Align Left, Align Vertical Centers, Align Right, Align Top, Align Horizontal Centers, Align Bottom, and Align Baselines. When you choose these Alignment menu options, the set of selected controls align accordingly.

Table 6-1 describes each alignment menu option.

Table 6-1	Flex Builder Alignment Options
Option	*Description*
Align Left	Aligns the left edges of all selected controls with the left edge of the first component that was selected.
Align Vertical Centers	Aligns the vertical centers of all selected controls with the vertical centers of the first component that was selected.
Align Right	Aligns the right edges of all selected controls with the right edge of the first component that was selected.
Align Top	Aligns the top edges of all selected controls with the top edge of the first component that was selected.
Align Horizontal Centers	Aligns the horizontal centers of all selected controls with the horizontal center of the first component that was selected.

(continued)

Table 6-1 *(continued)*

Option	Description
Align Bottom	Aligns the bottom edges of all selected controls with the bottom edge of the first component that was selected.
Align Top	Aligns the top edges of all selected controls with the upper edge of the first component that was selected.
Align Baselines	Aligns the text of all selected controls with the text of the first component that was selected. If any of the selected controls doesn't have text, the bottom edge of the control is considered its text baseline.

Figures 6-9 and 6-10 demonstrate how alignment works. Figure 6-9 shows components that we dragged from the Components view and placed haphazardly next to each other. We chose the Align Right option to align the right edges of all the controls with the top Button, as shown in Figure 6-10. We selected the top Button first to force the rest of the components to align their right edges with its right edge.

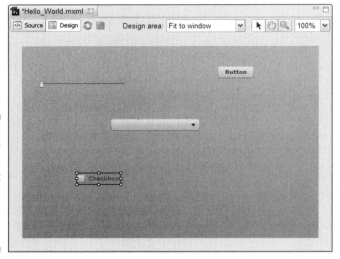

Figure 6-9:
A set of controls that aren't aligned respective to each other.

Sizing and resizing controls

Controls can be resized directly on the design stage or through the properties inspector, and this resizing is reflected visually as well as in the generated code in Source mode.

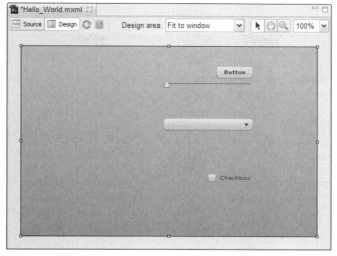

Figure 6-10:
A set of
controls that
have their
right edges
aligned with
each other.

To resize a control directly on the design stage, follow these steps:

1. **Select the control you want to resize.**

   It becomes decorated with resize handles.

2. **Hover the cursor over one of the resize handles.**

   Depending on the angle of resizing, you see a double-headed arrow.

3. **Click and drag the resize handle to resize the control.**

   To help you in deciphering the new size of the control after the resize action has completed, a ToolTip next to the resizing component displays the new width and height values.

You can also resize controls by modifying the `width` and `height` values in the properties inspector. You can enter pixel or percentage sizes in the `width` and `height` input fields.

Inserting Components with the Components View

Flex Builder Components view, shown in Figure 6-11, is often docked to the left of the stage area in Design mode. If it's not there, you can open it by choosing Window⇨Components. You can drag Flex components and containers from the Components view and drop them on the stage.

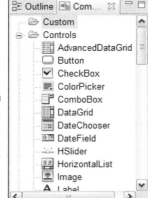

Figure 6-11:
Components
view in Flex
Builder
Design
mode.

Flex Builder Components view is organized into four folders of components, as described in the following list:

✔ **Custom:** The Custom folder holds references to any custom components written in either MXML or ActionScript files in the current project or the source path of the current project. When you drag a custom component to the stage, Flex adds the corresponding code to Source mode to indicate that the component has been added to the application.

✔ **Controls:** The Controls folder contains a list of all Flex user interface controls, such as Button and TextInput. When you drag controls from the Controls folder to the stage, the controls assume a default size and appearance. For example, dragging a Button from the Controls folder creates a button large enough to display the label 'Button'.

✔ **Containers:** The Containers folder contains a list of all Flex layout containers, such as HBox and Panel. After you drag any of the relative layout containers to the design stage, a sizing dialog box appears (similar to Figure 6-12). In this dialog box, you can specify how the container should be sized.

Here are your sizing options, based on the type of container:

• *For the Form, HBox, HDividedBox, VBox, and VDividedBox containers:* The default sizing option is to give the container 100 percent of its parent's `width` and a default `height`. To change this behavior, enter values into the dialog box to specify either a pixel or percentage size value for the container's `width` and `height`.

• *When dragging a Tile container:* The default sizing option is to size the Tile container to its contents. You specify a pixel or percentage size value for the container's `width` and `height`.

• *When dragging a Grid container:* The dialog box lets you determine how many rows and columns the Grid container should contain.

- *For all other options in the Containers folder (such as Panel and Canvas):* Flex Builder chooses a default pixel size that can be resized however you want.

✔ **Navigators:** The Navigators folder contains a list of all navigator controls, such as Accordion and TabNavigator. When you drag a Navigator to the design stage, it's decorated with a little toolbar displaying + and – buttons. You use these buttons to add and remove child views. (For more on Flex Navigators, see Chapter 10.) When adding new child views, you can use the dialog box that opens after you click the + button to specify the child view container and its label. Similarly, the – button can be used to delete the selected child view.

Figure 6-12:
The sizing dialog box for the HBox container.

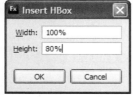

Viewing the Contents of Your Application in Outline View

When you use Flex Builder Outline view, shown in Figure 6-13, you can inspect the structure of your MXML application. Outline view is often the sibling pane to Components view and is usually docked to the left of the design stage. If the Outline View pane isn't open, you can manually open it by choosing Windows⇨Outline.

Outline view lists all Flex components created in MXML that exist in your Flex application. It gives you a neat way to view the hierarchy and organization of your Flex application. You can select single components or multiple components by Ctrl+clicking in Windows or ⌘+clicking on the Mac; the controls appear as selected in the design stage. This selection allows you to

✔ Adjust the position of a single component or a set of components en masse.

✔ Delete controls en masse.

✔ Edit properties in the Flex Builder properties inspector.

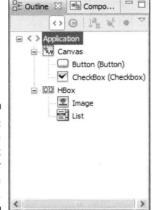

Figure 6-13:
Outline view in Flex Builder Design mode.

Working with States in States View

Flex uses the states concept, which you can use to create different views of your application. The Flex Builder States view, shown in Figure 6-14, is a handy interface for creating, deleting, and editing Flex states. (To find out more about Flex states, refer to Chapter 17.)

New State button

Edit State button

Delete State button

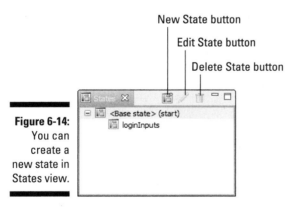

Figure 6-14:
You can create a new state in States view.

When creating Flex states, you first need to create a base state. Subsequent states are created atop the base state — that is, the base state can always be derived from other states. To create a new state, follow these steps:

1. **In the States View pane, click the New State button, shown in Figure 6-14.**

   The *base state* of your Flex application consists of all Flex elements defined in the Flex application up to the point where the new state is created.

2. **In the States dialog box, name the state and choose which existing state the new state should be based on. Then click OK.**

   The new state appears in the States View pane.

As you create new states, the hierarchy is displayed visually in the States view. For example, if State 1 is based on State 2 and State 2 is based on State 3, States view lists the states in such a way that State 1 is the parent of State 2, which is the parent of State 3.

Suppose that your application needs a login view that people use to log in with a username and password. The base state of the login view is simply a Panel container with a Login button. When users click the Login button, a different view appears, where they can enter their usernames and passwords. In this case, the base state of the login view is simply the Panel container with the Login button, as shown in Figure 6-15.

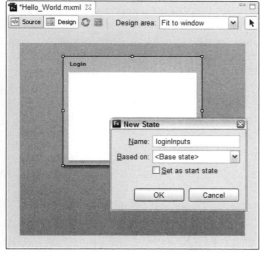

Figure 6-15: The base state of the login panel — you build subsequent states based on this state.

Using the New State button, you create a second state: loginInputs. In this view of the login panel, application users can enter their usernames and passwords. After you create this new state, which is based on the base state, notice that the States view shows the hierarchy of states — namely, that loginInputs is based on the base state, as shown in Figure 6-16.

New state

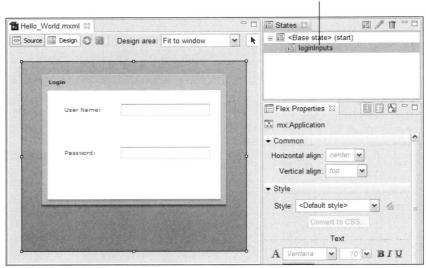

Figure 6-16:
Flex displays
a second
state for the
login panel
component,
loginInputs,
where appli-
cation users
can enter
their
information.

The following list gives you the lowdown on how to delete or edit a state:

- **To delete a state:** Select the state entry in States view and use the trash-can icon (Delete State button) on the States toolbar to delete the state. The state is then removed from States view, and the corresponding code is removed from the application.

- **To edit a state:** Click the pencil icon (Edit State Properties Button) on the States toolbar. In the Edit dialog box that appears, edit the name of the state and the existing state it's derived from. Remember that what-ever is on the design state and associated with a defined state encom-passes the view of that state in the application.

Configuring Controls with the Flex Builder Properties Inspector

Using the Flex Builder properties inspector, you can visually set properties, styles, and event handlers for all components defined in your application. The properties inspector is traditionally located to the right of the stage area in Flex Builder Design mode, in the Flex Properties pane, as shown in Figure 6-17. If you don't see the Flex Builder properties inspector, you can open it by choosing Window⇨Flex Properties.

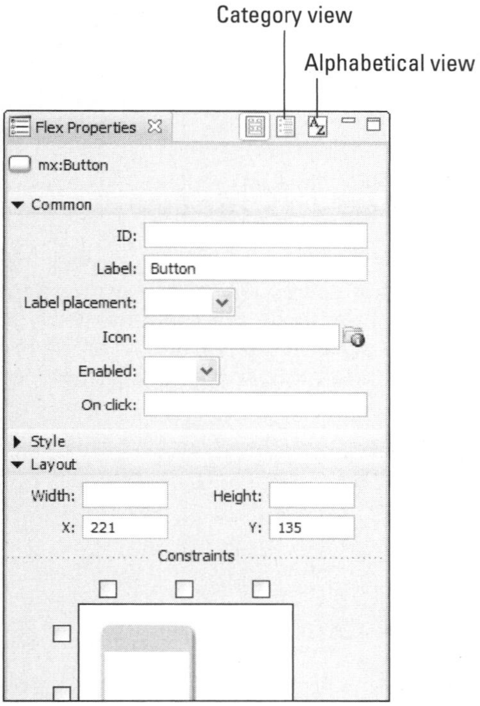

Category view

Alphabetical view

Figure 6-17:
The
properties
inspector
shows all
properties,
styles, and
events that
you can set
for the con-
trol that's
selected on
the design
stage.

Choosing a properties inspector view

The properties inspector has three different views for setting properties, styles, and events on controls selected in the stage area:

✔ **Standard:** This view is displayed by default, as shown in Figure 6-17. The properties inspector's Standard view splits the pane into properties, styles, and events that are commonly set on that control (in the Common pane), those that are style related (set in the Style pane), or those that are layout related (set in the Layout pane).

Standard view is the easiest view of the properties inspector to use, so we recommend it.

✔ **Category:** In this view, elements that can be set on the selected component in the design stage are grouped in common categories along with their set values. That is, all events that are valid on the selected component are located in the Events category; similarly, style-related properties are in the Styles category.

You can switch to Category view by clicking the Category View icon at the top of the properties inspector panel (refer to Figure 6-17).

✔ **Alphabetical:** This view simply lists all properties, events, and styles that can be set on the selected component on the design stage in alphabetical order along with their values. It's the last button in the upper-right corner of the properties inspector panel (refer to Figure 6-17).

Using the properties inspector

When a control is selected on the design stage, the properties inspector is updated to display input items that correspond to the properties, styles, and events that you can set for that component. For example, when you select a DataGrid control, the Common panel in Standard view of the properties inspector shows the properties and events commonly settable for a DataGrid control (see Figure 6-18).

Figure 6-18: When you select a DataGrid control, the properties inspector shows the properties, events, and styles that you can set on that control.

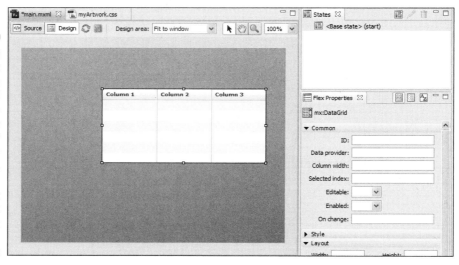

When multiple controls are selected on the design stage, the properties inspector is updated to display only the properties, events, and styles that are common among all selected components.

As you enter values for properties in the input fields, the selected component on stage is updated in real time to reflect the changes. For example, when you enter a value in the Column Width field and then press Enter, the DataGrid control on the stage is updated to display the new column widths.

Setting constraints visually with the Constraints Control

When you select a control or multiple controls that reside in an absolute-positioning container, the Layout pane in the properties inspector displays the special control named Constraints, as shown in Figure 6-19. You can use this control to create new layout constraints or edit existing layout constraints on the controls selected in the design stage. (To find out more about constraint-based layout and how you can use it to build reflowing layouts, check out Chapter 10.)

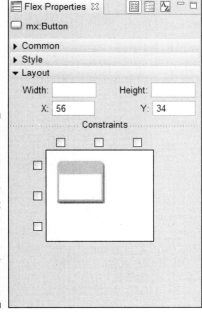

Figure 6-19: Use the Constraints control to visually set layout constraints on child controls relative to their parenting container.

The check boxes in the Constraint control correspond to the setting of the `left`, `right`, `top`, `bottom`, `horizontalCenter`, and `verticalCenter` layout constraints. When you select one of these check boxes, Flex calculates a constraint value that anchors the selected control on the stage to the edge of its parent.

For example, if you select the rightmost check box on top of the Constraint control, Flex sets the `right` layout constraint so that the selected control doesn't move its position and is anchored to the right edge of its parent container. The pixel value of the constraint — which is calculated when a constraint check box is selected — appears in the text box in the constraint control. You can also enter values into the text box, and Flex adjusts the position of the selected control to match the new constraint value. When you switch to Source mode, you see that the selected control, which had layout constraints set on it by way of the Constraint control, has the appropriate code set in the component tag corresponding to the newly created constraints.

For example, in Figure 6-20, the selected control has a `left` constraint set to 50 pixels and a `verticalCenter` constraint set to 100 pixels. In Source mode, the component tag looks like this:

```
<mx:Button left="50" verticalCenter="100" />
```

One neat thing that Flex Builder Design mode does is track the changes you make to your application, in either Design mode or Source mode. Whenever a change is made to the state of your application, such as adding a new component from Components view or setting a property on a component from the properties inspector, this change is tracked. You can then easily undo the action by either pressing Ctrl+Z (or ⌘+Z on the Mac) on the keyboard or choosing Edit⇨Undo. To redo the action, simply press Ctrl+Y (or ⌘+Y on the Mac) on the keyboard or choose the Edit⇨Redo menu option in the top-level Flex Builder menu.

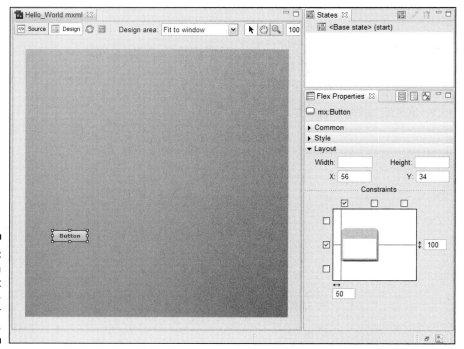

Figure 6-20:
A Button with a left and verti-calCenter constraint set.

Working with Style Sheets in CSS Design Mode

New in Flex Builder 3 is the powerful feature: CSS Design mode. You can use it to visually display and edit the contents of a CSS style sheet whose style blocks are used to style your Flex components. To use CSS Design mode, you need to open a CSS style sheet in Flex Builder. To switch to CSS Design mode, simply click the Design button in Source mode in the upper-left corner of the code editor.

CSS Design mode shows the different states that a component can enter and allows you to visually customize what the control looks like in those states. When you make edits in CSS Design mode, Flex updates the resulting style blocks in the CSS style sheet with the corresponding code that results in the visual appearance you chose. (To find out more about using CSS style sheets, class selectors, and type selectors in your Flex applications, see Chapter 18.)

To create new style blocks in your CSS style sheet, follow these steps:

1. **Click the New Style button in the toolbar at the top of CSS Design mode, as shown in Figure 6-21.**

   The New Style dialog box appears, as shown in Figure 6-22.

New Style

Delete Style

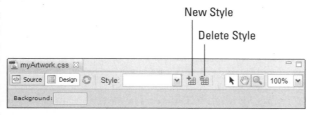

2. **Choose one of these selector types:**

   • *All Components (global):* Create a style block that (if possible) affects all components in the application. This is an easy way to create a font style or size that's percolated down to every component in the Flex application.

   • *All components with style name:* Create a new type selector of a particular name.

   • *Specific component:* Create a new class selector for all components of a specific type.

- *Specific component with style name:* Create a style block for all particular types of components that you chose to apply the style name to.

You can create a new style selector, either a class selector that can be applied to all Flex components of a particular type (such as all Buttons) or a type selector that can be a custom style block you define and apply to components of your choice.

Figure 6-22:
Choose which type of style block you want to create in your CSS style sheet.

3. **Depending on which selector type you chose in Step 2, choose which component you want to use to visualize the style entries. (If you selected All Components in Step 2, you can skip this step.)**

   For example, if you want to create a class selector or a type selector for Button-related controls, ensure that the Button control is selected as the Component option.

4. **Click OK to close the dialog box.**

After you click OK, the component that the style block is based on shows up on the design stage in all the different states it can assume. For example, when you're creating a type selector for the Flex Button control, different buttons representing the different various states the Button can enter (such as up, down, over, and selected) are displayed on the design stage. You can use the properties inspector (shown in Figure 6-23) to customize and edit all styles that dictate how the Button looks when it enters that state.

As you create new style blocks, the Style drop-down list on the top toolbar becomes populated with the names of the style blocks. You can use this drop-down list to determine which style block is visualized on the design stage. Also, if you open an existing CSS style sheet that already has style blocks created, the style drop-down list is populated with the style names, and you can select and further modify them with the properties inspector.

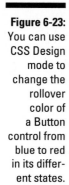

Figure 6-23:
You can use
CSS Design
mode to
change the
rollover
color of
a Button
control from
blue to red
in its differ-
ent states.

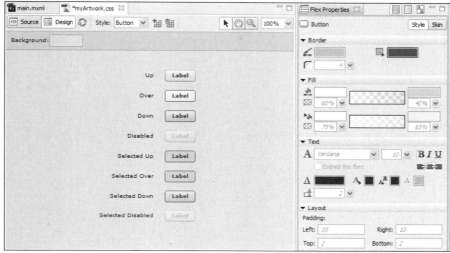

To delete a style block from your CSS style sheet, chose the style entry from
the Style drop-down list in the top toolbar and click the Delete Style button
(refer to Figure 6-21).

As you dive further into the topic of styling your Flex components, you find
that CSS Design mode is a powerful tool to visualize the specific look of components and modify them in detail.

Part III

The Flex Framework and Charting Components

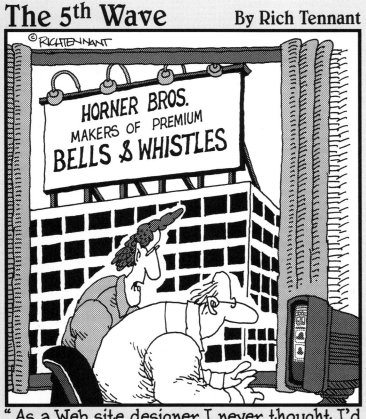

The 5th Wave   By Rich Tennant

HORNER BROS.
MAKERS OF PREMIUM
BELLS & WHISTLES

"As a Web site designer I never thought I'd say this, but I don't think your site has enough bells and whistles."

In this part . . .

Prepare to dive headfirst into the Flex framework and power all the way through. This part covers everything from a simple Button control to the data-driven DataGrid and List and all the charting components. There's a reason that Part III is the longest part in this book: It contains the meat of the Flex framework. At some point in your Flex career, you will use every component covered in Chapters 7 through 11.

We begin in Chapter 7 with some of the simplest components, such as Label and TextInput, and then we move to Chapter 8 to cover controls such as DataGrid and Tree, which are driven by underlying data models. We then cover Forms in Chapter 9 and Containers in Chapter 10. We finish this part by describing the charting components, which are sure to impress the executives in your organization.

Chapter 7

Simple User Interface Controls

● ●

In This Chapter

▶ Creating clickable user interface controls, such as Button and ComboBox

▶ Working with text controls, such as Label and TextInput

▶ Using media display controls, such as Image and VideoDisplay

▶ Building a media controller, such as a video player

● ●

he Flex framework offers a wide set of user interface controls for you to use while building your Flex application. *User interface controls* are the visual elements that appear in a Flex application. A large number of Flex user interface controls are available for you to use, and you can customize all of them based on the functionality or visual appearance you want.

In this chapter, we discuss how to create, display, and make common customizations to clickable controls, text display controls, and media display controls. These controls are some of the most essential building blocks in the Flex framework, and you use them repeatedly. The following list shows the user interface controls discussed in this chapter:

Button	CheckBox	ColorPicker
ComboBox	DateChooser	DateField
HSlider	Image	Label
LinkButton	PopUpButton	PopUpMenuButton
ProgressBar	RadioButton	RadioButtonGroup
RichTextEditor	Scrollbars	SWFLoader
Text	TextArea	TextInput
Video Display	VSlider	

Taking a Look at Simple Clickable Controls

Flex comes replete with a rich set of clickable user interface controls. These controls range from a simple Button and CheckBox to controls that encapsulate advanced functionality, such as ComboBox. The ComboBox control pops open a drop-down list prepopulated with options. You can easily define these clickable user interface controls in your Flex application and subsequently build a rich user interface. You can customize their functionality and visual appearance by setting properties and styles. In the following sections, we describe how to create and customize all the clickable user interface controls available in Flex.

The following sections discuss the various user interface controls that you use to build Flex applications. But before jumping into reading about these controls, you should understand the inheritance hierarchy of Flex controls. The Flex framework was written with *extensibility* in mind, which means that any Flex control can be extended to add new functionality or to create a whole new control. Extension is possible because Flex controls already *inherit* from each other. If you look at the Flex framework source code available in your FlexBuilder installation directory, you see that the `mx.controls.CheckBox` class *extends* the `mx.controls.Button` class. Because of this relationship, a CheckBox control inherits all the properties, events, methods, and styles declared in the Button class. This concept of inheritance is very powerful for Flex developers to understand. For a more in-depth review of the Flex inheritance hierarchy, check out Chapter 3.

For the most part, visual Flex components inherit from a single, basic class: `mx.core.UIComponent`. A UIComponent control represents the most basic Flex control. It provides properties, styles, and events that can be set to customize the control's visual appearance or functionality. All visual Flex controls can eventually trace their inheritance hierarchy back to UIComponent, thus making UIComponent the ancestor of all Flex controls! This inheritance hierarchy is shown in Figure 7-1.

Creating button-based controls

The Flex framework offers a variety of button-based controls. *Button-based* means that all controls in this section can trace their inheritance hierarchy back to the `mx.controls.Button` class. A user can click a button-based control to perform a new action or make a selection. These types of button-based controls include the Button, CheckBox, RadioButton, RadioButtonGroup, LinkButton, PopUpButton, and PopUpMenuButton controls. These controls are described in more detail in the following sections.

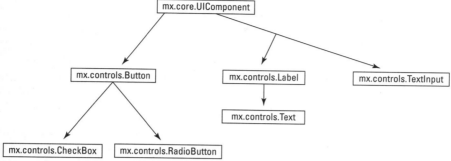

Figure 7-1:
Inheritance
hierarchy
for a subset
of Flex
components.

Button

The Button control is what you would expect: a simple, rectangular button that the user can click. You create a Button control in a Flex application by using the `<mx:Button>` MXML tag. You can customize a Button control to display a label, an icon, or both a label and an icon together. As with all other Flex controls, you can customize a Button control's visual appearance to its fine-grain detail.

You can also add event listeners to the Button control to detect when the button has been clicked and then perform an action in response to that click. The most common event that's listened to on a Button control is `click`. This event is fired by the button every time the user presses and releases a Button with the mouse or keyboard. To refresh your knowledge of events and event listeners, refer to Chapter 3.

You can set properties and styles for the Button control as described in the following list:

- ✔ **Add a text label:** You can set the `label` property on the Button control to specify which text should be displayed on the button. Then, to control the placement of the label, use the `textAlign` style. Its default value is `center`: The label appears in the center of the button. You can customize the button to display the label as left-aligned or right-aligned by setting the `textAlign` style to `left` or `right`.

- ✔ **Display an icon:** In addition to being able to add a label, you can have the Button control display an icon. To specify an icon, you set the `icon` style. The icon style expects an image that's embedded in the Flex application at compile time. (For more on the types of images you can embed in a Flex application, and the correct syntax to do so, see Chapter 18.)

- ✔ **Position the label and icon:** You can control the placement of the button's label with respect to the icon with the `labelPlacement` property. By default, the label is placed to the right of the icon. However, you can set `labelPlacement` to `left`, `right`, `top`, or `bottom` to set the orientation of the label with respect to the icon. Figure 7-2 shows buttons with different `labelPlacement` values in use.

Figure 7-2:
Label-
placement
orientations.

The example shown in the following code snippet shows a Trash button that you might use in a Flex application (see Figure 7-3).

```
<mx:Button id="trashButton" label="Trash"
        labelPlacement="bottom" icon="@Embed('assets/
        trash.jpg')" click="trash();" />
```

Figure 7-3:
A Button
control with
an icon and
a label.

An icon is displayed above the label, and this orientation is configured by using the properties and styles just described. This example includes a `click` event listener, which listens for the `click` event to be dispatched by the Button and then invokes the `trash` method to handle the response.

The `toggle` property controls whether a button supports *toggling,* which means that when someone clicks the button, it stays selected until someone clicks it again. If the `toggle` property is set to `false`, the button doesn't stay pressed after the user finishes clicking it. If you choose to use the `toggle` property, the `selected` property may also come in handy. The `selected` property takes effect only when the `toggle` property is set to `true`. The `selected` property, when set to `true`, visually renders the button as selected.

This property makes more sense with some of the other Button-based controls, such as CheckBox and RadioButton. When `selected` is set to `true` in these controls, CheckBox appears with a check mark displayed in the box, and RadioButton appears with the radio icon filled in. Figure 7-4 shows what the Button, RadioButton, and CheckBox controls look like when the `toggle` property and `selected` properties are set to `true`.

Figure 7-4:
Selected
and toggled
controls.

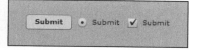

CheckBox

A CheckBox control displays a descriptive label and a box that can show a check mark to indicate selection. The CheckBox control extends from the Button control and thus inherits all properties, styles, methods, and events declared on the Button control. You can create a CheckBox control in a Flex application by using the <mx:CheckBox> MXML tag. Similar to how you work with a Button control, you often add a click event listener to detect when a user clicks the CheckBox control. The clicking of the check box causes the selection to take place and the check mark to be drawn in the box. The following example shows a CheckBox control that, when clicked, visually indicates that the user will receive a copy of his order in e-mail form (see Figure 7-5).

Figure 7-5:
A selected
CheckBox
control.

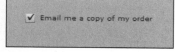

We added a click event handler so that when the CheckBox control is selected, the emailReceipt method is called. Notice that the CheckBox MXML tag has its selected property set to true, which means that the check box is initially displayed as selected, with the check mark drawn in the box:

```
<mx:CheckBox label="Email me a copy of my
        order"selected="true" click="emailReceipt();"
        />
```

RadioButton

The RadioButton control is another extension of the Button control, so it inherits all properties, styles, methods, and events defined by the Button control. You can create a RadioButton control in a Flex application by using the <mx:RadioButton> MXML tag. A RadioButton control displays a label and a circle that are filled in with a radio icon when selected. You can use event listeners to determine when the RadioButton control has been selected. Like all button-based controls, the click event is the most common event that is listened for. The click event is dispatched when the user clicks a radio button to select it.

Normally, you allow only one RadioButton control in a set of RadioButton controls to be selected at a time. Application users can select a single radio button from a set of mutually exclusive radio buttons. Selecting another RadioButton control deselects the previously selected radio button. You can make your radio buttons act like this by using the same `groupName` property for all buttons you want to group.

The following example shows two RadioButton controls that let users report their gender (see Figure 7-6). Because we used the same `groupName` property for both controls, only one radio button can be selected at a time:

```
<mx:RadioButton label="Female" groupName="gender" />
<mx:RadioButton label="Male" groupName="gender" />
```

Figure 7-6:
Two
RadioButton
controls.

RadioButtonGroup

If you want to take the concept of grouped RadioButton controls a step further than just RadioButton, you can create a RadioButtonGroup. It gives you more control over how your set of RadioButton controls behaves. You can define a RadioButtonGroup in MXML by using the `<mx:RadioButtonGroup>` tag. However, the RadioButtonGroup control isn't a visual control, so the `<mx:RadioButtonGroup>` tag doesn't render anything in your Flex application. This makes the control *faceless* in Flex. The special RadioButtonGroup control indicates that a set of RadioButton controls should be treated as a group. You create a RadioButtonGroup when you want the same action to occur when any of the RadioButton controls within the group is selected. In this manner, RadioButtonGroup "governs" the selection of each individual RadioButton control defined within the group.

When a radio button that's part of a RadioButtonGroup is selected by using the mouse or keyboard, the RadioButtonGroup receives a `change` event. By adding an event listener for the `change` event, you can ensure that all radio button selections are proxied through to the action specified by the `change` event handler.

The following example shows a RadioButtonGroup that is governing the behavior of a set of payment-option radio buttons. Whenever any of the radio buttons is selected, the RadioButtonGroup's `change` event handler is invoked. You can then define a single `change` event handler on the

RadioButtonGroup control rather than have to define `click` event handlers on each individual RadioButton control:

```
<mx:RadioButtonGroup id="paymentType" change=
        "handlePaymentOption(event);"/>
<mx:RadioButton groupName="paymentType" id="check"
        value="check" label="Check"/>
<mx:RadioButton groupName="paymentType" id="creditCard"
        value="creditCard" label="Credit Card"/>
<mx:RadioButton groupName="paymentType" id="moneyOrder"
        value="moneyOrder" label="Money Order"/>
```

LinkButton

The simple button-based LinkButton control is used to show links in a Flex application. As the user hovers over the LinkButton, its contents are highlighted. You can create a LinkButton control in your Flex application by using the `<mx:LinkButton>` MXML tag. As with all other button-based controls, you can detect when a user clicks the LinkButton by adding an event listener for the `click` event.

You can control the visual appearance of the LinkButton as the application user is interacting with it by setting a couple of styles in the LinkButton tag:

- `rollOverColor`: Controls the color of the entire LinkButton as the user hovers the mouse over it.

- `textRollOverColor`: Controls the color of just the label as the user hovers the mouse over it.

The following example shows a LinkButton control that, when clicked, navigates the user's browser to the Adobe Systems Incorporated home page:

```
<mx:LinkButton label="Adobe Systems Inc"
        click="navigateToURL(new URLRequest('http://
        www.adobe.com'));" textRollOverColor="white"
        rollOverColor="red"/>
```

As the user hovers over the LinkButton, shown in Figure 7-7, the background of the control becomes red and the text is white. You achieve this effect by setting the `textRollOverColor` and `rollOverColor` styles.

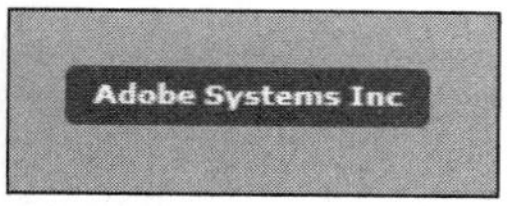

Figure 7-7:
Navigating
to Adobe.
com.

Adobe Systems Inc

The `navigateToURL` method is useful for launching links to other Web sites from within your Flex application. However, you cannot simply pass a URL string to `navigateToURL`. Instead, you must pass a `URLRequest` object that specifies the URL to navigate to. The previous example shows you how to do this.

You often use LinkButton controls in conjunction with a LinkBar control to provide a set of clickable links that can be used to navigate within a Flex application. For more information on how to create a LinkBar control and to find out more about navigation controls, see Chapter 9.

PopUpButton

You can use the PopUpButton control to pop up any Flex user interface control when a user clicks the PopUpButton control. A PopUpButton looks similar to a Button control, except that a second button with a downward arrow is affixed to the side of the Button control. When the user clicks this arrow button, a new Flex component pops up. You can create a PopUpButton control in your Flex application by using the `<mx:PopUpButton>` MXML tag.

You set the `popUp` property to specify which Flex control is used as the pop-up when a user clicks the arrow button. The `popUp` property expects an object that is of type `mx.core.IUIComponent`. `mx.core.IUIComponent` is the interface that all Flex controls implement, which means that you can set the `popUp` property to any visual control available in the Flex framework library.

Because all visual Flex controls in the Flex framework implement the `mx.core.IUIComponent` interface, any Flex method that expects an object of type `mx.core.IUIComponent` as a parameter, can accept any visual Flex control.

Every interface class in the Flex framework has an `I` prepended to its class name; for example, `mx.core.IContainer`, `mx.core.IFlexDisplayObject`, and `mx.core.IUID`. When you see the `I` in front of a class name, you know that the class is an interface.

The following example shows how to create a PopUpButton control that pops up a Flex button when a user clicks the arrow button (see Figure 7-8):

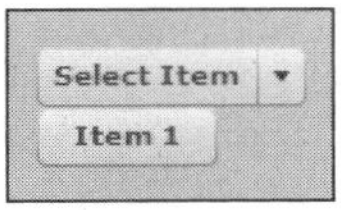

Figure 7-8:
A pop-up
Button
control.

```
<mx:PopUpButton label="Select Item">
   <mx:popUp>
      <mx:Button label="item 1" />
   </mx:popUp>
</mx:PopUpButton>
```

Notice that the `popUp` attribute is set as a child MXML tag of the PopUpButton MXML tag. A Button control is passed in as the value of the `popUp` MXML tag. That Button is the Flex control that's displayed when a user clicks the PopUpButton control's arrow.

Often, the pop-up control needs to be initialized in some way. For example, you might need to populate the pop-up control with data or add event listeners so that the pop-up responds to user interaction. Sometimes this means that you create the pop-up control in ActionScript and then set that newly created control as the value of the `popUp` property on the PopUpButton control. For the most part, you can always create the pop-up control with MXML tags, as the preceding example shows, but sometimes the pop-up control must be created in ActionScript for fine-grain control of the pop-up. The following example shows how to create a PopUpButton control where the pop-up is created in ActionScript:

```
<mx:PopUpButton id="popUpBtn" label="Select Animal"
         creationComplete="createPopUp();" />
<mx:Script>
   <![CDATA[
      import mx.controls.List;
      private var listPopUp:List;

      // Initialize the List control, and specify it as
      // the pop up object of the PopUpButton control.
      private function createPopUp ():void {
         listPopUp = new List();
         var dp:Object = [{label: "Cat"}, {label: "Dog"},
         {label: "Mouse"}];
         listPopUp.dataProvider = dp;
         popUpBtn.popUp = listPopUp;
      }
   ]]>
</mx:Script>
```

Figure 7-9 shows a PopUpButton control that displays a prepopulated List control.

First look at the `createPopUp` method. In this method, you first create the List control in ActionScript by using the ActionScript `new` operator. After you create the List control, you set its `dataProvider` property so that it's populated with data items. After the List control is created and populated with data, you can safely set the PopUpButton's `popUp` property to the newly created List control.

Figure 7-9:
A prepopu-
lated List
control.

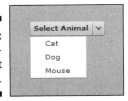

Now, how is the `createPopUp` method invoked? Notice that the PopUpButton tag has an event listener for the `creationComplete` event. This event is dispatched when any Flex control has been completely created. In the preceding example, after the `creationComplete` event has been dispatched, the `createPopUp` method is called, which safely creates the pop-up and assigns it to the PopUpButton's `popUp` property.

For more information about creating and using the List control, see Chapter 8.

Because a PopUpButton control extends the Flex Button control, it can follow all the same customizations available to a Button control. You can therefore customize the PopUpButton control to show just a label, an icon, or a label and an icon together.

PopUpMenuButton

The PopUpMenuButton control is similar to the PopUpButton control, except that the former always pops up a menu-like control. The PopUpMenuButton control creates a PopUpButton control and pops up a single-level Flex Menu control. You can create a PopUpMenuButton control in your Flex application by using the `<mx:PopUpMenuButton>` MXML tag. You can populate the pop-up menu with data directly in the PopUpMenuButton MXML tag. (For more information on creating and customizing the Flex Menu control, see Chapter 8.)

The following example shows how to create a PopUpMenuButton control that displays a menu pop-up when a user clicks the arrow button. The menu pop-up allows users to select a color from three color options, as shown in Figure 7-10.

Figure 7-10:
A pop-up
with three
color
choices.

The menu pop-up is populated with data directly as a child tag of the `PopUpMenuButton` tag. To populate the PopUpMenuButton with data, you set the `dataProvider` property. In this example, the `dataProvider` property is set to an array of data that's declared with MXML tags. This data is displayed by the menu pop-up:

```
<mx:PopUpMenuButton>
    <mx:dataProvider>
        <mx:Array>
            <mx:String>Red</mx:String>
            <mx:String>Blue</mx:String>
            <mx:String>Purple</mx:String>
        </mx:Array>
    </mx:dataProvider>
</mx:PopUpMenuButton>
```

To determine when an item on the pop-up menu has been selected, you add an `itemClick` event listener. The event object that's passed to the `itemClick` event listener has information in it that can tell you which menu item was selected. For more information on event objects and how to glean useful information from them, refer to Chapter 3.

Popping open controls with ComboBox and ColorPicker

In this section, we discuss ComboBox and ColorPicker, two controls that display their data in subcomponents that pop up as a result of user interaction in order to allow users to make selections.

ComboBox

The simple Flex ComboBox control lets users click an arrow button to open a drop-down list from which they can make choices. You create a ComboBox control by using the `<mx:ComboBox />` MXML tag. This control is similar to the HTML `<select>` element. The key property to set on a ComboBox control is the `dataProvider` property, which tells the ComboBox which data to display in its drop-down list. You can set the `dataProvider` property to any Flex or Flash data object, and the ComboBox tries to display the data in a clear fashion. After a user has selected an item from the drop-down list, the properties that track user selection are updated to represent the value that the user selected. To find the index of the item the user selected, you can inspect the `selectedIndex` property. To decipher the actual data item that the user selected from the list, you can inspect the `selectedItem` property. After a user selects an item from the drop-down list, the ComboBox dispatches the `change` event to signal that a selection has been made.

To find out more about the `dataProvider` property, data display, and selection, see Chapter 8, where these topics are discussed in-depth in relation to the Flex list controls (which the ComboBox control resembles).

The following code shows a ComboBox that can be used to make a credit-card choice:

```
<mx:ComboBox dataProvider="{['MasterCard', 'American
          Express', 'Visa']}" />
```

Data binding is used to set the `dataProvider` property. See Chapter 12 for more information on data binding.

ColorPicker

The Flex ColorPicker control lets users select color information. By default, the Flex ColorPicker opens a color swatch with many color entries that the user can select. A ColorPicker control can be created with the `<mx:ColorPicker />` MXML tag. When the user makes a selection, the `change` event is dispatched to signal that a color choice has been made. You can query the `selectionColor` property, which is set to the chosen value after the user chooses a color. To decipher the index of the color chosen in the color swatch, the `selectedIndex` property can be queried. You can use the `showTextField` property to determine whether a text box that displays the current color choice appears. By default, `showTextField` is set to `true`.

Making dates: Using calendar controls in Flex

In many applications, users need to enter and display date-related information. Maybe you're building a hotel reservation application and you need a calendar control to allow users to choose the length of their hotel stay. Or, perhaps you're building a scheduling application and need to display which days are fully booked and which are open for scheduling. Flex has two native user interface controls to deal with date-related information: DateChooser and DateField. The following sections discuss how to create and customize these calendar controls.

DateChooser

The powerful DateChooser control ties together the ability to display and select individual dates, multiple dates, or a range of dates. You can create a DateChooser control in your Flex application by using the `<mx:DateChooser>` MXML tag. A DateChooser control displays year, month, and day information. The DateChooser control provides a set of properties that can be used to customize the date information it displays. For example, DateChooser can show the current date, multiple dates, or a range of dates as selected or as disabled. A DateChooser control has arrow buttons that let users navigate to the next month or back to the previous month.

By default, DateChooser displays the current year and current month. You can customize which month and year DateChooser initially displays by setting the displayedMonth and displayedYear properties. The following example shows a default DateChooser control, displaying the current month and year for when this example was written and a DateChooser control that's preinitialized to show the calendar information for December 1999 (see Figure 7-11).

Figure 7-11:
Two Date
Chooser
controls
showing
calendar
information.

Notice that the number set to the displayedMonth property is zero-based, which means that the month numbers go from January represented by the number 0 all the way to December represented by the number 11:

```
<mx:DateChooser />
<mx:DateChooser displayedYear="1999" displayedMonth="11"
            />
```

You can control whether the current date is visually shown as selected when the current month and year are in view: Set the showToday property to true or false.

Sometimes you need to disable individual days or a range of dates so that those dates cannot be selected and they appear as grayed out. Days in a week or a range of dates can be disabled for selection by setting the disabledDays or disabledRanges properties:

- disabledDays: Set the disabledDays property to an array of numbers that are zero-based, such that Sunday corresponds to the number 0, Monday to the number 1, and so on. The days matching the numbers specified in the disabledDays array cannot be selected and are grayed out.

- disabledRanges: Similarly, you can disable a range of dates by setting the disabledRanges property to an array of ActionScript Date objects. The ActionScript Date objects defined in the array can correspond to a single date or to a range of dates.

  When specifying a range of dates to disable, you need to specify the rangeStart and rangeEnd properties.

The following example shows a DateChooser control displaying the date information for the month of February, 2008. The dates from February 5, 2008, to February 28, 2008, are disabled. The second DateChooser control shows date information for the month of February 2008, where Saturdays and Sundays are disabled from user selection (see Figure 7-12):

```
<mx:DateChooser displayedMonth="1"
        disabledRanges="{[{rangeStart: new Date(2008,
        01, 05), rangeEnd: new Date(2008, 01, 28)}]}"/>
<mx:DateChooser displayedMonth="1" disabledDays="[0, 6]"
        />
```

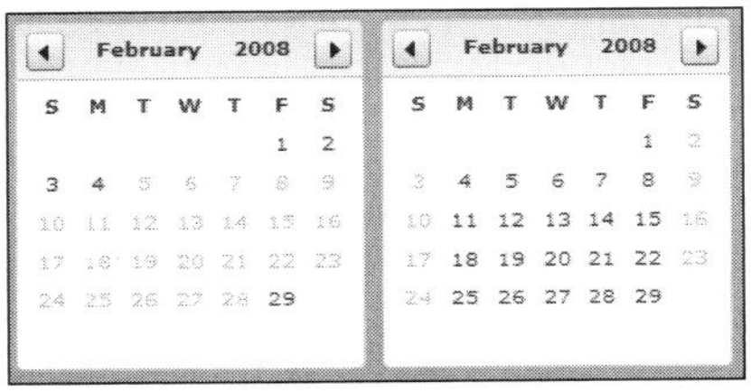

Figure 7-12:
Individual days and date ranges are disabled.

When the user selects single dates, multiple dates, or a range of dates, DateChooser updates some selections. You can query the selection properties to determine which selections the user has made. For example, when the user clicks July 4, 2007, the selectedDate property immediately is set to an ActionScript Date object representing July 4, 2007. Similarly, if the user holds down the Shift key and selects a range of dates, the selectedRanges property is set to an array of Date objects describing the ranges of dates that were selected.

DateField

The simple DateField control displays date information and allows the user to pop up a DateChooser control for more advanced calendar information. For example, you might use a DateField control to conserve visual space in your application because the DateField control takes up much less space then a DateChooser control. You can create a DateField control in your Flex application by using the <mx:DateField> MXML tag. When a DateField control is created, a text box displays date information and a calendar icon. The user can click the calendar icon to pop up a DateChooser control. If the user selects a date in the DateChooser control, the date displayed in the DateField control's text box updates to show that date.

All customizations available to a DateChooser control, such as the ability to disable dates from user selection, can be set on the DateField control. When these properties are set in the DateField MXML tag, they affect the DateChooser pop-up control. As with the DateChooser control, you can use the selectedDate and selectedRanges properties to determine which dates the user selected. The following example shows a DateField control where the user selected the date July 4, 2008 (see Figure 7-13):

```
<mx:DateField selectedDate="{new Date(2008, 08, 04)}" />
```

Figure 7-13:
A DateField control.

Scrolling around

Flex controls have an enormous amount of scrolling functionality built into them natively. For example, when a List control contains more items than it can display in its allotted space, it sprouts a vertical scrollbar by default. For the most part, scrollbars are created by each individual control, and you can set properties to control the scrolling policy. (For more information on configuring the scrolling behavior of individual controls, refer to the Chapter 8 sections that talk about `horizontalScrollPolicy` and `verticalScroll-Policy`.) However, in some cases, you may need to create individual scrollbar controls by using the `<mx:HScrollBar>` and `<mx:VScrollBar>` MXML tags in your Flex application. The HScrollBar control creates a horizontal scrollbar, and the VScrollBar control creates a vertical scrollbar.

A scrollbar consists of scroll arrows, a scroll thumb, and a scroll track. The thumb sits in the track and displays the scrolling progress. Users can grab and drag the thumb to scroll through larger "chunks" of information or click the scroll arrows to move the thumb in smaller "chunks." You can set the `width` property on a HScrollBar control to limit its width, and set the height property on a VScrollBar control to limit its `height`.

When a user scrolls a scrollbar component, a `scroll` event is dispatched. You can add an event listener for the `scroll` event in order to be notified when the scrollbar has been scrolled by way of the scroll arrows, scroll thumb, or scroll track. Certain scrolling properties can be set on the scrollbar controls in order to control where the scroll thumb appears and how far one click of either scroll arrow moves the scroll thumb. The properties `minScrollPosition` and `maxScrollPosition` are set to numbers that represent the minimum and maximum scroll positions. The `scroll Position` property is set to a number that represents the current scroll position within the range defined by `minScrollPosition` and `maxScroll Position`. Figure 7-14 shows a HScrollBar on the left and a VScrollBar on the right. The scrollbars are created with a minimum and maximum scroll position, and the scroll thumb is set to the halfway point. Notice the different parts of the scrollbars, such as the scroll arrows, scroll thumb, and scroll track.

```
<mx:HScrollBar width="100" minScrollPosition="0"
        maxScrollPosition="100" scrollPosition="50"/>

<mx:VScrollBar height="100" minScrollPosition="0"
        maxScrollPosition="100" scrollPosition="50"/>
```

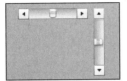

Figure 7-14:
Horizontal
and vertical
standalone
scrollbars.

Sliding around with Slider controls

The Flex framework offers a pair of handy controls that allow users to make choices by sliding a user interface control. Users can choose a value by dragging the slider thumb between endpoints that sit on either a horizontal axis or a vertical axis, as shown in Figure 7-15. For example, you may create a Flex application that's an MP3 player. You might use the Flex slider controls to let users control the volume of the MP3 playback. You can create a vertical slider by using the `<mx:VSlider>` MXML tag or a horizontal slider by using the `<mx:HSlider>` MXML tag.

ToolTip   Slider thumb

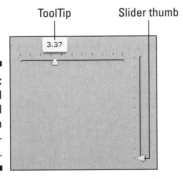

Figure 7-15:
Horizontal
and vertical
sliders with
limited slid-
ing range.

As a user drags the thumb, a ToolTip appears above it to indicate which value would be chosen if the dragging were terminated at that point (refer to Figure 7-15). You can control the range of values a user can select by setting the `maximum` and `minimum` properties, which limit users to a particular range of values to choose from. The values displayed in the ToolTip are calculated based on the range of values specified by `minimum` and `maximum`. These intervals can be visually displayed with tick marks. You can control the tick mark increments by setting the `tickInterval` property.

The following example shows a horizontal slider control and a vertical slider control (refer to Figure 7-15). You can move the horizontal slider's thumb anywhere between the values 0 through 10, and the slider shows a tick mark at each whole number between 0 and 10. You can move the vertical slider's thumb anywhere between 0 and 100, and a tick mark is shown at intervals of 10 between 0 and 100.

```
<mx:HSlider minimum="0" maximum="10" tickInterval="1" />
<mx:VSlider minimum="0" maximum="100" tickInterval="10" />
```

The `liveDragging` property controls whether the sliding of the slider thumb results in the real-time dispatching of value selection events and the setting of value selection properties. Because `liveDragging` is set to `false` by default, Flex sets value selection properties and dispatches value selection events when the user stops sliding the slider thumb. If `liveDragging` is set to `true`, Flex sets value selection properties and dispatches value selection events continuously as the user drags the slider thumb. When value selection has occurred, a `change` event is dispatched by the slider control. You can add an event listener for the `change` event in order to be notified when the user has selected a value.

Introducing Text Controls

Your Flex application needs to convey information to users, and even though a picture is worth a thousand words, sometimes you can't rely on icons and images to get your point across. When you need to spell it out, you can use a number of text controls. In this section, you find out how to use the Label and Text controls to display text, and also how to use TextInput, TextArea, and RichTextEditor controls to allow users to submit text to your application.

Displaying text in Flex

You have a few options for displaying text in your Flex applications. Many controls in the Flex framework have text built into their interfaces. For example, Panel has a title text field, and Button shows a label. But if you want to simply show some text on your own, you use either the Label control or the Text control.

Using Label

When you want to display a single line of text, use the Label control. It's the most basic text control in the Flex framework and does little more than display a single line of text. The main property you use is the `text` property, which sets the text to be displayed. You can add a simple Label control to your application by using the following MXML:

```
<mx:Label text="My super label" />
```

Figure 7-16 shows the result of creating a Flex Label control to display text to users.

Figure 7-16:
Displaying
text to
users.

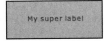

Label supports the truncation of text, which means that if you set the width of the label and the text can't fit within that width, Label displays an ellipsis (...) at the end of the text, indicating that the label has more text than can be shown. You can control whether this truncation occurs by setting the truncateToFit property, which is true by default. You can style the font your label uses by setting the text styles, such as fontWeight, fontSize, fontStyle. The fontWeight style controls whether the text that's displayed is boldface and can be set to normal or bold. By default, fontWeight is set to normal in all Flex text controls. The fontSize style controls the pixel height of the displayed text. By default, fontSize is set to 10. The fontStyle style controls whether text is italicized. By default, fontStyle is set to normal and can be set to italic to italicize the text.

Text versus Label

The Text control is nearly identical to the Label control, except that it can span multiple lines. A Flex Text control can be created with the <mx:Text> MXML tag. Label is limited to a single line, so if you need to show a block of text, you have to use the Text control. Other than that, it's pretty much the same control as Label, and you can use all the same properties and styles. The lone notable difference is that the Text control never truncates its text by using the ellipsis (...) format, like Label does.

Label and Text both have a selectable property that allows users to select the text. By default, selectable is false for Label and true for Text.

Exploring text-input controls

Sometimes you can't just talk at users — every once in a while, you need to listen too. When it's time to hear what application users have to say, you can let them type into the Flex application by using the text-input controls:

TextInput, TextArea, and RichTextEditor. These controls are the easiest way to receive input from a user, such as letting the user tell you his or her name, or even submit a credit card number.

TextInput

Think of TextInput as an editable Label control. Or, if you're from the HTML world, TextInput is just like the `<input type="text" />` tag. A TextInput control can be created with the `<mx:TextInput>` MXML tag. When you use TextInput, you're limited to a single line of text, so this text control should be used for simple input fields that don't require multiple lines of input.

You can get and set the text that's displayed in the control by accessing the aptly named `text` property. To create a basic text-input control, use the following MXML code:

```
<mx:TextInput id="myTextField" text="Hello World"/>
```

Then you can access the text that the user has typed by referencing `myText-Field.text`. Here's a complete MXML application to demonstrate accessing the text of a TextInput control:

```
<?xml version="1.0" encoding="utf-8"?>
<mx:Application
    xmlns:mx="http://www.adobe.com/2006/mxml">

    <mx:Script>
    <![CDATA[
        import mx.controls.Alert;

        private function showAlertMessage():void {
            Alert.show("Your name is: " + myTextField.text);
        }
    ]]>
    </mx:Script>

    <mx:Label text="Please enter your name:" />
    <mx:TextInput id="myTextField" />
    <mx:Button click="showAlertMessage()" label="Submit" />

</mx:Application>
```

This Flex application lets an application user enter her name in the TextInput control (see Figure 7-17). When the user clicks the Submit button, an alert message pops up and displays the text the user entered in the `myTextField` control.

Figure 7-17:
Using a
TextInput
control to
receive user
input.

If the user is entering a password, you can set the displayAsPassword property to true, which displays asterisks to hide what the user is typing. This strategy also works on the TextArea control.

TextArea

If you need the user to enter more than a single line of text, use the TextArea control rather than TextInput. This distinction is similar to the distinction between Label and Text, discussed a little earlier in this chapter. If we continue our comparison to HTML controls, it should be apparent that TextArea is similar to the HTML <textarea> tag. A Flex TextArea control can be created with the <mx:TextArea> MXML tag. In a TextArea control, a user can enter any amount of text, and if the text exceeds the width and height of the control, scrollbars appear.

RichTextEditor

Flex has a built-in control designed to let users add rich formatting to the text they enter. The RichTextEditor control consists of a TextArea control and several buttons and options for formatting the text that's entered, as shown in Figure 7-18. This control can be useful if you want to let a user enter text to be displayed later in your Flex application with the same formatting in place. A Flex RichTextEditor control can be created with the <mx:RichTextEditor> MXML tag. Because RichTextEditor is used for richly formatted text, you should always access the htmlText property of this control as opposed to the text property, which accesses plain text.

Figure 7-18:
The
RichText
Editor con-
trol provides
HTML
formatting
tools for text
editing.

Working with HTML text

All Flex text controls have two properties you can use to set the text shown in the control: `text` and `htmlText`. Any of the text controls can display basic HTML text, which allows you to use HTML tags such as <b>, <i>, and <u> to format your text. If you want to use HTML formatting in your text, you have to set the `htmlText` property rather than the `text` property.

The number of HTML tags supported in the Flex text controls is determined by the Flash Player's ability to render HTML. There are some limitations to what HTML tags the Flash Player can render. For a full list of supported HTML tags, see Table 7-1.

Table 7-1		Supported HTML Tags		
<a>	<b>	 	<font>	<img>
<i>	<li>	<p>	<textformat>	<u>

Notice that complex HTML tags, like <table>, aren't supported. This is a limitation in Flash Player 9.

Showing Off with the Flex Media Controls

Because Flex applications run on the Flash Player, you can take advantage of some of the rich media capabilities that Flash provides. You can load static images, animations, audio, and video into your applications by using media controls. The image and video controls are visual components that can be created with MXML or ActionScript to display the loaded media. Sound controls, on the other hand, aren't visual controls and must be created and controlled with ActionScript.

Displaying images

Flex supports the following image formats: GIF, JPEG, PNG, SVG, and SWF. Image assets with these extensions can easily be added to your Flex application.

Image control

The easiest way to display images in your application is to use the Flex Image control, which can be created with the <mx:Image> MXML tag. You use the source property to tell the control where it can find the image file to load. The location of the image file can be specified by a relative URL or an absolute URL. A relative URL specifies the location of the image file relative to the current location of the Flex MXML file.

The other notable properties of the Image control that you use are autoLoad and scaleContent, described in the following list:

✔ autoLoad: If autoLoad is set to true, which is the default setting, the image control downloads the source image immediately after the source property is set. Otherwise, you have to call the load() method explicitly in ActionScript to load the image file.

✔ scaleContent: You control the scaling of the source image by setting the scaleContent property, which is true by default. If you specify a width and height for the Image control, the image is either scaled (scaleContent = true) or cropped (scaleContent = false) to fit within the width and height you set.

If you need to load a Scalable Vector Graphics (SVG) file, you must embed it in your application. You cannot simply set the source property to the URL of your SVG file. To embed the file inline in your MXML tag, you use the @Embed syntax and embed an asset specified by a relative or absolute location:

```
<mx:Image source="@Embed('graphic.svg')" />
```

This line embeds the bytes of the SVG file in your main application SWF file. Embedding assets adds to the file size of your SWF, so be aware when you embed any multimedia.

SWFLoader versus Image

You should use the Image control when displaying noninteractive media. You can also load interactive SWF files, which can even be other Flex or Flash applications, by using the SWFLoader component. To create SWFLoader Flex control, you can use the <mx:SWFLoader> MXML tag. SWFLoader works just like Image but preserves interactivity in the SWF file you're loading. Generally, use the Image control to load all your images and use the SWFLoader to load interactive SWFs. You can create a simple SWFLoader control by using this bit of MXML code:

```
<mx:SWFLoader id="loader" source="@
          Embed(source='myLocalSWF.swf')" height="200"
          width="500"/>
```

In terms of object-oriented component architecture, Image is an extension of SWFLoader. Image adds a little extra functionality that lets it display well when used in some of the Flex List controls, such as List and DataGrid. Other than that, Image and SWFLoader are almost the same component.

Playing video

You can use the Flex VideoDisplay control to play back video files that have been encoded as either Flash Video (FLV) videos or MPEG-4 videos with H.264 encoding. The VideoDisplay control can display both progressive download video and streaming video. A Flex VideoDisplay control can be created with the <mx:VideoDisplay> MXML tag.

The Flex framework comes with only the most basic video controls, which is the video playback control. It doesn't include a prebuilt video player with play and pause buttons or a volume control. You can easily build your own, simple playback controls, but just be aware that the VideoDisplay control displays only video.

FLV files can be encoded with different compression algorithms for various quality and size results. Typical encoding options for FLV files are Sorenson Spark or On2 TrueMotion VP6.

Playing audio

You can play MP3 files in your Flex application by using the Sound class. But, just as the Flex framework doesn't contain an out-of-the-box video player component, it also has no prebuilt user interface for an audio-playing component. Instead, you get the essential elements that you need to play audio files, and you can hook them up to your own interface controls you have created.

Flex has no user interface components for playing sounds, so you have to get your hands dirty with ActionScript if you want to make audio work. You create a new instance of the Sound class in ActionScript and call the load() method to tell the Sound object which MP3 file to load. The load method takes a URLRequest object, which is a utility class in ActionScript that you use when working with URLs.

In the first line of the following code snippet, you create a new URLRequest object that points to the sound file you want to load — in this case, a file named audio.mp3. Notice that a relative URL is used to specify the location of the audio.mp3 file, which means that the file lives in the same directory as the Flex application. In the next line, you create a new Sound object, and in the third line you load the audio file into the Sound object. After you load the audio file, you can call the play method to start playback:

```
var urlRequest:URLRequest = new URLRequest("audio.mp3");
var sound:Sound = new Sound();
sound.load(urlRequest);
```

The Sound class has a `play()` method, but it doesn't have a `stop()` method. Never fear: If you don't want to force users to sit through the whole audio clip, you can stop it whenever you like, although it involves using the SoundChannel class. The `play` method of the Sound object returns a SoundChannel object that you need to keep track of if you ever want to stop the sound or adjust volume.

To expand on the previous code snippet, the following code listing creates two buttons that allow users to start and stop playing an audio file:

```
<mx:Application xmlns:mx="http://www.adobe.com/2006/mxml" layout="vertical">
    <mx:Script>
        <![CDATA[
        private var soundChannel:SoundChannel;

        private function playSound():void {
            var urlRequest:URLRequest = new URLRequest("audio.mp3");
            var sound:Sound = new Sound();
            sound.load(urlRequest);

            if(soundChannel != null) {
                soundChannel.stop();
            }

            soundChannel = sound.play();
        }

        private function stopSound():void {
            soundChannel.stop();
        }
        ]]>
    </mx:Script>

    <mx:Button click="playSound()" label="Play" />
    <mx:Button click="stopSound()" label="Stop" />

</mx:Application>
```

In this example, you first define a variable to hold the SoundChannel object that you will use to stop the sound after it has started playing. This variable, named `soundChannel`, is referred to in the `stopSound()` method when you want to stop the audio. The `playSound()` method creates a new Sound object and begins playing it. When you call `sound.play()`, you save the returned `SoundChannel` object in the `soundChannel` variable. If you didn't do this, you would never be able to stop the sound after you start playing it.

Next, we explain how to adjust the volume of sound that's already playing. To adjust the volume, you have to use another class: SoundTransform. Each SoundChannel object has a `soundTransform` property that is an instance of SoundTransform. You can change the `volume` property of a SoundTransform object to adjust the volume of the playing clip. So, in the previous example, you can adjust the volume to 50 percent by making the following call before calling `sound.play`:

```
soundChannel.soundTransform.volume = .5;
```

Using this line of code, you access the current SoundTransform of the playing clip and set the volume, which can range from 0 to 1.

Your options for working with audio within a Flex application also include streaming audio (or video) from a server. Streaming live audio or video requires a streaming server and is thus outside the scope of this book.

Showing progress with ProgressBar

The ProgressBar control isn't really a "media" control, but because the most typical use for ProgressBar is to show the progress of a media file that's loading, it is included in this section. A Flex ProgressBar control can be created with the `<mx:ProgressBar>` MXML tag. The ProgressBar control can be used to show the progress of any operation, whether it's loading an image file from a server or indicating which percentage of a video has played (see Figure 7-19).

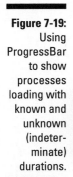

Figure 7-19: Using ProgressBar to show processes loading with known and unknown (indeterminate) durations.

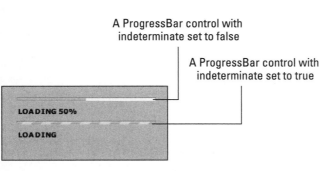

A ProgressBar control with indeterminate set to false

A ProgressBar control with indeterminate set to true

LOADING 50%

LOADING

You can get a ProgressBar to show progress in three ways, which you can set by using the mode property of the control. The three possible values for mode are event, polled, and manual. For both event and polled modes, you have to specify a source control by setting the source parameter. Here's the lowdown on these three values:

- ✔ event mode assumes that the control you set as the source property will dispatch ProgressEvent events to let the ProgressBar know to update itself. Controls such as Image and SWFLoader dispatch these events when loading data.

- ✔ polled mode assumes that the source control has properties named bytesLoaded and bytesTotal. If a ProgressBar is in polled mode, it checks these properties every 30 milliseconds and updates its progress.

- ✔ manual mode doesn't require a source control. Instead, you must manually call setProgress(bytesLoaded, bytesTotal) in ActionScript, on the ProgressBar, to set the progress.

The language used in the ProgressBar documentation often refers to bytesLoaded and bytesTotal, which indicates that a common use of ProgressBar is for loading files. But you can use the ProgressBar for any other progress events, such as indicating the percentage of a processing task that has completed: Just call ProgressBar.setProgress and pass in the current amount completed and the total amount.

Tying It Together: A Video Player Example

As we mention earlier in this chapter, the Flex framework doesn't contain a component with play and pause buttons to control a video. In Listing 7-1, you create a simple application to control a video by combining the Label, Button, VideoDisplay, and ProgressBar controls. The result is shown in Figure 7-20.

Listing 7-1: Creating a Simple Video Player Application

```
<?xml version="1.0" encoding="utf-8"?>
<mx:Application xmlns:mx="http://www.adobe.com/2006/mxml" layout="vertical"   → 2
              verticalGap="0">
  <mx:Script>                                                                 → 4
    <![CDATA[
      import mx.events.VideoEvent;
```

```
        private function playheadUpdated(event:VideoEvent):void {
            progress.setProgress(video.playheadTime, video.totalTime);      → 8
        }
     ]]>
   </mx:Script>


   <mx:Label text="My Awesome Video" fontStyle="italic" />                  → 12
   <mx:VideoDisplay width="150" height="150" id="video" source="video.flv"
             playheadUpdate="playheadUpdated(event)"/>
   <mx:ProgressBar mode="manual" id="progress" label="Playing: %3%%"        → 15
             labelPlacement="center" width="150" height="18"/>
   <mx:HBox>
       <mx:Button label="Play" enabled="{video.playing == false}"           → 18
             click="video.play()" />
       <mx:Button label="Pause" enabled="{video.playing == true}"
             click="video.pause()" />                                        → 21
   </mx:HBox>
</mx:Application>
```

Figure 7-20:
The output
from the
video-
display
example.

Here's how the code in Listing 7-1 breaks down:

→ **2**   Stepping through Lines 2–3, you see that an Application is created, and its layout is set to `vertical`. This layout places the items vertically so that each control is one above the other.

→ **4**   When you include a `Script` block at the top of the file, you combine MXML and ActionScript. We cover the ActionScript code contained within the `Script` tags momentarily, but first look at the MXML composition of this Application.

→ **12**   A Label control displays a title for the video — in this case, My Awesome Video. Then the VideoDisplay control shows the video, which has been set to play at 150-by-150 pixels (Line 13). The `source` property points to the video file that will play, and an event listener gets called every time the VideoDisplay control fires a `playheadUpdate` event (Line 14).

→ **15** A ProgressBar control shows the percentage of the video that has played. Because you're using the ProgressBar in manual mode, you have to explicitly set the progress as the video plays.

REMEMBER

You can use the ProgressBar to show any kind of progress event, not just bytes loading. In this case, you show the progress of the video playing. You do this by calling `setProgress(amount Completed, totalAmount)` whenever you want to update the progress that's shown. In this example, the current playhead time and the total time of the video are passed in Line 8.

→ **18** Near the end of the example are a few Button controls to start and stop the video playback (Lines 18–21). You add your calls to `video.play()` and `video.stop()` inline in the `click` event handler for each Button control.

Notice that you're using the HBox control to lay out the Button controls horizontally. If you're interested in finding out more about layout containers, see Chapter 10.

We also use data binding to bind the `enabled` property of each `Button` to the `playing` property on the VideoDisplay. If `playing` is `false`, the play button is disabled, and the pause button is enabled. After `playing` becomes `true`, the enabled properties are toggled, and the stop button becomes enabled while the play button is disabled.

We cover data binding in more depth in Chapter 12, so feel free to jump there for more information. Otherwise, just be aware that the curly braces in the following line indicate that the `enabled` property of Button is being bound to the `playing` property of VideoDisplay.

```
enabled="{video.playing == true}"
```

This line ensures that whenever the `playing` property of the VideoDisplay changes, the `enabled` properties of the Buttons are updated.

Chapter 8

Data-Aware User Interface Controls

. . . .

In This Chapter

▶ Creating simple controls to display flat data, like List and DataGrid

▶ Creating simple controls to display hierarchical data, like Tree and Menu

▶ Creating advanced controls like the AdvancedDataGrid

▶ Creating item renderers to customize the look of data-aware controls

. . . .

With Flex, you can build rich applications that display data and enable users to interact with data. Users of your application will interact with data primarily through a set of *data-aware controls*. These controls have a built-in mechanism that allows the user interface controls to be updated whenever the underlying data powering the control is modified. Having this mechanism built directly into the Flex controls saves you, the Flex developer, a lot of work because managing updates to data can be tedious.

In this chapter, we first discuss the mechanism that the data-aware controls use to interact with the data powering their display. Then we describe the library of data-aware controls that the Flex framework offers. The following table lists the controls that we cover in the chapter:

AdvancedDataGrid	DataGrid
HorizontalList	List
Menu	MenuBar
TileList	Tree

Recognizing That Awareness Comes from the dataProvider

Data-aware Flex controls all specify a data object that provides the data that the control displays. You associate this data object with the user interface control by setting the `dataProvider` property. It's defined in the `mx.controls.listClasses.ListBase` class, and that ListBase class is the parent class for all data-aware controls in Flex.

Because of the Flex inheritance hierarchy, all data-aware controls have a `dataProvider` property because they all extend the ListBase class. Because the `dataProvider` property lets you use most types of data objects as data sources for Flex controls, you can set the `dataProvider` object to any of the native Flash data types, such as Array, XMLList, XML, or any of the Flex data collections like ArrayCollection or XMLListCollection. (To find out more about inheritance, check out Chapter 3, and to find out more about collections, check out Chapter 13.)

We walk you through some examples of these different types of data objects in this chapter. Similarly, you can set the `dataProvider` to any of the Flex framework data objects, such as ArrayCollection or XMLListCollection. For a more in-depth explanation of Flex collections, please check out Chapter 13.

Creating Flash Data Objects in MXML and ActionScript

You can create all the different types of data objects available in Flash and Flex in either MXML or ActionScript. First, take a look at some examples of how to create Flash data objects, such as arrays, XML objects, and XMLList objects in MXML and ActionScript.

Array

An *array* is a data structure that holds elements that can be accessed by an index. Here is the code to create an array of strings describing a set of colors, in MXML:

```
<mx:Array id="colors">
    <mx:String>Red</mx:String>
    <mx:String>Blue</mx:String>
    <mx:String>Green</mx:String>
</mx:Array>
```

You can also use ActionScript to create the same data structure:

```
<mx:Script>
    <![CDATA[
        public var colors:Array = ["Red", "Blue",
            "Green"];
    ]]>
</mx:Script>
```

These two examples are equivalent.

XML

XML is a common markup language, and XML objects can be created in Flash to store XML data. You can create a Flash XML object describing a set of colors in MXML:

```
<mx:XML id="colors">
    <node label="Colors">
        <node label="Red" />
        <node label="Blue" />
        <node label="Green" />
    </node>
</mx:XML>
```

You can also create the object in ActionScript:

```
<mx:Script>
    <![CDATA[
        public var colors:XML = <node
        label='Colors'><node label='Red'/><node
        label='Blue'/><node label='Green'/></node>;
    ]]>
</mx:Script>
```

Again, these two examples are equivalent.

An XML object is often used to describe *hierarchical data,* which is data that has a parent-child relationship. In the `colors` XML object, the Colors node acts as the parent node to the Red, Blue, and Green child nodes. Child nodes with no descendants, such as the Red, Blue, and Green nodes, are also called *leaf* nodes. An XML object must have a *root* node, which is a parent node that wraps up all subsequently defined child nodes, for the object to be considered valid XML.

XMLList

You can express an XMLList object by using MXML tags or by using ActionScript. An XMLList object is similar to a snapshot of part of an XML object. Unlike an XML object, an XMLList object doesn't need a root node to wrap up all descendant nodes. To create an XMLList object that describes a set of colors, you can do the following:

```
<mx:XMLList id="colors">
    <node label="Red" />
    <node label="Blue" />
    <node label="Green" />
</mx:XMLList>
```

Or, you can use ActionScript:

```
<mx:Script>
    <![CDATA[
        public var colors:XMLList = <><node
        label='Red'/><node label='Blue'/><node
        label='Green'/></>;
    ]]>
</mx:Script>
```

Creating Flex Data Objects in MXML and ActionScript

Flex offers a rich set of data management classes, called *collections,* that handle modifications, additions, and deletions to the data set. These collections wrap the Flash data objects we discussed above. These changes are managed by the Flex collection classes, and user interface controls displaying collections update seamlessly to reflect any changes to data.

Using collections and data-aware controls together is powerful! You can create Flex collections yourself, or you can let Flex wrap up noncollection data objects that you create (such as Arrays, XML, and XMLList objects) into the correct type of collection. Thankfully, this capability is built into all data-aware controls, so you don't have to do much to enable the updating mechanisms.

Even if your user interface control displays data from an XML object, the control is updated when changes have been made to the underlying data object, because the XML object gets wrapped into a collection by the control itself.

The following sections look at some examples of how you can create Flex collections in MXML and ActionScript. (To find out more about collections, refer to Chapter 13.)

ArrayCollection

The following example shows an ArrayCollection created in MXML, and it wraps an Array object as its data source:

```
<mx:ArrayCollection id="colors">
    <mx:source>
            <mx:Array id="colors">
            <mx:String>Red</mx:String>
            <mx:String>Blue</mx:String>
            <mx:String>Green</mx:String>
            </mx:Array>
    </mx:source>
</mx:ArrayCollection>
```

Here's the same ArrayCollection object created in ActionScript:

```
<mx:Script>
    <![CDATA[
    import mx.collections.ArrayCollection;

    private var colorsArray:Array = ["Red", "Blue",
        "Green"];

    public var colors:ArrayCollection;
    private function createArrayCollection():void
    {
      colors = new ArrayCollection();
      colors.source = colorsArray;
    }
    ]]>
</mx:Script>
```

XMLListCollection

The following example shows how you can create an XMLListCollection in MXML or ActionScript by wrapping an XMLList object as its data source:

```
<mx:XMLListCollection id="colors">
    <mx:source>
    <mx:XMLList>
      <node label="Red" />
      <node label="Blue" />
      <node label="Green" />
    </mx:XMLList>
    </mx:source>
</mx:XMLListCollection>
```

You can create the same XMLListCollection object in ActionScript:

```
<mx:Script>
    <![CDATA[
        import mx.collections.XMLListCollection;

    private var colorsXMLList:XMLList = new XMLList<node
        label='Red'/><node label='Blue'/><node
        label='Green'/>");

    private var colors:XMLListCollection;
    private function createXMLListCollection():void
    {
      colors = new XMLListCollection();
      colors.source = colorsXMLList;
    }
    ]]>
</mx:Script>
```

Of course, you don't have to code the data objects from scratch in MXML or ActionScript. In most real-world Web applications, a back-end database exists, and your application queries it for data. Most data querying occurs by using remote procedural calls or services to fetch data back to the Flex application. In Flex, you do this by using the pre-existing data-management libraries available like WebService and HTTPService. To find out more about fetching data for your Flex application, check out Chapter 14.

Powering Your Data-Aware Control with Data

Regardless of how you create your data object, you associate the data object with the data-aware user interface control by setting the control's `dataProvider` property. You can do this in MXML by using data binding or in ActionScript. (For a more in-depth explanation of data binding, refer to Chapter 12.)

In the following example, data binding is used to set the `dataProvider` property on the first List control, and the second List control sets `data Provider` in a Script block. Both examples are valid, though the more common scenario is the first example, using data binding to associate a data object with a user-interface control:

```
<mx:Array id="names">
    <mx:String>Sam</mx:String>
    <mx:String>Ammu</mx:String>
    <mx:String>Suguna</mx:String>
</mx:Array>

<mx:List id="nameList1" width="100"
        dataProvider="{names}"/>

<mx:List id="nameList2" width="100" creationComplete=
        "setDataProvider();" />
<mx:Script>
    <![CDATA[
        private function setDataProvider():void
        {
            nameList2.dataProvider = names;
        }
    ]]>
</mx:Script>
```

Voilà! The List controls have been created and display the name data. Both Lists look identical because they are bound to the same data object. Figure 8-1 shows what one of those Lists looks like.

Figure 8-1:
A List
control
displaying
names as its
data.

Scrolling List Controls

The Flex framework offers a set of simple List controls that do the following:

- ✔ Display items either vertically or horizontally
- ✔ Demonstrate built-in scrolling behavior
- ✔ Provide single-selection and multiselection capabilities
- ✔ Offer additional customizations for fine-grain control of the display and interaction with data

List controls are often used to show numerous items in an organized fashion. Applications often use List controls to display a number of items, such as in a product catalog.

Exploring the scrolling List controls

Flex's three scrolling List controls are described in the following list:

- ✔ `mx.controls.List`: The simplest List control; displays a list of vertical items
- ✔ `mx.controls.HorizontalList`: Displays a list of horizontal items
- ✔ `mx.controls.TileList`: Displays any number of items in a tile-like fashion

The following sections describe how to create List controls, hook them up to data, manage their selection, and customize their visual appearance.

mx.controls.List

The `mx.controls.List` control is the simplest data-aware control that the Flex framework offers. You use this control in a Flex application by using the `<mx:List />` MXML tag. A Flex List displays items vertically and sprouts a vertical scrollbar when the number of data items exceeds the number of visible rows. Horizontal scrollbars can also be created, and scrollbars have scroll policies that control that behavior.

As described earlier in this chapter, the `dataProvider` property binds a list to the data it should display. Here's an example of a List control bound to a data object storing some U.S. state names:

```
<mx:List width="150" height="200" dataProvider="{states}"
    />
```

In Figure 8-2, notice that the List control has a vertical scrollbar that enables users to access state names that are off-screen. This scrolling support, which is built into all List controls by default, is discussed in further detail in the "Scrolling in List, DataGrid, and hierarchical data controls" section, later in this chapter.

Figure 8-2:
A List control displaying states as its data.

mx.controls.HorizontalList

The `mx.controls.HorizontalList` control is the same as the List control except that it displays items horizontally. When the number of data items exceeds the number of visible columns, the HorizontalList control sprouts a horizontal scrollbar, as shown in Figure 8-3. The following example shows a HorizontalList control displaying some states in the United States of America:

```
<mx:HorizontalList dataProvider="{states}" />
```

Figure 8-3:
A Horizontal List control.

mx.controls.TileList

The `mx.controls.TileList` control is similar to the List and HorizontalList controls, except in the following ways:

- ✔ It displays items in a tile-like fashion.
- ✔ You can control the layout direction by using the `direction` property.
- ✔ You can control the height and width of individual tiles by setting the width of the TileList columns or the height of the TileList rows.

The following two examples show a horizontal TileList component (see Figure 8-4) and a vertical TileList component (see Figure 8-5). The vertical TileList is limited to two rows, and the horizontal TileList is limited to four rows; the column and row dimensions are controlled by the `rowHeight` and `columnWidth` properties.

```
<mx:TileList direction="vertical" dataProvider="{states}"
             rowCount="2" rowHeight="100"/>
```

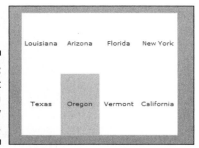

Figure 8-4:
A TileList control with specific row heights.

```
<mx:TileList direction="horizontal"
        dataProvider="{states}" columnCount="3"
        columnWidth="100"/>
```

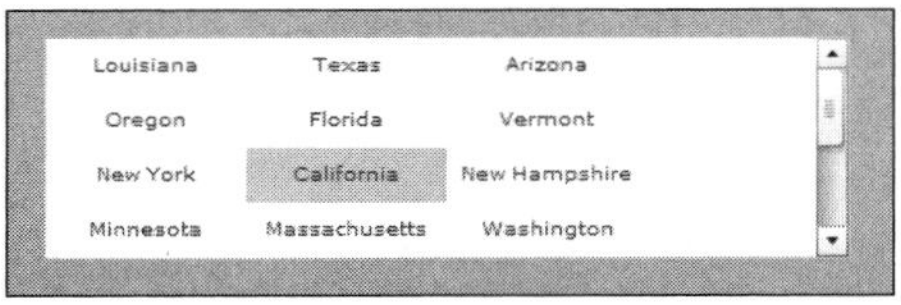

Figure 8-5:
A TileList
control with
specific col-
umn widths.

Louisiana	Texas	Arizona
Oregon	Florida	Vermont
New York	California	New Hampshire
Minnesota	Massachusetts	Washington

Making List controls display text

By default, the List controls try to display the data bound to them as accu-
rately as possible. They look on the data item for a property named `label`
(if the data is an array entry) or an attribute named `@label` (if the data is an
XML entry).

Often, your data doesn't follow this format. Suppose that your data back-end
is configured to send employee data information to your application, where
the employee's name lives in a field named `name`. You can use the `label-
Field` property, available on all List controls, to dictate which data field in
every data item should be used to display as the label. Remember that if the
data is XML, the `labelField` property expects an attribute name, which
must be qualified with the @ sign.

Let's take a look at some examples to see exactly how to use the `label
Field` property to display the correct label. In the first example, an object-
based data set is bound to a List control. You want the list to display the data
contained in the name field:

```
<mx:ArrayCollection id="employeeData">
  <mx:Object employee="John Jeffries" phone="510 555 3419"
        sex="Male"/>
  <mx:Object employee="Mary Smith" phone="415 555 2309"
        sex="Female"/>
  <mx:Object employee="Ned Martin" phone="408 555 4309"
        sex="Male"/>
</mx:ArrayCollection>
  <mx:List dataProvider="{employeeData}"
        labelField="employee" />
```

The second list has an XML-based data set, so you have to use the @ quali-
fier to indicate that the labels should be read from the employee attribute on
each XML node:

```
<mx:XMLListCollection id="employeeData">
  <mx:XMLList>
    <node employee="John Jeffries" phone="510 555 3419"
          sex="Male"/>
    <node employee="Mary Smith" phone="415 555 2309"
          sex="Female"/>
    <node employee="Ned Martin" phone="408 555 4309"
          sex="Male"/>
  </mx:XMLList>
</mx:XMLListCollection>
<mx:List dataProvider="{employeeData}" labelField="@
          employee" />
```

Both examples produce the List control shown in Figure 8-6. This control configures its display with a `labelField` property.

Figure 8-6:
Configuring
the display
with label
Field.

Sometimes you want finer grain control over how to configure the label displayed by the List control for each data item. For example, you might want to add *Ms.* or *Mr.* to each employee name, depending on whether the name is male or female. You can access the employee sex field to determine if an employee is male or female. You need a way to inspect this `sex` field and then determine the resulting label for that data item. Luckily, the handy `labelFunction` property, available on all Flex List controls, does that.

You can specify a function as the value to the `labelFunction` property, and this function is called on every data item that the list displays. The `label Function` property is often used to perform runtime label modification, formatting, and localization. `labelFunction` takes a data item that is of type Object and returns the String that is the label to be displayed for that data item.

The following example shows how you add the *Ms.* or *Mr.* label to the employee name displayed by the List control. The `handleEmployee NameDisplay` method takes an Object as a parameter, and you cast it to XML and then query the `sex` field to determine whether the employee is male or female. Depending on the result, you build up a String that is used as the label for that data item in the List control:

```
<mx:XMLListCollection id="employeeData">
  <mx:XMLList>
    <node employee="John Jeffries" phone="510 555 3419"
          sex="Male"/>
    <node employee="Mary Smith" phone="415 555 2309"
          sex="Female"/>
    <node employee="Ned Martin" phone="408 555 4309"
          sex="Male"/>
  </mx:XMLList>
</mx:XMLListCollection>
<mx:List dataProvider="{employeeData}" labelFunction=
          "handleEmployeeNameDisplay" />
<mx:Script>
  private function handleEmployeeNameDisplay(item:Object):
          String
          {
            if (XML(item).@sex == "Female")
              return "Ms. " + XML(item).@employee;
            else if (XML(item).@sex == "Male")
              return "Mr. " + XML(item).@employee;
            else return XML(item).@employee;
          }
</mx:Script>
```

Figure 8-7 shows the result of this example.

Figure 8-7:
Configuring
the label
display
with label
Function.

DataGrid Controls for Powerful Data Display

DataGrid controls are often used to display large sets of information, such as flight information or employee data. They're similar to List controls (described in the "Scrolling List Controls" section), except that they can show data in multiple columns. DataGrid controls enable application users to sort data numerically or alphabetically by clicking column headers. Users can also resize and drag DataGrid columns into different orderings.

The DataGrid controls are perfectly suited to show data with different properties. For example, you can use a DataGrid control to display employee information where one column shows the employee's name, the next column shows the employee's phone number, and the final column displays the employee's title. Application users can then easily see a large set of related data in a simple and clear user interface control.

DataGrid

The simplest DataGrid control is `mx.controls.DataGrid`, which you can create by using the `<mx:DataGrid />` MXML tag in your application. Because the DataGrid control is an extension of the List control, it needs to have its `dataProvider property` set in order to display user data. Because a DataGrid control displays multiple properties defined on a single data item, the data bound to a DataGrid control needs to be *complex* (where a single data item has multiple fields).

For example, the following code snippet shows a complex data object bound to a DataGrid control. Each Object defines a row on the DataGrid, and properties of the Object define the column entries for that row. The DataGrid control displays three columns: one apiece for the employee's name, phone number, and title, as shown in Figure 8-8:

```
<mx:ArrayCollection id="employeeData">
  <mx:Object employee="John Jeffries" phone="510 555 3419"
        title="Engineering Manager" />
  <mx:Object employee="Mary Smith" phone="415 555 2309"
        title="Director of Sales" />
  <mx:Object employee="Ned Martin" phone="408 555 4309"
        title="Marketing Manager" />
</mx:ArrayCollection>
<mx:DataGrid dataProvider="{employeeData}" />
```

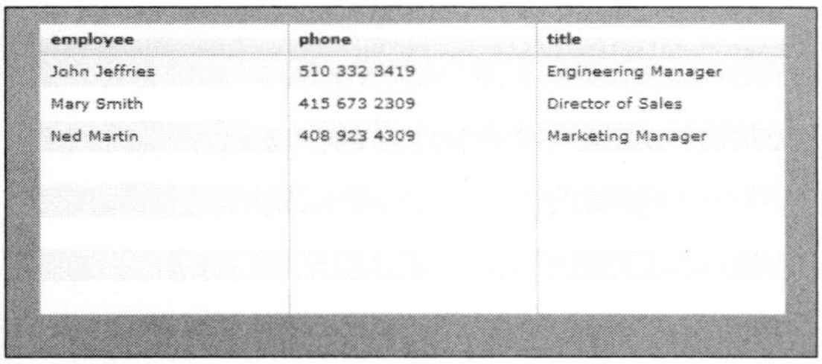

Figure 8-8:
A DataGrid control displaying employee data in multiple columns.

employee	phone	title
John Jeffries	510 332 3419	Engineering Manager
Mary Smith	415 673 2309	Director of Sales
Ned Martin	408 923 4309	Marketing Manager

DataGridColumn

If you want to increase your control over the display or naming of columns, you can specify the order of the DataGrid columns: Use the `<mx:DataGridColumn />` tag in MXML. DataGridColumns live in the `columns` property of the DataGrid control. If the DataGrid columns aren't specified, the DataGrid tries to display the data as well as possible, and the property names on each individual data item correspond to a column. When creating a DataGridColumn, you can decide how the header text appears and give the column sizing information.

For example, in the DataGrid displayed in Figure 8-8, say you want the employee column to say *Adobe Systems Employee* and the column to always be 200 pixels wide. To accomplish this task, create a DataGridColumn and do the following:

1. **Set the `dataField` property to the property on the data object that the column is supposed to display.**

2. **Use the `headerText` property on the DataGridColumn to customize the text that's displayed in that column's header.**

3. **Set the `width` property on the DataGridColumn to ensure that the column width is what you want (in this case, you want the column displaying the employee name to be 200 pixels).**

The resulting code is shown here:

```
<mx:DataGrid dataProvider="{employeeData}">
  <mx:columns>
    <mx:DataGridColumn dataField="employee"
          headerText="Adobe Systems Employee" width="200"
          />
    <mx:DataGridColumn dataField="title" />
  </mx:columns>
</mx:DataGrid>
```

The result is shown in Figure 8-9.

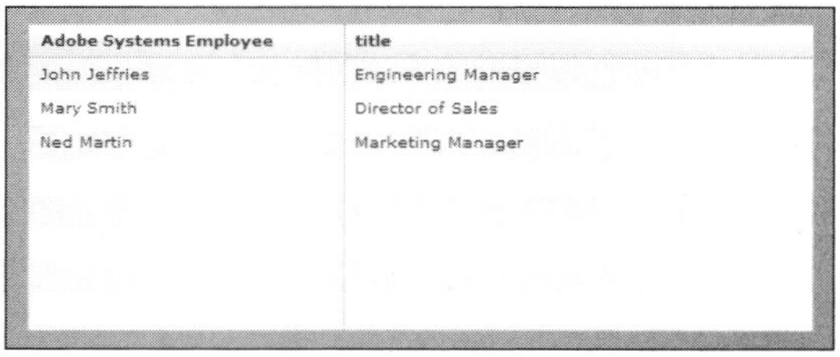

Figure 8-9:
A DataGrid
Column
control
displaying
employee
data.

Adobe Systems Employee	title
John Jeffries	Engineering Manager
Mary Smith	Director of Sales
Ned Martin	Marketing Manager

AdvancedDataGrid

A new feature in Flex 3 is the AdvancedDataGrid control, which is an extension of the DataGrid control. AdvancedDataGrid is offered only with Flex Builder Professional (which includes, in addition to the AdvancedDataGrid component, such advanced visualization components as charts). To learn more about Flex Builder Professional, check out Chapter 4.

The AdvancedDataGrid control has extra features that support better data visualization, aggregation, and formatting. Its main use is to show a hybrid control in which data is contained in rows (similar to a DataGrid) but that can display a hierarchy like a Tree component. The AdvancedDataGrid can also be used to create *summary rows,* which are extra rows that display summary information about the preceding rows. Additionally, the AdvancedDataGrid offers multicolumn sorting, which you can use to sort entries in your DataGrid with different columns as sorting parameters.

You can create an AdvancedDataGrid control in your Flex application by using the `<mx:AdvancedDataGrid />` MXML tag. An AdvancedDataGrid control takes a special type of data object as its dataProvider: a GroupingCollection. A GroupingCollection transforms *flat* data (data with no parent/child relationship) into hierarchical data that can be grouped based on common data fields. When you create an AdvancedDataGrid control, you must specify how you want your data to be grouped, by setting the `grouping` property on a GroupingCollection and passing in a Grouping object. This Grouping object expects data fields to be specified, by setting the `name` property, and AdvancedDataGrid groups data based on these fields. Like a regular DataGrid control, the AdvancedDataGrid control lets you specify columns (called AdvancedDataGridColumn) where you can customize the header label by setting the `headerText` property, and specify the field in each data item that should be displayed by setting the `dataField` property.

Listing 8-1 shows an application in which employee data is grouped in an AdvancedDataGrid according to which offices the employees work in and their genders. Figure 8-10 shows what this AdvancedDataGrid looks like.

Listing 8-1: An AdvancedDataGrid Control Group's Employee Information

```
<?xml version="1.0"?>
<mx:Application xmlns:mx="http://www.adobe.com/2006/mxml">

    <mx:ArrayCollection id="employeeData">
        <mx:Object employee="John Jeffries" phone="510 555 3419"
            title="Engineering Manager" sex="Male" office="Townsend"/>
        <mx:Object employee="Mary Smith" phone="415 555 2309" title="Director of
            Sales" sex="Female" office="Townsend"/>
```

(continued)

Listing 8-2 *(continued)*

```
            <mx:Object employee="Ned Martin" phone="408 555 4309" title="Marketing
                Manager" sex="Male" office="Townsend"/>
            <mx:Object employee="Michelle Camp" phone="415 555 9876" title="Quality
                Assurance" sex="Female" office="Townsend"/>
        </mx:ArrayCollection>


    <mx:AdvancedDataGrid id="adg" width="100%" height="200" initialize="gc.
            refresh();">
        <mx:dataProvider>
            <mx:GroupingCollection id="gc" source="{employeeData}">
                <mx:grouping>
                    <mx:Grouping>
                        <mx:GroupingField name="office"/>
                        <mx:GroupingField name="sex"/>
                    </mx:Grouping>
                </mx:grouping>
            </mx:GroupingCollection>
        </mx:dataProvider>

        <mx:columns>
            <mx:AdvancedDataGridColumn dataField="employee"
                headerText="Employee"/>
            <mx:AdvancedDataGridColumn dataField="office" headerText="Office"/>
            <mx:AdvancedDataGridColumn dataField="sex" headerText="Gender"/>
            <mx:AdvancedDataGridColumn dataField="title" headerText="Title"/>
        </mx:columns>
    </mx:AdvancedDataGrid>

</mx:Application>
```

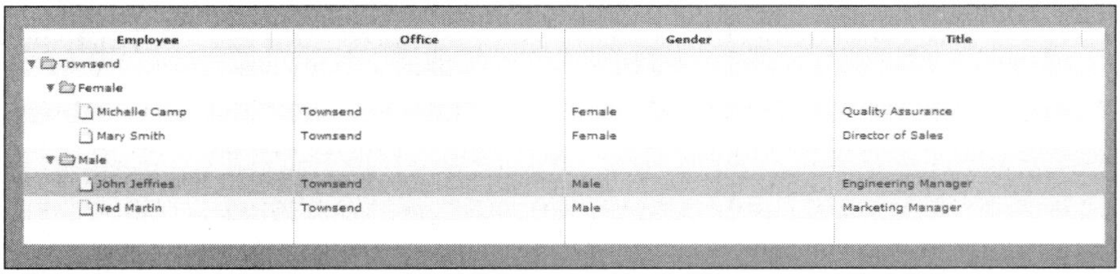

Figure 8-10:
An
Advanced
DataGrid
control
displays
grouped
data.

Given that the AdvancedDataGrid control is a complex component, the online
Flex documentation is a helpful resource for finding out how to customize the
data display of an AdvancedDataGrid control.

Hierarchical Data Controls

Sometimes the data you want to display in a data-aware control isn't flat in nature, but is in fact *hierarchical*, which means that each data item has a parent/child relationship. For example, menu options in most applications are hierarchical in order to show relationships like this: File⇨New⇨Document.

The Flex framework has a set of controls perfectly suited to displaying this kind of hierarchical data, including the Flex Tree, Menu, and MenuBar controls, all of which extend from List. Like all other List controls, the hierarchical data controls require a `dataProvider` to bind data to the user interface control for display.

Growing a Flex Tree

To create a Flex Tree control, use the `<mx:Tree />` MXML tag in your Flex application. The Tree control displays hierarchical data as well as it can. As with all other List controls, you can use the `labelField` and `labelFunction` properties to customize the display of labels for each item in the tree.

The tree creates expandable nodes for those data items that act as *parent* nodes — data items that have one or more child data items to display. These parent nodes, or *branch* nodes, appear by default with a folder icon that the user can click to either open and display child nodes or to close and hide child nodes. Child nodes that have no data items as children are considered *leaf nodes* and are endpoints of the tree. Leaf nodes appear as little file icons. The child nodes that are displayed when a branch node is opened, or hidden when a branch node is closed, can be either another branch node, or a leaf node.

All icons that the tree uses to display parent and leaf nodes can be customized:

- ✔ **Parent node icons:** You can set the `folderOpenIcon` and `folderClosedIcon` styles to customize the icon displayed when a branch node is opened or closed. Because these styles are on the Tree control, you can set them in-line in the MXML tag by embedding an asset. (See Chapter 18 for more on embedding graphical assets in a Flex application.)

- ✔ **Leaf node icons:** The `defaultLeafIcon` style can be used to customize the icon displayed next to leaf nodes.

Figure 8-11 shows a Tree control with the default folder and leaf icons (left) and with customized folder and leaf icons (right).

Often, the data bound to a Tree control is wrapped up in a *root* node, one that encompasses all data that the Tree control displays. Whether this root node is displayed is determined by the `showRoot` property on the Tree control.

Setting the property to true shows the root node of the dataProvider; setting it to false doesn't show the root node, and only the children of the root node are displayed. By default, showRoot is set to false. Figure 8-12 shows a Tree control with showRoot set to true (on the left) and false (on the right).

Figure 8-11: Tree controls with default icons and customized icons.

Figure 8-12: Setting showRoot to true (left) and to false (right).

Navigating Flex applications with Menus and MenuBars

Often, you want to create a pop-up Menu control or MenuBar control to assist users in navigating your Flex application. As menu options are chosen, you can trigger code to run that can change the state or view of your application.

Another set of useful hierarchical data-aware controls, similar to the Tree control, are described here:

- ✔ **Flex Menu:** Creates a pop-up menu that displays data with a parent/child relationship.

- ✔ **Flex MenuBar:** Creates a standalone menu bar that can be affixed to a part of your application layout to display pop-up menus as users navigate the menu items.

Menu

The Flex Menu control is one of the only user-interface elements that isn't created by using an MXML tag. Instead, the Flex Menu control must be created in

ActionScript, with a few lines of code. The format is similar to what you write in an MXML tag when creating any other data-aware control. You create the control, specify its `dataProvider` property, and optionally customize the display of the label by applying the `label` and `labelFunction` properties.

Listing 8-2 shows how to create a Flex Menu control and customize its behavior and appearance. The result is shown in Figure 8-13.

Listing 8-2: Creating a Pop-Up Menu Control in ActionScript

```
<?xml version="1.0" encoding="utf-8"?>
<mx:Application xmlns:mx="http://www.adobe.com/2006/mxml" layout="vertical">

<mx:Script>
<![CDATA[
  import mx.controls.Menu;                                            → 5
  import mx.events.MenuEvent;                                         → 6

        private function createMyMenu():void                          → 8
        {
            var m:Menu = Menu.createMenu(this, fileData, false);      → 10
            m.labelField="@label";                                    → 11
            m.addEventListener(MenuEvent.CHANGE, handleChange);       → 12
            m.show(100, 100);                                         → 13
        }

        private function handleChange(event:MenuEvent):void           → 16
        {
            selection.text = event.item.@label;
        }

]]>
</mx:Script>
<mx:XML xmlns="" id="fileData">
        <node label="root">
          <node label="File">
          <node label="New" />
          <node label="Open">
            <node label="New Flex Project" />
            <node label="New ActionScript Project" />
          </node>
          <node label="Exit" />
          </node>
        </node>
        </mx:XML>

        <mx:Button label="Pop Up a Menu" click="createMyMenu();" />   → 37
        <mx:Label id="selection" />

</mx:Application>
```

Figure 8-13:
A popped-
up Menu
control.

In the following list, we walk you through the steps to create the Menu control, assign it to a data source, pop it up, and use the change event to discern when a menu item has been chosen and determine what the menu item is:

→ **5**   On Lines 5–6, import the Menu and MenuEvent classes into the Script block.

→ **8**   The createMyMenu method, which creates the Menu control, is assigned to the click handler of the Button declared on Line 37.

→ **10**   Using the Menu class's createMenu method, you create a Menu control and assign it to the local variable m. The first parameter to the createMenu method is the parent, which in this case you set to this. The Flex Application then acts as the parent of the Menu control. The second parameter is the data you want to set as the dataProvider for the Menu control, which you set to the XML object declared on Line 24. The last parameter indicates whether you want to show the root node of the data set bound to the Menu control, which you set to false.

→ **11**   Set the labelField of the Menu control so that the labels for each data item are read from the label attribute.

→ **12**   Add an event listener for the change event, which is dispatched when the user makes a selection from the menu. When the change event is fired, the handleChange event handler is invoked.

→ **13**   After you create the Menu control and add the necessary event listeners, you show the pop-up menu. Invoke the show method and pass in the x and y parameters to indicate where the menu should pop up.

→ **16**   On Lines 16–19, the handleChange event handler is invoked in response to a change event being fired. This method checks the event object for the label of the menu item that has been selected and displays that label as the text property of the Label control declared on Line 28.

MenuBar

Unlike a Flex Menu control, you can create the Flex MenuBar control in MXML by using the `<mx:MenuBar />` MXML tag in your application. Like all other List controls, the MenuBar control displays, as adequately as it can, a `dataProvider` that encompasses hierarchical data. You can use the `label-Field` and `labelFunction` properties to customize the display of labels for individual data items.

The following example shows a MenuBar control that can be used to navigate a Flex application:

```
<mx:MenuBar dataProvider="{fileData}" labelField="@label"
            showRoot="false"/>
```

The result is shown in Figure 8-14.

Figure 8-14:
A MenuBar
control.

As with a Flex Menu control, when an application user selects a menu item, the `change` event is fired. The event object can be inspected to determine which menu item has been selected. Using that information, you can invoke code to change the state or view of your application.

Selection in List, DataGrid, and hierarchical data controls

Because data-aware controls have selection mechanisms built into them, the List controls use a selection highlight to indicate selection visually and to let you easily determine which items a user selects by using the keyboard or the mouse. The visual appearance of selected items is built into the List controls. When a user selects an item in a List control, the selection highlight is, by default, a blue rectangle drawn over the selected item or items. You can control this color with the selectionColor style, which can be set to any color value.

List controls support the single or multiple selection of items. By default, multiple selection is turned off, but it can be turned on by setting the `allowMultipleSelection` property to true.

To figure out which items in the List control were selected, you can query a variety of selection properties that are set when the user makes a selection by using the keyboard or the mouse:

✔ `selectedIndex`: A useful property that returns the index of the selected item within the list of data items. For example, if you select the third item in a list of five items, `selectedIndex` is set to 2.

✔ `selectedIndices`: The property that returns the set of indices within the list of data items when multiple items in the List control are selected. The property holds an array of values that represent the selected items, where the first item in the array is the first selected item's index and the last item in the array is the last selected item's index.

If you need the data items that were selected rather than just the index of the selected items, you can query the `selectedItem` or `selectedItems` properties:

✔ `selectedItem`: Keeps a reference to the data item that was selected.

✔ `selectedItems`: Keeps a reference to an array of items that were selected. The ordering matches the same order as the `selected Indices` property.

In the following example, we show you what each of the selection properties would hold based on the selections made in Figures 8-15 and 8-16.

Figure 8-15:
A List control with a single selection.

```
selectedIndex: 1
selectedItem.employee: Mary Smith
```

Figure 8-16:
A List control with multiple selections.

```
selectedIndices: [1, 3]
selectedItems: [{employee:'Mary Smith', phone:'415
        673 2309', title:'Director of Sales'},
        {employee:'Felicia Styles', phone: '408 786
        7645', title:Director of Marketing'}]
```

Editable List, DataGrid, and hierarchical data controls

List controls can be put into an *editable* state, which allows application users to edit directly within the user interface control the data that's displayed. This editing of the data is then committed to the data object that the List control is displaying so that the user's changes are saved. By default, Flex List controls aren't editable but can be put into the editable state by setting the `editable` property to true.

If a List control has `editable` set to true and a user presses Tab or clicks to select a list entry, the item in the cell is selected, and a blinking cursor appears. If the user starts typing, the data that's entered appears in the list cell; when the user clicks out of that entry into another entry, that information is saved in the data object that is displayed by the List control.

When an editing session begins, the following events are dispatched:

- ✔ `itemEditBegin`: Dispatched when the editing session begins — when the user has selected an item or pressed the Tab key to select an item, and the list entry starts accepting edits.
- ✔ `itemEditEnd`: Dispatched when the editing session has ended.

In Figures 8-17 and 8-18, we show what a List and DataGrid look like during an editing session.

Figure 8-17: A List control with an active editing session.

employee	phone	title
John Jeffries	510 332 3419	Engineering Manager
Mary Smith	415 673 2309	Director of Sales
Ned Martin	408 923 4309	Marketing Manager

Figure 8-18: A DataGrid control with an active editing session.

Advanced Functionality in Data-Aware Controls

The following sections describe some of the advanced functionality that's available in the data-aware controls.

Scrolling in List, DataGrid, and hierarchical data controls

List controls have scrolling behavior built into them and automatically sprout horizontal scrollbars when the number of data items exceeds the number of visible items. The number of visible items is usually determined by the height of the List control, although if the rowCount property is set, it determines the number of visible rows. The appearance of the horizontal scrollbar indicates the number of items that are off-screen. For example, if several items are off-screen, the scroll thumb is small, to indicate that there are many pages of data to scroll.

For the most part, you don't need to do much to control the scrolling behavior of your application's List controls. Scrollbars appear and disappear as needed. If you need control over the appearance of scroll bars, though, you can use the horizontalScrollPolicy and verticalScrollPolicy properties. These two properties can be set to On, Off, or Auto on any List control:

- **On:** The corresponding scrollbar always appears on the List control.
- **Off:** The scrollbar never appears on the List control.
- **Auto:** The scrollbar appears when needed — when off-list data items can be accessed only with a scrollbar.

Often, you want to programmatically set the selection of the List control and have that selected item scroll into view. This task is easy to do if you use the verticalScrollPosition property, which sets the scrolling position of the vertical scrollbar. In the following example, the verticalScroll Position is set to 20: When a user clicks the button, the List selects the 20th item in the data set and scrolls the scrollbar to that item.

```
<mx:List dataProvider="{states}" id="stateList"
        width="150" height="100"/>
<mx:Button click="stateList.selectedIndex = 20; stateList.
        verticalScrollPosition = 20;" />
```

Dragging and dropping in List, DataGrid, and hierarchical data controls

Because the Flex data-aware controls all have built-in *drag-and-drop* functionality, users can drag single or multiple data items within the same List control or from one List control to another. For the most part, dragging between the same type of List controls is recommended because you have to do some extra custom coding to support dragging between different types of List controls.

You can control the drag-and-drop behavior by using a set of drag-related properties:

✔ To turn on dragging functionality in a List control, set `dragEnabled` to `true`. By default, this property is `false`.

✔ To enable a List control as a drop target that accepts dropped items, set `dropEnabled` to `true`. By default, this property is `false`. As items are dragged and dropped, copies of the data are made, and the underlying data object is updated with these copies.

✔ If you simply want users to be able to move an item in a data-aware control, rather than copy the item, make sure that `dragMoveEnabled` is set to `true`.

When participating in a dragging or dropping operation, the List controls have some built-in identifiers to help in visualizing the drag operation. When you drag an item, a *drag proxy* is drawn. This ghosted replication of the item being dragged helps to visually identify the data item that's part of the drag operation.

If a List control is open to accepting drop inputs (that is, if its `dropEnabled` property is set to `true`), the drag proxy has a little green plus sign in a circle affixed to it, as shown in Figure 8-19. If a List control isn't open to accepting drop inputs (if its dropEnabled `property` is `false`), the drag proxy has a red *x* in a circle affixed to it (see Figure 8-20); and, when the item is dropped, the item zooms back into the originating List control because the drop action was rejected.

Figure 8-19:
Accepting
a valid drop
item.

Figure 8-20: Not accepting a drop item.

The List control dispatches a variety of drag events that indicate when a drag operation has begun, has been terminated, or the item was successfully dropped. The event objects associated with these drag events tell you exactly which item was dragged, from which List control the drag operation originated, and where the data item was eventually dropped. This information can be handy when trying to augment the built-in drag functionality, although for the most part, the built in drag-and-drop behavior is sufficient. For a list of these drag events, refer to Chapter 15.

Multiple items can be dragged and dropped in the List controls. When a user multiselects noncontiguous items (by holding the Ctrl key) or multiselects contiguous items (by holding the Shift key), all selected items move as part of the drag operation.

Setting variable list row heights

You may have noticed that all the rows in Flex List controls are standard in size. In fact, the Flex List controls support creating rows of variable height where the contents of each individual row can wrap. You control this behavior by setting a couple of key properties to true:

- ✔ variableRowHeight: Individual rows in the List, DataGrid, Tree, and AdvancedDataGrid controls can have differing heights. By default, this property is set to false.

- ✔ wordWrap: The text in the row is wrapped. Note that wordWrap works only when set to true *and* when variableRowHeight is also set to true.

The following example shows a List control with variable row height and text wrapping turned on (see Figure 8-21).

```
<mx:List dataProvider="{loremIpsum}"
         variableRowHeight="true" wordWrap="true"
         width="200" />
```

Figure 8-21:
Rows of
variable
height
with text
wrapping
turned on.

Data-Aware Controls for Customizing the Display of Items

The powerful Flex concept of *item rendering* allows you to customize List control entries. All earlier examples in this chapter simply show text entries for the List controls. You can jazz up the display of list entries with non-text entries, such as Images and Buttons and CheckBoxes. In fact, any data-aware control can show any Flex user interface controls within its row! Imagine displaying a product catalog in a TileList control where each tile has an image of the product, a label describing the product, and a link to a review of the product. This kind of enhanced customization is made possible by taking advantage of item renderers, which requires simply setting the item Renderer property on a List control.

A few different types of item renderers are available to use, from simple to complex. They are covered in the following sections.

Drop-in renderer

The basic kind of item renderer is the *drop-in* model, where you use one of the built-in Flex user interface controls to augment the display of individual list entries in a List control. You can set the `itemRenderer` property on any of your List controls to the class name of one of the out-of-the-box Flex user interface controls.

The following code example shows how to use an `mx.controls.Image` control to display an image as the item renderer for one of the columns in a DataGrid. Notice that the DataGridColumn's `dataField` property is associated with the image field in the data set — the column that displays the image field uses an Image control to load in the image described by the image field (in this case, JPG files of the employee):

```
<mx:DataGrid variableRowHeight="true"
        dataProvider="{dataProvider}"
    >
        <mx:columns>
            <mx:DataGridColumn
                dataField="image" headerText="Image"
                itemRenderer="mx.controls.Image" />
            <mx:DataGridColumn headerText="Name"
          dataField="name"/>
        </mx:columns>
    </mx:DataGrid>
<mx:XML id="data">
<employees>
    <employee>
        <name>John Jeffries</name>
        <image>imgs/employee109.jpg</image>
    </ employee >
    < employee >
        <name>Martha Martin</name>
        <image>imgs/employee87.jpg</image>
    </ employee >
</ employees >
</mx:XML>
```

In-line item renderer

Using a standard Flex control out of the box as the renderer for your row may not customize the display enough for your needs. You may need to interact with the data more or composite a number of Flex controls to create the layout for the row you want. In this case, you can use an *in-line* item renderer to build a special component that's used as the renderer for a row. You use the special <mx:Component /> tag, which defines an MXML component that dictates the layout of each row.

The following code example shows how to use the <mx:Component /> tag to create an in-line item renderer for a List control that lays out a Label control specifying the employee's name and an Image control specifying the employee's image in a vertical layout container:

```
<mx:List variableRowHeight="true"
        dataProvider="{dataProvider}">
  <mx:itemRenderer>
    <mx:Component>
      <mx:VBox width="100%" height="150"
            horizontalAlign="center"
            verticalAlign="middle">
        <mx:Label text="{data.name}" />
        <mx:Image text="{data.image}" />
```

```
        </mx:VBox>
      </mx:Component>
    </mx:itemRenderer>
</mx:List>
```

Notice that the data object is used to specify the source for the Image control or the text of the Label control. The data object represents the data model sourcing the List control. By specifying the source of the Image control as `data.image`, you instruct the control to introspect the data item's image field for the source of the asset that the Image control should render.

Tying It All Together: A DataGrid Control with Multiple Inline Item Renderers

Listing 8-3 creates a DataGrid control and uses three different inline item renderers to customize the display of the cells. Two of the most common questions that beginning Flex developers ask involve using editable item renderers in a DataGrid and conditional formatting of DataGrid items. The following example touches on both issues by using an editable ComboBox control as an item renderer and displaying one cell in bold, depending on the underlying data. The result is shown in Figure 8-22.

Listing 8-3: An Example of a Multiple Item Renderer

```
<?xml version="1.0" encoding="utf-8"?>
<mx:Application xmlns:mx="http://www.adobe.com/2006/mxml">

    <mx:ArrayCollection id="employeeData4">                          → 4
        <mx:Object employee="John Jeffries" phone="5105553419"
            title="Engineering Manager" director="false" sex="Male"/>
        <mx:Object employee="Mary Smith" phone="4155552309"
            title="Director of Sales" director="true" sex="Female"/>
        <mx:Object employee="Ned Martin" phone="4085554309"
            title="Marketing Manager" director="false" sex="Male"/>
        <mx:Object employee="Felicia Styles" phone="4085557645"
            title="Director of Marketing" director="true" sex="Female" />
    </mx:ArrayCollection>


    <mx:DataGrid dataProvider="{employeeData4}" width="400">         → 16
        <mx:columns>

            <mx:DataGridColumn headerText="Employee">               → 19
                <mx:itemRenderer>
                    <mx:Component>
                        <mx:VBox verticalGap="0">                    → 22
```

(continued)

Listing 8-3 *(continued)*

```
                    <mx:Label text="{data.employee}" fontSize="12"
                        fontWeight="{data.director == true ? 'bold' :
                        'normal'}" />
                    <mx:Label text="{data.title}" textIndent="10"
                        fontStyle="italic" width="100%" />
                </mx:VBox>
            </mx:Component>
        </mx:itemRenderer>
    </mx:DataGridColumn>

    <mx:DataGridColumn headerText="Phone #">
        <mx:itemRenderer>                                          → 31
            <mx:Component>
                <mx:Label text="{formatter.format(data.phone.toString())}">
                    <mx:PhoneFormatter id="formatter" formatString="(###)
                        ###-####" />
                </mx:Label>
            </mx:Component>
        </mx:itemRenderer>
    </mx:DataGridColumn>

    <mx:DataGridColumn headerText="Gender">
        <mx:itemRenderer>
            <mx:Component>
                <mx:Canvas>
                    <mx:ComboBox id="combo"                         → 44
                        selectedIndex="{data.sex == 'Male' ? 0 : 1}"
                        change="data.sex = combo.selectedItem">
                        <mx:dataProvider>
                            <mx:Array>
                                <mx:String>Male</mx:String>
                                <mx:String>Female</mx:String>
                            </mx:Array>
                        </mx:dataProvider>
                    </mx:ComboBox>
                </mx:Canvas>
            </mx:Component>
        </mx:itemRenderer>
    </mx:DataGridColumn>

    </mx:columns>
  </mx:DataGrid>

</mx:Application>
```

Here's an explanation of the sample application in Listing 8-3:

→ **4**   You define the data that will be displayed in the DataGrid. In this
          example, you create an ArrayCollection of Objects that holds the
          details about a few employees.

→ **16**   You create a DataGrid control and bind the ArrayCollection you created (`employeeData4`) to the `dataProvider` property of the DataGrid.

→ **19**   Lines 19–28 define the first column in the DataGrid, which displays the employee's name and job title. You create a DataGridColumn and assign a custom item renderer, which is defined on Lines 22–25. The custom item renderer you use is a VBox container that contains two Label controls. The first Label control displays the employee's name. The second Label control displays the job title in italics.

→ **23**   Notice on Line 23 that you set the `fontWeight` of the Label control based on the value of the `director` property of the data. If `director` is set to true, the Label control is rendered in bold; otherwise, it uses the normal font weight. This single item renderer displays three data fields: `employee`, `title`, and `director` (by way of the bold formatting).

→ **31**   You use a custom item renderer to format the phone number by using the PhoneNumberFormatter. For more information about using formatters, see Chapter 9.

→ **44**   In the third column, you use a ComboBox control to display the employee's gender. You bind the `selectedIndex` of the ComboBox to the value of the `sex` property of the data item. Notice that, in the `change` handler for the ComboBox, you modify the underlying data. Whenever you're working with editable item renderers, you always want to edit the underlying data when the user changes something.

Figure 8-22:
A DataGrid with three different item renderers.

Chapter 9

Forms, Formatters, and Validators

In This Chapter

▶ Creating simple form layouts

▶ Applying a validator control to a user interface control to validate user input

▶ Applying formatting controls to format data into customizable strings

*I*n this chapter, we discuss how to build form layouts and how to use validator and formatter controls. Form layouts are often used to collect information such as billing and shipping addresses, credit card information, and names and birthdates from application users. You can use *form layout containers* to arrange user interface controls in a form-like manner to make it easier to collect information from users.

Additionally, you can use *validator controls* to make a form field required in such a way that a user must enter input in a correct format or else validation of that form field fails. For example, a form text field expecting a valid e-mail address would use an `EmailValidator` to ensure that the user enters a valid e-mail address.

You can use *formatter controls* to perform one-way conversions of raw data into customized strings for display. For example, a label that needs to display today's date can use a `DateFormatter` to customize the display of the date.

The following table shows the form layout elements and the validator and formatter controls available in Flex that we discuss in this chapter:

CreditCardValidator	CurrencyFormatter	CurrencyValidator
DateFormatter	DateValidator	EmailValidator
Form	Formatter	FormHeading
FormItem	NumberFormatter	NumberValidator
PhoneFormatter	PhoneNumberValidator	RegExpValidator
SocialSecurityValidator	StringValidator	ValidationResult
Validator	ZipCodeFormatter	ZipCodeValidator

Delving into Form Layouts

A common use of Flex forms is to collect information from users. For example, you can create a checkout page asking users to enter their names, billing information, and shipping addresses. The Flex form containers have built-in functionality that enables you to mark certain form fields as required or optional. Additionally, you can use validator controls (described later in this chapter) to validate the information entered by users.

Figure 9-1 shows a simple Flex form used to gather general information about an application user. The First Name text field and Last Name text field are required, as denoted by the asterisks. An EmailValidator control validates the e-mail address that the user enters.

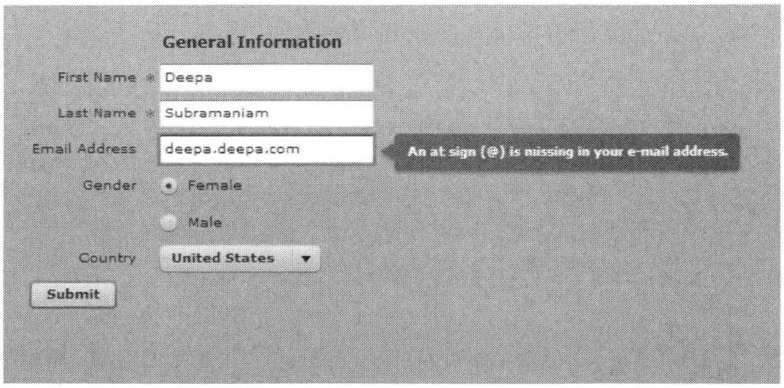

Figure 9-1:
A simple checkout form created by using the Flex form container.

Listing 9-1 shows how, in just 20 lines of MXML, this simple yet powerful form can be culled together.

Listing 9-1: A Simple Flex Form Created in MXML

```
<?xml version="1.0" encoding="utf-8"?>
<mx:Application xmlns:mx="http://www.adobe.com/2006/mxml"
         layout="vertical">

   <mx:EmailValidator source="{email}" property="text"/>
   <mx:Form width="100%" height="100%"
        defaultButton="{submitButton}">
      <mx:FormHeading label="General Information" />
      <mx:FormItem label="First Name" required="true">
         <mx:TextInput />
      </mx:FormItem>
      <mx:FormItem label="Last Name" required="true">
         <mx:TextInput />
      </mx:FormItem>
      <mx:FormItem label="Email Address">
         <mx:TextInput id="email" />
      </mx:FormItem>
```

```
        <mx:FormItem label="Gender">
            <mx:RadioButton label="Female" />
            <mx:RadioButton label="Male" />
        </mx:FormItem>
        <mx:FormItem label="Country">
            <mx:ComboBox dataProvider="{['United
                States']}" />
        </mx:FormItem>
        <mx:Button label="Submit" id="submitButton"/>
    </mx:Form>
</mx:Application>
```

In Figure 9-1, the user entered an invalid e-mail address, so the Email Address text field places a red highlight around the control and displays the following validation failure message:

> An at sign (@) is missing in your e-mail address.

Creating and arranging a form layout are discussed in the following sections.

Form: Recognizing the top dog

The top-level MXML tag for creating a Flex form is `<mx:Form />`. The Form tag creates a Form container, which means that the Form follows all rules expressed by any Flex container. (To find out more about Flex containers and their layout rules, check out Chapter 10.) The form elements, such as FormHeading and FormItem, and any Flex user interface control, such as Button, TextInput, and CheckBox, can be added as children of the `<mx:Form />` tag. (The FormHeading and FormItem form elements are discussed in the following two sections.)

You can set the dimensions of the Form container to an explicit pixel dimension or to a percentage of its parent container; or, the Form container can measure its contents and decide its dimensions accordingly. To set explicit pixel dimensions, set the `width` and `height` properties to numerical values:

```
<mx:Form width="300" height="300" />
```

To set percentage-based dimensions, set the `width` and `height` properties to percentage values, like this:

```
<!--The Form container will grow to fit the full size of
        its parenting container -->
<mx:Form width="100%" height="100%" />
```

To allow the Form container to measure its contents and determine the correct size on its own, simply omit the width and height properties, and the Form container takes care of measurement on its own:

```
<!—Let the Form container determine its own size -->
<mx:Form />
```

If a Form container has the `width` and `height` properties set to either a pixel or percentage value and the contents of the Form container exceed those dimensions, Flex takes care of "sprouting" scrollbars automatically so that users can scroll to the content that's beyond the boundaries of the Form container. Two properties control this behavior: `horizontalScrollPolicy` and `verticalScrollPolicy`. You can set these two properties to values of `auto`, `on`, or `off`, as described in this list:

✔ `auto`: The scrollbar appears as determined by the Form container; it's the default scroll policy in both directions.

✔ `on`: The scrollbar is always on in either direction.

✔ `off`: The scroll bar is never displayed in either direction.

FormHeading: Creating labels for different content areas

A FormHeading form element is used to create an optional label for items in the Form container. Often, a Flex form is divided into different content areas. For example, a form may have one section for a user's personal information (such as first name, last name, and phone number), another section for payment information, and a third section for shipping information. These different sections correspond to different content areas and can be labeled as such by using FormHeading controls. You create a FormHeading control by using the `<mx:FormHeading />` MXML tag. The following FormHeading depicts the form we just described:

```
<mx:Form>
    <mx:FormHeading label="General Information" />

    <!-- FormItems corresponding to the general
         information content area -->

    <mx:FormHeading label="Payment Information" />

    <!-- FormItems corresponding to the payment
         information content area -->

    <mx:FormHeading label="Shipping Information" />
```

```
    <!-- FormItems corresponding to the shipping
            information content area -->
</mx:Form>
```

The left side of the FormHeading labels is aligned with the left side of the user interface controls in the form. Additionally, by default, the FormHeading labels are bolded. In Figure 9-1 you can see that a FormHeading control is used to display the General Information label.

You can control the look of the FormHeading labels by using these styles:

- ✔ color: To draw the FormHeading labels in a different color, set the color style to a string or hexadecimal color value, such as color="red" or color="0xFF0000".

- ✔ fontSize: To modify the size of the FormHeading labels, set the fontSize style to a different numerical value. By default, the font size of a FormHeading control is 12.

- ✔ fontWeight: Use this style to determine whether the FormHeading label is bolded. By default, the fontWeight of a FormHeading control is bold, and setting it to normal removes the boldface.

FormItem: Creating individual form elements

The FormItem form element comprises the guts of a Flex form container. The FormItem container controls the identification and layout of individual form elements. A single FormItem container draws a label describing the purpose of that form entry and containing the control (or multiple controls) making up that form entry. Additionally, a FormItem container can designate a form entry as required or optional. To create a FormItem container in a Flex Form, you use the <mx:FormItem /> MXML tag.

To specify the label for a FormItem, you set the label property on the FormItem tag to any string. This label primarily describes the purpose of that particular form entry. The following code snippet defines several FormItem controls. Notice that the FormItem labels are vertically aligned with the first child item of the FormItem container. Figure 9-2 shows the resulting form.

```
<mx:Form width="100%" height="100%">
    <mx:FormHeading label="Shipping Information" />
    <mx:FormItem label="Street Address">
        <mx:TextInput width="100%"/>
        <mx:TextInput width="100%"/>
    </mx:FormItem>
    <mx:FormItem label="State">
```

```
                <mx:ComboBox dataProvider="{['United States']}" />
        </mx:FormItem>
        <mx:FormItem label="Zip Code">
            <mx:TextInput />
        </mx:FormItem>
</mx:Form>
```

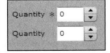

Figure 9-2:
Several
FormItem
containers
in a Flex
form.

You can mark required input fields in a Flex form. To designate a field as required, set the `required` property on a FormItem container to `true`. If this property is `true`, all the child user interface controls of the FormItem container are drawn with a red asterisk between the FormItem label and the user interface control. By default, the `required` property is set to `false`. As shown in Figure 9-3, the upper FormItem container designates its child fields as required, and the lower designates its child fields as optional.

```
<mx:FormItem label="Quantity" required="true">
    <mx:NumericStepper />
</mx:FormItem>
<mx:FormItem label=" Quantity ">
    <mx:NumericStepper />
</mx:FormItem>
```

Figure 9-3:
Two types
of child
fields.

By default, Flex doesn't enforce the filling of required fields with information. Instead, you can use validator controls to auto-enforce requirements on form fields. Validators are described in detail later in this chapter, in the section "Validate Me."

Default Button: Helping out the end user

Often you want to create a Flex form where, after the user finishes filling in information, pressing the Enter key causes a default action to occur. For example, take a look at the General Information form section, shown earlier in this chapter (refer to Figure 9-1). Typically, users press the Tab key to move into the first FormItem container and then enter their first name, press the Tab key again to move into the next FormItem container and enter their last name, and so on. After they tab into the Country FormItem container and select their country, they press Enter. Flex offers a way for that keystroke to be the equivalent of clicking the Submit button.

You determine this type of interaction by setting the `defaultButton` property on the Form container to the `id` of a button control that is a child of the Form container. Then when the user presses Enter after entering information, that action triggers the clicking of that particular button. The `id` property can be set on any Flex control to a unique string, and that `id` can be used anywhere in MXML or ActionScript code to refer to that particular control.

The following code snippet shows how the Submit button in the General Information form is wired to be the form default button:

```
<mx:Form width="100%" height="100%"
         defaultButton="{submitButton}">
    <mx:FormHeading label="General Information" />
    <mx:FormItem label="First Name" required="true">
        <mx:TextInput />
    </mx:FormItem>
    <mx:FormItem label="Last Name" required="true">
        <mx:TextInput />
    </mx:FormItem>
    <mx:FormItem label="Email Address">
        <mx:TextInput id="email" />
    </mx:FormItem>
    <mx:FormItem label="Gender">
        <mx:RadioButton label="female" />
        <mx:RadioButton label="male" />
    </mx:FormItem>
    <mx:FormItem label="Country">
        <mx:ComboBox dataProvider="{['United States']}" />
    </mx:FormItem>
    <mx:Button label="Submit" id="submitButton"/>
</mx:Form>
```

Validate Me

Flex provides a rich variety of validator controls that can be used to validate user entry data, such as e-mail addresses, dates, Social Security numbers, zip codes, currency, numbers, and strings. These powerful controls ensure that the data users enter into a Flex form is valid.

Customizing visual cues for validation errors

When validation of a form field fails, the visual appearance of the user interface control changes. By default, Flex draws a red border highlight around the perimeter of the control. Additionally, when the user hovers the mouse cursor over the control, a red ToolTip appears and displays a validation failure message. These visual cues indicate that the control failed validation.

You can customize these visual cues. For example, Figure 9-4 shows a TextInput control failing validation by a ZipCodeValidator control. The validation-failure message tells the user which type of input was expected — in this case, a valid zip code.

Figure 9-4:
A validation
failure.

Zip Code	9410B	The ZIP+4 code must be formatted '12345-6789'.

Changing the validation failure border highlight

To customize the border highlight that appears around a Flex control that fails validation, you can set the `errorColor` style, which can be set on any Flex user interface control that extends from `mx.core.UIComponent`. That includes all controls contained in the `mx.controls` package, such as Button, TextInput, CheckBox, and List.

If you want a black border highlight to appear around a TextInput control that failed validation, set the `errorColor` style to the string `black` or to the hexadecimal color value for black, like so:

```
<mx:TextInput id="ti" errorColor="black" />
<mx:TextInput id="ti" errorColor="0x000000" />
```

Customizing the validation failure message

Additionally, you can customize the failure message in the ToolTip that appears when the user hovers the mouse cursor over the control that failed validation. By default, Flex displays an error message that indicates which type of input was expected.

To display your own validation failure message, you can set the `error Message` property, which can be set on any Flex control that extends from `mx.core.UIComponent`. The following example shows a custom validation failure message when a TextInput control fails validation by an EmailValidator:

```
<mx:TextInput id="ti" errorMessage="You have entered an
          incorrect email address. Please try again." />
```

Clearing the validation error

Sometimes you want to clear the validation error and all the accompanying validation failure visual cues. It's simple: You clear out the source object's value that's being validated and set the `errorString` property on the user interface control that failed validation to the empty string, "".

The following code snippet shows, after an incorrect zip code has been entered in the zipCode TextInput, how pressing the Reset button clears the value entered in the zipCode TextInput and removes all validation failure cues:

```
<mx:Script>
    <![CDATA[
        private function resetZipCode():void
        {
            zipCode.text = "";
            zipCode.errorString = "";
        }
    ]]>
</mx:Script>
<mx:ZipCodeValidator source="{zipCode}" property="text" />
<mx:Form width="300" height="200">
    <mx:FormItem label="Zip Code">
        <mx:TextInput id="zipCode" />
    </mx:FormItem>
    <mx:Button label="Reset" click="resetZipCode();" />
</mx:Form>
```

Setting important properties on validators

Validators have a few key properties that need to be set in order for validation to be successfully triggered:

✔ source: The most important property that's set on every validator. The source property indicates which object is the source of the validation. It must be set to an object reference, so the curly-brace data binding syntax is used to bind in the object reference as the value of the source property. To refresh your knowledge of data binding, refer to Chapter 12.

✔ property: The second-most-important property that needs to be set on any validator. It defines which property field on the source object contains the value that needs to be validated.

The following code snippet shows a ZipCodeValidator where the source object is set to the TextInput control whose id is zipCode. The property property specifies that the text property on the zipCode TextInput contains the value that needs to be validated by the ZipCodeValidator:

```
<mx:ZipCodeValidator source="{zipCode}" property="text" />
<mx:Form>
    <mx:FormItem label="Zip Code">
        <mx:TextInput id="zipCode" />
    </mx:FormItem>
</mx:Form>
```

Flex validators enable you to specify that a missing or empty value in a user interface control causes a validation failure. This behavior is dictated by the required property, which can be either true or false, and can be set on any validator control. Suppose that you have a form with three elements: name, date of birth, and e-mail. You can create a validator with required set to true to indicate that the user must enter a date of birth, and not doing so causes a validation failure.

In Figure 9-5, the user left the Date of Birth field empty, triggering a validation error. To customize the error message that's displayed when a field has a missing or empty value, set the requiredFieldError property to the string you want displayed. The following code snippet displays the custom error message shown in Figure 9-5:

Figure 9-5:
An empty
form field
fails
validation.

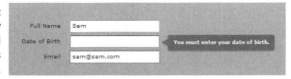

```
<mx:DateValidator source="{dob}" property="text"
        required="true" requiredFieldError="You must
        enter your date of birth."/>
<mx:Form width="300" height="300">
    <mx:FormItem label="Full Name">
        <mx:TextInput />
    </mx:FormItem>
    <mx:FormItem label="Date of Birth">
        <mx:TextInput id="dob"/>
    </mx:FormItem>
    <mx:FormItem label="Email">
        <mx:TextInput />
    </mx:FormItem>
</mx:Form>
```

Another useful property available on all validator controls is `listener`. Sometimes you may want to validate one control but have the validation visual cues applied to another control. In that case, you employ the `listener` property to indicate which component should have the validation results applied to it. Figure 9-6 shows a ZipCodeValidator validating one text field and drawing the validation error around another text field.

Figure 9-6:
Applying
validation to
a different
control.

The following code snippet shows how the entry in the zipCode TextInput contains the user information that's validated, but the zipError TextArea control shows the validation-failure message:

```
<mx:ZipCodeValidator source="{zipCode}" property="text"
        listener="{zipError}" />
<mx:Form width="300" height="300">
    <mx:FormItem label="Zip Code">
        <mx:TextInput id="zipCode" />
        <mx:TextArea id="zipError" />
    </mx:FormItem>
</mx:Form>
```

Triggering validation

Validation of a Flex control is event driven and occurs by way of *triggering.* Triggering is basically a way of invoking the validator to validate a value expressed by the `source` object. Validators can be triggered by associating them with a particular event or programmatically. The following sections discuss triggering validation in response to a particular event and invoking validation programmatically.

Event-based validation

With event-based validation, you can set up validation so that it occurs in response to an event dispatched because of some user action. When this event is dispatched, validation of the validator's `source` object occurs.

Two properties are necessary to set up an event-based validation trigger:

- ✔ `trigger`: Defines the control that generates an event that triggers the validator. It must be set to an object reference, so the curly-brace syntax must be used to bind in an object reference.

- ✔ `triggerEvent`: Specifies the event dispatched by the `trigger` control that should trigger the validation.

By default, Flex takes care of invoking validation when the user enters a value in a user interface control that's associated with a validator:

- ✔ **If the `trigger` property isn't set on the validator control:** The trigger is the value of the `source` object.

- ✔ **If the `triggerEvent` property is omitted:** Flex uses the `valueCommit` event, which is dispatched by all Flex user interface controls when the user selects or enters a value.

For example, the TextInput control dispatches the `valueCommit` event after the user has entered text and the control no longer has mouse or keyboard focus. Or, the DateChooser control dispatches the `valueCommit` event after the user has selected a date. For the most part, this default pairing of `trigger` and `triggerEvent` is sufficient, but sometimes you may want to invoke validation upon particular user action, and that's when these properties should be set to something other than their default values.

The following code snippet shows how validation occurs based on the user's clicking a button. The `trigger` property on the ZipCodeValidator is set to the `id` string of the Submit button, and the `triggerEvent` is set to the `click` event. After the Submit button is clicked, therefore, and its `click` event is dispatched, the ZipCodeValidator validates the Social Security number TextField:

```
<mx:SocialSecurityValidator source="{social}"
        property="text" trigger="{submit}"
        triggerEvent="click" />
<mx:Form width="250" height="300">
    <mx:FormHeading label="Personal Information" />
    <mx:FormItem label="Name" required="true">
        <mx:TextInput />
    </mx:FormItem>
    <mx:FormItem label="Phone Number">
        <mx:TextInput id="phone" />
    </mx:FormItem>
    <mx:FormItem label="Social Security Number">
        <mx:TextInput id="social" />
    </mx:FormItem>
    <mx:Button id="submit" label="Submit" />
</mx:Form>
```

Programmatic validation

In addition to event-based validation, validator controls can be triggered programmatically. This is necessary in cases where you may have to perform conditional validation based on the information the user enters. Programmatically triggering a validator control is easy — you simply invoke the `validate` method, available on all validators. The following example shows how clicking the Submit button triggers EmailValidator programmatically:

```
<mx:EmailValidator id="emailValidator" source="{email}"
        property="text" />
<mx:Form width="200" height="200">
    <mx:FormItem label="Email">
        <mx:TextInput id="email" />
        <mx:Button label="Submit" click="emailValidator.
        validate()"/>
    </mx:FormItem>
</mx:Form>
```

Listening for validation events

A few important validation events are dispatched when any Flex user interface control has been validated. Listening for these events may come in handy if you need to do additional processing based on a validation result. When a Flex user interface control is validated, the validator dispatches one of these events:

✔ `valid`: If the validation was successful

✔ `invalid`: If the validation failed

To capture these events, you can add an event listener directly to the validator tag. These events are `ValidationResultEvent` objects, which have properties related to the validation.

The following example shows how you can listen for, and catch, validation events. Depending on the type of validation event, the example pops up an alert window that describes whether the validation failed or succeeded:

```
<mx:EmailValidator id="emailValidator" source="{email}"
        property="text" valid="handleValidationResult(e
        vent)" invalid="handleValidationResult(event)"/>
<mx:Form width="200" height="200">
    <mx:FormItem label="Email" id="emailField">
        <mx:TextInput id="email" />
    </mx:FormItem>
</mx:Form>
<mx:Script>
<![CDATA[
    import mx.controls.Alert;
    import mx.events.ValidationResultEvent;

    private function handleValidationResult(event:
        ValidationResultEvent):void
    {
        var message:String = "";
        if (event.type == ValidationResultEvent.VALID)
            message = "Validation succeeded";
        else if (event.type == ValidationResultEvent.
          INVALID)
            message = "Validation failed";
        Alert.show(message);
    }
]]>
</mx:Script>
```

Furthermore, individual validators have specific properties that hold the error message string when a particular parameter is invalid; for example:

✔ `ZipCodeValidator`: Has a `wrongLengthError` property. You can set this property to a string representing the custom validation error message to display when a user enters a zip code that is not the expected length.

✔ `CreditCardValidator`: Has the `invalidNumberError` that can be set to a custom error string that's displayed when the user enters an invalid credit card number.

For more information about the individual error string properties for each validator, see the online Flex documentation.

Checking out out-of-the-box Flex validators

Now that you understand how validators work and which properties are necessary to set to get the type of validation you want, take a brief look at the set of standard validators that Flex offers. These validators are used to validate all sorts of common data that come up frequently in Web applications.

CreditCardValidator

The CreditCardValidator allows you to validate a credit card number by ensuring that it is the correct length, has the proper prefix, and passes the Luhn mod10 algorithm for the specified card type. The *Luhn mod10 algorithm* is a simple formula used to validate credit card number authenticity.

These important properties need to be set when using a CreditCardValidator:

- ✔ `cardNumberSource`, `cardNumberProperty`: Specifies which Flex object and which property on that object represent the credit card number

- ✔ `cardTypeSource`, `cardTypePropery`: Indicates which Flex object and which property on that object represent the type of credit card

Run the following code and validate one of your own credit cards. If the credit card number doesn't match the credit card type, or it fails the Luhn mod10 algorithm, validation fails:

```
<mx:CreditCardValidator id="cv" cardTypeSource="{card}"
        cardTypeProperty="selectedItem"
        cardNumberSource="{number}"
        cardNumberProperty="text" trigger="{btn}"
        triggerEvent="click"
/>

<mx:Form>
    <mx:FormItem label="Credit Card Type">
        <mx:ComboBox id="card" dataProvider="{['American
            Express', 'Diners Club', 'Mastercard',
            'Discover', 'Visa']}" />
    </mx:FormItem>
    <mx:FormItem label="Credit Card Number">
        <mx:TextInput id="number"/>
    </mx:FormItem>
    <mx:FormItem>
        <mx:Button id="btn" label="Submit"/>
    </mx:FormItem>
</mx:Form>
```

NumberValidator

The NumberValidator validates a string representing a valid number based on the properties you set. The properties available dictate whether a number is valid based on the appearance of a decimal point, the appearance of the thousands separator, whether the number falls within a given range, whether it's an integer, whether it's negative, and whether it has the correct decimal precision.

Table 9-1 describes a subset of the properties available to set on NumberFormatter to control the validation of a string representing a number. For the full set of properties, see the online Flex documentation.

Table 9-1	Properties That Can Be Set on a NumberValidator	
Property	**Allowable Values**	**What It Determines**
allowNegative	Boolean: true, false	Whether negative numbers are valid; defaults to true
maxValue	Any number	The maximum value allowed; defaults to NaN
minValue	Any number	The minimum value allowed; defaults to NaN
Precision	Any number	The maximum number of digits allowed after the decimal point

The following example shows validation of a user's birth year. The expected value is a four-digit number corresponding to the user's year of birth:

```
<mx:NumberValidator minValue="1900" maxValue="2008"
        source="{birthYearText}" property="text"/>
<mx:TextInput id="birthYearText" />
```

CurrencyValidator

The CurrencyValidator validates a string as an authentic currency expression. Several properties can be used to govern the validation, such as

- ✔ The format of the currency value
- ✔ Whether negative values are allowed
- ✔ Which precision is used to validate currency values

Properties necessary to customize the simple validation of a currency value are described in this list:

- ✔ alignSymbol: Specifies whether the currency symbol appears to the right or left of the currency expression (set to left by default)

✔ currencySymbol: Displays the currency symbol (set to $ by default)

✔ decimalSeparator: Used as the decimal point character (. by default)

✔ thousandsSeparator: Used as the thousands separator character (, by default)

In addition to these properties, the CurrencyValidator contains the same properties specified in Table 9-1 for NumberValidator.

The following example shows a CurrencyValidator that validates text based on whether it has two decimal places after the decimal point and is between 0 and 10:

```
<mx:CurrencyValidator id="cv" source="{currency}"
        property="text" minValue="0" maxValue="10"
        precision="2"/>
<mx:TextInput id="currency" />
```

DateValidator

The Flex DateValidator enables you to validate a date string as a correct date-and-date format. The DateValidator validates whether the month that's entered is between 1 and 12 (January and December), whether the day is between 1 and 31, and whether the year is a number. The following properties are important when creating a DateValidator control:

✔ daySource, dayProperty: Specifies on which property the source Flex object displays the day information that's validated

✔ monthSource, monthProperty: Specifies on which property the source Flex object displays the month information that's validated

✔ yearSource, yearProperty: Specifies on which property the source Flex object displays the year information that's validated

The allowedFormatChars property is set to a string that represents all the formatting characters that are valid for the date expression being validated. The string / \ - . . is the default.

The following code example shows how to validate a user entering a birth month and birth year. The month must be a number between 1 and 12, and the year must be a valid value:

```
<mx:DateValidator id="dv" monthSource="{month}"
        monthProperty="text" yearSource="{year}"
        yearProperty="text" trigger="{btn}"
        triggerEvent="click"/>
<mx:Form width="200" height="200">
    <mx:FormItem label="Birth Month">
        <mx:TextInput id="month" />
    </mx:FormItem>
```

```
        <mx:FormItem label="Birth Year">
                <mx:TextInput id="year" />
        </mx:FormItem>
        <mx:Button id="btn" label="Submit" />
</mx:Form>
```

EmailValidator

The Flex EmailValidator makes the validation of e-mail strings quite simple. The e-mail string is validated based on the appearance of a single @ sign, a period in the domain name, and an e-mail suffix that has two, three, four, or six characters. The EmailValidator doesn't authenticate whether the e-mail address exists.

The EmailValidator has several properties that you can use to customize the error string that appears when the validation criteria isn't met. The `tooMany AtSignsError` can be set to a custom error string that's displayed when more than one @ sign is encountered. Similarly, the `invalidDomainError`, `invalidIPDomainError`, `invalidPeriodsInDomainError`, `missing AtSignError`, `missingPeriodInDomainError`, and `missingUsername Error` can be set to strings that are displayed when the attribute case isn't met.

The following example shows an EmailValidator validating an e-mail address entered by the user:

```
<mx:EmailValidator id="ev" source="{email}"
         property="text" />
<mx:Form width="250" height="200">
    <mx:FormItem label="Email">
        <mx:TextInput id="email" />
    </mx:FormItem>
</mx:Form>
```

PhoneNumberValidator

The Flex PhoneNumberValidator validates a string representing a valid phone number. The validation parameters ensure that the phone number is at least ten digits long and potentially has formatting strings. The PhoneNumberValidator doesn't ensure that the phone number is a real, active phone number. The `allowedFormatChars` property, which defaults to the string ()- .+, can be augmented to include more formatting characters. Additionally, if the string being validated is the wrong length, you can set the `wrongLengthError` to a custom string that's displayed as the validation error.

The following example shows how to create a PhoneNumberValidator to validate a string representing a user's phone number:

```
<mx:PhoneNumberValidator id="pv" source="{phoneNumber}"
         property="text" />
```

```
<mx:Form width="250" height="200">
    <mx:FormItem label="Phone Number">
        <mx:TextInput id="phoneNumber" />
    </mx:FormItem>
</mx:Form>
```

RegExpValidator

The RegExpValidator validates a string based on a regular expression you specify. Here are the important properties for using RegExpValidator:

- ✔ `expression`: When set to a valid regular expression of your choice, the associated string is validated against that regular expression. The validation is successful if the RegExpValidator can find a match for the regular expression in the string. A validator failure occurs if no match is found.

- ✔ `flags`: This property lets you specify regular expression flags when the expression matching is taking place.

- ✔ `noMatchError`: To customize the error message that's displayed when no match is found, set this property to a string value that is the error message of your choice.

The following example lets the user enter a regular expression of their choice in the first TextInput, and the text entered in the second TextInput is validated against the regular expression entered by the user:

```
<mx:RegExpValidator id="rev" expression="{regExp.text}"
        source="{regExpEntry}" property="text" />
<mx:Form width="250" height="200">
    <mx:FormItem label="Regular Expression">
        <mx:TextInput id="regExp" />
    </mx:FormItem>
    <mx:FormItem label="Text to Match">
        <mx:TextInput id="regExpEntry" />
    </mx:FormItem>
</mx:Form>
```

SocialSecurityValidator

The SocialSecurityValidator is a handy control that validates a string representing a U.S. Social Security number. The SocialSecurityValidator doesn't check whether the Social Security number is valid, just that it follows the pattern expected of a valid Social Security number. The Social Security number must be a nine-digit number. It can use the minus sign (–) to split up the number, often like so: ###-##-####. Whether other characters are allowed to be used to split up the Social Security number is controlled by the `allowedFormatChars` property, which defaults to the ()- .+. string.

The following example validates a nine-digit U.S. Social Security number:

```
<mx:SocialSecurityValidator id="sv" source="{social}"
        property="text" />
<mx:Form width="400" height="200">
    <mx:FormItem label="Social Security Number">
        <mx:TextInput id="social" />
    </mx:FormItem>
</mx:Form>
```

StringValidator

The Flex StringValidator validates a string based on length. You can set the `minLength` and `maxLength` properties to bound the length of the string being validated. The following example shows how to validate a string based on whether it's greater than zero characters long and less than five characters long. A string with six characters fails validation:

```
<mx:StringValidator id="sv" minLength="0" maxLength="5"
        source="{entry}" property="text" />
<mx:Form width="200" height="200">
    <mx:FormItem label="String Entry">
        <mx:TextInput id="entry" />
    </mx:FormItem>
</mx:Form>
```

ZipCodeValidator

The Flex ZipCodeValidator allows for the validation of U.S. and Canadian zip codes. One key property needed to customize your ZipCodeValidator is the `domain` property. You can set it to either the string `US Only` (only a U.S. zip code is being validated) or `US or Canada` (the zip code could be a U.S. or Canadian zip code).

Additionally, you can set the following two properties to a custom string that's displayed in certain circumstances:

✔ `wrongCAFormatError`: When an invalid Canadian zip code is encountered

✔ `wrongUSFormatError`: When an invalid U.S. zip code is encountered

By default, these two properties have descriptive validation error messages that are displayed.

The following example shows the validation of a six-digit Canadian postal code or a five- or nine-digit U.S. postal code. Entering, for example, a three- or seven-digit value causes a validation failure:

```
<mx:ZipCodeValidator id="zv" source="{zip}"
        property="text" domain="US or Canada" />
<mx:Form width="400" height="200">
    <mx:FormItem label="Canadian or US Zip Code">
        <mx:TextInput id="zip" />
    </mx:FormItem>
</mx:Form>
```

Format Me

Flex offers a diverse set of formatting controls that allow one-way, automatic conversions of raw data — which is either entered by an application user or returned from a back-end data source — into a formatting string. The formatting controls are useful in displaying data in a meaningful way to the application user because data returned from a data source often isn't formatted in a way that's human readable. Flex offers a wide array of formatters to format common data values such as dates, currencies, and zip codes as well as a general number formatter that can be customized to your exact specification by setting formatting properties.

The formatter controls are triggered to format data. That is, you can decide when the formatting should take place and trigger the formatting to occur. Often, you use data binding to trigger a formatter to format its input and display the formatted data in any of the Flex text controls, such as Label, TextInput, or TextArea. (To find out more about data binding, refer to Chapter 12.)

Formatting data

To format raw data with a Flex formatter, two important steps are necessary. First, a formatter MXML tag must be written in order to create a Flex formatter. The following Flex formatters are available out of the box for easy uses:

- `<mx:CurrencyFormatter />`
- `<mx:DateFormatter />`
- `<mx:NumberFormatter />`
- `<mx:PhoneFormatter />`
- `<mx:ZipCodeFormatter />`

The examples in this section show how formatters are used in general, and the following sections describe how to use each individual formatter in more detail.

Then, after a formatter has been written in MXML, you set an `id` on it. It's by this `id` that the formatter is invoked to format data. As is the general rule when setting the `id` property, you can often increase the readability of your application code by making the `id` on Flex controls meaningful and human readable.

Setting formatter properties

The next step is to set the formatter-specific properties that customize how the data should be formatted. We discuss these formatter properties in the individual descriptions of each Flex formatter in the later section "Handling formatting errors."

Now, how does a Flex formatter know what to convert the raw data to? Well, some Flex formatters use a `formatString` property to describe the pattern that that the formatter formats against. The DateFormatter, PhoneFormatter, and ZipCodeFormatter use the `formatString` property. For example, the `formatString` for a DateFormatter is a set of letters that describes the way the date and time can be described. By default, `formatString` for a DateFormatter is MM/DD/YYYY, meaning that the date February 28, 1981, is formatted as 02/28/1981. You can set the format string to produce the output you want. The `formatString` possibilities for each formatter are described in the next section.

Applying the formatter to raw data

After all the properties that govern the formatting of data have been set on your Flex control, the formatter is ready to be applied to raw data. This application usually occurs by way of data binding. It is often the case that the formatter is used to format text, and this text is often contained in the `text` property available on all Flex text controls, such as Label, TextInput, and TextArea.

To associate the text contained in the `text` property as the raw data that your formatter must format, you write a data binding expression that expresses this and set that data binding expression as the `text` of another Flex text control. That way, one Flex text control is displaying the formatted data entered by another Flex text control. This data binding expression instructs the Flex control to display, as its text, the original, raw data that is run through the formatter's `format` method.

The following code snippet illuminates this concept. First, you define a Zip CodeFormatter, whose `id` is `zipCodeFormatter`. You also a have a Text Input control whose `id` is `zipCode`. You want the `zipCode` TextInput to display, as its text, zip code data that has been formatted by the zipCode Formatter. The zip code data is coming from, in this case, a string that is defined above the ZipCodeFormatter. This zip code data could come from anywhere: It could be data entered by the user somewhere in the application or from fetching data from an external data source:

```
<mx:String id="zipText">337014</mx:String>
<mx:ZipCodeFormatter id="zipCodeFormatter"
        formatString="### ###" />
<mx:TextInput id="zipCode" text="{zipCodeFormatter.
        format(zipText)}"/>
```

Sometimes you want to trigger the formatting of raw data not through a data binding expression that would result in automatic formatting, but rather from a button click or some other user gesture. It's simple: You programmatically invoke the formatter's `format` method when the user gesture of your choice occurs. The following example shows how to do it. The text contained in the zipCode TextInput gets formatted from the format Button's `click` event:

```
<mx:ZipCodeFormatter id="zipCodeFormatter"
        formatString="### ###" />
<mx:TextInput id="zipCode" text="337014"/>
<mx:Button label="format" click="zipCode.text =
        zipCodeFormatter.format(zipCode.text);" />
```

Handling formatting errors

If a formatting error occurs, Flex returns an empty string as well as a descriptive string, which describes the error, as the value of the `error` property on the formatter. A Flex formatter's `error` property is either the string "Invalid value," which means that an invalid value was passed to the formatter's `format` method, or "Invalid format," which means that the `formatString` is invalid in some way. This section describes the individual formatters available in the Flex framework.

NumberFormatter

The Flex NumberFormatter lets you format a number by setting properties that adjust the decimal point, thousands separator, and negative sign as you see fit. Here's a rundown of the properties you can set:

> ✔ rounding: This property determines the behavior when rounding to the nearest number. You can set the rounding property to none, up, down, or nearest. By default, rounding is set to none so that no rounding occurs.

✔ precision: Often used with rounding, this property can be set to a number that denotes how many decimal places to include in the formatted string. By default, precision is set to –1, meaning that no precision occurs.

✔ userNegativeSign: This property defaults to true and can be set to true or false to designate whether a negative sign is displayed when a negative number is formatted. If useNegativeSign is set to false, formatting a negative number such as –12 is outputted with parentheses around it, as in (12). The useThousandsSeparator property, which defaults to true, determines whether the number is split into thousands increments with a separator character (that is, by default, ',').

✔ decimalSeparatorFrom, thousandsSeparatorFrom: decimal SeparatorFrom defaults to '.', and thousandsSeparatorFrom defaults to ','. These properties can be set to determine which character is interpreted as a decimal point or thousands separator marker when parsing an input string by the formatter.

✔ decimalSeparatorTo, thousandsSeparatorTo: decimalSepara- torTo defaults to '.', and thousandsSeparatorTo defaults to ','. These properties can be set to determine what the outputted text should use as a decimal point and thousands separator.

The following example shows how to round a decimal number to the tenth place:

```
<mx:NumberFormatter id="nf" rounding="up" precision="2" />
<mx:TextInput text="{nf.format('1.234567')}" />
```

CurrencyFormatter

The Flex CurrencyFormatter allows you to format currency values. You can regulate the decimal rounding and precision, set the thousands separator, set a negative sign, and add a currency symbol. The CurrencyFormatter uses all properties specified on NumberFormatter to control the decimal and thousands place behavior, so refer to the earlier section "NumberFormatter."

To specify the currency symbol, you can set the currencySymbol property to a string, usually a single character, that's used when formatting the currency value. By default, currencySymbol is set to '$'. The placement of the currency symbol is determined by the alignSymbol property, which can either be set to left or right. By default, alignSymbol is left so that the currency symbol appears like American currency values rather than European currency values. The following example shows a conversion of a number to a European currency value:

```
<mx:CurrencyFormatter id="cf" currencySymbol="EURO"
            alignSymbol="right" rounding="up"
            precision="2"/>
<mx:TextInput text="{cf.format('2.3')}" />
```

DateFormatter

The DateFormatter enables you to format date values — represented as either strings or ActionScript Date objects — into customized date strings. You can set the `formatString` to determine how the raw data should be formatted. The `formatString` needs to be set to a pattern string composed of letters that control the date parsing behavior.

Table 9-2 captures some of the different formatting patterns and specifies what they mean when parsing a Date. The DateFormatter can also be used to format and display time information. For descriptions of the pattern letters governing time formatting, refer to the online Flex documentation.

Table 9-2	Date and Time Format Patterns
Pattern Letter	*What It Does*
Y	Determines display of Year
	YY = 98
	YYYY = 1998
	YYYYY = 01998
M	Determines display of Month
	M = 1
	MM = 01
	MMM = Jan
	MMMM = January
D	Determines display of Day
	D = 1
	DD = 01
	DD = 12
E	Determines display of the day of week
	E = 5
	EE = 05
	EEE = Fri
	EEEE = Friday

The following example shows how to use a DateFormatter to format an ActionScript Date object into a human-readable string:

```
<mx:DateFormatter id="df" formatString="MMMM DD, YYYY" />
<!-- Displays as February 28, 1981 -->
<mx:TextInput text="{df.format(new Date(1981, 01, 28))}"
         />
```

PhoneFormatter

The PhoneFormatter enables you to format strings into a valid seven-digit United States phone number. The formatString property, by default, is '(###) ###-####'. You can change the order as desired. When parsing the formatString, you can indicate which characters are valid for the pattern by setting the validPatternChars to a string with all the characters you want included in the pattern. By default, validPatternChars is '+()#- .'. The areaCodeFormat property can be set to format the appearance of the area code in a phone number. By default, areaCodeFormat is set to '(###)'.

The following example shows how a phone number is formatted to have no miscellaneous characters or spaces:

```
<mx:PhoneFormatter id="pf" formatString="###-###-####" />
<!-- Displays as 408-123-4567 -->
<mx:TextInput text="{pf.format('4081234567')}" />
```

ZipCodeFormatter

The ZipCodeFormatter allows the formatting of strings into a five-digit, six-digit, or nine-digit zip code. The formatString can be set to the values shown in Table 9-3.

Table 9-3	Format Patterns for Formatting Zip Codes
Pattern	*Length of Zip Code*
#####-####	Nine digits with hyphen
##### ####	Nine digits with space
#####	Five digits
### ###	Six digits with space

The following code example shows how to format a number into a six-digit Canadian zip code:

```
<mx:ZipCodeFormatter id="zf" formatString="### ###" />
<!-- Displays as 123 456 -->
<mx:TextInput text="{zf.format('123456')}" />
```

Tying It All Together: Creating an E-Commerce Form

Listing 9-2 ties together forms, validators, and formatters. The sample application is a classic e-commerce checkout form that validates the information as the user enters it (see Figure 9-7). Formatters are used to format the date displayed at the top of the form as well as the label at the bottom, which is tracking the number of visitors to the page.

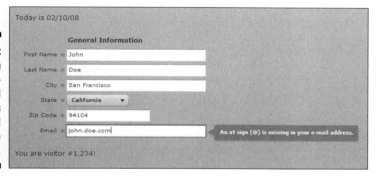

Figure 9-7:
A Flex form using validators and formatters to verify and customize data.

Listing 9-2: Checkout Form Highlighting Validators, Formatters, and Forms

```
<?xml version="1.0" encoding="utf-8"?>
<mx:Application xmlns:mx="http://www.adobe.com/2006/mxml" layout="vertical">
<mx:Script>
    <![CDATA[
        private var currentDate:Date = new Date(2008, 01, 10);        → 5
        private var currentVisitor:int = 1234;                        → 6
    ]]>
</mx:Script>

<mx:ZipCodeValidator source="{zipCode}" property="text" />           → 10
<mx:EmailValidator source="{emailTxt}" property="text" />            → 11
<mx:DateFormatter id="df" formatString="MM/DD/YY" />                 → 12
<mx:NumberFormatter id="nf" useThousandsSeparator="true" />          → 13

<mx:VBox>
    <mx:Label text="Today is {df.format(currentDate)}" fontSize="12" />   → 16
    <mx:Form width="100%" height="100%">
        <mx:FormHeading label="General Information" />               → 18
        <mx:FormItem label="First Name" required="true">            → 19
            <mx:TextInput width="250"/>
```

(continued)

Listing 9-2 *(continued)*

```
        </mx:FormItem>
        <mx:FormItem label="Last Name" required="true">          → 22
            <mx:TextInput width="250" />
        </mx:FormItem>
        <mx:FormItem label="City" required="true">               → 25
            <mx:TextInput width="250"/>
        </mx:FormItem>
        <mx:FormItem label="State" required="true">              → 28
            <mx:ComboBox dataProvider="{['California', 'Washington',
                'Arizona']}" />
        </mx:FormItem>
        <mx:FormItem label="Zip Code" required="true">           → 32
            <mx:TextInput id="zipCode" width="150"/>             → 33
        </mx:FormItem>
        <mx:FormItem label="Email" required="true">              → 35
            <mx:TextInput id="emailTxt" width="250" />           → 36
        </mx:FormItem>
    </mx:Form>
    <mx:Label text="You are visitor #{nf.format(currentVisitor)}!"
        fontSize="12"/>                                          → 40
</mx:VBox>
</mx:Application>
```

Here's an explanation of the sample application in Listing 9-2:

→ **5** The Date object capturing today's date. You format this date object with a DateFormatter for display in the form.

→ **6** The private variable capturing the current visitor value. This is displayed with a NumberFormatter at the bottom of the form.

→ **10** The ZipCodeValidator MXML tag. This tag validates the zip code the user enters in the zipCode TextInput on Line 33.

→ **11** The EmailValidator MXML tag. This tag validates the e-mail address that the user enters in the e-mail TextInput on Line 36.

→ **12** The DateFormatter MXML tag. This tag formats the current date that's displayed at the top of the form.

→ **13** The NumberFormatter MXML tag. This tag formats the current visitor number displayed at the bottom of the form.

→ **16** Where the current date is formatted. The formatting occurs because data binding is used to trigger the formatter and invoke the format method converts the date object into a human-readable, formatted date string.

→ **18**   A FormHeading control is used to denote general information section on the form. The FormHeading label shows up bolded and in larger text than the FormItem labels.

→ **19**   In Lines 19, 22, 25, 28, 32, and 35, the `required` attribute is set to true on each FormItem tag so that a red asterisk appears between the FormItem label and the FormItem children. It's a visual cue to the user that the field is requires an entry.

→ **40**   Where the current visitor number is formatted. The formatting occurs because data binding is used to trigger the formatter and invoke the format method that converts the number into a string with a comma delimiting the thousands place.

In this example alone, you can see the use of the Form and FormItem container, FormHeading control, NumberFormatter, DateFormatter, EmailValidator, and ZipCodeValidator.

Chapter 10

Containers and Navigators

- -

In This Chapter

▶ Laying out an application with canvases and boxes

▶ Getting complex with the Tile, Panel, and TitleWindow containers

▶ Navigating with Accordion, TabNavigator, and ViewStack

▶ Using the ButtonBar, LinkButtonBar, and TabBar navigation bars

- -

*C*ontainers are components designed specifically to hold other components. You use containers to control the layout of your Flex application. All the controls you use in the application are in some form of a container; even the base `<mx:Application>` MXML tag is a container. In this chapter, we cover all the container controls in the Flex framework. We also cover *navigators*, which are special kinds of containers that let users switch back and forth between different child components. We also touch on the navigation bar controls, which aren't containers themselves but have been specifically designed to work with some of the navigator controls.

In this chapter, we cover the following containers and controls:

Accordion	Alert	ApplicationControlBar
ButtonBar	Canvas	ControlBar
Grid	HBox	HDividedBox
LinkBar	Panel	TabBar
TabNavigator	Tile	TitleWindow

Introducing Basic Containers

The basic container you use is Canvas, which at its fundamental level lets you place components by setting x and y coordinates. A few more containers, such as HBox and VBox, handle the task of laying out child components in more useful ways. In this section, we discuss these containers and how to control the layout of your application.

All containers discussed in this chapter extend `mx.core.Container`, which is the base container class in the framework that handles most of the core functionality of the container classes. The inheritance of many of the Flex containers is shown in Figure 10-1. Container is responsible for such fundamental tasks as adding and removing children and clipping and scrolling content. Typically, you don't ever use the `mx.core.Container` class itself; instead, you use one of the containers we cover in this chapter.

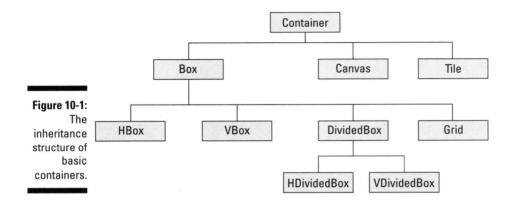

Figure 10-1:
The inheritance structure of basic containers.

Understanding common container behavior

Because all container classes extend `mx.core.Container`, they all have some of the same functionality. All containers discussed in this chapter support adding and removing children in the same ways and have common CSS styles and skins to control the container display.

Adding and removing children

You can add children to, and remove them from, any container by using either MXML or ActionScript. By nesting components within the MXML tag of a container, you automatically add the components as children of the container.

In this example, you create a new Canvas that contains two children — a Text Input control and a Button control with `Submit` as the label (see Figure 10-2):

```
<mx:Canvas width="400" height="400">
   <mx:TextInput x="0" y="0" />
   <mx:Button x="0" y="30" label="Submit" />
</mx:Canvas>
```

Figure 10-2:
Two controls within a Canvas container.

The TextInput control and Button control are nested within the opening tag (`<mx:Canvas>`) and closing tag of the Canvas (`</mx:Canvas>`), so they're added as children. Containers can also contain additional containers, so you can create fairly complex layouts by nesting MXML tags.

You can add and remove children in ActionScript by using the `addChild` and `removeChild` methods. The following application adds check boxes to a VBox container (we cover the VBox container in the later section "Managing your layout with box layout containers"; for now, just note the use of the `addChild` method in the Script block):

```
<?xml version="1.0" encoding="utf-8"?>
<mx:Application xmlns:mx="http://www.adobe.com/2006/mxml" layout="vertical">
    <mx:Script>
    <![CDATA[
        import mx.controls.CheckBox;
        private function addCheckBox():void {
            var checkBox:CheckBox = new CheckBox();
            checkBox.label = "Checkbox " + (myVBox.numChildren + 1);
            myVBox.addChild(checkBox);
        }
    ]]>
    </mx:Script>
    <mx:Button label="Add Checkbox" click="addCheckBox()" />
    <mx:VBox id="myVBox" />
</mx:Application>
```

Getting to know common styles

All containers support border and background styles, the most common of which are

- ✔ borderStyle
- ✔ borderThickness
- ✔ borderColor
- ✔ backgroundColor
- ✔ backgroundAlpha
- ✔ cornerRadius

These styles let you change the look of any of the container classes.

By default, the basic containers in this section draw no borders or backgrounds. You can enable borders on containers by setting the `borderStyle` property, which can be set to `none`, `solid`, `inset`, or `outset`. Setting the `borderStyle` property to `solid` draws a solid line as the border. Using `inset` or `outset` gives your border the effect of being raised or depressed. Figure 10-3 illustrates these four settings.

If you don't set the `borderStyle` style and try to set the `borderThickness` or `borderColor` styles, you will be disappointed. You *must* explicitly set `border Style` to `solid`, `inset`, or `outset` if you want the border to be drawn.

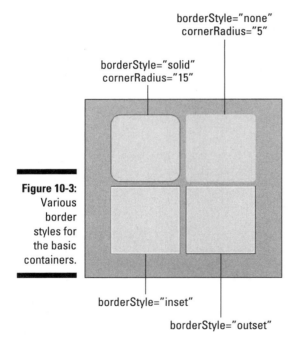

borderStyle="none"
cornerRadius="5"

borderStyle="solid"
cornerRadius="15"

Figure 10-3:
Various
border
styles for
the basic
containers.

borderStyle="inset"

borderStyle="outset"

Using percentage widths and heights

When you nest children within a container, you can set the size of the children in two ways:

- Set the `width` and `height` properties in pixels.
- Set `width` and `height` to percentage values. By using percentages rather than exact pixel values, the container sizes the child components to a percentage of its own width and height.

If you're using ActionScript to set the width or height of a component to a percentage value, you must use different properties: `percentWidth` and `percentHeight`. These properties are used only when you're setting them in ActionScript. You cannot set `percentWidth` or `percentHeight` in MXML, but if you're using MXML, you can simply type `width="100%"` to use a percentage width.

Starting with a blank Canvas

The Canvas container is the simplest container in the Flex framework. You can use a Canvas to hold collections of components. Children within a Canvas are positioned by setting the `x` and `y` properties, which are relative to the upper-left corner of the Canvas.

Because of the relative positioning of children within a Canvas container, you can reposition entire groups of controls without repositioning each individual control. In Listing 10-1, you see a nested set of Canvas containers. Each of the two inner Canvas containers contains different controls that are positioned relative to the Canvas that holds them. The result is shown in Figure 10-4.

Listing 10-1: Canvas Layout Example

```
<mx:Canvas>

    <mx:Label text="Short Survey" />

    <mx:Canvas x="0" y="20">                                              → 4
        <mx:Label text="How old are you?" x="0" />
        <mx:RadioButton x="10" y="20" groupName="ageGroup" label="Under 30"/>
        <mx:RadioButton x="10" y="40" groupName="ageGroup" label="30-59"/>
        <mx:RadioButton x="10" y="60" groupName="ageGroup" label="60-89"/>
        <mx:RadioButton x="10" y="80" groupName="ageGroup" label="Over 90"/>
    </mx:Canvas>

    <mx:Canvas x="110" y="20">                                           → 12
        <mx:Label text="Which technologies have you used?" />
        <mx:CheckBox x="10" y="20" label="HTML" />
        <mx:CheckBox x="10" y="40" label="JavaScript" />
        <mx:CheckBox x="10" y="60" label="Java" />
        <mx:CheckBox x="10" y="80" label=".NET" />
    </mx:Canvas>

</mx:Canvas>
```

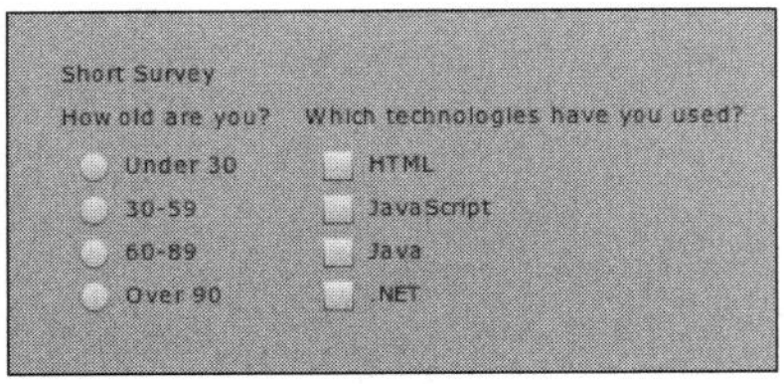

Figure 10-4:
The output
of the exam-
ple shown in
Listing 10-1.

Take a closer look at the listing:

→ **4**   On this line, the first inner Canvas container is created and placed
at (0, 20). The container contains a group of four radio buttons.

→ **12**   The second inner Canvas container is located at (110, 20) and contains four check boxes.

By changing the x and y properties of the inner Canvas containers, you can
move the sets of controls as a group, without worrying about the layout of all
controls within the containers. The x and y coordinates of the radio buttons
and check boxes remain the same even as the Canvas container that holds
the controls changes position.

Positioning items by using constraint-based layout

You have two options for controlling the placement of children in a Canvas
container: Use the x, y, `width`, and `height` properties or use constraint-
based layout.

Constraint-based layout uses the `left`, `right`, `top`, and `bottom` styles:

✔ `left`, `right`: The values for `left` and `top` are similar to setting x and
y because the values you specify position the component a certain
number of pixels from the upper-left corner of the Canvas.

✔ `right`, `bottom`: The `right` and `bottom` styles are slightly different;
these styles determine the width and height of the component, relative
to the parent Canvas:

• Setting `right` to a value of 0 makes the component stretch all the
way to the right edge of the Canvas. Setting `right` to 5 sizes the
component to reach 5 pixels from the right edge.

• The `bottom` style is used the same way to determine the height of
the child component.

The `left`, `right`, `top`, and `bottom` constraints are styles, not properties, like x and y. If you try to modify them in ActionScript, you cannot simply write `component.left = 10`, as you would for a normal property. Instead you have to call `component.setStyle("left", 10)`.

The following code shows two Canvas components, each with an HSlider and a Button control. The HSlider is positioned 10 pixels from the top and 10 pixels from the left of the Canvas and stretches to reach 10 pixels from the right. The Button is positioned 10 pixels from the lower-right corner of the Canvas.

```
<mx:Canvas width="200" height="100" borderStyle="solid">
   <mx:HSlider x="10" y="10" width="180" />
   <mx:Button width="60" height="20" x="130" y="70"/>
</mx:Canvas>

<mx:Canvas width="200" height="100" borderStyle="solid">
   <mx:HSlider left="10" right="10" top="10" />
   <mx:Button width="60" height="20" right="10" bottom="10"/>
</mx:Canvas>
```

Both Canvas containers in this example lay out their children in exactly the same way:

- **Example 1:** Uses absolute x, y, `width`, and `height` values to position child components. Because the Canvas container is 200 pixels wide, you can determine the appropriate absolute values to set for x, y, `width`, and `height`.

- **Example 2:** Uses `top`, `bottom`, `left`, and `right` styles to position the children. In this example, both Canvases look exactly the same because they both have the same 200-pixel width.

What happens if you want the Canvas to be 300 pixels wide? In the first example, you have to manually adjust the positioning and dimensions of the HSlider and Button if you want them to still be positioned in the corners of the Canvas. In the second example, which uses constraint-based layout, you don't need to change anything to keep the controls positioned in the corners.

Managing your layout with box layout containers

Rather than manage positions within a container manually, as you have to do with Canvas, you can use one of the box controls to manage child positions automatically. Two simple box containers, HBox and VBox, lay out the child controls horizontally or vertically.

If you rewrite Listing 10-1, the example created with Canvas containers, and simplify it by using HBox and VBox containers, the resulting code is shown in Listing 10-2.

Listing 10-2: Combining the HBox and VBox Containers

```
<mx:VBox>
    <mx:Label text="Short Survey" />
    <mx:HBox>
        <mx:VBox verticalGap="0">
            <mx:Label text="How old are you?" />
            <mx:RadioButton groupName="ageGroup" label="Under 30"/>
            <mx:RadioButton groupName="ageGroup" label="30-59"/>
            <mx:RadioButton groupName="ageGroup" label="60-89"/>
            <mx:RadioButton groupName="ageGroup" label="Over 90"/>
        </mx:VBox>
        <mx:VBox verticalGap="0">
            <mx:Label text="Which technologies have you used?" />
            <mx:CheckBox label="HTML" />
            <mx:CheckBox label="JavaScript" />
            <mx:CheckBox label="Java" />
            <mx:CheckBox label=".NET" />
        </mx:VBox>
    </mx:HBox>
</mx:VBox>
```

Notice that all references to x and y properties are removed from the new example. The box containers lay out the components, so you don't need to worry about positioning. If you want to reorder the check boxes, therefore, you can simply move one above the other in MXML and recompile the application.

Both the HBox and VBox containers have properties that control the spacing placed between the children. This property is verticalGap for a VBox and horizontalGap for an HBox. The default value for both verticalGap and horizontalGap is 4 pixels. In the example, the verticalGap property is set to 0 for VBox containers, which removes the extra spacing between the radio buttons and check boxes.

VBox and HBox extend the same base class: mx.containers.Box. You can even use the Box container itself, if you're so inclined. The direction in which the contents of a Box container are positioned depends on the direction property of the container, which can be either vertical (the default) or horizontal. The only benefit to using Box rather than HBox or VBox is that you can change the direction property in ActionScript while your application is running if you want to switch layout directions on the fly. In most cases, though, you can just stick to either HBox or VBox.

Building a dynamically resizable layout with divided boxes

The divided box containers, which are similar to the box containers, come as a pair of containers, HDividedBox and VDividedBox, which allow you to specify either a horizontal or vertical layout. The difference between the divided box containers is that users can drag the divider bar, which appears between the children, to resize the child components (see Figure 10-5).

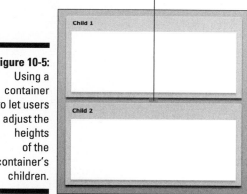

Divider bar

Figure 10-5: Using a container to let users adjust the heights of the container's children.

For the most part, divided box containers are used just like the normal HBox and VBox containers. You can nest the child components in MXML to add them to the container, or you can add children by using ActionScript. A divider bar placed between each child in the container can be dragged to resize the children. When the user drags the divider between two children, the child on the top and the child on the bottom of the bar are resized.

The liveDragging property of the divided box containers can be set to true to perform the resizing of the children in real time as the user drags the divider bar. The default setting for liveDragging is false, which means that as the user drags the divider, an indicator helps visualize how the children will be resized after the user releases the divider bar.

Just as the HBox and VBox properties use the horizontalGap and vertical-Gap properties to determine the spacing of child elements, the divided boxes use the same properties. However, the divided boxes require slightly more space to display the divider bar — 6 pixels, by default. If you set the vertical Gap or horizontalGap properties to fewer than 6 pixels, not enough space remains to draw the divider bars, and they aren't shown.

You can use percentage widths and heights in addition to exact dimensions, which can often come in handy when using the divided boxes. The following example creates an Application with a Tools pane on the left and a main content area on the right, which occupies the bulk of the Application's width. The resulting application is shown in Figure 10-6. Because you're using HDividedBox, the user can customize the interface by adjusting the width of the left pane:

```xml
<?xml version="1.0" encoding="utf-8"?>
<mx:Application xmlns:mx="http://www.adobe.com/2006/mxml">
   <mx:HDividedBox width="100%" height="100%">
      <mx:Panel width="200"  height="100%" title="Tools" />
      <mx:Panel width="100%" height="100%" title="Main Content"  />
   </mx:HDividedBox>
</mx:Application>
```

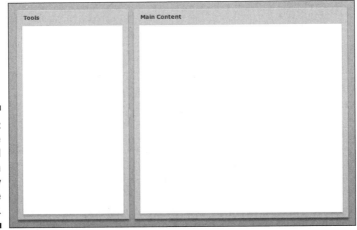

Figure 10-6:
Using the HDivided Box for a dynamically resizable layout.

Creating a tiled layout with the Tile container

The Tile container, which is a bit like a combination of HBox and VBox, lays out child components in rows and columns. Figure 10-7 shows the Tile container used to lay out a series of CheckBox controls. You can specify the direction in which the container should start laying out child components by setting the direction property, which can be either horizontal or vertical. The default value is horizontal, which lays out the components by placing them horizontally until Flex runs out of space, at which point it creates a new row below the last one. If you set an explicit width for the Tile container, it automatically calculates how many columns and rows it must create, based on the dimensions of the child components. If you don't specify the width or height of a Tile container, it attempts to lay out the children by using an equal number of rows and columns.

Figure 10-7:
CheckBox
controls in
a Tile
container.

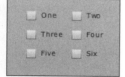

Figure 10-7:
CheckBox
controls in
a Tile
container.

You can override the automatic calculation of the row and column dimensions by setting the `tileWidth` and `tileHeight` properties. If you set these two properties, the Tile container is forced to use these measurements to lay out the children, even if the children don't fully fit within these dimensions. You can also set only one of the `tileWidth` or `tileHeight` properties and let the Tile container compute the other one automatically.

The Tile container isn't the same as the TileList control. The Tile container is a simple container that holds a collection of child user interface components. TileList, on the other hand, is a data-driven list control. For more information on the TileList control, see Chapter 8.

Using the Grid container

The Grid container is similar to the Tile container, but Grid gives you more control over the sizes of grid rows and columns. A Grid container is the closest container in the Flex framework to the HTML `<table>` tag. A Grid contains one or more GridRow containers, each of which can contain one or more GridItem containers. The basic nested structure of a Grid looks something like this:

```
<mx:Grid>
    <mx:GridRow>
        <mx:GridItem />
        <mx:GridItem />
    </mx:GridRow>
    <mx:GridRow>
        <mx:GridItem />
        <mx:GridItem />
    </mx:GridRow>
</mx:Grid>
```

This example shows the nested hierarchy of a Grid control. Notice that you don't specify grid columns. They're determined by the placement of GridItem containers within the rows. In this example, the Grid is a 4-by-4 grid with two rows and two columns. In a real-world example, you add the contents of the Grid into the individual GridItem objects. The GridItem container itself acts just like the HBox container, so if you add multiple controls to a GridItem, the default behavior lays them out horizontally within that grid square.

If you don't set explicit dimensions of the Grid or the nested GridRow or GridItem containers, the Grid automatically sizes itself to fit the contents. Each row of the grid is as high as the highest child in that row, and each column is as wide as the widest child in that particular column. You can override this default measurement by specifying widths or heights on the GridRow containers or the GridItem containers. You then gain slightly more control than when you're using the Tile container, which allows you to set only `tileWidth` and `tileHeight` for the entire Tile container, not on an individual, row-by-row basis.

The following example illustrates this difference:

```
<mx:Grid>
    <mx:GridRow>
        <mx:GridItem>
            <mx:Button width="55" label="One" />
        </mx:GridItem>
        <mx:GridItem>
            <mx:Button width="55" label="Two" />
        </mx:GridItem>
        <mx:GridItem>
            <mx:Button width="100" label="Three" />
        </mx:GridItem>
    </mx:GridRow>
    <mx:GridRow>
        <mx:GridItem>
            <mx:Button width="55" label="Four" />
        </mx:GridItem>
        <mx:GridItem>
            <mx:Button width="55" label="Five" />
        </mx:GridItem>
        <mx:GridItem>
            <mx:Button width="100" label="Six" />
        </mx:GridItem>
    </mx:GridRow>
</mx:Grid>
```

This chunk of code produces a Grid container with two rows and three columns, as shown in Figure 10-8. The columns size themselves to fit the content, which makes the first two columns 50 pixels wide and the third column 100 pixels wide. If you try to mimic this same layout using a Tile container, you end up with three columns, all of which are 100 pixels wide because the Tile container forces all rows and columns to be the same width and height.

Figure 10-8:
A grid with
two rows
and three
columns.

Discovering Panel Containers and Control Bars

In this section, we discuss two closely related containers, Panel and TitleWindow, which add a title bar above their contents and some additional border styles to wrap around the content.

Panel

All the containers discussed earlier in this chapter are almost invisible. The divided box containers have minimal visual components (the divider bar between children), and Canvas and the normal box containers are invisible unless border and background properties are set. The *Panel* container, on the other hand, is a visual container that displays the child contents within a skinned window and the title bar at the top, as shown in Figure 10-9.

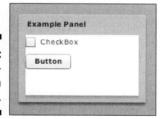

Figure 10-9:
Child con-
trols in a
Panel.

A Panel can automatically lay out its children by using three layout methods: absolute, vertical, or horizontal. You can set the `layout` property to determine which layout algorithm is used. By default, a Panel lays out its children vertically. Because Panel supports absolute, vertical, and horizontal layouts, you can avoid unnecessarily putting a Canvas, VBox, or HBox in a Panel just to get this functionality.

The title bar at the top of a Panel can contain three elements: title text, status text, and an icon. You can set the `title` property of the Panel to change the text that's shown on the title bar. By default, this text is left-aligned and bold, but you can style it however you like. The following example sets the `titleStyleName` style of the Panel to `customTitleStyle`, which is a CSS style defined in the `<mx:Style>` block. The result is shown in Figure 10-10.

```
<?xml version="1.0" encoding="utf-8"?>
<mx:Application xmlns:mx="http://www.adobe.com/2006/mxml">
    <mx:Style>
        .customTitleStyle {
            font-size: 16;
            font-weight: normal;
            text-align: center;
            font-style: italic;
        }
    </mx:Style>

    <mx:Panel title="Panel Title" titleStyleName="
            customTitleStyle" width="200" height="200">
        <mx:Label text="Panel content goes here" />
    </mx:Panel>
</mx:Application>
```

Figure 10-10:
Using a custom style for a Panel's title text.

You use a few other styles and properties to customize a Panel:

✔ `status`: In addition to supporting the `title` property, Panel supports a `status` property, which displays status text in the title bar. The status text is, by default, right-aligned and in a lighter, unbolded font. You can change the look of the status text just like you change the title text by setting the `statusStyleName` style to a custom CSS style.

✔ `titleIcon`: To set the icon in the title bar of a Panel, you have to use the `titleIcon` property, not the `icon` property. All containers have the `icon` property, which is used when the container is shown in a parent navigator, such as TabNavigator or Accordion (discussed later in this chapter). But setting the `icon` property of a Panel doesn't place an icon in the title bar, even though it would intuitively seem like the right property.

✔ `headerHeight`: You can change the height of the title bar by setting the `headerHeight` style to a pixel value.

✔ `headerColors`: You can further adjust the header by setting the `header Colors` style, which should be set to an Array of two colors, used to draw the gradient in the header.

For example, to create a Panel with a 40-pixel-high header that fades from white to black, you can use the following MXML code:

```
<mx:Panel title="Panel Title" headerHeight="40"
    headerColors="[0xffffff, 0x000000]"
    width="200" height="200" />
```

By default, a Panel draws the upper-left and upper-right corners as rounded corners, and the bottom corners are square. You can make the Panel round the bottom corners as well by setting `roundedBottomCorners` to `true`. A few other fairly self-explanatory styles you can use to customize the look of the Panel container are `dropShadowEnabled`, `dropShadowColor`, `shadow-Direction`, and `shadowDistance`.

TitleWindow

The Flex framework contains an additional TitleWindow container, which is almost identical to Panel except for one feature: It can have a Close button in the upper-right of the Panel. When you use the TitleWindow container, you have to tell it to show the Close button by setting the `showCloseButton` property to `true`. After you do that, you notice a little X button in the upper-right corner. But clicking the Close button doesn't automatically do anything. When the user clicks the Close button, the TitleWindow dispatches a `close` event. *You* perform an action after the `close` event is dispatched.

The most common use of the TitleWindow and the Close button is to launch a popup window, such as a Preferences pane, that the user can interact with and then close. The example in Listing 10-3 launches a TitleWindow as a popup and then removes it when the user clicks the Close button. We haven't discussed the PopUpManager yet, so feel free to jump to Chapter 15 to find out more; for now, just know that the PopUpManager is used to launch pop-ups in your Flex application.

Listing 10-3: Launching and Closing a TitleWindow Pop-up

```
<?xml version="1.0" encoding="utf-8"?>
<mx:Application xmlns:mx="http://www.adobe.com/2006/mxml">
    <mx:Script>
        <![CDATA[
            import mx.events.CloseEvent;
            import mx.containers.TitleWindow;
            import mx.managers.PopUpManager;

            private function launchPopUp():void {                        → 9
                var titleWindow:TitleWindow = new TitleWindow();         → 10
                titleWindow.width = titleWindow.height = 200;
                titleWindow.title = "This is my TitleWindow";            → 12
                titleWindow.showCloseButton = true;                     → 13

                titleWindow.addEventListener(CloseEvent.CLOSE, closeClicked); → 15

                PopUpManager.addPopUp(titleWindow, this);                → 16
                PopUpManager.centerPopUp(titleWindow);
            }

            private function closeClicked(event:CloseEvent):void {       → 20
                var titleWindow:TitleWindow = event.currentTarget as TitleWindow;
                PopUpManager.removePopUp(titleWindow);                   → 22
            }
        ]]>
    </mx:Script>

    <mx:Button label="Launch TitleWindow PopUp" click="launchPopUp()" /> → 27

</mx:Application>
```

Here's a closer look at Listing 10-3:

→ **9**   The `launchPopUp` method is called when the user clicks the Button defined in MXML on Line 27.

→ **10**   On Lines 10–11, you create a new TitleWindow container and set a few properties, such as `width` and `height` and the `title` that should be displayed in the title bar.

→ **13**   You explicitly set the `showCloseButton` property to `true` so that the Close button is displayed.

→ **15**   You add an event handler that's called whenever the Close button is clicked. To find out about the event model, see Chapter 3.

→ **16**   Using the PopUpManager, you open the TitleWindow as a pop-up in your application and center it on-screen.

→ **20**   After the Close button is clicked in the TitleWindow, a Close event occurs, which triggers the `closeClicked` method.

→ **22**   You use the PopUpManager again to remove the TitleWindow from the application.

Alert

The Alert control is a specialized version of the Panel container, which you use to easily display dialog box notification messages to users. You use the Alert control for warning messages or simple notifications when you want the user to click OK or Cancel. You can also use the Panel container to create an element similar to the default Alert component — Alert just gives you an easier method of displaying messages to users without having to write much custom code.

The default Alert behavior shows a window that displays a title, a message, and an OK button. When the user clicks the OK button, the Alert dialog box disappears. The Alert control is different from most normal Flex controls because you create it by calling a static method rather than creating a new instance of the control. The Alert class has the static method `show`, which you use to pop up new Alert controls. When you call `Alert.show()`, you pass in the message that the Alert will display in the Alert window. Listing 10-4 creates an Alert dialog box when the user clicks the Button control.

Listing 10-4: Displaying an Alert

```
<?xml version="1.0" encoding="utf-8"?>
<mx:Application xmlns:mx="http://www.adobe.com/2006/mxml">
   <mx:Script>
      <![CDATA[
         import mx.controls.Alert;

         private function showAlert():void {
            Alert.show("You did something really, really
            bad!", "Warning");
         }
      ]]>
   </mx:Script>

   <mx:Button label="Show Alert" click="showAlert()" />

</mx:Application>
```

You can also customize the buttons shown in the Alert dialog box. By default, an Alert contains a single OK button, but you can make the Alert show OK, Cancel, Yes, and No buttons. To do so, you pass in the combination of buttons that you want displayed as the third parameter when you call `Alert.show()`.

The Alert class has a few static variables that define each of the valid buttons that can be shown: `Alert.OK`, `Alert.CANCEL`, `Alert.YES`, and `Alert.NO`. When you create an Alert with a customized set of buttons, you use the pipe operator (|) and pass in each of the static variables you want to use. Listing 10-5 creates an Alert with Yes and No buttons.

Listing 10-5: Customizing the Alert Buttons

```xml
<?xml version="1.0" encoding="utf-8"?>
<mx:Application xmlns:mx="http://www.adobe.com/2006/mxml">
    <mx:Script>
        <![CDATA[
            import mx.events.CloseEvent;
            import mx.controls.Alert;

            private function showAlert():void {
                Alert.show("Are you sure you want to do
                    that?", "Really?", Alert.YES | Alert.NO,
                    this, alertCloseHandler);
            }

            private function alertCloseHandler(event:Close
              Event):void {
                if(event.detail == Alert.YES) {
                    //do something for the Yes response
                }
                else if(event.detail == Alert.NO) {
                    //do something for the No response
                }
            }
        ]]>
    </mx:Script>

    <mx:Button label="Show Alert" click="showAlert()" />

</mx:Application>
```

Notice that you pass `Alert.YES | Alert.NO` as the third parameter in the call to `Alert.show()`. Also notice the fifth parameter, which is `alert-CloseHandler`. This function is executed when the user clicks one of the buttons to close the Alert control. You can query the `detail` property of the CloseEvent to determine which button the user clicked.

Control bars

A *control bar* is a container that typically contains various button controls, similar to the toolbars you're familiar with in your software programs, such as a word processor or an image editor. A word processor might have a toolbar that contains formatting controls to let you change the font size and color and other properties. The Flex framework contains two containers to serve this purpose:

- ✔ ControlBar: Can be used on its own, but is specifically designed to work with the Panel container by docking to the bottom of the Panel
- ✔ ApplicationControlBar: A container designed to dock to the top or bottom of your main Flex application

These two containers are discussed in detail in the following sections.

Adding a ControlBar to a Panel

To add a ControlBar container to a Panel, you can simply include a ControlBar as a child of a Panel in MXML. The Panel container treats the ControlBar slightly differently from the way it treats other children and docks it to the bottom of the Panel, below the content area that holds other children. The following example adds to a Panel a ControlBar that contains two Button controls:

```
<mx:Panel width="200" height="200" title="Example Panel">

    <mx:Text text="The content of your panel goes here."
            width="100%" />

  <mx:ControlBar horizontalAlign="center">
    <mx:Button label="Cancel" />
    <mx:Button label="Save" />
  </mx:ControlBar>

</mx:Panel>
```

The result is shown in Figure 10-11.

Figure 10-11: A Panel container with a ControlBar docked to the bottom.

The ControlBar must be the last child defined in MXML within a Panel tag. If the ControlBar isn't the last child, it's added to the content area of the Panel rather than docked to the bottom.

The ControlBar container is just a slightly modified Box container. The only real difference is that the Panel container is specifically designed to determine whether a ControlBar has been added as the last child of the Panel; if the ControlBar has been added, it's placed correctly along the bottom of the Panel. But the ControlBar container itself is basically just a Box and doesn't have any visual appearance of its own.

Using the ApplicationControlBar

The ApplicationControlBar container is designed to dock to the top of your main application (as shown in Figure 10-12); however, you can also use it in other contexts. You can dock the ApplicationControlBar to the top of the main application by setting the dock property to true. If dock is true, the ApplicationControlBar is placed at the top of the application and covers the entire width. You can also use the ApplicationControlBar without docking it to the top of your application, just as you would use any other container.

Figure 10-12:
Docking an Application ControlBar to the top of the application.

The following code snippet adds an ApplicationControlBar to a Flex application and docks it along the top:

```
<?xml version="1.0" encoding="utf-8"?>
<mx:Application xmlns:mx="http://www.adobe.com/2006/mxml">
    <mx:ApplicationControlBar  dock="true">
        <mx:Button label="Save" />
        <mx:Button label="Load" />
        <mx:Button label="New" />
    </mx:ApplicationControlBar>
</mx:Application>
```

Getting Up to Speed on Navigators

All containers discussed earlier in this chapter display, all at one time, all the child components that they hold. The containers might lay out those child components differently, but all children are visible at the same time. Sometimes, though, you need to navigate through a series of components and display one at a time in a certain order. The Flex framework contains a set of navigator controls for this specific purpose.

Switching between views with the ViewStack

The ViewStack is the simplest available navigator control. You can think of it as a stack of papers on a desk, with the uppermost sheet showing on top and all other sheets hidden underneath the top sheet. A ViewStack has a collection of child containers, but only one container is visible at any given time. You use the `selectedIndex` and `selectedChild` properties to specify which child container to show.

All Flex containers store references to their children by using *zero-based* indexing, which means that the first child in a container can be accessed in ActionScript by using `container.getChildAt(0)`. For navigators, to set the selected index to the first child, you set `selectedIndex = 0`. A value of `1` for `selectedIndex` refers to the second child.

Because all navigator controls must have only containers as children, you cannot add a control, such as Button, directly to a navigator. Instead, you add a container, such as Canvas or VBox (both of which are discussed earlier in this chapter).

You add children to a ViewStack just like you add them to a Canvas or any other container: by nesting MXML containers or by using ActionScript. The following example creates a ViewStack with four Panel containers. When the ViewStack initially loads, only the first Panel is visible in the application, and it's sized to fit the ViewStack size, which in this case is 200-by-200 pixels.

```
<mx:ViewStack id="vstack" width="200" height="200">
    <mx:Panel id="panel1" title="Panel 1" />
    <mx:Panel id="panel2" title="Panel 2" />
    <mx:Panel id="panel3" title="Panel 3" />
    <mx:Panel id="Panel4" title="Panel 4" />
</mx:ViewStack>
```

The other three Panel containers remain hidden until the `selectedIndex` or `selectedChild` properties of the ViewStack change. For example, you can select the second Panel by using ActionScript and calling either `vstack.selectedIndex = 1` or `vStack.selectedChild = panel2`.

Controlling a ViewStack with navigation bar controls

A ViewStack on its own doesn't have any user interface controls for switching between the children it contains. You can switch between children by using ActionScript to change the `selectedIndex` or `selectedChild` properties manually; however, for an easier way to let the user move between the children of a ViewStack, use the ButtonBar, ToggleButtonBar, LinkBar, or TabBar controls. All these controls are specifically designed to be hooked up to a ViewStack and to create buttons that let the user switch between children. The control you use determines which button is created (see Figure 10-13):

- ✔ **ButtonBar:** Creates simples buttons, one next to the other
- ✔ **ToggleButtonBar:** Just like a ButtonBar, but allows one button to be in a toggled state to show selection
- ✔ **TabBar:** Creates a series of tabs
- ✔ **LinkBar:** Uses LinkButtons

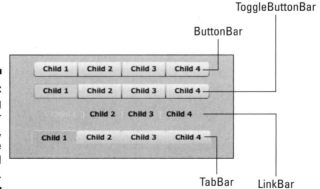

Figure 10-13: Comparing button bar controls, all with the first child selected.

The choice of which button bar control to use depends on the visual look you're hoping to achieve.

To use a navigation bar control with a ViewStack, you create the control that you want to use and assign the ViewStack that it controls as the `data Provider` of the navigation bar. After the navigation bar is wired up to the ViewStack, the navigation bar automatically displays one button for each child in the ViewStack, using the `label` and `icon` properties of the child container to draw the button. When the user clicks one of the buttons, the appropriate child in the ViewStack is shown.

The following chunk of code creates a ViewStack that holds four Panel children and adds a ToggleButtonBar to control the navigation:

```
<?xml version="1.0" encoding="utf-8"?>
<mx:Application xmlns:mx="http://www.adobe.com/2006/mxml">

    <mx:ToggleButtonBar dataProvider="{vStack}" />

    <mx:ViewStack id="vStack" width="200" height="200">

        <mx:Panel title="Panel 1" label="Child 1" />
        <mx:Panel title="Panel 2" label="Child 2"/>
        <mx:Panel title="Panel 3" label="Child 3"/>
        <mx:Panel title="Panel 4" label="Child 4"/>
    </mx:ViewStack>
</mx:Application>
```

The output is shown in Figure 10-14.

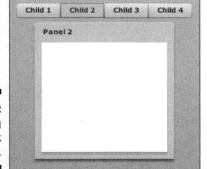

Figure 10-14:
Controlling
a ViewStack
container.

In this example, the Panel containers have both the `title` and `label` properties set. The ToggleButtonBar control uses the `label` property to create the navigation buttons. This property is different from the one that Panel uses for the title bar text.

Using navigation bars on their own

The navigation bar controls don't necessarily have to be used in conjunction with ViewStacks. You can create any of these controls separately and set the `dataProvider` property to control the buttons that are displayed. The `dataProvider` property can be an Array or ArrayCollection that's used to draw the buttons. If you aren't using the navigation bar in conjunction with a ViewStack, listen for the `itemClick` event that's dispatched when the user clicks one of the buttons. You can then perform a custom action when the user changes the selection. The following example creates a ButtonBar control and assigns an array of strings as the `dataProvider`, which is used to label the buttons. When a button is clicked, an Alert indicates which button was clicked.

```
<?xml version="1.0" encoding="utf-8"?>
<mx:Application xmlns:mx="http://www.adobe.com/2006/mxml">

    <mx:Script>
        <![CDATA[
            import mx.controls.Alert;
            import mx.events.ItemClickEvent;

            private function handleItemClick(event:ItemClickEvent):void {
                Alert.show("You selected button: " + ( event.index + 1 ), "Button
                    Clicked");
            }
        ]]>
    </mx:Script>

    <mx:ButtonBar itemClick="handleItemClick(event)">
        <mx:dataProvider>
            <mx:String>Button 1</mx:String>
            <mx:String>Button 2</mx:String>
            <mx:String>Button 3</mx:String>
            <mx:String>Button 4</mx:String>
        </mx:dataProvider>
    </mx:ButtonBar>

</mx:Application>
```

Improving navigation with an Accordion

The Accordion navigator displays its children as a set of expanding panels, stacked one above the other. Each child has a header button created for it that can be clicked to expand the child to make it visible. Only one child can be visible at any time, so expanding a new child minimizes the child that was previously selected. The following example illustrates the basic use of the Accordion navigator (see Figure 10-15):

```
<mx:Accordion width="300" height="200">
   <mx:Canvas label="Child 1">
      <mx:Label text="Contents of Child 1" />
   </mx:Canvas>
   <mx:Canvas label="Child 2">
      <mx:Label text="Contents of Child 2" />
   </mx:Canvas>
   <mx:Canvas label="Child 3">
      <mx:Label text="Contents of Child 3" />
   </mx:Canvas>
   <mx:Canvas label="Child 4">
      <mx:Label text="Contents of Child 4" />
   </mx:Canvas>
</mx:Accordion>
```

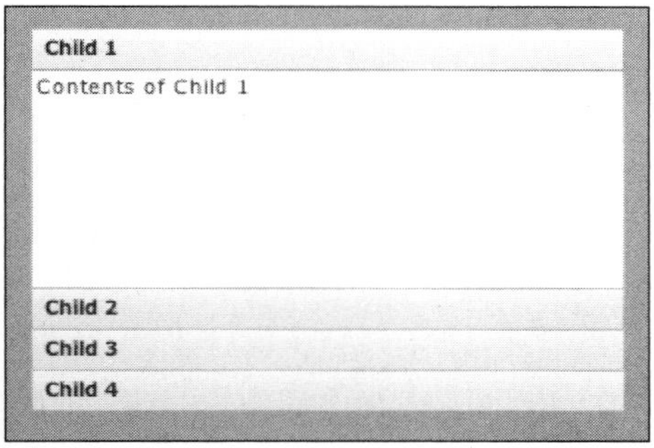

Figure 10-15:
An
Accordion
with the
first of four
children
selected.

In this example, four header buttons are created and stacked vertically, one for each child of the Accordion. Each header button displays a label that identifies the child container, which is determined by setting the label property on the child itself. In addition to showing the label for each child, a header button can display an icon, which you can enable by setting the icon property of each child. Each child can have its own unique label and icon.

The user can click any of the header buttons to select the corresponding child, which expands that child and minimizes the previously selected child. You can change the selected child yourself, just like you change the child in a ViewStack, by modifying either the selectedIndex or selectedChild property. The children open and close with an animation, and you can adjust the speed of this animation by changing the openDuration style, which is 250 milliseconds by default.

You can change the look of the Accordion by setting these styles:

✔ headerStyleName: To style the header buttons, set this style and specify a CSS style to use for the header button. Remember that the header button is just a Button control, so any of the CSS styles for Button should be applicable.

✔ `headerHeight`: Set this style on the Accordion to explicitly control the height of the header buttons. If the style isn't set, the headers are sized appropriately, depending on the size of the font used for the labels.

Listing 10-6 creates header buttons that are 35 pixels high, with custom font, border, and background styles to alter the default appearance.

Listing 10-6: Custom Styling for an Accordion Container

```
<?xml version="1.0" encoding="utf-8"?>
<mx:Application xmlns:mx="http://www.adobe.com/2006/mxml">
   <mx:Style>
       .customHeaderStyle {
           font-style: italic;
           text-decoration: underline;
           font-family: Arial;
           font-size: 16;
           text-align: right;

           color: #FFFFFF;
           text-roll-over-color: #EFEFEF;
           text-selected-color: #FFFFFF;

           border-color: #000000;
           fill-colors: #333333, #000000, #ff0000, #000000;
           fill-alphas: 1,1;
           selected-fill-colors: #666666, #333333;
           theme-color: #ff0000;
       }
   </mx:Style>
   <mx:Accordion headerStyleName="customHeaderStyle" headerHeight="35">
       <mx:Canvas label="Child 1">
           <mx:Label text="Contents of Child 1" />
       </mx:Canvas>
       <mx:Canvas label="Child 2">
           <mx:Label text="Contents of Child 2" />
       </mx:Canvas>
       <mx:Canvas label="Child 3">
           <mx:Label text="Contents of Child 3" />
       </mx:Canvas>
       <mx:Canvas label="Child 4">
           <mx:Label text="Contents of Child 4" />
       </mx:Canvas>
   </mx:Accordion>
</mx:Application>
```

This custom CSS style produces the Accordion shown in Figure 10-16.

Figure 10-16:
An
Accordion
with custom
CSS header
styles.

Creating tabs with the TabNavigator

The TabNavigator container is essentially just a ViewStack wired up with a Tab Bar that sits on top. For each child that's added to the TabNavigator, a tab is created in the TabBar that the user can click to select the child. The TabNavigator is shown in Figure 10-17.

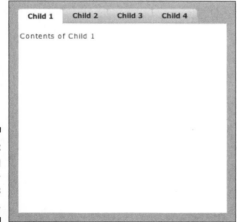

Figure 10-17:
Displaying
child com-
ponents as
tabs.

You use a few properties and styles to customize the TabNavigator:

✔ tabHeight, tab Width: Control the sizing of the tabs.

✔ horizontalAlign: Control whether tabs are docked to the left or right or in the center of the TabNavigator.

✔ `horizontalGap`: Determine the gap between tabs in the TabBar.

✔ `selectedIndex`, `selectedChild`: Change which tab is selected, just like changing the same properties on a ViewStack or Accordion.

Optimizing performance with deferred instantiation

All navigator containers support *deferred instantiation.* This concept means, fundamentally, that a navigator creates its children only as it needs them. When the navigator is created, one child is selected — usually, the first child in the list of children. The first child is created instantly because it needs to be shown immediately, and the other children are initially hidden from view, so they don't get created. Then, after a different child is selected, that child is created and displayed.

Performance is the primary reason that navigators use this method of deferred instantiation. When your Flex application is loading, it has to create all components that are visible on-screen. This process of creating and laying out components takes time, and anything you can do to minimize the number of components that must be created speeds up the load time and responsiveness of your application. If you were to create every child of a navigator all at once, your application would hang until all children were created. Deferred instantiation lets you break up that process into smaller chunks, each of which happens as needed.

Avoiding common pitfalls

Although deferred instantiation can significantly improve the performance of your application, you might run into some common pitfalls. If the children of a navigator haven't been created because they haven't yet been shown, you cannot access any properties or methods of those children. Only after those children are created can you access them directly. The following example shows a common error that illustrates this point:

```
<mx:ViewStack id="vstack" width="200" height="200">
  <mx:Panel label="Page 1">
    <mx:Label text="Enter your name:" />
    <mx:TextInput id="nameField" />
    <mx:Button label="Next"
        click="nameText.text = nameField.text; vstack.selectedIndex = 1;" />
  </mx:Panel>
  <mx:Panel label="Page 2">
    <mx:Label text="You entered:" />
    <mx:Label id="nameText" />
  </mx:Panel>
</mx:ViewStack>
```

Although this example is oversimplified, it illustrates the potential problem caused by deferred instantiation. In the example, two Panel containers are within a ViewStack, the first of which contains a TextInput control that lets the user type her name. The second Panel simply contains a label that displays whatever the user entered on the first Panel. When the user clicks the button on the first Panel, it sets the `text` property of the Label component on the second panel and shows the second Panel. But if you run this chunk of code, it produces an error when the button is clicked. The error occurs because the call to `nameText.text = nameField.text` happens before the `nameText` Label component on the second panel has been created. So, when you try to set the `text` property of `nameField`, `nameField` is still `null`, resulting in a runtime error.

One solution to this problem is to use data binding to bind the `text` property of the `nameText` Label on the second panel to the value entered on the first panel. (Data binding is covered in depth in Chapter 12.) The following bit of code binds the `text` property of Label on the second panel to the `text` property of the TextInput control on the first panel:

```
<mx:ViewStack id="vstack" width="200" height="200">
   <mx:Panel label="Page 1">
      <mx:Label text="Enter your name:" />
      <mx:TextInput id="nameField" />
      <mx:Button label="Next"
         click="vstack.selectedIndex = 1;" />
   </mx:Panel>

   <mx:Panel label="Page 2">
      <mx:Label text="You entered:" />
      <mx:Label id="nameText" text="{nameField.text}" />
   </mx:Panel>
</mx:ViewStack>
```

Using data binding is one solution to the problem, but you can accomplish the same goals by using one of a variety of other methods. The point of the example, however, is that you cannot access a property or method of a child component that hasn't yet been created. And, when you use the navigator components, only the initially selected child is created. The rest of the children are created only as they're individually shown.

Choosing between enabling and bypassing deferred instantiation

In general, your Flex applications should work with deferred instantiation. If it's absolutely necessary, however, you can force navigators to create all their children immediately and bypass deferred instantiation. You can use the `creationPolicy` property to change how the children of navigators are created. All possible values for `creationPolicy` are `auto`, `all`, `queued`, and `none`. We don't cover the `queued` or `none` settings because they're fairly advanced topics. You primarily need to set `creationPolicy` to only `auto` or `all`:

- ✔ `auto`: The default setting; enables deferred instantiation.

- ✔ `all`: Forces the creation of all children at the same time. This setting creates all children at the same time that the navigator is created, allowing you to access any children or properties on those children without worrying about whether the child has been shown yet.

Tying It Together: Building a Form with Multiple Parts

Listing 10-7 ties together forms, validators, containers, and navigators. The sample application is a multipart form for users to complete. Users are asked for information such as name and e-mail address. The form is divided into three distinct groupings, which divide the information logically and present it in a more consolidated space. You use an Accordion navigator to hold the three separate forms. Figure 10-18 shows the output of this code listing.

Listing 10-7: A Multipart Form Application

```
<?xml version="1.0" encoding="utf-8"?>
<mx:Application xmlns:mx="http://www.adobe.com/2006/mxml">

    <mx:Script>
    <![CDATA[
        import mx.events.ValidationResultEvent;
        import mx.controls.Alert;
        import mx.validators.Validator;

        private function validateAllFields():void {           → 10
            //loop over each validator and check to make sure it's valid
            for each(var validator:Validator in validators) {
                var validationResult:ValidationResultEvent = validator.validate();

                //if we get an invalid result we show an error
                if(validationResult.type == ValidationResultEvent.INVALID) {
                    Alert.show("There's an error in this form:\n" +
                        validationResult.message, "Error");
                    return;
                }
            }
        }
```

```
        Alert.show("Your form was submitted successfully.", "Success");    → 23
    }
]]>
</mx:Script>

<!-- Our data model that stores all the information we are collecting -->
<mx:Model id="model">                                                      → 29
   <information>
     <name>{nameInput.text}</name>
     <email>{emailInput.text}</email>
     <gender>{genderInput.selectedItem}</gender>
     <ssn>{ssnInput.text}</ssn>
     <pinCode>{pinInput.text}</pinCode>
   </information>
</mx:Model>

<!-- An Array of all the validators we will use to validate the data. -->
<mx:Array id="validators">                                                 → 41
   <mx:StringValidator  source="{model}" property="name"
     listener="{nameInput}"   requiredFieldError="Name is required." />
   <mx:EmailValidator    source="{model}" property="email"
           listener="{emailInput}"  requiredFieldError="Email is required."
           />
   <mx:SocialSecurityValidator source="{model}" property="ssn"
     listener="{ssnInput}" required="false" />
   <mx:NumberValidator source="{model}" property="pin"
     listener="{pinInput}" allowNegative="false"
     precision="0" required="false" />
</mx:Array>                                                                → 52

<!-- The actual form views. We have 3 panes of forms. -->
<mx:Panel width="400" title="Tell us about yourself">

   <mx:Accordion width="100%">                                             → 57

     <mx:Form id="personalForm" label="Personal Information">
        <mx:FormItem label="Name" required="true">
          <mx:TextInput id="nameInput" />
        </mx:FormItem>
        <mx:FormItem label="Email" required="true">
          <mx:TextInput id="emailInput" />
        </mx:FormItem>
     </mx:Form>

     <mx:Form label="Optional Information">
        <mx:FormItem label="Gender">
          <mx:ComboBox id="genderInput" prompt="Select your gender">
            <mx:dataProvider>
               <mx:String>Male</mx:String>
```

(continued)

Listing 10-7 *(continued)*

```
                <mx:String>Female</mx:String>
            </mx:dataProvider>
        </mx:ComboBox>
    </mx:FormItem>
</mx:Form>

<mx:Form label="Secret Information">
    <mx:FormItem label="SSN">
        <mx:TextInput id="ssnInput" />
    </mx:FormItem>
    <mx:FormItem label="ATM PIN Code">
        <mx:TextInput id="pinInput" width="60" />
    </mx:FormItem>
</mx:Form>

</mx:Accordion>

<mx:ControlBar horizontalAlign="right">                          → 90
    <mx:Button label="Submit" click="validateAllFields()" id="submit" />
</mx:ControlBar>
</mx:Panel>

</mx:Application>
```

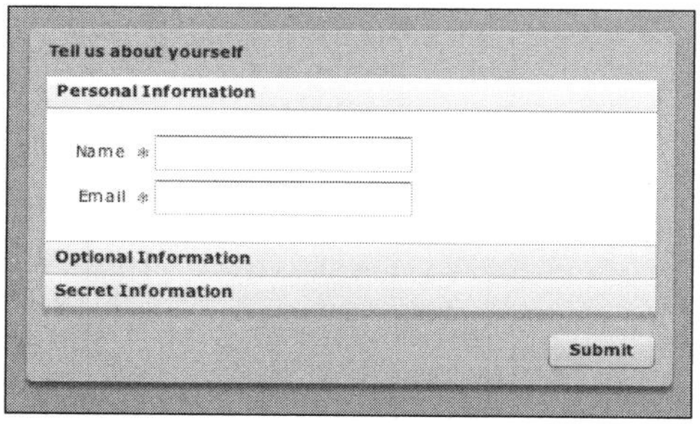

Figure 10-18:
Using an
Accordion
to break a
Form into
multiple
parts.

This list describes the sample application in Listing 10-7:

→ **29**   You define a Model to hold the data that will be submitted in the form. To find out more about using a Model to hold data, refer to Chapter 13.

→ **41**   Lines 41–52 define a collection of Validators that will be used to validate the user-submitted data in this application.

→ **57**   You create an Accordion to hold the forms. In this application are three pieces of the total form broken up into separate Form containers. Each of these forms is a child of the Accordion, so a separate header button is created for each one, allowing the user to move between the different parts.

→ **90**   The submit button for this form is docked to the bottom of the Panel by using a ControlBar. Remember that this ControlBar must be the last child in the Panel.

→ **91**   When the user clicks the Submit button, the `validateAll-Fields()` method is called, which is defined on Line 10. This method loops over all the validators that we have defined in Lines 41–52. If any of those validators don't validate correctly, then an error message is shown using the Alert component. If all the validators validate correctly the Alert component displays a success message.

In this example, you can see the use of the Panel container, ControlBar container, and Accordion navigator. The example also makes heavy use of forms and validators, which are covered in Chapter 9.

Chapter 11

Charting Components

· ·

In This Chapter

▶ Getting your data into charts

▶ Working with different chart types

▶ Adding interactivity and animation

▶ Adding legends to your charts

· ·

*T*here's no better way to impress the executives in your corporation than by showing them slick charts and graphs. Rather than simply display a list of data in a grid, you can make the data "come alive" by visualizing it in a column chart or pie chart or in any of the other charting options available in the Flex framework. Flex comes stocked with a full charting package that can make CEOs drool over the impressive data visualizations. If you're trying to impress one of the executives in your company, add a few animated charts to the application you're working on to showcase sales performance. In no time, you'll have everyone wondering how you created such amazing software — just don't tell anyone how easy it was.

In this chapter, we cover the following charting components:

AreaChart	BarChart
BubbleChart	CandleStickChart
ColumnChart	HLOCChart
Legend	LineChart
PieChart	PlotChart

The Flex charting components are available only if you purchased Flex Builder 3 Professional. In this chapter, we assume that you purchased the professional license.

Filling Your Charts with Data

Just like the other data-aware controls, such as List and DataGrid, described in Chapter 8, the charting controls use data providers that you use to load data into the charts. In addition to setting the data provider of a chart, however, you also need to tell the chart some specific information about how that data should be rendered.

Using the right series

Each type of chart you create requires the correct type of data *series* so that the chart knows how to draw the data. A charting series isn't the same as the underlying collection or model that you use to populate the series. For each chart you create, you use a combination of these two items:

✔ A data provider

✔ A specific chart series, such as ColumnSeries or PieSeries

You can set the `dataProvider` property of the individual series, or you can use the `dataProvider` of the chart itself.

Specifying the right fields

Each chart series has a few properties that you need to set to tell the series a bit more information about the data in the data provider. For the charts that use an x and y axis, which includes all charts except for the PieChart, you use the `xField` property or the `yField` property, or both, to tell the series how the data is supposed to be charted. The details about which field properties are required depend primarily on which kind of series you're charting and which kind of axes you're using.

We cover each chart series in the following sections as we discuss the different chart types. Later in this chapter, we also discuss the particular uses of different chart axes. For now, take a look at Listing 11-1, a simple example that displays a pie chart to show sales figures per employee. You use a `PieSeries` and specify the `field` property so that the chart knows which value to use to create pie wedges of the appropriate size. The resulting pie chart is shown in Figure 11-1.

In this example, you use a Model to hold the XML data that gets displayed in the chart. You create a PieChart that has a PieSeries set as the `series` property. Then you bind the `dataProvider` of the PieSeries to your data model. This populates the PieChart with the sales data in the model, and the chart handles the rest by figuring out how to draw wedges of the appropriate size based on the data.

The `<mx:series>` block of the example shows adding a PieSeries to the chart. The `series` property of the chart is an Array, and you can specify any number of series. Using multiple series is more useful with chart types other than the pie chart and is covered in more detail later in this chapter.

Always use the correct series for each chart you create. For a ColumnChart, you use a ColumnSeries and for a BarChart, you use a BarSeries, for example.

Listing 11-1: Creating a PieChart to Show Sales Data

```xml
<?xml version="1.0" encoding="utf-8"?>
<mx:Application xmlns:mx="http://www.adobe.com/2006/mxml">

    <mx:Model id="salesByEmployee">
        <employees>
            <employee name="Doug" sales="150000" />
            <employee name="Deepa" sales="75000" />
            <employee name="Darron" sales="30000" />
            <employee name="Ben" sales="60000" />
        </employees>
    </mx:Model>

    <mx:PieChart width="300" height="300" >
        <mx:series>
            <mx:PieSeries
                dataProvider="{salesByEmployee.employee}"
                field="sales" labelField="name"
                labelPosition="callout" />
        </mx:series>
    </mx:PieChart>

</mx:Application>
```

Figure 11-1:
Using a simple PieChart to show sales breakdown by employee.

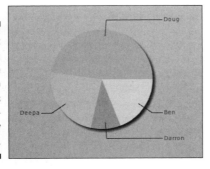

In this chapter, we use the `<mx:Model />` tag with XML data to populate the sample charts. The `<mx:Model>` tag is a simple way to hold XML data and is an excellent way to quickly put some test data into your Flex applications. All you need to do is add the `<mx:Model>` tag to your application and place an XML representation of your data within the tag. In more complex scenarios, you might load data from a Web service, as XML or in some other format. You can use the Flex framework collection classes, such as ArrayCollection or XMLListCollection, to populate your charts with data. To find out more about working with the collection classes, see Chapter 13.

Creating a ColumnChart and BarChart

You can create the typical column or bar charts, which display your data in either vertical columns or horizontal bars (see Figure 11-2). The BarChart and ColumnChart are closely related, and the only major distinction is the vertical or horizontal orientation. But even though the charts are similar, they are in fact two distinct controls, and each one needs to use the appropriate chart series, which is either ColumnSeries or BarSeries.

Both the ColumnChart and BarChart support clustering and stacking of the columns or bars. (See the following two sections.) You can control which type of rendering is used for the chart by specifying the `type` property, which can be set to `clustered`, `stacked`, `100%`, or `overlaid`. To customize the chart type, you have to use multiple data series in the same chart, such as a comparison of sales figures from different quarters.

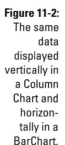

Figure 11-2: The same data displayed vertically in a Column Chart and horizontally in a BarChart.

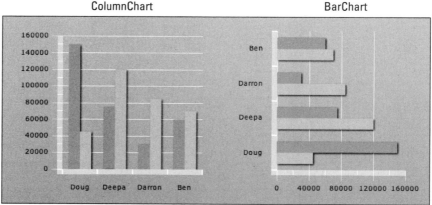

Clustering

Clustering, the default chart behavior, is the grouping of multiple data series along the x axis, in the case of the ColumnChart, or along the y axis, in the case of the BarChart. Clustering is useful for a side-by-side comparison of related numbers when you need to easily be able to see the values of each individual column. Listing 11-2 creates an example that adds two different series to a ColumnChart and uses the default clustering behavior. The resulting Flex application is shown in Figure 11-3.

Listing 11-2: Creating a ColumnChart with Clustered Series

```xml
<?xml version="1.0" encoding="utf-8"?>
<mx:Application xmlns:mx="http://www.adobe.com/2006/mxml">
   <mx:Model id="salesByEmployee">
      <employees>
         <employee name="Doug" salesQ1="150000" salesQ2="45000" />
         <employee name="Deepa" salesQ1="75000" salesQ2="120000" />
         <employee name="Darron" salesQ1="30000" salesQ2="85000" />
         <employee name="Ben" salesQ1="60000" salesQ2="70000" />
      </employees>
   </mx:Model>

   <mx:ColumnChart dataProvider="{salesByEmployee.employee}">

      <mx:series>
         <mx:ColumnSeries yField="salesQ1" />
         <mx:ColumnSeries yField="salesQ2" />
      </mx:series>

      <mx:horizontalAxis>
         <mx:CategoryAxis id="xAxis" categoryField="name" />
      </mx:horizontalAxis>

   </mx:ColumnChart>

</mx:Application>
```

Stacking

Stacking involves creating a combined bar or column for all the series you're comparing in your chart. Stacked charts can be useful for visualizing the combined aggregate value of each series and the breakdown within a group of values. You have the following two options when working with stacked series in column or bar charts, which you can use by setting the `type` property of the chart to either `stacked` or `100%`:

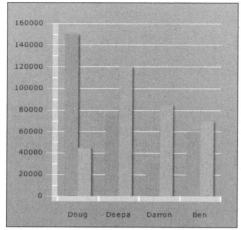

Figure 11-3:
Using a clustered Column Chart to compare two data series.

✔ stacked: Setting `type` to `stacked` places each column in the set on top of another to create a single column that indicates the total sum value. The length of each piece of a stacked column indicates that individual piece's numeric value, which can be determined by checking the axis along the side of the chart.

You can change Listing 11-2 to use stacked columns by simply changing the chart type in MXML:

```
<mx:ColumnChart type="stacked"dataProvider="{salesByEm
    ployee.employee}">
```

This change in the `type` property produces the stacked columns shown in Figure 11-4.

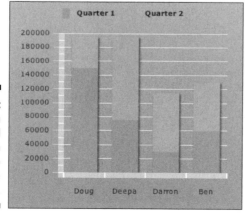

Figure 11-4:
Using a stacked Column Chart to compare data.

✔ 100%: Setting `type` to `100%` creates a stacked column that breaks down the individual pieces based on the percentage that each piece contributes to the total of the set. In a percentage-based stacked chart, all stacked columns in the chart are the same length because they all add up to 100 percent. This type of chart doesn't indicate the actual value of each piece of the stacked column, but allows you to easily visualize the relative breakdown.

In Figure 11-5, which uses the same sales data as the previous chart example, the percentage-based stacked columns show the relationship between first and second quarter sales for each employee. You can see that Doug had far more sales in the first quarter than in the second quarter, whereas Deepa had more sales in the second quarter than in the first. This type of chart doesn't indicate actual sales numbers, however. Understanding how employees contrast with each other is difficult by using this type of chart.

The appropriateness of the stacked and 100 percent chart types depends on the type of information you're trying to convey.

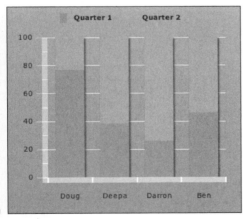

Figure 11-5: Comparing percentage differences in data series using the 100 percent stacked Column Chart.

Designing a LineChart and AreaChart

Rather than display your data as bars or columns, you can use the LineChart or AreaChart to display your data series as a solid line or filled area, respectively.

You can control the rendering of both the line and area charts by changing the `form` style of a LineSeries or AreaSeries. Possible values for `form` are

- ✔ segment
- ✔ tep
- ✔ reverseStep
- ✔ vertical
- ✔ horizontal
- ✔ curve

Each `form` renders the data differently, so experiment with the options to figure out which `form` is best for your chart's purpose.

LineChart

LineChart draws a solid line for each data series, which should be defined as a LineSeries, in the chart. LineCharts are useful for analyzing trends and can be used effectively to compare multiple series because you can easily see where the individual lines cross one another.

The example in Listing 11-3 displays two data series in a LineChart (see Figure 11-6). Each LineSeries has `form` set to `curve`, which makes the line a smooth curve (rather than a straight line) between data points, giving the chart a more fluid feel.

Listing 11-3: Adding Two Series to a LineChart

```
<?xml version="1.0" encoding="utf-8"?>
<mx:Application xmlns:mx="http://www.adobe.com/2006/mxml">

    <mx:Model id="salesByQuarter">
        <quarters>
            <quarter name="Quarter 1" dougSales="150000" deepaSales="75000" />
            <quarter name="Quarter 2" dougSales="45000" deepaSales="120000" />
            <quarter name="Quarter 3" dougSales="73500" deepaSales="67500" />
            <quarter name="Quarter 4" dougSales="68000" deepaSales="50000" />
        </quarters>
    </mx:Model>

    <mx:Legend dataProvider="{chart}" direction="horizontal" />

    <mx:LineChart id="chart" dataProvider="{salesByQuarter.quarter}"
        width="300" height="250">
        <mx:series>
            <mx:LineSeries form="curve"
```

```
          yField="dougSales" displayName="Doug" />
      <mx:LineSeries form="curve"
          yField="deepaSales" displayName="Deepa" />
    </mx:series>

    <mx:horizontalAxis>
      <mx:CategoryAxis categoryField="name" />
    </mx:horizontalAxis>
  </mx:LineChart>

</mx:Application>
```

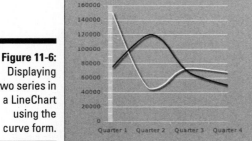

Figure 11-6:
Displaying
two series in
a LineChart
using the
curve form.

The default LineChart adds a drop shadow to each series in the chart. You can remove this shadow by setting the `seriesFilters` property of the LineChart. The following code sets the `seriesFilters` to an empty Array, which removes the shadow:

```
<mx:LineChart>
    <mx:seriesFilters>
       <mx:Array />
    </mx:seriesFilters>
    <mx:series>
       <mx:LineSeries xField="x" yField="y" />
    </mx:series>
</mx:LineChart>
```

AreaChart

An AreaChart is similar to a LineChart, except that each series is typically rendered as a solid area rather than as a line. One important difference, however, is that area charts support stacking, just as column and bar charts do (see the earlier section "Stacking"). By setting the `type` property of the

AreaChart to either `stacked` or `100%`, you can stack multiple-area series. You can use the following code to modify Listing 11-3 to use an AreaChart with an AreaSeries:

```
<mx:AreaChart id="chart" dataProvider="{salesByQuarter.quarter}"
    type="stacked"
    width="300" height="250">
    <mx:series>
        <mx:AreaSeries form="curve"
            yField="dougSales" displayName="Doug" />
        <mx:AreaSeries form="curve"
            yField="deepaSales" displayName="Deepa" />
    </mx:series>

    <mx:horizontalAxis>
        <mx:CategoryAxis categoryField="name" />
    </mx:horizontalAxis>
</mx:AreaChart>
```

The resulting chart is shown in Figure 11-7.

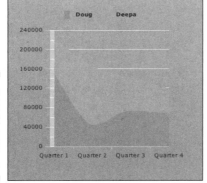

Figure 11-7:
A stacked
AreaChart
displaying
two curved
series.

Making a PieChart

PieChart is the only chart type that doesn't use an x and y axis to plot data. Instead, the data of a pie chart is drawn as wedges in a pie. The PieChart uses a PieSeries data series to populate its data. The only major difference between using a data provider with a pie chart versus the other chart types is that a pie chart uses only a single field of your data items to draw the wedge sizes. When you use the other types of charts that have an x axis and y axis, you need to specify which fields should be used for each axis. Because PieChart uses only a single field, this task is simplified by using a single field property on each PieSeries you create.

Going the simple route

To create a simple pie chart with a single series, you set the series of the PieChart to a PieSeries object pointing to the proper data provider for the chart, as in Listing 11-4. The resulting PieChart is shown in Figure 11-8.

Listing 11-4: Creating a Basic PieChart

```
<?xml version="1.0" encoding="utf-8"?>
<mx:Application xmlns:mx="http://www.adobe.com/2006/mxml">

    <mx:Model id="demographicData">
        <demographics>
            <gender name="Male" count="25" />
            <gender name="Female" count="34" />
        </demographics>
    </mx:Model>

    <mx:PieChart dataProvider="{demographicData.gender}">
        <mx:series>
            <mx:PieSeries field="count" labelField="name"
                labelPosition="inside" />
        </mx:series>
    </mx:PieChart>

</mx:Application>
```

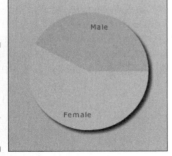

Figure 11-8:
Using a PieChart to show break-down by gender.

Notice these important points about Listing 11-4:

- ✔ field: The PieSeries you create has the field property set to count, which uses the count of each gender entry in the Model to size the pie wedges.

- ✔ labelField: You set the labelField property to name, which in this case is either "Male" or "Female." The labelField is used when labels are displayed for the wedges.

✔ labelPosition: You specify a labelPosition of inside, which draws the labels within the pie wedges. For a PieChart, you can specify various label positions by setting labelPosition to callout, inside, insideWithCallout, none, or outside. Some labelPosition options are shown in Figure 11-9.

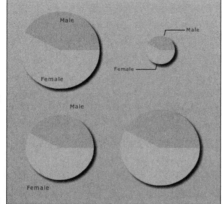

Figure 11-9:
Using the various label positions of the PieChart.

Doing a donut shape

You can create donut-shaped pie charts by using the innerRadius style of the PieChart. If you specify a value for innerRadius, the chart is rendered as a ring around a hole in the center. The value you specify for inner Radius represents a percentage of the entire circle, ranging from 0 to 1 (which equates to 100 percent). The example in Listing 11-5 creates a pie chart showing the breakdown of donut sales, with an innerRadius of 30 percent of the total pie chart radius. The chart that's created is shown in Figure 11-10.

Listing 11-5:   Using the innerRadius Property

```
<?xml version="1.0" encoding="utf-8"?>
<mx:Application xmlns:mx="http://www.adobe.com/2006/mxml">

    <mx:Model id="donutSales">
        <donuts>
            <donut type="Jelly Donut" numberSold="12" />
            <donut type="Bear Claw" numberSold="7" />
            <donut type="Chocolate Donut" numberSold="9" />
        </donuts>
    </mx:Model>

    <mx:PieChart innerRadius=".3"
            dataProvider="{donutSales.donut}" >
```

```
        <mx:series>
            <mx:PieSeries field="numberSold"
              labelField="type" labelPosition="outside" />
        </mx:series>
    </mx:PieChart>

</mx:Application>
```

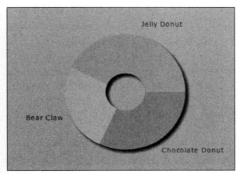

Figure 11-10:
Using the inner Radius style of a PieChart to create a donut chart.

Exploding wedges

You can customize the look of your pie charts by "exploding" wedges. An exploded wedge doesn't self-destruct; it simply sets itself apart a bit by sliding out from the whole pie chart. To customize the exploded wedges in a PieChart, you can set one of these properties on the PieSeries:

- explodeRadius: Explodes all wedges by an equal amount, which creates some spacing around each wedge. The values can range from 0 to 1, which indicates a percentage of the total pie chart radius that will be used to offset the wedge.

- perWedgeExplodeRadius: Gives you finer control over wedge placement by letting you specify different values for individual pie wedges. When you specify a value for the perWedgeExplodeRadius property, you use an Array of values, each ranging from 0 to 1, that corresponds with the data in your data provider. Ensure that the order of the explode radii in your Array matches the order of the data in the data provider.

By specifying the Array [0, 0, .3, 0] for perWedgeExplodeRadius in Listing 11-6, you tell the chart that the third wedge, which corresponds with Darron's sales, should be exploded out 30 percent of the pie chart's total radius. The resulting pie chart is shown in Figure 11-11.

Listing 11-6: Using the perWedgeExplodeRadius Property

```
<?xml version="1.0" encoding="utf-8"?>
<mx:Application xmlns:mx="http://www.adobe.com/2006/mxml">
    <mx:Model id="salesByEmployee">
        <employees>
            <employee name="Doug" sales="150000" />
            <employee name="Deepa" sales="75000" />
            <employee name="Darron" sales="30000" />
            <employee name="Ben" sales="60000" />
        </employees>
    </mx:Model>

    <mx:PieChart width="300" height="300" >
        <mx:series>
            <mx:PieSeries
                perWedgeExplodeRadius="{[0,0,.3,0]}"
                dataProvider="{salesByEmployee.
                employee}" field="sales" labelField="name"
                labelPosition="callout" />
        </mx:series>
    </mx:PieChart>

</mx:Application>
```

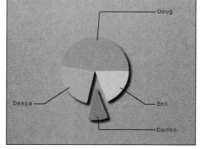

Figure 11-11:
Exploding
an individual
wedge of a
PieChart.

The values in the `perWedgeExplodeRadius` property are independent of the data in the data provider. If you set `perWedgeExplodeRadius` to explode out a particular wedge and you then update the underlying data in the data provider, `perWedgeExplodeRadius` is still set to its original setting. To illustrate this issue, imagine that a data provider originally has six items, you explode the fourth item, and then you remove the third item. After the removal of the third item, the `perWedgeExplodeRadius` still indicates that the fourth item is supposed to be exploded, so a different wedge than you originally intended is exploded. Keep this concept in mind so that the data in your chart and the explode settings for the data stay synchronized.

Building a PlotChart and a BubbleChart

The PlotChart is similar to the LineChart and AreaChart (both described earlier in this chapter) in that it plots one or more data series as a collection of points along the x and y axes. The PlotChart, however, renders the data points as individual, unconnected markers and uses different marker shapes to represent the unique data series. The PlotChart renders your first data series as diamond markers, the second series as circle markers, and the third series as square markers, as shown in Figure 11-12. If you have more than three series in a chart, the markers start over with the diamond marker, and the color of each series continues to change.

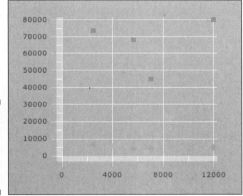

Figure 11-12:
Using the
PlotChart to
plot multiple
data series.

The PlotChart uses both the `xField` and the `yField` of a PlotSeries to determine the position of each data point. Therefore, you should specify both `xField` and `yField` and ensure that your data provider has the appropriate fields for plotting the data.

The BubbleChart is similar to the other charts, except that it adds another visualized data field to each data series. You can think of the BubbleChart as a PlotChart that draws circles of different sizes for each data point. In a BubbleChart, your data should have x and y coordinates, just like in the PlotChart, but it should also have an additional field that is used to determine the size of the bubble marker. So, you define not only the `xField` and `yField` properties but also `radiusField`. The BubbleChart ensures that all bubble markers are sized correctly relative to each another based on the value of `radiusField` for each data point.

The example in Listing 11-7 defines a Model that contains quarterly sales data. However, unlike any of the previous examples, you now have an additional field for profit. In the resulting chart, shown in Figure 11-13, the x axis represents the financial quarter, the y axis represents the sales for that quarter, and the size of the bubble marker represents that quarter's profit.

Listing 11-7: Creating a BubbleChart

```xml
<?xml version="1.0" encoding="utf-8"?>
<mx:Application xmlns:mx="http://www.adobe.com/2006/mxml">

    <mx:Model id="salesByQuarter">
        <quarters>
            <quarter name="Q1" sales="80000" profit="5000" />
            <quarter name="Q2" sales="45000" profit="4500" />
            <quarter name="Q3" sales="73500" profit="6700" />
            <quarter name="Q4" sales="68000" profit="4000" />
        </quarters>
    </mx:Model>

    <mx:BubbleChart id="chart" width="400" height="250"
        dataProvider="{salesByQuarter.quarter}"
        maxRadius="20">
        <mx:series>
            <mx:BubbleSeries xField="name" yField="sales"
                radiusField="profit"/>
        </mx:series>
        <mx:horizontalAxis>
            <mx:CategoryAxis categoryField="name" />
        </mx:horizontalAxis>
    </mx:BubbleChart>
</mx:Application>
```

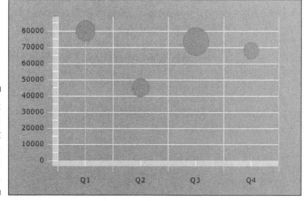

Figure 11-13: Using a BubbleChart to render a third data field.

Introducing the CandleStickChart and HLOCChart

Two charts in the Flex charting package are used for complex representations of financial data: CandleStickChart and HLOCChart. HLOC, which stands for High Low Open Close, refers to the high, low, opening, and closing values of financial stocks; you can see an example of this chart type in Figure 11-14. Because of the complex nature of these types of charts, we don't discuss them here. Just remember that if you need to present stock market data in your Flex application, these two chart types are the ones to explore. For more information about them, refer to the Flex documentation.

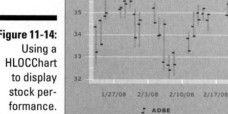

Figure 11-14:
Using a
HLOCChart
to display
stock per-
formance.

Working with Axes

Most chart types, with the exception of the PieChart, use x and y axes to plot data. You can control the layout of the axes and the chart itself by using different kinds of axes: CategoryAxis, LinearAxis, LogAxis, and DateTimeAxis.

Listing 11-2, earlier in this chapter, shows how you can use the CategoryAxis, which is typically used when values along an axis are nonnumeric values. In this chart of sales per employee, the x axis displays the name of the employee because you use a CategoryAxis and set the `categoryField` to the proper field on the data provider, which is `name`:

```
<mx:horizontalAxis>
   <mx:CategoryAxis id="xAxis" categoryField="name" />
</mx:horizontalAxis>
```

When the field you're displaying in the axis is a numeric field, however, you use one of the numeric axes:

✔ **LinearAxis, LogAxis:** Designed to work with ordered numbers and automatically plot your data on the chart in the correct order. (Both axes are shown in Figure 11-15.) LinearAxis creates an axis that ranges from the minimum value to the maximum value in equally spaced increments. For some data sets, however, plotting data on a logarithmic scale is more useful, which you can do with LogAxis. It makes the distance between tick marks on the low end of the scale greater than on the high end.

✔ **DateTimeAxis:** Appropriately named and should be used when working with data that occurs through time. The DateTimeAxis handles the details, such as formatting labels for the axis based on the total time range. If the data provider of your chart has a field that's an actual ActionScript Date object, the DateTimeAxis easily understands the data. If not, it attempts to parse the field you specify and determine the Date value itself.

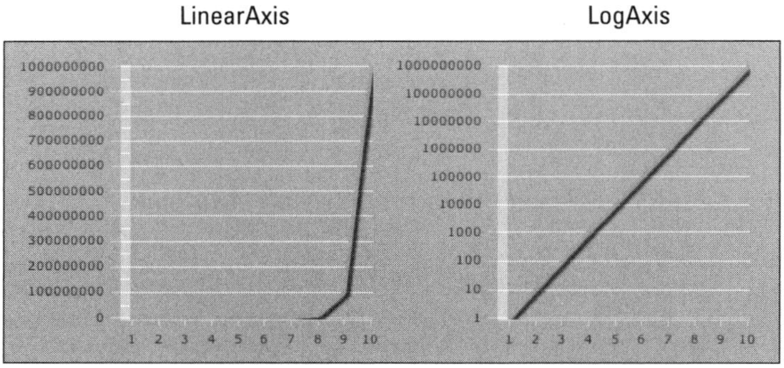

Figure 11-15: Comparing the same data set by using a LinearAxis and a LogAxis.

Listing 11-8 provides a Model that contains a date field that will be used for the x axis. The data in the model, however, is simply a text representation of a Date. The DateTimeAxis automatically parses it and converts it to a proper Date object for use in the axis. The resulting chart is shown in Figure 11-16.

Listing 11-8: Using the DateTimeAxis

```
<?xml version="1.0" encoding="utf-8"?>
<mx:Application xmlns:mx="http://www.adobe.com/2006/mxml">
    <mx:Model id="salesByMonth">
        <data>
            <month date="01/01/2008" sales="30400" />
            <month date="02/01/2008" sales="28000" />
            <month date="03/01/2008" sales="75000" />
            <month date="04/01/2008" sales="120000" />
```

```
                <month date="05/01/2008" sales="110000" />
                <month date="06/01/2008" sales="80500" />
                <month date="07/01/2008" sales="65000" />
                <month date="08/01/2008" sales="100000" />
                <month date="09/01/2008" sales="125000" />
                <month date="10/01/2008" sales="105400" />
                <month date="11/01/2008" sales="95000" />
                <month date="12/01/2008" sales="70000" />
            </data>
        </mx:Model>

        <mx:AreaChart dataProvider="{salesByMonth.month}" width="400" height="250">
            <mx:series>
                <mx:AreaSeries xField="date" yField="sales" />
            </mx:series>
            <mx:horizontalAxis>
                <mx:DateTimeAxis id="xAxis" displayLocalTime="true" />
            </mx:horizontalAxis>
            <mx:horizontalAxisRenderers>
                <mx:AxisRenderer axis="{xAxis}" canStagger="true" canDropLabels="false"
                    />
            </mx:horizontalAxisRenderers>
        </mx:AreaChart>

    </mx:Application>
```

If you have more complex date strings in your model that the DateTimeAxis can't automatically parse, you can use the `parseFunction` property, which should be set to a custom function you define. Your function should take the data field from your model and return a proper Date representation of that value. You can then do whatever complex parsing you need in order to convert your data for use in the DateTimeAxis.

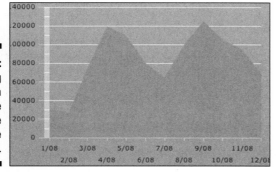

Figure 11-16: Displaying data through time by using the DateTime Axis.

Adding Legends to Your Charts

Each chart in the Flex framework supports adding a legend to display the name and color of each series in the chart. You can add the Legend control to your application by using the `<mx:Legend />` MXML tag. Each legend you create should be linked to a specific chart by setting the `dataProvider` property of the Legend control to a chart instance. The chart and legend handle the rest, and each series you include in your chart shows up with a marker indicating the color and a label in the Legend control.

You can control the direction in which the Legend control places the labels by setting the `direction` property, which can be either `vertical` or `horizontal`. Previous examples in this chapter use a horizontal Legend control to indicate which colors in the chart corresponded with which quarter's sales figures. You do so by adding the following line of MXML code to the application:

```
<mx:Legend dataProvider="{chart}"
    direction="horizontal" />
```

The Legend control uses the label specified as the `displayName` property of each series in the chart. Note that this property is different from the `label Field` or `name` properties of the series, so if you're having trouble making your legend show the correct names, ensure that you're setting the `display-Name` property of the series in your chart. In the examples in this section, you define the `displayName` of each series with the following MXML code lines:

```
<mx:ColumnSeries yField="salesQ1" displayName="Quarter 1" />
<mx:ColumnSeries yField="salesQ2" displayName="Quarter 2" />
```

Refer to Listing 11-3 to see how a Legend control is used to visually identify two data series.

Using a Legend control is more appropriate for some chart types than for others. If you're using a single series in a chart, the legend information is often unnecessary, such as in a ColumnChart or LineChart, because the chart is self-explanatory, assuming that some kind of title is provided. But after you add multiple series in a chart, each series is rendered in a different color, and the only way to distinguish between series is to use either rollover data tips or a Legend control.

The `PieChart` has added functionality to draw labels either within the wedges or by using callouts. By using the `labelPosition` property of the `PieChart`, you might be able to label your chart without needing to explicitly add a Legend control.

Adding Interactivity

You can use all charts in the Flex charting package to create complex interactions between the chart data. Fundamentally, each data item dispatches mouse events, whether the item is rendered as a bar in a BarChart or as a wedge in a PieChart. The events that are dispatched are slightly different from normal MouseEvents. When a user rolls over or clicks the data displayed in a chart, or has any other mouse interaction with the data, a ChartItemEvent is dispatched that contains details about the underlying chart and chart data.

When your mouse handler receives notification of a ChartItemEvent, you can access the `hitData` property of the event, which is a HitData object that contains details about the item with which the user interacted. If the multiple items were affected, the `hitSet` property of the ChartItemEvent contains an Array of HitData objects. After you have a reference to a HitData object, you can use the `item` property to access the underlying data item from the data provider.

Mouse events and chart item events aren't the same events. Because charts are normal Flex components, they have their own mouse events, and you can add typical mouse listeners on charts, such as `click`, `mouseDown`, and `mouseUp`. But these events aren't the item click events that tell you about specific mouse interactions on chart items. For chart item interactions, make sure to use ChartItemEvent events, such as `itemClick`, `itemMouseDown`, and `itemMouseUp`. If you're wondering why you aren't notified of chart data in your event handler, double-check that you're listening for the right events.

In addition to dispatching mouse events for each item in the chart, the Flex chart controls also have built-in functionality to let users select specific chart items. The charts all have a `selectionMode` property that can be set to `none`, `single`, or `multiple`. If you set `selectionMode` to either `single` or `multiple`, you enable item selection in that chart. After the user selects an item in the chart, the chart dispatches a `change` event to notify you. You can then access selected items by using the `selectedItem` or `selectedItems` properties of the chart.

The example in Listing 11-9 sets the `selectionMode` of the chart to `single` and displays an Alert notification when an item is selected.

Listing 11-9: Creating Interactive Charts

```
<?xml version="1.0" encoding="utf-8"?>
<mx:Application xmlns:mx="http://www.adobe.com/2006/mxml">
  <mx:Script>
```

(continued)

Listing 11-9 *(continued)*

```
    <![CDATA[
      import mx.controls.Alert;
      import mx.charts.events.ChartItemEvent;

      private function itemClickHandler(event:ChartItemEvent):void {
        var item:Object = chart.selectedChartItem.item;

        Alert.show("You selected: " + item.name, "Employee Selected");
      }
    ]]>
  </mx:Script>

  <mx:Model id="salesByEmployee">
    <employees>
      <employee name="Doug" salesQ1="150000" />
      <employee name="Deepa" salesQ1="75000" />
    </employees>
  </mx:Model>

  <mx:ColumnChart id="chart" dataProvider="{salesByEmployee.employee}"
    change="itemClickHandler(event)" selectionMode="single"
    width="300" height="300">
    <mx:series>
      <mx:ColumnSeries yField="salesQ1" />
    </mx:series>
    <mx:horizontalAxis>
      <mx:CategoryAxis categoryField="name" />
    </mx:horizontalAxis>
  </mx:ColumnChart>
</mx:Application>
```

Animating Your Charts

After you discover how to create attractive-looking charts, you can make
them "move," to add extra punch to your application. The Flex charting components support animation through the use of these three effects:

✔ **SeriesSlide:** Slides new data in and out of the chart as it is added or
  removed

✔ **SeriesZoom:** Zooms each data renderer in or out, depending on whether
  you're showing or hiding the data in the chart

✔ **SeriesInterpolate:** Animates the data from one location to another as
  the data is updated

You apply these effects individually to each series you want to animate by
setting either the `showDataEffect` or the `hideDataEffect` on the series.

The first two effects, SeriesSlide and SeriesZoom, can be applied when the data is either shown or hidden. When data is *shown,* it means that the data in the data provider for the series gets set. The data is hidden every time the data provider is changed for that series. If you swap data providers or update values within the data provider, the old data is first hidden, and then the new data is shown. The SeriesInterpolate effect, unlike SeriesSlide and SeriesZoom, can be applied only when the data is shown.

The example in Listing 11-10 allows the user to select a quarter's sales data to show. The ColumnSeries has a SeriesSlide effect applied to the `hide` `DataEffect` so that the columns slide down when hiding the data. A second SeriesSlide effect slides the data up when it's being shown.

Listing 11-10: Sliding Data In and Out

```
<?xml version="1.0" encoding="utf-8"?>
<mx:Application xmlns:mx="http://www.adobe.com/2006/mxml">

   <mx:Script>
      <![CDATA[
         import mx.events.ItemClickEvent;

         private function toggleButtonSelected(event:ItemClickEvent):void {
            if(event.index == 0) {
               series.yField = "salesQ1";
            }
            else {
               series.yField = "salesQ2";
            }
         }
      ]]>
   </mx:Script>

   <mx:Model id="salesByEmployee">
      <employees>
         <employee name="Doug"   salesQ1="150000" salesQ2="45000"  />
         <employee name="Deepa"   salesQ1="75000"  salesQ2="120000" />
         <employee name="Darron" salesQ1="30000"  salesQ2="85000"  />
         <employee name="Ben"    salesQ1="60000"  salesQ2="70000"  />
      </employees>
   </mx:Model>

   <mx:ToggleButtonBar dataProvider="{['Quarter 1', 'Quarter 2']}"
      itemClick="toggleButtonSelected(event)" />

   <mx:ColumnChart dataProvider="{salesByEmployee.employee}"
      width="300" height="250">

      <mx:series>
```

(continued)

Listing 11-10 *(continued)*

```
        <mx:ColumnSeries id="series" yField="salesQ1" >
            <mx:hideDataEffect>
                <mx:SeriesSlide direction="down" />
            </mx:hideDataEffect>
            <mx:showDataEffect>
                <mx:SeriesSlide direction="up" />
            </mx:showDataEffect>
        </mx:ColumnSeries>
    </mx:series>

    <mx:horizontalAxis>
        <mx:CategoryAxis id="xAxis" categoryField="name" />
    </mx:horizontalAxis>

    </mx:ColumnChart>

</mx:Application>
```

By using two SeriesSlide effects, you can achieve a fluid transition that clears the chart and animates your new data as it moves into place. The previous example makes the first data set slide down and out of view before sliding the new data set into view. You can also simply animate the data directly from the first data set to the second data set by using the SeriesInterpolate effect. This effect is helpful when you apply it as the `showDataEffect` of any of the chart types for an easy way to create smooth data transitions. You would have to modify the previous example only slightly in order to use the SeriesInterpolate effect:

```
<mx:ColumnSeries id="series" yField="salesQ1" >
    <mx:showDataEffect>
        <mx:SeriesInterpolate />
    </mx:showDataEffect>
</mx:ColumnSeries>
```

Tying It Together

The example in Listing 11-11 uses the concepts discussed in this chapter to create an interactive, animated charting dashboard. The example first presents a pie chart with total yearly sales per employee. The user can select an individual pie wedge in the chart, which explodes that wedge to highlight the data and to load a second chart with the quarterly breakdown for the selected employee, as shown in Figure 11-17.

Listing 11-11: An Interactive, Animated Charting Dashboard Application

```
<?xml version="1.0" encoding="utf-8"?>
<mx:Application xmlns:mx="http://www.adobe.com/2006/mxml"
   verticalAlign="middle" horizontalAlign="center">

   <mx:Script>
      <![CDATA[
         import mx.charts.chartClasses.IAxis;
         import mx.charts.HitData;
         import mx.formatters.CurrencyFormatter;
         import mx.charts.events.ChartItemEvent;
         import mx.charts.chartClasses.Series;

         private function calculateTotalSales(series:Series,          → 13
            item:Object, fieldName:String):Object {
            return  item.salesQ1 + item.salesQ2 + item.salesQ3 + item.salesQ4;
         }

         private function calculateTotalLabel(data:Object, field:String,   → 18
            index:Number, percentValue:Number):String {
            var totalSales:Number = data.salesQ1 + data.salesQ2
               + data.salesQ3 + data.salesQ4;

            var label:String = data.name + "\n";
            label += "Total sales: " + formatter.format(totalSales);

            return label;
         }

         private function pieChartClickHandler(event:ChartItemEvent):void {→ 29
            var item:Object = event.hitData.item;
            var index:int = event.hitData.chartItem.index;

            var explodeRadii:Array = new Array();
            for(var i:int=0; i<pieChart.dataProvider.length; i++) {
               if(i==index) {
                  explodeRadii.push(.3);
               }
               else {
                  explodeRadii.push(0);
               }
            }

            pieSeries.perWedgeExplodeRadius = explodeRadii;          → 43

            var individualSales:Array = new Array();                 → 45
            individualSales.push({quarter:"Q1", sales:item.salesQ1});
            individualSales.push({quarter:"Q2", sales:item.salesQ2});
            individualSales.push({quarter:"Q3", sales:item.salesQ3});
            individualSales.push({quarter:"Q4", sales:item.salesQ4});
```

(continued)

Listing 11-11 *(continued)*

```
            selectedEmployeeSales = individualSales;

            selectedName = item.name;
        }

        private function getWedgeDataTip(hitData:HitData):String {      → 56
            var item:Object = hitData.item;

            var tip:String = item.name + "\n";
            tip += "Q1: " + formatter.format(item.salesQ1) + "\n";
            tip += "Q2: " + formatter.format(item.salesQ2) + "\n";
            tip += "Q3: " + formatter.format(item.salesQ3) + "\n";
            tip += "Q4: " + formatter.format(item.salesQ4) + "\n";

            return tip;
        }

        private function getAxisLabel(labelValue:Object, previousValue:Object,
            axis:IAxis):String {
            return formatter.format(labelValue);                        → 70
        }

        [Bindable]
        private var selectedName:String;                                → 74

        [Bindable]
        private var selectedEmployeeSales:Object;                       → 77
    ]]>
</mx:Script>

<mx:Model id="salesByEmployee">                                        → 81
    <employees>
        <employee name="Doug" salesQ1="150000" salesQ2="45000"
            salesQ3="23500" salesQ4="6800" />
        <employee name="Deepa" salesQ1="75000" salesQ2="120000"
            salesQ3="67500" salesQ4="5000" />
        <employee name="Darron" salesQ1="30000" salesQ2="85000"
            salesQ3="12000" salesQ4="7000" />
        <employee name="Ben" salesQ1="60000" salesQ2="70000"
            salesQ3="90500" salesQ4="100000" />
    </employees>
</mx:Model>

<mx:CurrencyFormatter id="formatter" />                                 → 94

<mx:HBox width="100%" height="100%"
    verticalAlign="middle" horizontalAlign="center">

    <mx:Panel title="Yearly sales per employee" moveEffect="Move"
        width="100%" maxWidth="450" height="100%" maxHeight="450">
```

(continued)

Listing 11-11 *(continued)*

```
        <mx:PieChart id="pieChart" width="100%"
            dataProvider="{salesByEmployee.employee}"                    → 103
            showDataTips="true" dataTipFunction="getWedgeDataTip"        → 104
            itemClick="pieChartClickHandler(event)" >                    → 105

            <mx:series>
                <mx:PieSeries id="pieSeries" dataFunction="calculateTotalSales"
                    labelPosition="callout" labelFunction="calculateTotalLabel">
                    <mx:showDataEffect>
                        <mx:SeriesInterpolate />                         → 111
                    </mx:showDataEffect>
                </mx:PieSeries>
            </mx:series>

        </mx:PieChart>

    </mx:Panel>

    <mx:Panel title="Quarterly sales: {selectedName}"
        width="100%" height="100%" maxHeight="450" showEffect="Fade"
        includeInLayout="{selectedEmployeeSales != null}"
        visible="{selectedEmployeeSales != null}">                      → 123

        <mx:ColumnChart id="columnChart" width="100%" height="100%"
            dataProvider="{selectedEmployeeSales}">

            <mx:series>
                <mx:ColumnSeries yField="sales">                        → 129
                    <mx:showDataEffect>
                        <mx:SeriesInterpolate />                        → 131
                    </mx:showDataEffect>
                </mx:ColumnSeries>
            </mx:series>

            <mx:horizontalAxis>
                <mx:CategoryAxis id="xAxis" categoryField="quarter" />  → 137
            </mx:horizontalAxis>

            <mx:verticalAxis>
                <mx:LinearAxis labelFunction="getAxisLabel" />          → 141
            </mx:verticalAxis>

        </mx:ColumnChart>
    </mx:Panel>
  </mx:HBox>

</mx:Application>
```

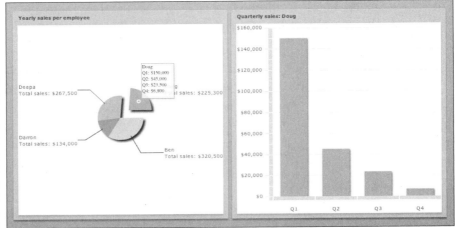

Figure 11-17:
The
interactive
chart
example
after an
employee
has been
selected.

This example is lengthy, but it highlights, all at one time, how to tie together multiple chart types, interactivity, and animation. Here's a breakdown of Listing 11-11:

→ **81**   You define a Model in MXML that drives both the PieChart and the ColumnChart in this application. This Model contains quarterly sales data for four employees.

→ **103**   You create a PieChart and set the `dataProvider` of the PieSeries to bind to the Model that's created on Line 81.

→ **108**   The PieChart displays the total sales per employee for the entire year, but the Model contains only individual quarterly sales figures. You define a `dataFunction` that returns the value that will be used to size the pie wedge. This function is defined on Line 13. Notice how the `calculateTotalSales` function adds each quarterly sales amount and returns the total. This is an alternative way, rather than specify a `field` property, of defining the size of the pie wedges.

→ **105**   You add a listener to listen for `itemClick` events. When the user clicks on a pie wedge, the `pieChartClickHandler` function on Line 29 is executed.

In the `pieChartClickHandler` function, you set the `per WedgeExplodeRadius` on Line 43, which tells the PieChart to explode the wedge that was selected, offsetting it from the rest of the pie wedges. You also create a new Array that acts as the data provider for the second chart that is shown after a pie wedge has been selected. Lines 45–51 create the new data provider and assign it to the `selectedEmployeeSales` variable.

→ **123** You bind the visibility of the Panel that contains the ColumnChart to the conditional statement `selectedEmployeeSales = null`, so after `selectedEmployeeSales` is set to anything other than null, this Panel is shown.

→ **131** When a new employee is selected, the ColumnChart animates the data because `showDataEffect` has been set to a SeriesInterpolate effect.

→ **141** Because the data in this chart shows sales in dollars, we use a custom function to return the labels that should be shown on the vertical axis. A custom `labelFunction` is defined to point to the `getAxisLabel` function, which is defined on Line 70. This function uses the CurrencyFormatter defined on Line 94, which produces labels such as `$1,000` rather than `1000`.

Part IV
Working with Data in Flex

In this part . . .

One of the most powerful features of Flex is its ability to create user interface controls that are driven by underlying data models. Data binding, covered in Chapter 12, makes it easy to link your UI components to the underlying data that your application is displaying. After you get used to using data binding to automatically populate MXML components, you won't be able to live without it. Then, in Chapter 13, we dive into the collection classes that you use to store and manipulate data in your applications. And, in Chapter 14, we show you how to pull in data from external sources using XML and Web services.

Chapter 12

The Power of Data Binding

*F*lex provides a very smart and robust mechanism for associating data contained in one object with another object. This association is called *data binding.* By using data binding, you can very simply pass data between different elements of your application without writing a lot of code. Because the data binding infrastructure is easy to use, requires little code, and is baked into all the Flex controls at a very low level, you can use data binding to invoke some powerful control over connecting the data in your application to the user interface controls.

Here are some examples of ways you might use data binding:

✔ To bind data from one Flex user interface control to another

✔ To bind data returned from a data service request, such as an HTTPService result, to user interface controls, such as a DataGrid control

This chapter explains how to add data binding into your applications. Data binding is one of the most powerful features of Flex, and you will surely use it often.

Understanding the Data Binding Expression

In data binding, you associate a certain property of a *source* object with a property of a *destination* object by creating a data binding expression. Key elements of this data binding expression include the source and destination properties:

✔ **Source property:** The property of the source object that contains the data that should be copied to the destination object

✔ **Destination property:** The property of the destination object that receives the copied data

When data binding copies data from the source property to the destination property, the data binding expression is said to *fire*. If the data from the source object gets successfully set on the destination object, the firing was successful; otherwise, your application encounters an error, and the data was not properly set.

You can create a data binding expression several different ways. Most often, you write a data binding expression in-line within an MXML tag. When data binding is expressed in MXML, you can easily recognize the data binding expression because it uses a special curly-brace syntax ({}) to create the binding. Most often, data binding occurs in MXML via the curly-brace syntax, but you can also create data binding expressions by using a special <mx:Binding/> MXML tag. We discuss all these mechanisms in this chapter.

Using Data Binding in MXML

You can create a data binding expressions within an MXML document very easily. The most common (and easiest) way to construct a data binding expression is by using the special data binding–specific curly-brace syntax: {}. You can also create data binding expressions in MXML by using the special <mx:Binding /> MXML tag. In the following sections, we discuss these two approaches.

Going curly: Creating data binding expressions in-line in MXML tags

You can use the special curly-brace syntax to create a data binding expression in-line within an MXML tag. By *in-line,* we mean that the curly-brace expression is used within the value of an attribute expressed in an MXML tag. The special curly-brace syntax tells the MXML compiler that a data binding expression has been created, and the MXML compiler generates some special ActionScript code behind the scenes so that the data binding expression can *fire* (pass data between a source and destination object) correctly.

To write a curly-brace-based data binding expression, you need to identify the source property and destination property. Take a look at the following example of a data binding expression:

```
<mx:TextInput id="userText" />
<mx:Label text="{userText.text}" />
```

This expression says that the Label control's text value should be whatever the user has typed into the userText TextInput control. The userText control acts as the source object, and the text property is the source property that will be automatically copied into the Label control's text property. The destination object is the Label control because that control gets its text from another object. The Label control's text property is the destination property because that property is getting its value from another control.

When you run this example in Flex Builder, whatever text you enter into the TextInput control appears, in real time, as the text in the Label control (see Figure 12-1). This text appears because the data binding expression successfully fires. Whenever the value of the source property changes (when userText.text changes), data binding copies the data from the source (userText.text) to the destination (the Label's text property).

Figure 12-1:
The text
entered
appears as
the Label
control's
text.

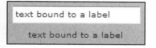

Creating data binding expressions with the <mx:Binding/> MXML tag

In addition to the curly-brace syntax (which we talk about in the preceding section), you can create data binding expressions within an MXML document by using the <mx:Binding/> tag. When you use the <mx:Binding /> tag, you explicitly define the source and destination properties as attributes in the tag, which are the only attributes that you need to set.

For both the source and destination of the Binding tag, you reference specific properties or variables that you are binding. You can use any property on any Flex control whose value can be read as the Binding tag's source property, and you can use any property on any Flex control whose value can be set as the Binding tag's destination property.

Take a look at the following example:

```
<mx:Binding source="userText.text" destination="labelText.
       text" />
<mx:TextInput id="userText" />
<mx:Label id="labelText" />
```

In this example, you create a data binding expression in which you bind the `labelText` Label control's `text` property to the text entered into the `userText` TextInput control. Whenever the value of the `source` property changes (`userText.text`), the data binding copies that value to the `destination` property (`labelText.text`).

If you run this example, while you type text into the TextInput control, the Flex Label control displays that text in real time.

Using ActionScript functions in the source of a data binding expression

The source and destination of a data binding expression can contain more than just properties. You can also invoke ActionScript methods on the data being passed into the destination object. For example, you may want to reformat the text of a label that is set with data binding. The following example shows how you can modify the text that the user enters into a TextInput control so that when the Label control displays that text, it's converted into uppercase letters. You simply call a method within your curly-brace expression:

```
<mx:TextInput id="userText" />
<mx:Label text="{userText.text.toUpperCase()}" />
```

Invoking ActionScript methods on the data being passed from the source to the destination lets you easily format the data, concatenate multiple pieces of text, or perform other calculations on the data without needing a separate block of ActionScript code. Because you can use ActionScript within the data binding curly braces, you can invoke any type of ActionScript method when you construct your binding.

You can also reference the return value from an ActionScript function in a data binding expression. For example, you can have a text user interface control display the return value of an ActionScript method that does some conditional evaluation. Just include the ActionScript method in the data binding expression. The following example shows this approach in action. Depending on the day of the week, the Label control displays Happy Weekday or Happy Weekend:

```
<mx:Script>
    <![CDATA[

    private function dayOfWeek():String
    {
        var date:Date = new Date();
        if ( (date.day >= 1) && (date.day <= 5) )
            return "Weekday"
        else return "Weekend";
    }
    ]]>
</mx:Script>

<mx:Label text="Today's date is Wednesday, May 28" />

<mx:Label text="{'Happy ' + dayOfWeek()}" />
```

The data binding expression in the preceding example (which configures the Label's `text` to display) concatenates `Happy` with the results of the `dayOfWeek` ActionScript method. Figure 12-2 shows the result.

Figure 12-2:
Using an
ActionScript
function
within data
binding.

Today's date is Wednesday, May 28

Happy Weekday

What Properties Support Data Binding?

For data binding to work in Flex, the source property needs to emit a property change event when its value changes. This event triggers the Flex data binding infrastructure to copy the new value from the source to the destination. If a property emits a change event (which means you can use it for data binding), the Flex documentation refers to it as a *bindable property*.

Most properties on Flex user interface controls are bindable properties. If a property is bindable, the ActionScript Flex Language Reference documentation that comes with Flex includes the statement "This property can be used as the source for data binding."

One of the most common uses for data binding is populating the data of a Flex list-based user interface control. (To find out more about the list-based controls available in Flex, check out Chapter 8.) Flex list-based controls have a `dataProvider` property that controls what data is displayed, and you can often most easily set this property by using a data binding expression because the dataProvider property is bindable. The following example shows how an ArrayCollection of state names is bound into the List control (see Figure 12-3):

```
<mx:ArrayCollection id="stateList">
    <mx:Array>
        <mx:String>California</mx:String>
        <mx:String>Arizona</mx:String>
        <mx:String>Nevada</mx:String>
        <mx:String>Washington</mx:String>
    </mx:Array>
</mx:ArrayCollection>

<mx:List width="200" dataProvider="{stateList}" />
```

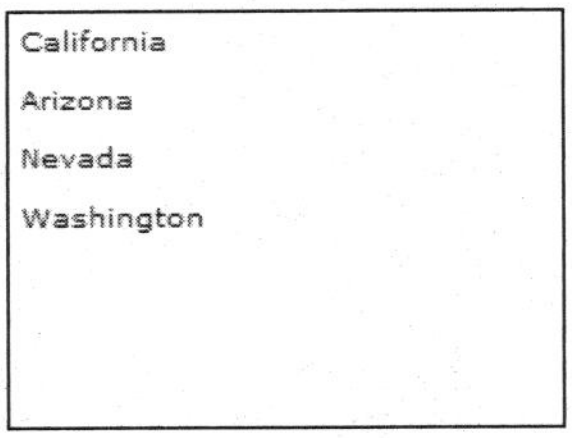

Figure 12-3:
Populate a
List control
with an
Array
Collection.

California

Arizona

Nevada

Washington

Moving Forward: Advanced Data Binding

After you understand the basics of Flex data binding (which we cover in the section "Using Data Binding in MXML," earlier in this chapter), you can move on to more advanced uses of data binding, such as binding a single source property to multiple destinations or multiple source properties to a single destination. Also, Flex developers often use two-way data binding expressions in which two expressions are used to keep two user interface controls synchronized. The following sections show how to construct these more advanced data binding expressions.

Binding to multiple destinations or sources

Often, certain data models drive the data that is displayed in several different user interface controls. In those cases, you may need to have data binding expressions in which a single source property is associated with multiple destinations. The following example shows how you can bind a source property to multiple destinations in a data binding expression that you create by using both the curly-brace syntax and the <mx:Binding/> MXML tag:

```
<mx:Model id="empModel">
    <employees>
        <name>Ellen O'Malley</name>
    </employees>
</mx:Model>

<mx:Label text="{empModel.name}" />
<mx:Label text="{empModel.name}" />
```

In this example, you have a data model that contains employee information. You have multiple destination objects — the different Label controls — that reference the employee data model in the data binding expression that drives what they display.

Now, rather than using the curly-brace syntax, create the same data binding expression by using the `<mx:Binding/>` MXML tag:

```
<mx:Model id="empModel">
    <employees>
        <name>Ellen O'Malley</name>
    </employees>
</mx:Model>

<mx:Binding source="empModel.name" destination="text1.
        text" />
<mx:Binding source="empModel.name" destination="text2.
        text" />

<mx:Label id="text1" />
<mx:Label id="text2" />
```

Both the preceding examples show how a single source property can drive the association of data in multiple destinations.

So, now that you understand how to bind a single source property into multiple destination properties, do the reverse. Setting up this type of data binding relationship is a little trickier. You can set up one of the data binding expressions by using the curly-brace syntax, but you must set up the subsequent binding expressions by using the `<mx:Binding />` tag.

In the following example, two data binding expressions bind the values of two different TextInput controls into a single Label control:

```
<mx:Binding source="text1.text" destination="myLabel.
        text"/>

<mx:TextInput id="text1" />
<mx:TextInput id="text2" />

<mx:Label id="myLabel" text="{text2.text}"/>
```

The two TextInput controls — text1 and text2 — act as the source objects, and the Label control's text property is the destination property for the binding expression. If the user enters text into text1, the data binding expression created by the <mx:Binding /> tag fires, and the Label control updates. If the user enters text into text2, the data binding expression created with the curly braces fires, and the Label control updates.

And *voilà* — by using this simple code, you create a data binding relationship in which multiple sources are bound to a single destination control.

Constructing a bidirectional data binding expression

In the data binding examples we've shown thus far in the chapter, the binding has all been one way. This means that you bind a source property to a destination property, and changes to the source property affect the destination property, but changes to the destination property don't affect the source property. Sometimes, you may want to construct a two-way data binding expression, in which the data binding goes both ways. The following example shows how to construct this type of expression:

```
<mx:TextInput id="text1" text="{text2.text}" />
<mx:TextInput id="text2" text="{text1.text}" />
```

In this example, you have two TextInput controls: text1 and text2. If the value of text1.text changes, that new value gets copied into the text property of text2. Similarly, if the value of text2.text changes, that new value gets copied into the text property of text1.

Bidirectional data binding expressions can sometimes get tricky and cause a *circular loop,* in which one event triggers a binding firing, which then emits its own event and triggers another binding firing, and so on and so forth. This infinite loop could freeze your Flex application and cause it to hang. But never fear, the Flex framework takes care of this for you. The Flex data binding infrastructure ensures that two-way data binding expressions don't create infinite loops by making sure the data binding expression is triggered only once when the source property is modified.

Debugging Data Binding Expressions

You may need to debug your data binding expression if, for example, the destination property didn't properly update. In the following list, we offer a few simple tips to ensure you set up your data binding expression correctly:

✔ **Pay attention to warnings that the MXML compiler in Flex Builder's code editor provides.** These warnings often appear in Flex Builder's Problems view. These warnings may indicate that the data binding expression will initially display correctly, but subsequent changes to the source property won't cause the destination property to update. You can resolve these warnings by adding the appropriate Bindable metadata, which is discussed in the "Using Bindable Metadata" section.

✔ **If your data binding expression isn't firing, make sure that the source property is actually changing.** If the source property doesn't change, the binding expression doesn't get triggered.

✔ **Use the Flex Builder debugger to test whether the event that triggers the binding fires.** Because data binding is an event-based mechanism, the event that triggers the source property to copy its data into the destination property needs to actually fire. Use the Flex Builder debugger to debug whether a call to dispatchEvent() actually gets invoked. dispatchEvent() is the code that gets run when an event is fired, so you can use the debugger to see whether the right event gets dispatched to trigger the binding.

Using Bindable Metadata

A certain bit of "magic" must happen to signal to Flex that a source property has changed and the new value needs to be copied to the destination. This magic happens by way of a piece of Flex metadata called Bindable.

Metadata is extra information added to ActionScript or MXML code to signal to the Flex compiler that some special processing needs to occur. Many types of metadata exist in Flex, and the Flex documentation lists these. In Flex, the *Bindable* metadata registers a property as being able to be a source property in a data binding expression to the Flex compiler. The Bindable metadata has the following form: [Bindable]. And you must add it in the following cases:

✔ Before a public, protected, or private property defined as a variable in order to signal to Flex that that property supports binding

✔ Before a public class definition

✔ Before a public, protected, or private property defined with a get or set method

For example, the following code produces a warning by the MXML compiler:

```
<mx:Script>
    <![CDATA[
        private var temp:String = "bindable";
    ]]>
</mx:Script>

<mx:Label text="{temp}"/>
```

The `temp` variable does not have the Bindable metadata so the Flex compiler does not know it can be used as a source property in the Label text's data binding expression. If you run this code in Flex Builder, the Problems pane shows the following warning:

```
Data binding will not be able to detect assignments to
          "temp"
```

To rectify this problem, simply add the Bindable metadata above the `temp` variable declaration like so:

```
<mx:Script>
    <![CDATA[
        [Bindable]
        private var temp:String = "bindable";
    ]]>
</mx:Script>
```

By doing this, the compilation warning and the warning in Flex Builder's Problems view will disappear.

Tying It Together: Building an Interactive Form with Data Binding

Listing 12-1 ties together the different ways that you can create data binding expressions so that data is customized for display. This simple example takes user-entered input and displays a friendly greeting. You create a data binding expression by using the curly-brace syntax to bind in property values and to invoke an ActionScript method for conditional display. The interactive form that this code creates is shown in Figure 12-4.

Listing 12-1: Multi-Part Data Binding Example

```
<?xml version="1.0" encoding="utf-8"?>
<mx:Application xmlns:mx="http://www.adobe.com/2006/mxml">

    <mx:Form>
        <mx:FormHeading label="User Information" />
            <mx:FormItem label="First Name">
                <mx:TextInput id="firstName" text="Lucy"/>                    → 7
            </mx:FormItem>
            <mx:FormItem label="Last Name">
                <mx:TextInput id="lastName" text="Pearson"/>                  → 10
            </mx:FormItem>
            <mx:FormItem label="Gender">
                <mx:RadioButton id="femaleBtn" label="Female" selected=
                "true"/>                                                      → 13
                <mx:RadioButton id="maleBtn" label="Male" />                 → 14
            </mx:FormItem>
    </mx:Form>

    <mx:Label text="Welcome to San Francisco {getGenderString(femaleBtn.
        selected)} {firstName.text} {lastName.text}" />                      → 18

    <mx:Script>
    <![CDATA[
    private function getGenderString(isFemale:Boolean):String               → 22
    {
        if (femaleBtn.selected)
            return "Ms.";
        else
            return "Mr.";
    }
    ]]>
    </mx:Script>
</mx:Application>
```

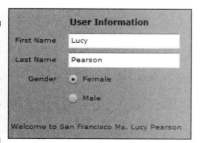

Figure 12-4:
Use data
binding to
customize
data for
display.

Here's an explanation of the example application in Listing 12-1:

→ **7** You create a TextInput control for the user to enter his or her first name.

→ **10** You create a second TextInput control for the user to enter his or her last name.

→ **13** You create RadioButton controls for the user to select his or her gender. You query the RadioButtons to see which button is selected so you can customize the text that is displayed.

→ **18** This is the meat of the example. On Line 18, you have a Label control that uses data binding to determine whether to show Ms. or Mr. in the greeting, based on the return value of the getGenderString function. Because you pass the value of femaleButton.selected to getGenderString, the binding will update and call the method whenever the RadioButton is changed. The next data binding expression binds to the text held in the firstName TextInput control, and the last data binding expression binds in the text held in the lastName TextInput control.

→ **22** The ActionScript function that is used in the data binding expression on Line 18 checks which gender was selected and returns the correct string to display (Mr. or Ms.).

In this example, you can see how you can use data binding by binding directly to property values as well as to the return value of an ActionScript function. This example also makes heavy use of forms, which we cover in Chapter 9.

Chapter 13

Working with Data Collections

*N*o matter how well you skin and style your Flex application, it needs data. Data is the engine behind every Flex application, and without data and data management techniques, a Flex application will most likely fail.

In this chapter, we cover functionality provided by Flex data collections, which you can use to manage your data. You can find out how to create Flex data collections, use them for uniform and easy access of data items, allow data collections to manage the updating of data items, and add sorting and filtering capabilities to modify the view of your data. All the Flex List controls are built to accept Flex data collections as a data source, which makes it a cinch to visualize data in Flex. If you're writing real-world, data-heavy Flex applications, you can find out some useful data management techniques in this chapter.

Why Use Flex Data Collections?

Flex uses data collections to manage sets of data so that user interface controls and your ActionScript code can access that data easily. Flex data collections offer a consistent and straightforward way to access, add, delete, or modify individual data items. All Flex List controls can accept Flex data collections as a data source, and those List controls can display the data collections and respond to changes to items in the data collection appropriately. If you use Flex data collections as the data provider for any of your Flex List controls, the List control always updates automatically if the underlying data changes.

Flex data collections wrap themselves around a data source. This data source contains the items that the Flex data collection exposes to the application so that the data collection can sort, filter, access, and modify those items. You can use two types of Flex data collections in the Flex framework:

✔ `mx.collections.ArrayCollection`: Use ActionScript Arrays as the data source

✔ `mx.collections.XMLListCollection`: Use ActionScript XML and XMLList objects as the data source

Usually, depending on what kind of data back-end you set up and what kind of objects that back-end returns, you can choose the type of Flex collection you would create pretty easily. If your data back-end request, such as a WebService or HTTPService call, returns an Array or Array-based data structure, you would create an ArrayCollection to manage that data because an ArrayCollection handles Array data well. Similarly, if your service call returns XML, you would create an XMLListCollection to manage that data set.

The rest of this chapter explains how to create Flex data collections, access individual data items, modify data items, and apply sorting and filtering capabilities to those data collections.

Creating ArrayCollections

You use ArrayCollections to represent and manipulate an ActionScript Array, which you can use as the data source for any Flex List control. You create an ArrayCollection from an ActionScript Array object, and the ArrayCollection wraps around the Array so that it can access, add to, delete, or modify the individual data items in the Array. The ArrayCollection can also sort or filter the individual data items in the Array. (Though the actual Array does not get sorted or filtered, the ArrayCollection presents a separate view of the sorted or filtered data items.)

You can create a Flex ArrayCollection in MXML by using the `<mx:ArrayCollection/>` tag or in ActionScript. You must set the `source` property on an ArrayCollection to an Array, and that Array is what the ArrayCollection wraps itself around.

Using MXML to create an ArrayCollection

The code in Listings 13-1 and 13-2 shows how to create an ArrayCollection that wraps an Array of data items representing different foods. Listing 13-1 shows how to create an ArrayCollection in MXML. In this example, the `source` property is bound to the `foods` Array.

Listing 13-1: An ArrayCollection in MXML

```
<mx:Array id="foods">
    <mx:Object name="Broccoli" type="Vegetable" />
    <mx:Object name="Apple" type="Fruit" />
    <mx:Object name="Orange" type="Fruit" />
    <mx:Object name="Beets" type="Vegetable" />
    <mx:Object name="Brussels Sprouts" type="Vegetable" />
</mx:Array>

<mx:ArrayCollection id="foodCollection" source="{foods}"
            />
```

Listing 13-2 shows how to create the same ArrayCollection without setting the `source` property explicitly. Instead, because the `source` property is the default property of an ArrayCollection, you can just create the `foods` Array as the first child of the ArrayCollection MXML tag, and the ArrayCollection uses that Array as the `source` data object. Listings 13-1 and 13-2 create identical ArrayCollections.

**Listing 13-2: An ArrayCollection in MXML without the Source
Property Explicitly Set**

```
<mx:ArrayCollection id="foodCollection">
    <mx:Array id="foods">
        <mx:Object name="Broccoli" type="Vegetable" />
        <mx:Object name="Apple" type="Fruit" />
        <mx:Object name="Orange" type="Fruit" />
        <mx:Object name="Beets" type="Vegetable" />
        <mx:Object name="Brussels Sprouts"
            type="Vegetable" />
    </mx:Array>
</mx:ArrayCollection>
```

Using ActionScript to create an ArrayCollection

In addition to creating ArrayCollections in MXML, you can create Array Collections in ActionScript. Listing 13-3 shows how to create an ArrayCollection in ActionScript by using the ArrayCollection constructor and passing in an ActionScript Array as the `source` data object for the collection. In this example, you first import the mx.collections.ArrayCollection class because it's not linked into the Flex application by default.

Listing 13-3: An ArrayCollection in ActionScript

```
import mx.collections.ArrayCollection;

private var foodCollection:ArrayCollection;
private var foods:Array =
    [{name:"Broccoli", type:"Vegetable"},
        {name:"Apple", type:"Fruit"},
        {name:"Orange", type:"Fruit"},
        {name:"Beets", type:"Vegetable"},
        {name:"Brussels Sprouts", type:"Vegetable"}];

private function createFoodCollection():void
{
    foodCollection = new ArrayCollection(foods);
}
```

You can create ArrayCollections in both MXML and ActionScript that you can use to display and interact with Array data.

Creating XMLListCollections

You use XMLListCollections to represent and manipulate an ActionScript XML or XMLList object, which you can use as the data provider for any Flex List control. (For more on XML and XMLList objects, refer to Chapter 8.) You can create an XMLListCollection from an ActionScript XMLList object, and the XMLListCollection wraps around the XMLList so that it can access, add to, delete, and modify data items from the XMLList. Additionally, an XMLListCollection can sort or filter the individual data items in the XMLList. (Although the XMLList itself is not sorted or filtered, instead the XMLListCollection provides a separate view of the sorted or filtered data.)

You can create a Flex XMLListCollection in MXML by using the `<mx:XMLListCollection/>` tag or in ActionScript. The key property to set is the `source` property, which identifies the XMLList that the newly created XMLListCollection should wrap.

Using MXML to create an XMLListCollection

The code in Listings 13-4 and 13-5 shows how to create an XMLListCollection that wraps an `XMLList` data object representing different foods. Listing 13-4 shows how to create an XMLListCollection in MXML. In this example, the `source` property is bound to the `foods` XMLList object.

Listing 13-4: An XML ListCollection in MXML

```
<mx:XMLList id="foods" xmlns="">
    <food name="Broccoli" type="Vegetable" />
    <food name="Apple" type="Fruit" />
    <food name="Orange" type="Fruit" />
    <food name="Beets" type="Vegetable" />
    <food name="Brussels Sprouts" type="Vegetable" />
</mx:XMLList>

<mx:XMLListCollection id="foodCollection" source="{foods}"
        />
```

Listing 13-5 shows how to create the XMLListCollection in Listing 13-4 without setting the `source` property explicitly. Instead, because the `source` property is the default property of an XMLListCollection, you can just create the `foods` XMLList object as the first child of the XMLListCollection MXML tag, and the XMLListCollection uses that XMLList object as the `source` data object. Listings 13-4 and 13-5 create identical XMLListCollections.

Listing 13-5: An XMLListCollection in MXML without the Source Property Explicitly Set

```
<mx:XMLListCollection id="foodCollection">
    <mx:XMLList id="foods" xmlns="">
        <food name="Broccoli" type="Vegetable" />
        <food name="Apple" type="Fruit" />
        <food name="Orange" type="Fruit" />
        <food name="Beets" type="Vegetable" />
        <food name="Brussels Sprouts" type="Vegetable" />
    </mx:XMLList>
</mx:XMLListCollection>
```

Using ActionScript to create an XMLListCollection

In addition to creating XMLListCollections in MXML, you can create them in ActionScript. Listing 13-6 shows how to create an XMLListCollection in ActionScript by using the XMLListCollection constructor and passing in an ActionScript XMLList as the `source` data object for the collection. In this example, you import the mx.collections.XMLListCollection class because that class isn't linked into the Flex application by default.

Additionally, when you create the `foodCollection` object with the `new` operator, you pass in an XMLList object that's represented by `foods.children()`. An XMLListCollection takes an XMLList object as its `source` data object. When you create an XMLListCollection from an XML ActionScript object, you must access the child elements of that XML object (which creates a new XMLList object) and pass that XMLList object as the source data object for the XMLListCollection.

Listing 13-6: An XMLListCollection in ActionScript

```
import mx.collections.XMLListCollection;

private var foodCollection:XMLListCollection;
private var foods:XML =
    <foods>
        <food name="Broccoli" type="Vegetable"/>
        <food name="Apple" type="Fruit"/>
        <food name="Orange" type="Fruit"/>
        <food name="Beets" type="Vegetable"/>
        <food name="Brussels Sprouts" type="Vegetable"/>
    </foods>;

private function createFoodCollection():void
{
    foodCollection = new XMLListCollection(foods.
        children());
}
```

You can create XMLListCollections in both MXML and ActionScript that you can use to display and modify XML data.

Common Collection Properties You Should Know

After you know how to create different Flex data collections, you need to get familiar with some of the common properties that can help you out when you need more information about your collection. Every Flex collection has a `length` property, which you can query for the number of data items contained in the collection. In the `foodCollection` examples in the preceding sections of this chapter, all the collections have a `length` value of 5 because each collection contains five food items.

Similarly, every Flex collection has a `sort` property, which lets you apply a native Flex `Sort` object to sort your collection numerically or alphabetically, and a `filterFunction` property, which lets you apply a function that filters your collection at runtime. The following section discusses both the sorting and filtering capabilities built into Flex data collections.

Sorting and Filtering Collections

Flex data collections allow you to sort and filter data items so that they can display a reordered subset of the main collection. When you sort or filter a Flex collection, you don't change the underlying data. Instead, the collection creates a view of that data which matches the sort or filter criterion. The following sections discuss how to sort and filter Flex collections in MXML and ActionScript.

Sorting Flex collections

A main `Sort` object, which defines what fields in the data items to sort and by what criterion, drives every Flex collection's sorting functionality. You need to understand how to create this `Sort` object, specify the fields, and customize the properties so that your data collection's sorting works correctly.

You set the `Sort` object needed to sort a data collection as the value of the collection's `sort` property. Every Flex collection has a `sort` property that takes a `Sort` object. After you specify the `Sort` object, you must set the `Sort` object's `fields` property to any number of `SortField` objects. A `SortField` object specifies which field in the individual data items the sorting functionality must be applied to. The `name` property on a `SortField` object governs this behavior. You must set the `name` property to the name of the field on each data item you want sorted.

In Listing 13-7, you create a `Sort` object with `SortField` objects, in which you specify the `name` field as the field in each data item that's actually sorted. You refer to the `name` field as `@ name` because `name` is an XML attribute (not a child node). The example binds the `foodCollection` data collection to a Flex List control so that you can see how the sorted collection looks. Because of the Sort object, the `foodCollection` sorts all the vegetable names alphabetically. Figure 13-1 shows how the sorted collection looks when it appears in a Flex List control.

Listing 13-7: Sorting a Collection by Name

```
<mx:XMLListCollection id="foodCollection">
    <mx:XMLList id="foods" xmlns="">
        <food name="Broccoli" type="Vegetable" />
        <food name="Apple" type="Fruit" />
        <food name="Orange" type="Fruit" />
        <food name="Beets" type="Vegetable" />
        <food name="Brussels Sprouts" type="Vegetable" />
    </mx:XMLList>
```

(continued)

Listing 13-7 *(continued)*

```
    <mx:sort>
        <mx:Sort>
            <mx:fields>
                <mx:SortField name="@name" />
            </mx:fields>
        </mx:Sort>
    </mx:sort>
</mx:XMLListCollection>

<mx:List dataProvider="{foodCollection}" labelField=
        "@name" />
```

Figure 13-1:
The food
collection
is sorted
alphabeti-
cally.

The SortField object has properties that you can set to customize the sort-ing functionality further. Here are a few examples:

- ✔ caseInsensitive: You can set the caseInsensitive property to true or false, depending on whether you want the Sort object to take case into account when it sorts data items. By default, the SortField.caseInsensitive property is set to false, meaning the Sort object doesn't take the case of the sorted data item into consideration.

- ✔ numeric: You can set the numeric property to control whether the field being sorted contains numeric values or string representations of numeric values. By default, the numeric property is set to false, meaning the Sort object sorts the field as if it's a string representation of numeric values. In this case, the Sort object evaluates the number 11 as a string as less than the number 9 as a string because 11 is a lower string value then 9. If the numeric property is set to true, the Sort object evaluates the field being sorted as a number. And, if the numeric prop-erty is set to a value of null, the Sort object evaluates the sort based on whether the first item is a number or string.

- ✔ descending: You can set the descending property to true or false to control whether the Sort object sorts the field in descending or ascending order. By default, descending is set to false, meaning the sorting occurs in an ascending order.

Filtering Flex collections

To filter Flex collections, you apply a function that determines whether each individual data item in the collection should be allowed into the filtered view. If the item is allowed, it appears in the resulting view after the data collection applies the `filter` function.

To apply a `filter` function to a Flex collection, simply set the property `filterFunction` to the name of an ActionScript function that you write to manage the filtering functionality. The ActionScript `filterFunction` method you write must follow a particular signature:

```
private function filter(item:Object):Boolean
```

So, the function you write, whatever you call it, must take an Object as its parameter and return a Boolean value. It returns `true` if the specified item should remain in the resulting collection or `false` if it should be filtered out of the resulting collection. This is the function you set as the value of the data collection's `filterFunction` property.

Listing 13-8 shows a filter applied to an ArrayCollection that represents a list of fruits and vegetables. The `filterFunction` method — `veggieFilter` — filters out all data items that have a Fruit type and allows the Vegetable-type foods to stay. Figure 13-2 shows what a List control displays when bound to the filtered data collection.

Listing 13-8: Applying a filterFunction Method That Filters Data in an ArrayCollection

```
<mx:Script>
   <![CDATA[

   private function veggieFilter(item:Object):Boolean
   {
       return String(item.type) == "Vegetable";
   }

   ]]>
</mx:Script>

<mx:ArrayCollection id="foodCollection"
         filterFunction="veggieFilter">
   <mx:Array id="foods">
       <mx:Object name="Broccoli" type="Vegetable" />
       <mx:Object name="Apple" type="Fruit" />
       <mx:Object name="Orange" type="Fruit" />
       <mx:Object name="Beets" type="Vegetable" />
```

(continued)

Listing 13-8 *(continued)*

```
        <mx:Object name="Brussels Sprouts" type="Vegetable"
                />
    </mx:Array>
</mx:ArrayCollection>

<mx:List dataProvider="{foodCollection}" labelField="name"
            />
```

Figure 13-2:
The food
collection
is filtered to
show only
vegetables.

Accessing Data Items

You will often need to access data items in your collections. Both of the collections classes, ArrayCollection and XMLListCollection, have a set of methods that you can use to get, add, and remove a data item. When you use these methods to modify the collection, the underlying source data object also gets affected. The following list covers some of the common ActionScript methods you will use to modify data in your data collections.

When you modify your data collection with the following methods, the underlying source object gets modified as well. So, if any other user interface controls are dependent on that source object for their data, be careful when adding, removing, and updating items in any data collection wrapping that source object.

- ✔ addItem(item:Object):void: Takes as its only parameter the object you want added to the data collection. This method adds the object to the end of the data collection, thus increasing the length of the collection by 1.

- ✔ addItemAt(item:Object, index:int):void: Takes as its parameters the object you want added to the data collection as well as the zero-based index of where that item should be added. For example, to add a new item into the third position of a collection with five data items, the index value would be 2.

- ✔ getItemAt(index:int):Object: Returns the object found at the zero-based index parameter passed in. In a collection with five data

items, passing an index value of 2 to a `getItemAt` call will return the
data item in the third position.

✔ `getItemIndex(item:Object):int`: Returns the zero-based index of
the item that is passed in as a parameter to the method.

✔ `removeAll():void`: Removes all the data items from a data collection. It
essentially empties the data collection, and the collection length is set to 0.

✔ `removeItemAt(index:int):Object`: Removes an item from the data
collection at the specified index. All data items after the removed item
have their index decreased by 1 to account for the removal.

✔ `setItemAt(item:Object, index:int):Object`: Places the item
passed in as the first parameter at the index specified by the second
parameter. If a data item already lives at that index, the new item
replaces it.

You can use the code in Listing 13-9 to add and remove an item in the data
collection. If you run this code, you can see how as the data collection is
modified by these methods, the List control that is displaying the contents of
the data collection updates automatically.

Listing 13-9: Modifying a Data Collection with Collection Methods

```
<?xml version="1.0" encoding="utf-8"?>
<mx:Application xmlns:mx=http://www.adobe.com/2006/mxml"
        layout="vertical">

<mx:ArrayCollection id="foodCollection">
    <mx:Array id="foods">
        <mx:Object name="Broccoli" type="Vegetable" />
        <mx:Object name="Apple" type="Fruit" />
        <mx:Object name="Orange" type="Fruit" />
        <mx:Object name="Beets" type="Vegetable" />
        <mx:Object name="Brussels Sprouts"
            type="Vegetable" />
    </mx:Array>
</mx:ArrayCollection>

<mx:Object id="banana" name="Banana" type="Fruit" />

<mx:Button label="Add a Banana" click="foodCollection.
        addItemAt(banana, 2);" />
<mx:Button label="Remove a Banana" click="foodCollection.
        removeItemAt(2);" />

<mx:List dataProvider="{foodCollection}" labelField="name"
        />

</mx:Application>
```

Chapter 14

Working with Remote Data

· ·

In This Chapter

▶ Loading XML data into your application

▶ Using external APIs to load data

▶ Using Web services

▶ Understanding AMF remoting

· ·

Choosing Flex for your front-end user interface doesn't lock you into any particular back-end application server technology. Flex applications can talk to any back-end technology that can produce XML, JSON, plain text, or pretty much anything else a Web server can output, which means that you can connect your Flex applications to almost any server technology you run across, such as PHP, .NET, ColdFusion, Java, or Ruby on Rails.

Because you can choose any server technology to power your Flex application, you can also use any database you want, such as MySQL, Oracle, Microsoft SQL Server, or PostgreSQL. Your Flex application doesn't communicate directly with these database products, but instead always talks to the application server.

This chapter explains how to consume data from a Web server, regardless of which back-end technology you might be using. A discussion of specific back-end server languages is outside the scope of this book, so we don't provide server-side code examples.

Connecting with HTTP

The simplest, and often most appropriate, method for loading data into your application is to use HTTPService class in the Flex framework to load XML data using HTTP, which is the standard transfer protocol for Web pages. You use the HTTPService class to load text data from a Web server. This data can be a simple text string, a JSON-encoded string, XML, or any other type of formatted text. Because XML is probably the most common method for transmitting data, the examples in this section focus on loading XML data.

Loading your own XML file

Say that you've been tracking how much money various people owe you so that you can remember to bug the friends who owe you money (and so that you can avoid those whom you owe). You use an XML file to keep tabs on all the debts, and the XML file looks similar to Listing 14-1.

Listing 14-1: An XML File

```
<?xml version="1.0" encoding="utf-8"?>
<debts>
    <person name="Eliah" amount="1200" />
    <person name="Russ" amount="500" />
    <person name="Jocelyn" amount="-300" />
    <person name="David" amount="100" />
    <person name="Jonas" amount="50" />
    <person name="IRS" amount="-50000" />
</debts>
```

The data is stored in a file named `debts.xml`. You load the XML file by creating the HTTPService tag in your application and setting the `url` property, as shown in Listing 14-2.

Listing 14-2: Loading the XML File

```
<?xml version="1.0" encoding="utf-8"?>
<mx:Application xmlns:mx="http://www.adobe.com/2006/mxml"
    creationComplete="service.send()">

    <mx:HTTPService id="service" url="debts.xml"/>

</mx:Application>
```

In Listing 14-2, you create HTTPService and point it to the `debts.xml` file. It uses a relative URL, so the `debts.xml` file needs to be deployed in the same directory as the SWF file when you put it on a server. You can use either a relative or absolute URL when you specify the `url` property.

The sample application in Listing 14-2 creates a new HTTPService by using MXML and calls the `send()` method on that service when the application has completed loading by using the `creationComplete` event of the application.

HTTPService can return results in a variety of formats, which changes how you access the data in the returned result. You can set the `resultFormat` property of the HTTPService to any of the following values: `object`, `array`, `xml`, `flashvars`, `text`, or `e4x`. Changing `resultFormat` changes the format and structure of the data that's returned. The default value is `object`, which converts XML to a hierarchical list of ActionScript objects. If you change the `resultFormat` property, the underlying data is still the same, but the way you access that data in your application is slightly different. In this chapter, we stick with the default `object` format.

Listing 14-2 creates a new HTTPService object and calls the `send()` method to load the XML file, but it doesn't do anything with that data after it loads. Listing 14-3 adds a DataGrid to that simple example to display the data, showing the name of the person who owes you money in one column and the amount of the debt in another (see Figure 14-1).

Listing 14-3: Adding a DataGrid to Display the Data

```
<?xml version="1.0" encoding="utf-8"?>
<mx:Application xmlns:mx="http://www.adobe.com/2006/mxml"
    creationComplete="service.send()">

    <mx:HTTPService id="service" url="debts.xml" />

    <mx:DataGrid dataProvider="{service.lastResult.debts.person}" >
        <mx:columns>
            <mx:DataGridColumn dataField="name" headerText="Name" />
            <mx:DataGridColumn headerText="Debt">
                <mx:itemRenderer>
                    <mx:Component>
                        <mx:Canvas backgroundColor="0xff0000"
                            backgroundAlpha="{data.amount > 0 ? 0 : .5}">

                            <mx:Label text="{formatter.format(data.amount)}" />

                            <mx:CurrencyFormatter id="formatter" />
                        </mx:Canvas>
                    </mx:Component>
                </mx:itemRenderer>
            </mx:DataGridColumn>
        </mx:columns>
    </mx:DataGrid>
</mx:Application>
```

Figure 14-1:
The results
of an HTTP
Service
call in a
DataGrid.

Name	Debt
Eliah	$1,200
Russ	$500
Jocelyn	-$300
David	$100
Jonas	$50
IRS	-$50,000

Listing 14-3 shows how you can use data binding to bind to the last returned result from the HTTPService call. You can access the lastResult property, which always contains the last set of data that was loaded by that particular HTTPService. You set the dataProvider of the DataGrid to {service.last Result.debts.person}, which is the array of person entries in the XML file.

Listing 14-3 also uses a custom item renderer for the second column in the DataGrid to draw a red background on the cells that have negative values (indicating that you owe somebody money). For more information on using item renderers with the DataGrid and other list controls, see Chapter 8.

You can access the data in two ways after you load it with an HTTPService:

✔ Use the lastResult property, as in Listing 14-3.

✔ Add an event handler using the result event.

If you add a handler to the result event, your event handler receives a ResultEvent event, which has a result property that contains the loaded data. Listing 14-4 adds an event handler to the result event to call an ActionScript function after the data is loaded.

Listing 14-4: Adding an Event Handler to the result Event

```
<mx:Script>
<![CDATA[
   import mx.rpc.events.ResultEvent;

   private function handleResult(event:ResultEvent):void {
      var result:Object = event.result;

      //do something with the result data
   }
]]>
</mx:Script>

<mx:HTTPService result="handleResult(event)" url="debts.
         xml" />
```

Asking for what you want

When you send a request for remote data, you often need to specify certain parameters to tell the server what data it should return. This process might involve sending the ID of a specific user to retrieve that user's records or a zip code to retrieve weather data for a specific city. To send custom parameters with HTTPService, you set the parameters property of the request before calling the send() method. The code is shown in Listing 14-5.

Listing 14-5: Sending Custom Parameters

```
<?xml version="1.0" encoding="utf-8"?>
<mx:Application xmlns:mx="http://www.adobe.com/2006/mxml"
   creationComplete="sendRequest()">
   <mx:Script>
      <![CDATA[
         private function sendRequest():void {
            var parameters:Object = new Object();
            parameters.parameter1 = "value1";
            parameters.parameter2 = "value2";
            parameters.parameter3 = "value3";

            service.send(parameters);
         }
      ]]>
   </mx:Script>

   <mx:HTTPService id="service" url="myServiceURL.php" />

</mx:Application>
```

Loading someone else's data

Often, you load your own data from a database or files on your Web server, but you're not limited to loading data from only your server. Numerous Web services have APIs (application programming interfaces) that you can use to load data from different online services. You can create mash-ups in Flex by pulling in data from any number of different sources.

Listing 14-6 creates a simple Flex application that performs a keyword search of YouTube videos and displays thumbnails for the results in a tiled list. The result is shown in Figure 14-2.

Listing 14-6: Using a Web Service (YouTube) to Return a List of Data

```
<?xml version="1.0" encoding="utf-8"?>
<mx:Application xmlns:mx="http://www.adobe.com/2006/mxml">
   <mx:Script>
      <![CDATA[
         import flash.net.navigateToURL;

         private function searchYouTube():void {              → 7
            var searchTerm:String = searchInput.text;

            var parameters:Object = new Object();             → 10
            parameters.vq = searchTerm;
            parameters.orderby = "rating";
```

(continued)

Listing 14-6 *(continued)*

```
            youtubeService.send(parameters);
        }
    ]]>
</mx:Script>

<mx:HTTPService id="youtubeService" resultFormat="object"          → 19
    url="http://gdata.youtube.com/feeds/api/videos" />

<mx:VBox>
    <mx:HBox width="100%">
        <mx:TextInput id="searchInput" width="100%" />
        <mx:Button label="Search" click="searchYouTube()" />
    </mx:HBox>

    <mx:TileList id="videoList" width="100%"
        dataProvider="{youtubeService.lastResult.feed.entry}">      → 29

        <mx:itemRenderer>
            <mx:Component>
                <mx:Image source="{data.group.thumbnail[0].url}"
                    toolTip="{data.title.value}"
                    click="navigateToURL(new URLRequest(data.group.player.url))"
                    />
            </mx:Component>
        </mx:itemRenderer>

    </mx:TileList>
</mx:VBox>

</mx:Application>
```

Figure 14-2:
Loading
thumbnails
from
YouTube by
using the
XML API.

Here's a breakdown of the code in Listing 14-6:

→ **19**   You create an HTTPService object that points to the YouTube API URL, which is `http://gdata.youtube.com/feeds/api/videos`. This is the base URL, but you need to pass some search parameters with the request.

→ **7**   When the user clicks the Search button, the `searchYouTube` function runs, which grabs the text that the user entered in the `searchInput` text box.

→ **10**   You create an object, named `parameters`, to hold all search parameters that you send to the YouTube API. You add two parameters, `vq` and `orderby`, which are defined by the YouTube API and are required. The `vq` parameter holds the search term, and the `orderby` parameter specifies that you want the results ordered by the rating of the videos.

→ **29**   You bind the last returned result from the HTTPService to the `dataProvider` of the TileList component, which uses the Image component to render the first thumbnail (the API returns various sizes) of each result.

Listing 14-6 is a simple example that uses a single service to return a list of data. But imagine integrating more than just a single data source into your application. You could return a list of videos based on the tags found in the user's Flickr photos. The data mash-up possibilities are limited only by how many public APIs you can find and figure out how to use.

Understanding the Flash security restrictions

Flash Player imposes some security restrictions that limit what data sources your Flex applications can access online. All Flex applications live in the *Flash security sandbox,* which controls which Web site domains your application can access to load data. If you're loading an XML file from the same domain in which the SWF file resides, you don't have to worry about security restrictions because the data is in the same "sandbox." But if you try to load data from a different server, the other server needs to have a *cross-domain policy file* in place, which allows your application to access the data.

For example, if your SWF file is located at `http://domain1.com/MyApplication.swf` and you're trying to load an XML file located at `http://domain2.com/data.xml`, you will encounter a security error unless `http://domain2.com/crossdomain.xml` has a cross-domain policy file in place. The cross-domain policy file must be called `crossdomain.xml` and must be located at the Web server base directory. This file specifies which domains can access data that the domain containing the cross-domain policy file hosts. The following snippet is an example of a completely open cross-domain policy file that allows access from any external domain:

```
<cross-domain-policy>
   <allow-access-from domain="*"/>
</cross-domain-policy>
```

Some Web services have lenient cross-domain policy files, and some don't. For example, the Flickr API has an open cross-domain policy file (just like the one in the preceding example) located at `http://api.flickr.com/crossdomain.xml`, which means you can load data from Flickr into your Flex application, regardless of which server hosts your SWF file. If you're trying to load data across different domains, check to see whether the domain that you are trying to access has the appropriate cross-domain policy file.

Connecting with Web Services

In addition to supporting simple XML APIs, Flex supports Web services, which are defined by a *Web Services Definition Language* document *(WSDL)*. This document is an XML definition that tells you which API methods you can call and which parameters you should send. Communicating with Web services involves sending Simple Object Access Protocol, or SOAP, messages (specially defined XML documents) back and forth. Luckily, Flex takes care of the hard work for you, so you don't have to write complicated SOAP requests by hand.

To use a WSDL service to load data into your application, you can use the `<mx:WebService />` tag and specify the `wsdl` property to point to the WSDL URL. You can then manually call each method on the WSDL and handle the result. However, an easier way to work with Web services is to use the Flex Builder built-in wizard. The WSDL Import Wizard is the feature we focus on in this section. When you use the WSDL Import Wizard, Flex Builder examines the WSDL and generates a series of ActionScript classes to let you invoke each of the methods on the WSDL, without your having to worry about any of the behind-the-scenes work.

To start using the WSDL Import Wizard, create a new Flex project in Flex Builder and then follow these steps:

1. **Choose Data⇨Import Web Service (WSDL), as shown in Figure 14-3.**

   This step loads the Import Web Service Wizard, which walks you through the next three steps to automatically generate ActionScript code for working with the WSDL.

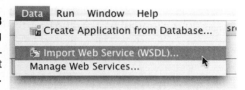

Figure 14-3
Launching
the WSDL
Import
Wizard.

2. **Select your current Flex project and then click Next.**

   You select a source directory, which contains the generated
   ActionScript classes that the Import Web Service Wizard will create.

3. **Enter the URL of the WSDL and then click Next.**

   Figure 14-4 shows how to specify the WSDL URL that the Import Wizard
   inspects. For this example, enter the URL **http://www.webservicex.net/
   WeatherForecast.asmx?WSDL**, which is a Web service that lets you
   retrieve weather forecast data for any zip code in the United States.

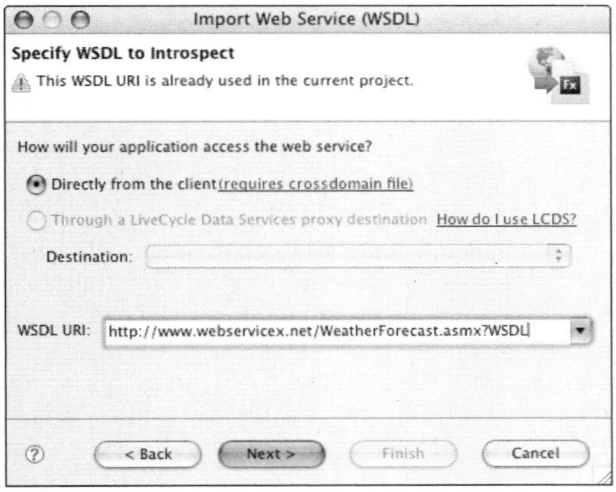

Figure 14-4:
Pointing
the WSDL
Import
Wizard to a
WSDL URL.

4. **Select which operations to use.**

   The Import Web Service Wizard examines the WSDL and presents you
   with a list of all operations that are available for the sample WSDL.
   Figure 14-5 shows you this list. You can select or deselect any operation.
   ActionScript code is generated for all selected operations.

5. **Click Finish to complete the wizard and generate the code.**

After you click Finish, the WSDL Import Wizard generates a bunch of ActionScript
classes in your project. These classes are meant to wrap the WSDL and create
classes that are easier to use than the generic WebService class in the Flex framework. Figure 14-6 lists the ten classes generated for this weather forecast Web
service. The WeatherForecast class is the main class you use for loading data.

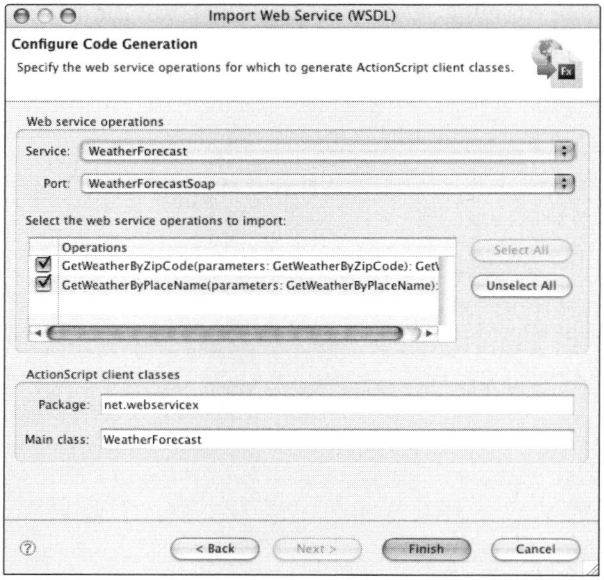

Figure 14-5:
Selecting
WSDL
operations.

Figure 14-6:
Auto-
matically
generated
ActionScript
classes.

After these classes are generated, you can use them to make your Web service calls. The WeatherForecast class, shown in Figure 14-6, is used in Listing 14-7 to make the `getWeatherByZipCode` call. Note that the code for the `getWeather ByZipCode` function was generated by the WSDL Import Wizard; the only code other than the automatically generated code is contained completely in Listing 14-7.

Listing 14-7 creates an application that queries the weather forecast Web service provided by WebserviceX.NET. This code uses the classes generated by using the WSDL Import Wizard and displays the forecast data for any given zip code in a DataGrid, as shown in Figure 14-7.

Listing 14-7: Loading Weather Forecast Data Using a Web Service

```xml
<?xml version="1.0" encoding="utf-8"?>
<mx:Application xmlns:mx="http://www.adobe.com/2006/mxml"
   xmlns:webservicex="net.webservicex.*">

   <mx:Script>
      <![CDATA[
         private function getForecast():void {
            service.getWeatherByZipCode(zipCodeInput.text);
         }
      ]]>
   </mx:Script>

   <webservicex:WeatherForecast id="service" />

   <mx:VBox>
      <mx:HBox width="100%">
         <mx:TextInput id="zipCodeInput" width="100%" />
         <mx:Button id="submitButton" label="Search" click="getForecast()" />
      </mx:HBox>

      <mx:DataGrid dataProvider="{service.getWeatherByZipCode_lastResult.
            Details}"
         rowHeight="58" width="100%" height="300">
         <mx:columns>
            <mx:DataGridColumn dataField="Day" >
               <mx:itemRenderer>
                  <mx:Component>
                     <mx:Text />
                  </mx:Component>
               </mx:itemRenderer>
            </mx:DataGridColumn>
            <mx:DataGridColumn dataField="MinTemperatureF" headerText="Low"
               width="40" />
            <mx:DataGridColumn dataField="MaxTemperatureF" headerText="High"
               width="40" />
            <mx:DataGridColumn dataField="WeatherImage" headerText="" width="50">
               <mx:itemRenderer>
                  <mx:Component>
                     <mx:Image />
                  </mx:Component>
               </mx:itemRenderer>
            </mx:DataGridColumn>
         </mx:columns>
      </mx:DataGrid>
   </mx:VBox>
</mx:Application>
```

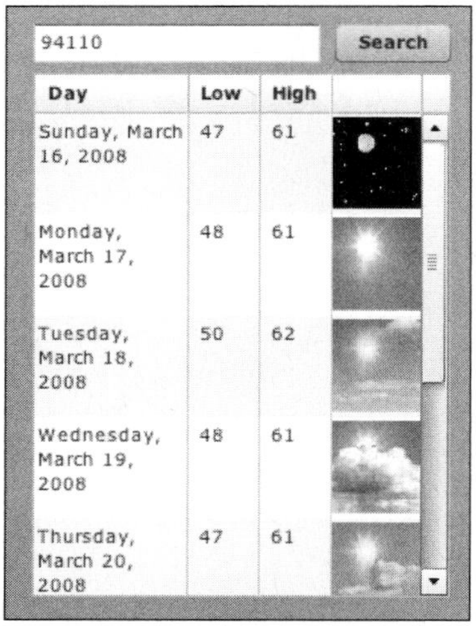

94110			Search
Day	**Low**	**High**	
Sunday, March 16, 2008	47	61	
Monday, March 17, 2008	48	61	
Tuesday, March 18, 2008	50	62	
Wednesday, March 19, 2008	48	61	
Thursday, March 20, 2008	47	61	

Figure 14-7:
Loading
weather
forecast
data by
using a Web
service.

Losing Weight with AMF Remoting

XML is a helpful way to exchange data because it provides a standard, human-readable way to format data. The major downside, however, is that the XML markup takes up space, and text can often be uncompressed when it's sent over the wire. You pay a price for the attractive formatting of XML by sacrificing bandwidth, which means slower transfer speeds.

The alternative is to not send data as text, but instead to efficiently compress it as binary data and then send it from the server to your application. Adobe created the binary transfer specification AMF (Action Message Format), which can be used to send compressed binary data to Flex applications. Data that's compressed using AMF is automatically uncompressed after it reaches your Flex application and is converted automatically into ActionScript classes. The result is a much smaller bandwidth footprint to transfer the same amount of data. You also have the added benefit of automatically receiving strongly typed ActionScript classes, as opposed to generic XML.

Adobe has created the open-source AMF server product Blaze DataSet, which can be used to send compressed AMF data from your server application to your client-side Flex application. A number of alternative implementations of the AMF protocol also exist in a number of server languages. A description of how to set up AMF on a server is a bit outside of the scope of this book, but you can read more about Blaze DataSet at `http://opensource.adobe.com`.

Part V

Exploring Advanced Flex Topics

The 5th Wave   By Rich Tennant

"What I'm looking for are dynamic Web applications and content, not Web innuendoes and intent."

In this part . . .

It's time to roll up your sleeves and dig a little deeper into what Flex has to offer. This part steps things up a notch and explores the inner workings of some of the more advanced Flex topics. This part is the only one that requires an understanding of the Flex framework before you begin, so wait to read this part until after you read Parts I through IV. We cover quite a few topics in Part V, including working with the Flex manager classes, using states and effects, and applying custom skinning.

Chapter 15

Working with Managers We Actually Love

In This Chapter

▶ Taking a look at the DragManager

▶ Understanding how the FocusManager manages the focus of components

▶ Using the PopUpManager to pop up components on top of your application

▶ Displaying ToolTips with the ToolTipManager

▶ Finding out more about the SystemManager — the engine behind your Flex application

*F*lex has a number of managers that oversee some useful built-in functionality in the Flex framework. These managers allow you to

✔ Drag and drop controls

✔ Manage focus on controls

✔ Create views that appear as modal or non-modal dialog boxes

✔ Create ToolTips that appear and disappear based on user action

✔ Create and prioritize cursors

✔ Update your application URL while the user navigates the application

✔ Add browser Back and Forward button support

Typically, the Flex managers — the DragManager, FocusManager, PopUpManager, ToolTipManager, and SystemManager — automatically take care of the management of these mechanisms, so you don't need to do anything special or write any code. When you tab through a set of components in an application and the blue focus highlight appears around each component when it gains focus, the FocusManager governs that behavior; you don't have to write any special code. Similarly, the DragManager governs dragging and dropping items in any of the List controls, such as List, DataGrid, and Tree. You only have to set the drag-and-drop properties on the List controls to true to enable that functionality.

Sometimes, however, you may want more control over these mechanisms or to use them in parts of your application in which the behavior isn't built in automatically. This chapter explains how to invoke the managers by using code to get the behavior that you want, such as programmatically setting focus on a component, reordering focus on a group of components, or popping up a custom component.

Dragging and Dropping with the DragManager

The Flex DragManager manages all the drag-and-drop interactions built into components or drag-and-drop interactions that you manually add to your Flex application. The DragManager governs the drag operation, such as making a Flex component dragable and dropable, creating the *drag proxy* (a ghost image) when you drag a component, and dispatching all the drag-related events.

You can drag and drop all Flex components by writing a little bit of code. There is some built-in drag and drop behaviors in certain Flex controls. The most robust drag-and-drop behavior is built into the Flex List controls. The List controls enable users to drag and drop data items within a single control or between multiple controls. The DragManager governs all this drag-and-drop behavior.

Figures 15-1, 15-2, and 15-3 show a drag-and-drop action. Figure 15-1 shows a drag proxy, a ghosted replica of the item the user is dragging. This drag proxy is created automatically by the DragManager when dragging and dropping in any list-based control. In Figure 15-2, the user is dragging a data item from one List control into another List control. The green plus sign indicates that the List control can receive a dragged data item. If the List control can't receive a dragged data item, a red X sign appears, as shown in Figure 15-3.

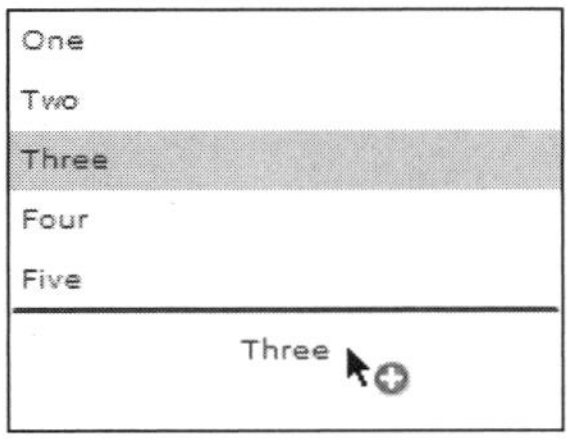

Figure 15-1:
This drag proxy is a ghosted replica of the item being dragged.

Figure 15-2:
The List
control can
receive the
dragged
data item.

 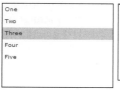 

Figure 15-3:
The List
control can't
receive the
dragged
item.

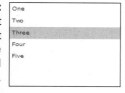 

As users drag and drop items within a Flex application, drag events are dispatched to signal what is going on. The following list describes these drag events and when they are dispatched:

- dragStart: This event is dispatched by the component where the drag operation is originating. This event signals the beginning of the drag-and-drop operation.

- dragEnter: This event is dispatched by any component that has the mouse hover over it during a drag operation (which means dragStart has already been dispatched).

- dragDrop: This event is dispatched by the component that has accepted the dragged item after the mouse has been released on top of it.

- dragComplete: This event is dispatched by the component that dispatched the dragStart event when the item has been dropped. This signals the end of the drag-and-drop operation.

The FocusManager: Managing Which Controls Have Focus

The FocusManager, for the most part, stays behind the scenes in a Flex application. Most Flex user interface controls — such as button-based controls and list-based controls — are focus-aware. A *focus-aware* control is notified by the FocusManager when users click it or navigate to it by pressing the

Tab key on their keyboard. For example, when the user presses the Tab key to move between different TextInput components, the component that currently has focus displays a highlighted border to notify the user. By default, this border highlight is blue.

Only one user interface control can have focus at a time. Focus-aware Flex user interface controls respond visually when they gain focus by drawing a focus highlight around their perimeters. Figure 15-4 shows two Flex buttons in which one has focus and one doesn't. By default, Flex draws a blue highlight around the Button control on the left that has focus.

Figure 15-4:
One control
has focus;
the other
doesn't.

The FocusManager's main responsibility is to govern a tab loop. When you initially press Tab in a Flex application, focus shifts to a component, and then if you keep pressing Tab, focus eventually comes back to that first component. The sequence in which components gain focus before the first component regains focus is called a *tab loop*. In Figure 15-5, each control is labeled with a number that indicates the focus order for the tab loop.

Figure 15-5:
This set of
components
constitutes
a tab loop.

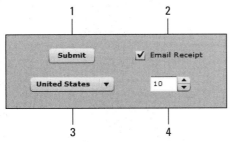

You can control the order of a tab loop by setting the `tabIndex` property on the set of components constituting that tab loop. The `tabIndex` property must be set to a number, where a lower number means that component gets focus prior to a component with a higher `tabIndex` value. You can reverse the tab loop displayed in Figure 15-5 by adding the following code, which sets the tab Index on each component in reverse order:

```
<mx:Tile width="342" height="83" horizontalGap="20"
        verticalGap="20" horizontalAlign="center">
   <mx:Button label="Submit" tabIndex="4"/>
   <mx:CheckBox label="Email Receipt" selected="true"
        tabIndex="3"/>
   <mx:ComboBox dataProvider="{['United States']}"
        tabIndex="2"/>
   <mx:NumericStepper value="10" tabIndex="1"/>
</mx:Tile>
```

A couple of focus-related events are dispatched when a Flex control has focus or focus moves to another control. When a Flex component gains focus — that is, the user has clicked into the component or pressed the Tab key to move to that component — the focusIn event is dispatched. Similarly when a component that has focus loses focus (that is, the user hits the Tab key to move to another component or clicks into another component), the focusOut event is dispatched. By listening to these two events, you can decipher whether a Flex control has gained or lost focus.

Popping Up Dialog Boxes with the PopUpManager

The Flex PopUpManager governs pop-ups in your application. *Pop-ups* are Flex components that you load and position as overlays over the rest of your Flex application. These pop-ups can be one of two types:

✔ With *modal* pop-ups, users cannot use the rest of your Flex application sitting behind the pop-up until they close the pop-up.

✔ *Non-modal* pop-ups are placed over the application, but users can still interact with the normal application behind the pop-up.

Pop-ups are also used for Flex controls that have built-in pop-up behavior (such as ToolTips, drop-down lists in components [such as ComboBox and ColorPicker], alerts, and Flex Menu controls). Pop-ups are similar in concept to HTML pop-up windows, but Flex pop-ups are different because they are overlays that sit on a special layer of your Flex application. Flex pop-ups do not open new browser windows. Figure 15-6 shows a custom MXML component that pops up on top of a Flex application and asks the user to log in.

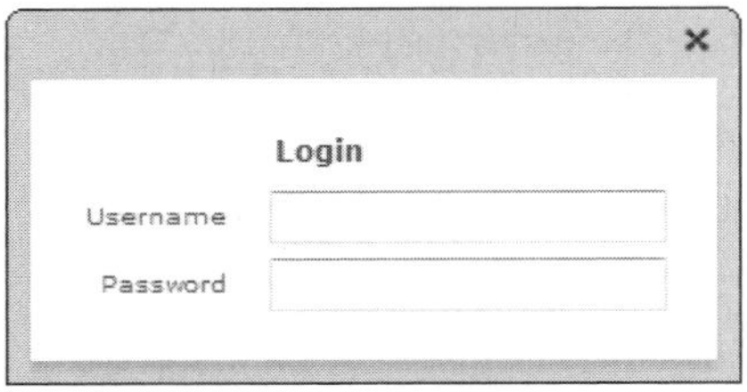

Figure 15-6:
The PopUp
Manager
pops up a
Login dialog
box.

To pop up a component, whether it's an individual Flex component, an ActionScript component, or an MXML component, you use the PopUpManager's `createPopUp` method. You pass three parameters to the `createPopUp` method (the last one is optional):

- ✔ `parent`: This parameter specifies the parent component over which the pop-up will be placed.

- ✔ `className`: You pass the name of a class, and the PopUpManager creates an instance of this class and adds it as a pop-up.

- ✔ `modal`: This optional parameter is a Boolean that indicates whether the pop-up should be modal (blocking other interaction with the application) or non-modal.

Typically, you use the TitleWindow container as the top-level tag of an MXML component when you pop up a dialog box. The TitleWindow container has the visual appearance that users expect from a dialog box, as well as a close button, which you can make appear by setting the TitleWindow's `show-CloseButton` property to `true`.

The following code shows how a button click can trigger the appearance of a modal MXML component, `registrationForm.mxml`. (See Chapter 16 for more on MXML components.)

```
<mx:Button label="Fill Out Registration Form"
           click="PopUpManager.createPopUp(Application.
           application as DisplayObject, registrationForm,
           true);" />
```

Now, suppose that you want an MXML component to pop up in a Flex application when the user clicks a button. The Button's `click` event triggers the code that pops up the component by calling the PopUpManager's `create-PopUp` method.

Listing 15-1 creates `Login.mxml`, the MXML component that represents the Login window. You use the PopUpManager to pop up this component.

Listing 15-1: The Login Window Pop-Up Component

```
<?xml version="1.0" encoding="utf-8"?>
<mx:TitleWindow xmlns:mx="http://www.adobe.com/2006/mxml"
        showCloseButton="true">
    <mx:Form>
        <mx:FormHeading label="Login" />
        <mx:FormItem label="Username">
            <mx:TextInput width="100%" />
        </mx:FormItem>
        <mx:FormItem label="Password">
            <mx:TextInput width="100%"
            displayAsPassword="true" />
        </mx:FormItem>
    </mx:Form>
</mx:TitleWindow>
```

To pop up the Login component in your main application, enter the code in Listing 15-2.

Listing 15-2: Popping Up the Login Window

```
<mx:Button label="Pop Up Login Component"
        click="popUpLoginComp();" />

<mx:Script>
  <![CDATA[
    import mx.core.IFlexDisplayObject;
    import mx.managers.PopUpManager;

    private var popUp:IFlexDisplayObject;

    private function popUpLoginComp():void
    {
        popUp = PopUpManager.createPopUp(this, Login);
    }
  ]]>
</mx:Script>
```

Listing 15-2 uses the popUp variable to keep track of a reference to the pop-up that the PopUpManager creates. You keep track of this reference to the pop-up if you want to remove the pop-up at a later time.

To remove a pop-up, just invoke the PopUpManager's removePopUp method, which takes a reference to the pop-up as its only parameter. So, if you want to remove the Login component when the user clicks a button, you simply write the following code:

```
<mx:Button label="Remove PopUp" click="PopUpManager.
        removePopUp(popUp);"/>
```

Note that when you call the `removePopUp` method, you pass the reference to the pop-up that you stored with the `popUp` variable.

And, finally, if you want to center your pop-up, use the PopUpManager's `centerPopUp` method. As with the `removePopUp` method, you need to pass a reference to the pop-up when you call the `centerPopUp` method. The following code shows how the PopUpManager centers the Login window relative to the parent after it pops up that window:

```
private function popUpLoginComp():void
{
    popUp = PopUpManager.createPopUp(this, Login);
    PopUpManager.centerPopUp(popUp);
}
```

Show Me the ToolTips: Using the ToolTipManager

You can invoke the Flex ToolTipManager to show and hide custom ToolTips. For the most part, ToolTip behavior is built into the Flex framework. For example, when you slide a Flex Slider control's arrow, a ToolTip calls out the value that'll be set if you drop the slider arrow at that point. Similarly, if a Flex Button control is too small to display its full label, hovering over the button displays the label in its full length as a ToolTip. These callouts use the ToolTipManager to create and destroy ToolTips.

You may want to create and show your own ToolTips in situations that the Flex framework doesn't manage by default. To do so, use the ToolTipManager to call the following methods:

✔ `createToolTip`: To create a custom ToolTip, use the `createToolTip` method. This method takes the following parameters:

- `text`: A String representing the text that you want to display in the ToolTip

- `x`: The horizontal location of the ToolTip

- `y`: The vertical location of the ToolTip

The `createToolTip` method returns a reference to the ToolTip created, and you need to save that reference to a variable so that you can use it later when you use the ToolTipManager to destroy the ToolTip.

✔ `destroyToolTip`: To remove the ToolTip, you call the `destroyTool Tip` method and pass in the reference to the ToolTip that you want to remove.

Listing 15-3 shows how to create a ToolTip when the user hovers over the Image control.

Listing 15-3: Manually Creating a ToolTip

```
<mx:Image source="my_image.jpg" id="img"
        mouseOver="showToolTip()"
        mouseOut="hideToolTip();"/>
<mx:Script>
    <![CDATA[
        import mx.core.IToolTip;
        import mx.managers.ToolTipManager;

        private var tooltip:IToolTip;

        private function showToolTip():void
        {
            tooltip = ToolTipManager.createToolTip('This
                is my image', img.x, img.y);
        }

        private function hideToolTip():void
        {
            ToolTipManager.destroyToolTip(tooltip);
        }
    ]]>
</mx:Script>
```

The `createToolTip` method is invoked when the Flex Image control dispatches the `mouseOver` event, and you save a reference to the ToolTip in the `tooltip` private variable.

When the user moves off the image, you hide the ToolTip by invoking the `destroyToolTip` method when the `mouseOut` event is dispatched.

You can set properties by using the ToolTipManager to control and customize the behavior of the ToolTip. For example, you can set the `showDelay` property to the number of milliseconds that you want the Flex control to wait before it shows the ToolTip. By default, the `showDelay` property is 500 milliseconds. Similarly, you can set the `hideDelay` property to the amount of time, in milliseconds, that you want Flex to wait before it hides the ToolTip. This code example shows how to set these properties:

```
    private function showToolTip():void
    {
        ToolTipManager.showDelay = 200;
        ToolTipManager.hideDelay = 500;
        tooltip = ToolTipManager.createToolTip('This is my
            image', img.x, img.y);
    }
```

When a Flex component is about to show (or hide) a ToolTip, several events are dispatched by the component displaying (or hiding) the ToolTip. When a ToolTip is about to be shown, the `toolTipShow` event is dispatched. Similarly, when the ToolTip is about to be hidden, the `toolTipHide` event is dispatched.

SystemManager: The Engine Behind Your Application

The Flex SystemManager is a very powerful and vital manager in the Flex framework. Though you'll most likely never need to interact with it, you may want to find out what it does. The SystemManager is really the engine behind getting your Flex application up and running. Here are some of the tasks it performs:

✔ Its most important job is creating the Application instance based on your `<mx:Application />` tag.

✔ It manages the display and removal of the preloader that appears when your Flex application is downloading and initializing.

✔ It manages all the top-level items in your application, such as pop-ups, ToolTips, and cursors, and it also handles the focus between top-level items.

Chapter 16

Custom Components and Component Architecture

* *

In This Chapter

▶ Understanding the basic life cycle of a Flex component

▶ Creating reusable custom Flex components in MXML

* *

*I*n this chapter, we look at the Flex component architecture and help you understand the different life cycle events of a Flex component, from initial creation to when it's rendered to the screen. Understanding this component life cycle architecture is an advanced concept that helps you immensely as you proceed with your Flex development.

You also find out in this chapter how to create reusable custom components for use in your Flex applications. Knowing how to create reusable components is an important design principle that's common in software because code sharing produces efficiency, maintainability, and good performance.

Looking at the Flex Component Life Cycle

All Flex components follow a life cycle recipe that dictates how the component is created, handles property changes, sizes and positions itself, and, finally, draws itself on the screen. Three ActionScript methods, defined in the `mx.core.UIComponent` class in the Flex framework, drive this component life cycle. Associated with these methods are life cycle events that are emitted to notify anyone listening that the component is progressing through its life cycle stages.

The three component life cycle methods are implemented by all visual components in the Flex framework, and it's customary to do the same if you write your own, custom ActionScript Flex component. These methods encapsulate a common pattern that exists in the Flex component architecture: an invalidation pattern. This *invalidation* pattern allows for property changes that affect the size, position, or visual display of a component to be batched up so that it's speedier. In the following sections, we briefly touch on these three methods and the purposes they serve.

To find out more about the component life cycle, apart from the following sections, step through the Flex component source code that's provided when you install Flex Builder. Using the Flex source code as a model when writing your own ActionScript components is always a good idea. To quickly jump to any of the source code for the Flex framework classes, hold the Ctrl key and click the MXML tag of the class, which will load the source code for that particular class.

Property invalidation: commitProperties

The goal of the `commitProperties` method is to process properties set on the component so that the new property values affect the current state of the component. If you look at the source code for any visual component in the Flex framework, a common pattern that's invoked is to use a Boolean property as a dirty flag to indicate that a property has changed, and then call an invalidation method that forces the component to call `commitProperties` down the line. In the method body for `commitProperties`, the dirty flags are checked to see whether they have been marked as *dirty* — that is, a new property value has been set and needs to be processed. If a dirty flag has been set and a property needs to be processed, the processing occurs in the method body of `commitProperties`.

The main goal of using dirty flags in the invalidation method is to allow multiple properties to all be changed at the same time, but only do the necessary layout changes once, after all the properties have been set. Changing various properties on a component often affects the visual appearance of the component, but you don't want to make the component redraw itself more than necessary. So instead of redrawing or remeasuring the component every time a property changes, you keep track of all the changed properties (by using dirty flags) and then process all of them at the same time in a batch.

This property invalidation pattern may be a little easier to understand when you look at an example. Let's look at how the enabled property is processed on a Flex Label component by using `commitProperties`.

You can access the source code of the Label control by holding the Ctrl key and clicking on any `<mx:Label />` MXML tag.

Listing 16-1 shows some of the code that is part of the Label class in the Flex framework. When the `enabled` property is set, it triggers an invalidation call that invokes the `commitProperties` method. Notice a `set enabled` method for setting the `enabled` property on the Label control. This property controls whether the component is enabled or disabled. In Listing 16-1, after the new value for `enabled` has been set, a Boolean flag named `enabled-Changed` is set to true, and the `invalidateProperties` method is invoked to force the Label component to make a new validation pass and execute the `commitProperties` code.

Listing 16-1: Triggering a Call to commitProperties()

```
override public function set enabled(value:Boolean):void
{
   if (value == enabled)
      return;

   super.enabled = value;
   enabledChanged = true;

   invalidateProperties();
}
```

The call to `invalidateProperties` tells the Flex framework that a property has changed and queues up a call to `commitProperties` that will happen before the component is re-rendered to the screen. But notice that the Label control does no processing other than setting the dirty flag (`enabledChanged`) and calling `invalidateProperties`. When the `commitProperties` code is executed during the component's next validation pass, the `enabledChanged` flag value is checked to see whether the `enabled` property needs further processing. In Listing 16-2, take a look at the code that handles that checking and processing.

Listing 16-2: Executing commitProperties()

```
override protected function commitProperties():void
{
    super.commitProperties();
    ...

    if (enabledChanged)
    {
        textField.enabled = enabled;
        enabledChanged = false;
    }
    ...
}
```

You can see that the pattern is straightforward. In `commitProperties`, the various Boolean dirty flags are checked to see whether they're true, which indicates the property is dirty and needs processing. In this case, when the `enabledChanged` flag is true, the `enabled` property is set on the underlying ActionScript TextField object, which is a child component that the Flex Label control uses to actually display the text. The final step is to toggle the property flag — in this case, the enabledChanged Boolean value — back to its original value to avoid reprocessing the property value during the next validation pass.

You must change the property Boolean flags back to their original values to avoid reprocessing property changes during subsequent validation passes. Also, remember to call super.commitProperties() whenever you override the commitProperties method.

Size invalidation: measure ( )

The goal of the measure method in mx.core.UIComponent — a method that all visual Flex components implement — is to dictate the size of the Flex component. When overriding the measure method, it's your job to set the measuredWidth and measuredHeight properties to the width and height you want for the component. The component uses these two properties to report its proper dimensions when it's sized and positioned by its parent component.

Like all the core component life cycle methods, the measure method is never directly invoked. Instead, a pattern of invalidation is used to trigger the method invocation. For the measurement part of the life cycle, the invalidateSize method is called to force the component to make a new measurement pass.

Take a look at some sample code from the Button class in the Flex framework to see this process in action. When a Button control's label property is set, the new text may require the Button control to be wider or narrower, which means the Button control needs to go through a new measurement pass. In Listing 16-3, take a look at the set label method in the mx.controls. Button class.

Listing 16-3: Triggering a Call to measure()

```
public function set label(value:String):void
{
    ...

    if (_label != value)
    {
        _label = value;
        labelChanged = true;

        invalidateSize();
        ...
    }
}
```

You can see, after the new value has been set, that the `invalidateSize` method is invoked to force the Button to go through a new measurement pass. Then, in the Button's `measure` method, the Button calculates its new `measuredWidth` and `measuredHeight` based on the new text width and other related factors (such as the icon and padding styles).

Drawing and layout invalidation: updateDisplayList()

The goal of the `updateDisplayList` method is to handle the layout and drawing of the visual component in response to changes in its state. Whenever any property that affects the visual appearance of a control is modified, the `updateDisplayList` method is invoked. The `updateDisplayList` method positions the child elements of the control by setting their x and y properties. If the component has no children, the only work that happens in `updateDisplayList` is the programmatic drawing of the component's visual appearance.

The `updateDisplayList` method is the only one of the three component life cycle methods that takes parameters. When `updateDisplayList` is called, it is passed `unscaledWidth` and `unscaledHeight`, which specify the unscaled width and height of the control. The component uses these parameters to draw the visual appearance of the component and to move and position child elements.

Creating Reusable Custom Components

The Flex framework is a collection of components developed by the engineers at Adobe. All these components fit together and work with each other to create complex applications. Every Flex application that you create is a collection of the various Flex framework controls. Your applications contain Buttons, DataGrids, and Sliders, for example. What makes each application different is the unique way in which you combine the components.

Some Flex components, such as the Label control, are extremely simple. Other components are a bit more complex and are composed of subcomponents. For example, the tab bar in the TabNavigator control is a collection of Buttons. But the TabNavigator doesn't have to re-create the code that defines a Button control — it simply reuses the same Button control. The Button control pops up in many other controls in the framework, such as the Sliders, the scrollbars for all the containers, and the header buttons for the Accordion. All framework controls are built with the concept of reuse in mind to try to minimize the amount of code that's needed and to simplify the design.

You can develop your own custom components along these same lines to create controls that you can reuse throughout your Flex applications. As you develop your applications, should always think about which parts you might be able to reuse, in both your current project and future projects. If you need to re-create some pieces repeatedly in multiple places in your application, you should probably create a custom component that you can use over and over again to solve the same problem. And, if you ever find that you're copying and pasting large chunks of code multiple times, you might want to consider breaking out those pieces into custom components.

In the following sections, you create a rating component that lets users rate items on a five-star scale. This rating is similar to the star rating widget you've probably seen on movie rental Web sites or video-sharing portals. The goal is to create the component shown in Figure 16-1. In the next few sections, you create the code for this custom component piece by piece. The entire code for the component is presented in Listing 16-5.

Figure 16-1:
A custom rating component used three times.

Defining the interface

Before you start writing code, you should map out the basic structure of the component and how it will be used. In this case, your rating component will have a property to keep track of the rating that the user has selected (a number between 0 and 5). In terms of communicating from the rating component back to your application, the component must notify the application whenever the user changes the rating. To accomplish this task, the component dispatches an event to let the other parts of the application know that the value has been changed.

For every component you create, you define a list of all properties, methods, and events that the component exposes. The rating component doesn't have any public methods that will be used, but it has a `rating` property and it dispatches a `change` event.

Choosing your base wisely

When you create a custom component, you extend a base class from the Flex framework. You choose a class as the starting point, therefore, and add functionality from there. Think about exactly what kind of functionality your component needs, and figure out whether an existing class already provides some of the required functionality. All custom Flex components extend the UIComponent class, which is the lowest-level component that you use. UIComponent is essentially a blank component that's invisible on its own, but it provides all the important behind-the-scenes invalidation functionality that's required for all components to work with the rest of the Flex framework. Simple components in the Flex framework, such as Button, Label, and TextInput, all extend UIComponent.

For the rating component, you need a series of stars in a horizontal line. These stars are fundamentally Button controls (although they will be skinned to look like stars). You have a few options for deciding which class to use as a base class, but because the component contains multiple Buttons, you should start with one of the Container classes to hold the buttons. You can use Canvas as the base, but then you have to control the positioning of the stars manually. Instead, start with the HBox control because it handles the positioning of child elements horizontally, which is exactly what you need.

You also need to choose a package structure to organize your custom components. In this example, the star rating component is named RatingSelector, and it's located in the com.dummies.controls package. We chose this package structure for this example because it mimics the structure of the Flex components (which use the mx.controls package). You can use any package structure that you want in your own applications.

To start creating your component, follow these steps:

1. **Choose File⇨New⇨MXML Component.**

   Alternatively, you can right-click the folder in your project and choose New⇨MXML Component.

   The New MXML Component dialog box appears, as shown in Figure 6-2.

2. **In the Filename text box, enter the name of your new component, and in the Based On text box, specify the base class that you want to extend.**

   In Figure 16-2, you can see that the RatingSelector component is extending the HBox container.

3. **Click Finish.**

   For the example, Flex Builder creates a file named RatingSelector.mxml in your project, and the MXML file initially is an empty HBox container, as shown here:

```
<?xml version="1.0" encoding="utf-8"?>
<mx:HBox xmlns:mx="http://www.adobe.com/2006/mxml"
         width="400" height="300">

</mx:HBox>
```

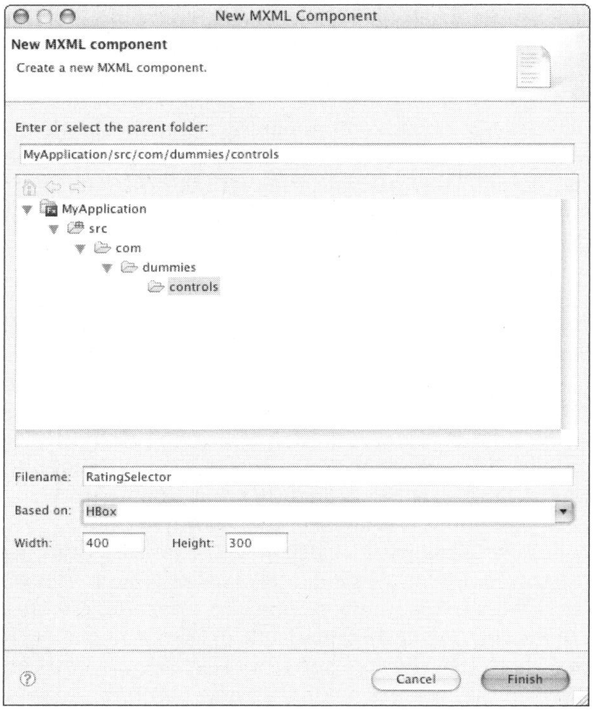

Figure 16-2:
Specify a
base class
to extend.

Notice that Flex Builder sets default `width` and `height` properties for custom MXML components. You can remove these tags because you will use the component's built-in measurement capabilities rather than explicit values for `width` and `height`.

Adding child components

The empty HBox MXML file is the start of the RatingSelector component, and you add the child components between the `<mx:HBox>` and `</mx:HBox>` tags. To begin with, the RatingSelector needs to have five Button controls. You can add these components by using the MXML Button tag. These buttons also need to be specially skinned to make them look like stars. Listing 16-4 adds five Button controls and applies a custom CSS style that uses two image assets to set the selected and unselected button states.

Also, remember to call `super.commitProperties()` whenever you override the `commitProperties` method.

This listing creates five Buttons that look like stars in a horizontal row. The image assets referenced in the `<mx:Style>` block (`star_unselected.png` and `star_selected.png`) are the unfilled and filled star images that make the buttons look like rating stars rather than the default Flex buttons. The images that you use for the button skins are located in the assets folder at the root folder of your project.

Listing 16-4: Adding Five Button Children with MXML

```
<?xml version="1.0" encoding="utf-8"?>
<mx:HBox xmlns:mx="http://www.adobe.com/2006/mxml">

    <mx:Style>
        .ratingStar {
            up-skin: Embed('/assets/star_unselected.png');
            down-skin: Embed('/assets/star_unselected.png');
            over-skin: Embed('/assets/star_unselected.png');
            selected-up-skin: Embed('/assets/star_selected.png');
            selected-down-skin: Embed('/assets/star_selected.png');
            selected-over-skin: Embed('/assets/star_selected.png');
        }
    </mx:Style>

    <mx:Button styleName="ratingStar" />
    <mx:Button styleName="ratingStar" />
    <mx:Button styleName="ratingStar" />
    <mx:Button styleName="ratingStar" />
    <mx:Button styleName="ratingStar" />

</mx:HBox>
```

Choosing between MXML and ActionScript

In this chapter, we cover creating a custom MXML component; however, you can create both custom MXML and custom ActionScript components. All components in the Flex framework (such as Button and TabNavigator) are ActionScript components. Because MXML is compiled down to ActionScript code by the compiler, if you can create a component by using MXML you can also create the same component by using ActionScript.

Creating ActionScript components is a more complicated process that involves a deeper understanding of the inner workings of the Flex framework. Advanced ActionScript components use the component validation life cycle that we discuss in the first half of this chapter, which handles such items as child creation, component measurement, and child layout. Creating MXML components is often easier than creating ActionScript components, but you have much finer and advanced control over components if you use pure ActionScript. Because creating ActionScript components is an advanced topic (we could write a book on it!), we cover only MXML components in this chapter.

Defining your properties

The RatingSelector allows the user to select a rating number between 0 and 5. You can access this public property from other parts of your application. To define custom properties on your MXML components, you need to add a `<mx:Script>` block to your MXML file that contains the properties that you want to expose.

To define the rating property, add a Script block that contains a public variable named `rating`:

```
<mx:Script>
    <![CDATA[
        [Bindable]
        public var rating:int;
    ]]>
</mx:Script>
```

Discovering how to talk with events

When a user changes a rating, you need to tell other parts of your application that the change has occurred. A rating change can trigger any number of different actions, such as saving that information to a database or adding the item to a list of user favorites. The rating component doesn't need to know what's supposed to happen after a change occurs; that information is completely outside of the scope of the component. All the component needs to do is announce the change event.

To announce the change, you use the `dispatchEvent` function from within your component. First, you need to pick exactly which kind of event you're dispatching. You can name your event anything you want, although in this case there's already a framework event for changes that some of the other components, such as TextInput, use to indicate that a change has occurred. You can dispatch a change event by adding the following ActionScript lines within a `<mx:Script />` block in your component:

```
var changeEvent:Event = new Event(Event.CHANGE);
dispatchEvent(changeEvent);
```

This code snippet creates a new event, which is of the type `Event.CHANGE`, and then dispatches the event you created. Anything outside the rating component that is listening for a change event is notified.

When you determine which events your custom component will dispatch, you also need to add some special metadata to your component so that Flex knows about these events. If you're creating an MXML component, you add a section to your MXML file that defines all the different events that your component can dispatch:

```
<mx:Metadata>
    [Event(name="change", type="flash.events.Event")]
</mx:Metadata>
```

By adding this `<mx:Metadata>` portion to your MXML file, you're telling the Flex compiler that your component dispatches the `change` event. This metadata lets you add an event listener to the RatingSelector component when you declare it with an MXML tag (see the example in Listing 16-5).

Putting it all together: The complete RatingSelector component

Your completed MXML component now defines a custom property (`rating`) and dispatches a `change` event when the user clicks one of the stars to set the rating. The full MXML component is shown in Listing 16-5.

Listing 16-5: Your Complete Custom Component

```
<?xml version="1.0" encoding="utf-8"?>
<mx:HBox xmlns:mx="http://www.adobe.com/2006/mxml" horizontalGap="0">
    <mx:Metadata>
        [Event(name="change", type="flash.events.Event")]
    </mx:Metadata>

    <mx:Script>
        <![CDATA[
            [Bindable]
            public var rating:int;

            private function setRating(newRating:int):void {
                this.rating = newRating;

                var changeEvent:Event = new Event(Event.CHANGE);
                dispatchEvent(changeEvent);
            }
        ]]>
    </mx:Script>

    <mx:Style>
        .ratingStar {
            up-skin: Embed('/assets/star_unselected.png');
            down-skin: Embed('/assets/star_unselected.png');
            over-skin: Embed('/assets/star_unselected.png');
            selected-up-skin: Embed('/assets/star_selected.png');
```

(continued)

Listing 16-5 *(continued)*

```
        selected-down-skin: Embed('/assets/star_selected.png');
        selected-over-skin: Embed('/assets/star_selected.png');
    }
</mx:Style>

<mx:Button styleName="ratingStar" selected="{rating >= 1}"
        click="setRating(1)" />
<mx:Button styleName="ratingStar" selected="{rating >= 2}"
        click="setRating(2)" />
<mx:Button styleName="ratingStar" selected="{rating >= 3}"
        click="setRating(3)" />
<mx:Button styleName="ratingStar" selected="{rating >= 4}"
        click="setRating(4)" />
<mx:Button styleName="ratingStar" selected="{rating >= 5}"
        click="setRating(5)" />

</mx:HBox>
```

Each `<mx:Button />` tag uses data binding to bind the `selected` property of the Button to a certain rating threshold. It's an easy way to make sure that when the `rating` property is set, the buttons reflect the current rating. You use the `click` event on each button to trigger the `setRating` function, which sets the `rating` property to the appropriate value and also dispatches the `change` event. So now when a user clicks one of the buttons, the rating is set, and a change event fires to notify any other parts of the application that are listening.

Using your shiny, new component

After you create the custom RatingSelector component, you can use it in your Flex application (and you can use it repeatedly). To use the component in your application, you can add it by using an MXML tag just as you do for all other components in the Flex framework. Listing 16-6 adds a single RatingSelector component to an application.

Listing 16-6: Using the Custom Component

```
<?xml version="1.0" encoding="utf-8"?>
<mx:Application xmlns:mx="http://www.adobe.com/2006/mxml"
    xmlns:controls="com.dummies.controls.*">

    <controls:RatingSelector />

</mx:Application>
```

When you run this application, you see one RatingSelector component that displays five stars, as shown in Figure 16-3.

Figure 16-3:
A single instance of the Rating Selector component.

Notice that the component tag uses the `<controls:` prefix for the namespace. This namespace is defined in the `<mx:Application>` tag by the `xmlns:controls="com.dummies.controls.*"` part of the tag. It's the default way that Flex Builder adds custom components. You probably don't need to add the `xmlns` line to the Application tag manually. If you simply start typing `<Rating` in your Application file, Flex Builder automatically suggests the rest of the MXML tag and automatically adds the `xmlns` line. You can then use the `<controls:RatingStar />` tag as many times as you want in your application.

After you add the RatingSelector component to your application, you can use the `rating` property and `change` event to interact with the component. Listing 16-7 is a more complete application that uses three instances of the RatingSelector to gather user feedback. You add an event listener to the `change` event of each component to recalculate the average rating whenever the user changes one of the ratings.

Listing 16-7: Creating an Application That Uses Your Custom Component

```
<?xml version="1.0" encoding="utf-8"?>
<mx:Application xmlns:mx="http://www.adobe.com/2006/mxml" xmlns:controls="com.
                dummies.controls.*">

    <mx:Script>
        <![CDATA[
            [Bindable]
            private var average:Number = 0;

            private function computeAverage():void {
                average = (rating1.rating + rating2.rating + rating3.rating) / 3;
            }
        ]]>
    </mx:Script>

    <mx:NumberFormatter id="formatter" precision="1" />

    <mx:Panel title="Session survey" fontSize="18">
        <mx:Form>
            <mx:FormItem label="Speaker was knowledgable">
```

(continued)

Listing 16-7 *(continued)*

```
            <controls:RatingSelector id="rating1" change="computeAverage()" />
        </mx:FormItem>
        <mx:FormItem label="Slides were helpful">
            <controls:RatingSelector id="rating2" change="computeAverage()" />
        </mx:FormItem>
        <mx:FormItem label="Speaker was engaging">
            <controls:RatingSelector id="rating3" change="computeAverage()" />
        </mx:FormItem>
    </mx:Form>
    <mx:ControlBar>
        <mx:Label text="Average rating: {formatter.format(average)}" />
        <mx:Spacer width="100%" />
        <mx:Button label="Submit" />
    </mx:ControlBar>
    </mx:Panel>

</mx:Application>
```

This sample application produces a form with three instances of the RatingSelector component, as shown in Figure 16-4.

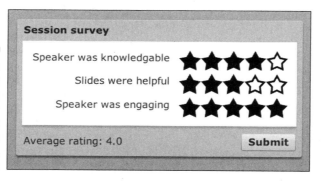

Figure 16-4: Using the Rating Selector component in an application.

Now, whenever you want to display a five-star rating component in your application, you can add the RatingSelector MXML tag. Always keep in mind this approach to thinking about your Flex application as individual reusable components. If you design your applications with reusable components, you can avoid duplicating code in your project. And, you never know: Later on down the line, you may find another use for a component that you created in an earlier project.

Chapter 17

Understanding States and Effects

*W*hen you build real-world Flex applications that are more advanced than your typical "Hello World" example, you're likely to have a few different screens, or views, that you present to the user. When we describe how the user moves through an application, we often use words like *views, pages, panels,* and *screens.* These words are often used interchangeably and refer to different sets of user interface controls that are presented to the user at a time. Flex has a few special features that make creating these different views easier. In this chapter, we introduce view states and explain how you create them with Flex Builder.

But we're not content with simply showing you how to move from one view state to another; we want to make things exciting! So we also cover using visual effects to animate your applications. You find out how to add some simple animated effects to your applications to spice things up a bit. Then you try combining view states with effects and add some slick animated effects as you transition from one view state to another.

Working with View States

States define different views of your application, such as different visual screens or pages that the user might move between. You can have different view states on your main application and on custom MXML components that you create. When you use view states, you can switch back and forth between related screens without necessarily creating completely separate MXML components for each screen.

Often, views are related; for example, a login form and a registration form might share a lot of similarities. The registration form probably has a few more fields than the login form, but they have much of the same structure.

By using view states, you can create a single multipurpose component that can switch between the login and registration states.

Creating a new view state is sort of like taking a snapshot of your application or MXML component. You can use that snapshot as the starting point and make changes to it for the specific view that you want to create. This snapshot-like view state is a *base state,* and you make modifications to this base state by doing any of the following:

✔ Adding and removing children

✔ Changing the layout

✔ Adjusting properties

You can create a new view that's slightly (or dramatically) different from the original base state. You can save this new view state without changing the original base state, so you can switch back and forth between the two.

Each state gets an identifying name, and your application can switch between states by setting the `currentState` property. Behind the scenes, the Flex framework takes care of doing all the necessary behind-the-scenes work, like creating and destroying the appropriate controls and changing labels and other properties. You can focus on designing the different views, hopefully without having to fiddle with the complex code required to move seamlessly from one state to another.

Creating view states with Design View

To start understanding view states, you can create a simple example that shows a login form. This example starts off with the code in Listing 17-1. This code listing doesn't define any states; you add those shortly.

Listing 17-1: A Login Form

```xml
<?xml version="1.0" encoding="utf-8"?>
<mx:Application xmlns:mx="http://www.adobe.com/2006/mxml" verticalAlign="middle">

    <mx:Panel id="loginPanel" title="Login"
        horizontalAlign="center" verticalAlign="middle">

      <mx:Form id="loginForm">
        <mx:FormItem label="Email">
          <mx:TextInput />
        </mx:FormItem>
        <mx:FormItem label="Password">
          <mx:TextInput displayAsPassword="true" />
        </mx:FormItem>
```

```
        <mx:FormItem>
            <mx:Button label="Login" />
        </mx:FormItem>
    </mx:Form>

  </mx:Panel>

</mx:Application>
```

When you switch to Design View in the Flex Development perspective, the code in Listing 17-1 creates the login form shown in Figure 17-1. In Design View, a States panel appears in the top-right corner of Flex Builder.

When you work with states, you can most easily start by using the States panel, which lets you use a WSYWIG editor to create and edit your view states. However, these states are really just defined in MXML code within your application (as you can see in the following section), so if you want to skip Design View altogether, you can manually code all the MXML.

States panel

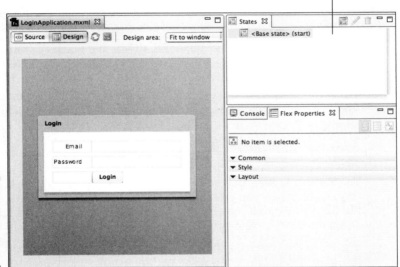

Figure 17-1:
Design
View shows
the States
panel.

In the example application, you want to create a view that shows a progress bar to let users know that you are performing the login action while they wait. This intermediate state helps provide visual feedback so users don't think the application isn't responding, and it also prevents users from trying to log in again while they're waiting for a response. Follow these steps to create this state:

1. **Right-click the <Base state> entry in the list of states and select New State from the menu that appears.**

   The New States dialog box, shown in Figure 17-2, opens. In this dialog box, you can name the new state you're creating and set a few properties.

2. **Enter** loggingln **as the name for the new state and then click OK.**

   The new state appears in the States panel. After you define a new state, you can select it from the list in the States panel and switch back and forth between all available states. In the Design panel of Flex Builder, the look of whichever state you select appears. Any changes you make in the Design panel affect only the selected state.

3. **With the `loggingIn` state selected, delete the Form container in the Panel container (but leave the Panel container itself) and add a ProgressBar control instead.**

   The ProgressBar control shows a loading animation while the login processes. You can complete the tasks in this step by using the WSYWIG editing of Design View.

4. **After you finish editing the `loggingIn` state, switch back to the base state.**

   The Form container that you deleted in the loggingIn state is still in the base state. When you edited the loggingIn state, you didn't change the base state at all. You can switch back and forth between states to compare the differences.

   In addition to removing and adding children, you can also edit properties of existing children to make certain properties change from one state to another.

5. **Switch back to the `loggingIn` state.**

   In the base state, the main login panel has a title of Login, so the loggingIn state also has that title.

6. **Change the `title` property of the Panel in the `loggingIn` state to** Logging In **to indicate the application's current status.**

After you make the modifications to the `loggingIn` state, it looks like Figure 17-3.

Figure 17-3:
The
loggingIn
state.

After you create the `loggingIn` state (as we outline in the preceding step list), follow these steps to create an `error` state that provides a notification when the user enters invalid login details:

1. **Right-click the <Base state> entry in the list of states and select New State from the menu that appears.**

   The New State dialog box appears (refer to Figure 17-2).

2. **Enter** error **as the name and click OK.**

   You now have an `error` state that looks the same as the original login form. Next, you need to add an error message to let users know they entered invalid credentials.

3. **To add an error message to the login form, drag a Label control from the Components panel onto the login Panel control and drop it directly above the Form container.**

4. **Edit the `text` property of the Label by setting it to Invalid Login! and setting the color to a scary red.**

   The new `error` state is shown in Figure 17-4.

Figure 17-4:
The error
state.

For this example, we keep it simple and stick with the base state, the logging in state, and the error state.

States under the hood

Behind the scenes, Flex Builder is generating a slew of MXML markup that defines the exact changes from one state to another. These changes consist of various MXML tags, such as `<mx:AddChild />` and `<mx:RemoveChild />`, which add and remove children from containers, `<mx:SetProperty />`, which changes a property of a component, such as the title of a Panel control, and `<mx:SetStyle />`, which modifies a style (such as font color).

The full MXML code that defines your `loggingIn` and `error` states (which you created in the preceding section) is shown in Listing 17-2.

Listing 17-2: Two States Defined in MXML

```
<mx:states>

    <mx:State name="loggingIn">
        <mx:RemoveChild target="{loginForm}"/>
        <mx:AddChild relativeTo="{loginPanel}" position="lastChild">
            <mx:ProgressBar label="Authenticating" indeterminate="true"
                labelPlacement="center" color="#000000" height="30"
                width="100%"/>
        </mx:AddChild>
        <mx:SetProperty target="{loginPanel}" name="title" value="Logging in..."/>
    </mx:State>

    <mx:State name="error">
        <mx:AddChild relativeTo="{loginForm}" position="before">
            <mx:Label text="Incorrect Login!" color="#FF0000" fontSize="13"/>
        </mx:AddChild>
        <mx:SetProperty target="{loginPanel}" name="title" value="Try again"/>
    </mx:State>

</mx:states>
```

Switching between states

After you define all your states in MXML, you can switch back and forth between them by using ActionScript to set the `currentState` property of your application. You set the `currentState` property to a string that matches the name of one of the available states. To return to the original base state, you can set the `currentState` property to `""`.

Listing 17-3 completes the basic login example by adding a click handler to the login button that will simulate a fake login attempt. This listing is a combination of the form created in Listing 17-1 (Lines 46 to 61), the states created in Listing 17-2 (Lines 25 to 43), and an additional `<mx:Script />` block that contains the ActionScript code that switches between states (Lines 4 to 23).

Listing 17-3: A Complete MXML Application with Three States

```
<?xml version="1.0" encoding="utf-8"?>
<mx:Application xmlns:mx="http://www.adobe.com/2006/mxml"
    verticalAlign="middle">
    <mx:Script>                                                        → 4
        <![CDATA[
            private function login():void {
                //switch to the loggingIn state to show the ProgressBar control
                this.currentState = "loggingIn";                       → 8

                //Create a fake timer to simulate logging in. In a real
                //application you might send a login request to a server
                //and wait for a response with success or failure
                var timer:Timer = new Timer(3000, 1);
                timer.addEventListener(TimerEvent.TIMER, fakeLoginHandler);
                timer.start();
            }

            private function fakeLoginHandler(event:TimerEvent):void {
                //For our example purposes we'll always switch to the error state
                this.currentState = "error";                           → 20
            }
        ]]>
    </mx:Script>                                                       → 23

    <mx:states>                                                        → 25
        <mx:State name="loggingIn">
            <mx:RemoveChild target="{loginForm}"/>
            <mx:AddChild relativeTo="{loginPanel}" position="lastChild">
                <mx:ProgressBar label="Authenticating" indeterminate="true"
                    labelPlacement="center" color="#000000" height="30"
                    width="100%"/>
            </mx:AddChild>
            <mx:SetProperty target="{loginPanel}" name="title"
                value="Logging in..."/>
        </mx:State>

        <mx:State name="error">
            <mx:AddChild relativeTo="{loginForm}" position="before">
                <mx:Label text="Incorrect Login!" color="#FF0000" fontSize="13"/>
            </mx:AddChild>
            <mx:SetProperty target="{loginPanel}" name="title" value="Try again"/>
        </mx:State>
    </mx:states>                                                       → 43

    <mx:Panel id="loginPanel" title="Login"                           → 46
        horizontalAlign="center" verticalAlign="middle">

        <mx:Form id="loginForm">
            <mx:FormItem label="Email">
                <mx:TextInput />
```

(continued)

Listing 17-3 *(continued)*

```
        </mx:FormItem>

        <mx:FormItem label="Password">
            <mx:TextInput displayAsPassword="true" />
        </mx:FormItem>
        <mx:FormItem>
            <mx:Button label="Login" click="login()" />
        </mx:FormItem>
    </mx:Form>

    </mx:Panel>
</mx:Application>
```
→ 61

When the user clicks the login button, the login() function sets the currentState property of the application to loggingIn on Line 8 of Listing 17-3. This state change switches the view state to show the ProgressBar control that's defined in the loggingIn state. In this example, you simply fake a login attempt by waiting for three seconds, then setting the currentState property to error on Line 20, which displays the invalid login message and allows the user to try again. You can set the currentState property at any time in your application to jump from view state to view state.

This example demonstrates using states to move back and forth between three related views: the initial login form, the login progress indicator, and the error notification. When you have multiple views that are related but have minor differences, you can use states to more easily manage these views.

Adding Effects to Your Application

You can use effects to animate containers and controls in your Flex applications. You might want to fly a Panel control in from the edge of your application, add a pulsating glow to a Button control when the user rolls over it with the mouse, or smoothly fade images in and out in a slide show. You can create all these animations by using the effect classes. In the following sections, we cover some of the main effect classes that you can use to add animated effects to your applications, such as the Move, Resize, Rotate, Zoom, and Wipe effects.

Pulling the trigger

You can trigger effects in two ways:

- By using an event trigger defined in MXML
- By manually calling the play() method of the effect in ActionScript

All the components in the Flex framework have effect triggers that use the naming convention *triggerEvent*Effect, such as moveEffect or resize-Effect. When you combine a trigger with a particular effect class, the combination is called a *behavior*. The available triggers include addedEffect, creationCompleteEffect, focusInEffect, focusOutEffect, hideEffect, mouseDownEffect, mouseUpEffect, moveEffect, removedEffect, resizeEffect, rollOutEffect, rollOverEffect, and showEffect.

Don't confuse triggers and events, such as the moveEffect trigger and the move event. To use an effect for movement, you set the moveEffect trigger; you use the move event to be notified when the component moves. If you try to assign an effect by setting the move event in MXML, you get a compiler error. This error appears if you use the other possible effect triggers, as well, such as using the resizeEffect trigger rather than the resize event.

Starting with simple movement

You can animate the movement of components in your application by using the Move effect. If you use the Move effect on a component, anytime the x or y properties are set or the move(x, y) method is called, the component smoothly animates from its location to the new position. If you use the Move effect, you can help guide the user and create a more fluid experience. Listing 17-4 uses the default behavior of the Move effect to smoothly animate each button when it's toggled on and off.

Listing 17-4: Using the Move Effect to Animate Buttons

```
<?xml version="1.0" encoding="utf-8"?>
<mx:Application xmlns:mx="http://www.adobe.com/2006/mxml">
   <mx:Script>
      <![CDATA[
         import mx.controls.Button;

         private function buttonClickHandler(event:MouseEvent):void {
            var button:Button = event.currentTarget as Button;

            if(button.selected)
               button.y = 30;
            else
               button.y = 0;
         }
      ]]>
   </mx:Script>
   <mx:HBox clipContent="false">
      <mx:Button label="Option 1" toggle="true"
         moveEffect="Move" click="buttonClickHandler(event)" />
```

(continued)

Listing 17-4 *(continued)*

```
        <mx:Button label="Option 2" toggle="true"
            moveEffect="Move" click="buttonClickHandler(event)" />
        <mx:Button label="Option 3" toggle="true"
            moveEffect="Move" click="buttonClickHandler(event)" />
    </mx:HBox>
</mx:Application>
```

Listing 17-4 places three Button controls in a horizontal box container. When a button is toggled on, the y property of the button is set to 30, which drops it down 30 pixels. When a button is toggled off, it returns to the normal position because y is set back to 0. If you didn't use the Move effect, the buttons would simply jump from one location to another. But by simply adding moveEffect="Move" to the Button controls, you can make each button smoothly animate whenever you change its position.

Figure 17-5 shows the application in Listing 17-4, with the first and third buttons selected. Unfortunately, this figure (and the figures in the rest of this chapter) can't capture the animated aspect of the effect, so run these examples yourself to watch the movement.

Listing 17-4 sets the moveEffect trigger of each Button control to the string Move. You don't actually define a <mx:Move /> tag anywhere in your application, but behind the scenes, Flex takes the "Move" string and figures out that it needs to create a Move effect. In this case, the default Move effect is created for each Button control. Using the "Move" string instead of creating a full <mx:Move /> tag is a sort of shorthand way to add the default effect behavior.

Sometimes, however, you need more control over the specific Move effect that you use. For example, you might want to change the duration property of the effect to make it run faster than it does by default. So, instead of setting moveEffect to the string "Move," you can define a <mx:Move /> tag within your application.

The following code defines a <mx:Move /> tag, sets the duration property (which is defined in milliseconds), and uses data binding to bind that particular effect to the moveEffect trigger for each Button control:

```
<mx:Move id="effect" duration="200" />

<mx:HBox clipContent="false">
    <mx:Button label="Option 1" toggle="true" moveEffect="{effect}" />
    <mx:Button label="Option 2" toggle="true" moveEffect="{effect}" />
    <mx:Button label="Option 3" toggle="true" moveEffect="{effect}" />
</mx:HBox>
```

Now the movement of your Buttons will take 200 milliseconds, as opposed to the default duration of 500 milliseconds.

Figure 17-5:
Animate
buttons in a
menu.

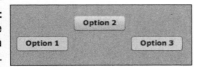

Whether you use the simple default behavior or create an instance of the effect class depends on how much control you want to have over how the effect plays. For simple animations, the default behavior might be all you need. But when you need to fine-tune that behavior, you have to create the MXML tags for the effects you want, like in the preceding block of code.

Turning your world upside down

Instead of just making things move from one spot to another, you can also spin them by using the `<mx:Rotate />` effect. You use the Rotate effect to smoothly animate the `rotation` property of any Flex control. Listing 17-5 creates a horizontal list of buttons just like Listing 17-4, but in this example, when a button is toggled on, it rotates 45 degrees. To achieve this effect, you create an instance of the `<mx:Rotate />` effect in MXML and then call the `play()` method in ActionScript.

The primary properties of the Rotate effect that you use to configure the rotation are `angleTo` and `angleFrom`. Listing 17-5 sets the `angleTo` property, but it doesn't set the `angleFrom` property, which means the Rotate effect starts with the current rotation of each button.

Listing 17-5: Applying the Rotate Effect

```
<?xml version="1.0" encoding="utf-8"?>
<mx:Application xmlns:mx="http://www.adobe.com/2006/mxml">
    <mx:Script>
        <![CDATA[
            import mx.controls.Button;

            private function clickHandler(event:MouseEvent):void {
                var button:Button = event.currentTarget as Button;
                rotate.target = button;
                rotate.angleFrom = button.rotation;

                if(button.selected)
                    rotate.angleTo = 45;
                else
                    rotate.angleTo = 0;

                rotate.play();
```

(continued)

Listing 17-5 *(continued)*

```
        }
    ]]>
  </mx:Script>

  <mx:Style>
    @font-face
    {
      font-family: boldVerdana;
      fontWeight: bold;
      src: local("Verdana");
    }

    Button {
      font-family: boldVerdana;
    }
  </mx:Style>

  <mx:Rotate id="rotate" />

  <mx:HBox clipContent="false">
    <mx:Button label="Option 1" toggle="true" click="clickHandler(event)" />
    <mx:Button label="Option 2" toggle="true" click="clickHandler(event)" />
    <mx:Button label="Option 3" toggle="true" click="clickHandler(event)" />
  </mx:HBox>
</mx:Application>
```

In the `clickHandler` function that executes when a button is clicked, you set the `target` property of the Rotate effect to the Button control that was clicked. Then, you set the `angleTo` property of the effect to either 45 or 0, depending on the selected state of the button. Finally, you call `play()`, which runs the effect and rotates the appropriate button.

You can see the result of Listing 17-5 in Figure 17-6, which shows the first and third buttons selected.

Figure 17-6:
Use the
Rotate
effect.

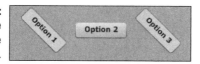

The <mx:Style /> block used in Listing 17-5 contains the @font-face section. This section embeds the Verdana font, which is used for the Button controls in the application. If you try to rotate any Flex component that has text labels, the text disappears when you rotate that component. This also applies when you want to fade any component in or out as well. If you run the example in Listing 17-5 after you remove the <mx:Style /> block, the label disappears when a button rotates. Always embed the fonts used by any controls that you rotate. For more on embedding fonts, see Chapter 18.

Zooming in and out

You can use the Zoom effect to magnify or shrink controls. Using the Zoom effect is like setting the scaleX or scaleY properties of a component. The primary properties of the Zoom effect that you use are zoomWidthTo, zoomWidthFrom, zoomHeightTo, and zoomHeightFrom. Each of these properties is specified as a percentage, in which 1 is equal to 100 percent scale.

Listing 17-6 uses the Zoom effect with the rollOverEffect and rollOutEffect triggers to create a fisheye menu effect, as shown in Figure 17-7. When the user hovers over a button, that button zooms to 150 percent of its original size. When the user moves off the button, that button zooms back to 100 percent.

Listing 17-6: Zooming Button with the Zoom Effect

```
<?xml version="1.0" encoding="utf-8"?>
<mx:Application xmlns:mx="http://www.adobe.com/2006/mxml">

  <mx:Zoom id="zoomIn"  zoomHeightTo="1.5" zoomWidthTo="1.5" />
  <mx:Zoom id="zoomOut" zoomHeightTo="1"   zoomWidthTo="1" />

  <mx:HBox clipContent="false">
    <mx:Button label="Option 1"
       rollOverEffect="{zoomIn}" rollOutEffect="{zoomOut}" />
    <mx:Button label="Option 2"
       rollOverEffect="{zoomIn}" rollOutEffect="{zoomOut}" />
    <mx:Button label="Option 3"
       rollOverEffect="{zoomIn}" rollOutEffect="{zoomOut}" />
  </mx:HBox>

</mx:Application>
```

Figure 17-7:
Use the
Zoom effect.

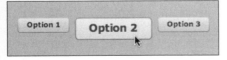

Wiping that look off your face

The Wipe effects come in four varieties: WipeUp, WipeDown, WipeLeft, and WipeRight. These Wipe effects are *masking effects,* meaning they mask the area of the component by making portions invisible. You can use these effects to make content appear or disappear by wiping across either vertically or horizontally, like a window washer wiping a squeegee across a window.

Listing 17-7 uses the WipeUp and WipeDown effects to transition between images contained in a ViewStack. These effects produce an animated slideshow transition.

Listing 17-7: Using Wipe Effects with a ViewStack

```xml
<?xml version="1.0" encoding="utf-8"?>
<mx:Application xmlns:mx="http://www.adobe.com/2006/mxml">

    <mx:Script>
        <![CDATA[
            private function nextImage():void {
                // if there are more children in the ViewStack just add 1
                // to the selectedIndex to move to the next child
                if(viewStack.selectedIndex < viewStack.numChildren - 1) {
                    viewStack.selectedIndex++;
                }
                // if we have reached the end we start over by
                // moving to the first child again
                else {
                    viewStack.selectedIndex = 0;
                }
            }
        ]]>
    </mx:Script>

    <mx:ViewStack id="viewStack" click="nextImage()">
        <mx:Canvas showEffect="WipeDown" hideEffect="WipeUp">
            <mx:Image source="assets/image1.jpg" />
        </mx:Canvas>
        <mx:Canvas showEffect="WipeDown" hideEffect="WipeUp">
            <mx:Image source="assets/image2.jpg" />
        </mx:Canvas>
        <mx:Canvas showEffect="WipeDown" hideEffect="WipeUp">
            <mx:Image source="assets/image3.jpg" />
        </mx:Canvas>
    </mx:ViewStack>

</mx:Application>
```

Running multiple effects

Two special effect classes aren't actual effects themselves — they let you run multiple effects, either one after the other or at the same time. You can wrap a few effects within the `<mx:Sequence />` tag, which runs each effect after the preceding effect in the list finishes, so that you can string together any number of different effects. Or you can use the <mx:Parallel /> tag, which lets you run effects simultaneously. You can even nest <mx:Sequence /> and <mx:Parallel /> tags within one another to create fairly complex effects.

Listing 17-8 uses the <mx:Sequence /> tag to wrap three separate Move effects. The resulting effect moves the target to the left, then to the right, then back to the original position. This movement produces a shaking effect. In this example, when the user clicks the login button, the entire form shakes back and forth.

Listing 17-8: Using the Sequence Effect to Make Things Shake

```xml
<?xml version="1.0" encoding="utf-8"?>
<mx:Application xmlns:mx="http://www.adobe.com/2006/mxml">

   <mx:Sequence id="shake" target="{loginPanel}">
      <mx:Move xBy="-10" duration="200" />
      <mx:Move xBy="20"  duration="200"  />
      <mx:Move xBy="-10" duration="200"  />
   </mx:Sequence>

   <mx:Panel id="loginPanel" title="Login">
      <mx:Form>
         <mx:FormItem label="Email">
            <mx:TextInput />
         </mx:FormItem>
         <mx:FormItem label="Password">
            <mx:TextInput displayAsPassword="true" />
         </mx:FormItem>
         <mx:FormItem>
            <mx:Button label="Login" click="shake.play()" />
         </mx:FormItem>
      </mx:Form>
   </mx:Panel>

</mx:Application>
```

One additional effect becomes useful only when placed within a sequence — the Pause effect. The Pause effect does absolutely nothing except pause the sequence of effects for a certain amount of time. You can insert pauses between each Move effect in Listing 17-8, which produces the following code:

```xml
<mx:Sequence id="shake" target="{loginPanel}">
   <mx:Move xBy="-10" duration="200" />
   <mx:Pause duration="200" />
   <mx:Move xBy="20"  duration="200"  />
   <mx:Pause duration="200" />
   <mx:Move xBy="-10" duration="200"  />
</mx:Sequence>
```

Combining States and Effects by Using Transitions

After you figure out how to create states in your application and how to create fluid animations by using the effect classes, you can combine both concepts by using transitions. The Transition class lets you add specific effects that control how your application moves from one view state to another. You can add a <mx:transitions> block to your application, just like you define your states in a <mx:states> block. Within the <mx:transition> MXML block, you can use the <mx:Transition /> tag to define which effects should play when moving from one state to another.

Each <mx:Transition /> tag has a fromState property and a toState property, which tell Flex when to play the effects. If you specify a state name for the fromState property and a second state name for the toState property, then the effect contained in that transition plays only when the state changes from the first to the second state. You can also use a wildcard (*) for the fromState or toState property, or for both properties.

Take the example login application in Listing 17-3 and add the transition in Listing 17-9. After you add the transition, when the login form changes from any state (because Listing 17-9 uses the wildcard) into the error state, the form first resizes smoothly to the new dimensions and then shakes to let the user know about the error.

Listing 17-9: Adding Transitions to Move from State to State

```
<mx:transitions>
   <mx:Transition fromState="*" toState="error">
      <mx:Sequence target="{loginPanel}">
         <mx:Resize duration="100" />
         <mx:Move xBy="-10" duration="200" />
         <mx:Move xBy="20"  duration="200"  />
         <mx:Move xBy="-10" duration="200"  />
      </mx:Sequence>
   </mx:Transition>

   <mx:Transition fromState="*" toState="loggingIn">
      <mx:Resize target="{loginPanel}" />
   </mx:Transition>
</mx:transitions>
```

Simply adding the 14 lines in Listing 17-9 produces a much more fluid, rich experience. States, effects, and transitions can produce extremely expressive applications when you use them correctly.

Chapter 18

Styling and Skinning Flex Components

In This Chapter

▶ Using MXML styles to customize your applications

▶ Styling with external style sheets

▶ Embedding fonts

▶ Creating graphical skins

*W*hen you start becoming more familiar with Flex, and create and deploy Flex applications of your own, the standard look and feel of a Flex application becomes easy to recognize. One of the benefits of Flex development is that you get great-looking components straight out of the box; wiring up a slick-looking application takes almost no time at all. Some would argue, however, that Adobe made the default Flex look and feel *too* sleek and polished, which leads to developers leaving the default visual appearance unchanged when they deploy their applications. You can end up with more and more Flex applications that look the same. But you can change all that.

Flex lets you control almost every aspect of the visual appearance of your applications, from the background colors and borders of your Panels all the way down to the color of the arrow that appears in a ComboBox. You can end up producing complete Flex applications that look and feel nothing at all like the default. You can change the visual appearance of Flex applications by using styling and skinning:

> ✔ **Styling:** Setting Cascading Style Sheets (CSS) styles on a component to change the way the component is drawn. For example, you can set the `border-color` style of a Button control to change the color that the border is rendered in. Styling gives you control over very specific aspects of the components, but it often doesn't let you drastically alter the complete look of the component. For example, styling lets you change the font color, background color, and rounded corners of a Button control, but it doesn't let you change the shape of the Button control to a five-pointed star.

✔ **Skinning:** A more complete modification of the component's look than styling allows. Skins can be either graphical or programmatic. Graphical skins use image assets (PNG, GIF, JPG, SWF, or SVG files) to completely replace the look and feel of the component. Programmatic skins use ActionScript code and the graphics capabilities of the Flash Player to draw all the parts of the component's visual appearance at runtime.

Nearly all the default skinning of the Flex component framework is done with programmatic skinning. So, when you see a Button control in your Flex application, ActionScript code drew all the elements of that Button control (such as the border, the background gradient, and the highlight) when the Button was created and added to your application at runtime. Programmatic skinning can be very powerful because you can use the graphics drawing methods of Flash for very finely detailed control; however, it is also very difficult to master.

In this chapter, we cover how to use CSS styling to customize the look and feel of your application, as well as how to apply image assets as graphical skins. Programmatic skinning can be tedious and fairly complicated, and it's outside of the scope of this book. If you're feeling adventurous, you can check out the source code of the Flex framework to see how Adobe created the default skins for all the controls.

Styling

To customize Flex components, you can use both properties and styles, which you set by using MXML markup or through ActionScript. In general, you use properties to change the functionality of a component, and you use styles to change the visual appearance. For instance, `toggle` is a property of the Button control that determines whether the Button control remains in the selected state after it's clicked. This property affects the functionality of the Button control. On the other hand, the background color or font size of the Button control's text affects the visual appearance but doesn't change the functionality. You control these changes by using styles — in the Button control example, the `fillColors` and `fontSize` styles.

Applying styles with MXML

You can apply styles by using MXML markup in the same way that you set properties with MXML. To change a Button control so that it no longer has rounded corners, you can use the following MXML code:

```
<mx:Button cornerRadius="0" label="My Button" />
```

You use the same syntax for setting both the `cornerRadius` style and the `label` property. But in this example, `cornerRadius` is a style, not a property. We explain this distinction in the section "Changing Styles with ActionScript," later in this chapter, when you need to change styles at runtime.

You can create fairly complex styling by using MXML. For example, Listing 18-1 produces an orange button that has a white border, as shown in Figure 18-1.

Listing 18-1: Applying MXML Styles to a Button

```
<mx:Button label="My Button"
    fontSize="14" fontWeight="normal" fontFamily="Georgia"
    fontStyle="italic" fillAlphas="[1.0, 1.0]"
    fillColors="[#FF9000, #BF5100]" cornerRadius="10"
    borderColor="#FFFFFF" textDecoration="underline" />
```

Figure 18-1:
A styled
Button
control.

All the styles that you define in MXML apply only to that single control. Listing 18-1 creates an orange button with a label in italic Georgia font, but all the other buttons in your application look like the default Flex buttons. You can copy all those styles and paste them into the MXML tag for each button that you want to apply the styles to. But that's tedious, and making even a slight change requires going back and finding each place you used those styles. Thankfully, you have an alternative way to define your styles that centralizes the style definitions and makes styles reusable across multiple controls; read on for details.

Using the <mx:Style> block

Instead of defining all your styles by using MXML tags, you can use a block of CSS styles in your application that apply to all the controls. Add the `<mx:Style>` block to your main MXML application file. Within the `<mx:Style>` block, you define all the CSS styles that will be used in your application. You can change Listing 18-1 to produce the modified example in Listing 18-2.

Listing 18-2: Using a Block of CSS Styles

```xml
<?xml version="1.0" encoding="utf-8"?>
<mx:Application xmlns:mx="http://www.adobe.com/2006/mxml">
   <mx:Style>
      Button {
         fontSize: 14;
         fontWeight: normal;
         fontFamily: Georgia;
         fontStyle: italic;
         fillAlphas: 1.0, 1.0;
         fillColors: #FF9000, #BF5100;
         cornerRadius: 10;
         borderColor: #FFFFFF;
         textDecoration: underline;
      }
   </mx:Style>

   <mx:Button label="My Button" />
</mx:Application>
```

Listing 18-2 defines a style for the Button control on Line 4. This style applies to all Button controls throughout your entire application. If you're trying to define a common style for a certain control, then using this approach lets you define the style in one place and have it apply everywhere.

Styles that you define in CSS can follow two naming conventions: *styleName* or *style-name*. For example, to set the corner radius of a Button control to 10 pixels, you can use either `cornerRadius: 10;` or `corner-radius: 10;`. But styles that you define in MXML must use the *styleName* syntax (like in Listing 18-1). Also, when you access styles via ActionScript, you must use the *styleName* syntax to reference those styles. The styles in Listing 18-2 follow the *styleName* syntax because we wanted the example to match the example in Listing 18-1 as closely as possible; but because we define these styles in a CSS block, we could have used either naming convention.

In addition to defining styles that apply to all controls of a certain type, such as Button or Panel, you can also define specific sets of styles and use style names to apply those styles to individual controls. By enclosing all the styles within the `Button { }` block in Listing 18-2, you're applying those styles to all buttons. But, instead of using the class name of a control, you can define a custom style name by adding a period character (`.`) before a custom name you choose. For example, Listing 18-3 defines two different styles, one named `blueButton` and one named `redButton`, which use different values for the `fill-colors` style.

Listing 18-3: Defining Two Named Styles with CSS

```
<mx:Style>
    .blueButton {
        fill-colors: #0000ff, #000033;
        fill-alphas: 1,1;
        color: #ffffff;
        border-color: #ff0000;
    }

    .redButton {
        fill-colors: #ff0000, 330000;
        fill-alphas: 1,1;
        color: #ffffff;
        border-color: #0000ff;
    }
</mx:Style>
```

By adding the period character before the name of the style, you create a custom style that you can reference in your application. After you add these two styles, you can assign them to a Flex control by setting the styleName property of any control in your application. In the following example, you apply the redButton style to the first Button control and the blueButton style to the second:

```
<mx:Button label="Red" styleName="redButton" />
<mx:Button label="Blue" styleName="blueButton" />
```

When you define the style names in the <mx:Style> block, you have to add the period character before the style name. However, when you assign the name by using the styleName property of a specific component, you don't use the period character.

You can also use a combination of styles that apply to a class name (such as Button), named styles (such as redButton), and MXML styles. The styles are all inherited and can override each other. So, you can have a <mx:Script> block that defines certain styles for Button (Listing 18-2) and also certain styles for redButton (Listing 18-3), and then you define a Button control in MXML like this:

```
<mx:Button styleName="redButton" fillColors="[0xFFFFFF,
           0xFFFFFF]" />
```

This button first inherits all the styles defined in the Button CSS block (Georgia font, orange fill colors, and so on); then the styles in the redButton CSS block, which override the fill and border colors; and finally, the MXML styles, which override the fill colors defined in CSS by defining a separate set of fillColors with MXML. The resulting button has a white background because MXML styles take priority, but it still has all the other inherited styles from the Button and redButton styles. With MXML styles, you can always override individual styles on specific controls, if needed.

Attaching an external style sheet

You can separate the visual styling of your application from your MXML source code even further by using external CSS files. Instead of including all your style blocks within your main application MXML file by using the `<mx:Style>` tag, you can put them all in a separate CSS file. This file contains all your CSS styles (no need for the `<mx:Style>` part, just add the styles themselves). Then, instead of using a long `<mx:Style>` tag, you can simplify it to point to the location of your external CSS file. You can change the code in Listing 18-2 by creating a separate file called `styles.css` and then referencing that file with a `<mx:Script />` tag in MXML and setting the `source` property to point to your external file, which reduces the amount of code in your main application file:

```
<?xml version="1.0" encoding="utf-8"?>
<mx:Application xmlns:mx="http://www.adobe.com/2006/mxml">
    <mx:Style source="style.css" />
    <mx:Button label="My Button" />
</mx:Application>
```

When you start using a lot of CSS styling and your main application MXML file gets bloated with CSS, you may want to separate out the CSS to make the MXML code more readable. Creating a separate CSS file also lets you create variations on the external style sheet and simply change the source property of the `<mx:Style>` tag to point to a new CSS style sheet file when you want to change the look and feel of your application.

Changing styles with ActionScript

In addition to setting styles with CSS style blocks and with MXML, you can also use ActionScript and set the styles at runtime. Two ActionScript functions let you work with styles: `getStyle(styleName:String)` and `setStyle(styleName:String, value:*)`. These two methods let you access individual styles and make changes. For example, you can adjust the corner radius of a Button control on the fly or change the Button control's font size when the mouse rolls over it.

The example in Listing 18-4 has a horizontal slider and a button. When the user drags the horizontal slider, the application calls the `setStyle` method of the Button control (`myButton`) and sets the value of the `cornerRadius` style to the current value of the slider.

Listing 18-4: Calling setStyle() to Set Styles at Runtime

```
<?xml version="1.0" encoding="utf-8"?>
<mx:Application xmlns:mx="http://www.adobe.com/2006/mxml">
    <mx:Script>
        <![CDATA[
```

```
        import mx.events.SliderEvent;

        private function sliderChangeHandler(event:SliderEvent):void {
            myButton.setStyle("cornerRadius", event.value);
        }
    ]]>
</mx:Script>

<mx:HSlider minimum="0" maximum="20" value="4"
    liveDragging="true" change="sliderChangeHandler(event)" />

<mx:Button id="myButton" label="MyButton" />
</mx:Application>
```

If you need to get the current value of any of the styles in your ActionScript code, you can use the getStyle method. So, to find out the current corner radius of the Button control in Listing 18-4, you can do something like this:

```
var radius:Number = myButton.getStyle("cornerRadius");
```

In addition to the getStyle and setStyle methods, you can also set the styleName property of any component at runtime by using ActionScript, which enables you to change the style name of a certain control at any time. When the styleName property of a control changes, its visual appearance changes to match the new set of styles defined in CSS.

Listing 18-5 changes the styleName property of the Button control from smallButton to bigButton when the mouse rolls over that control, which makes the font size of the label increase from 12 pixels to 20 pixels. When the mouse rolls off the control, the styleName property changes back to smallButton.

Listing 18-5: Setting the styleName property at Runtime

```
<?xml version="1.0" encoding="utf-8"?>
<mx:Application xmlns:mx="http://www.adobe.com/2006/mxml">
    <mx:Style>
        .smallButton {
            font-size: 12;
        }

        .bigButton {
            font-size: 20;
        }
    </mx:Style>

    <mx:Button id="myButton"
        label="My Button" styleName="smallButton"
        rollOver="myButton.styleName = 'bigButton'"
        rollOut="myButton.styleName='smallButton'" />

</mx:Application>
```

Working with fonts

If you're styling Flex components that display text, then you can set various styles that affect the font in which the text appears. You can set the `font-family` style to control which font the text appears in. The Flex framework uses the default font Verdana.

You can set the `font-family` style of a component to something other than Verdana, such as Arial or Courier, but the font must be installed on the user's computer for it to display correctly in your application. So, even though your custom-styled application might look great when you test it on your own computer, it might not look great when a user launches your application on a computer that doesn't have the required fonts installed. You can pretty safely assume nearly all computers have a few standard fonts (such as Times, Arial, and Courier), but after you start getting into other special fonts, you have to embed those fonts in your application to ensure that they look the way you want them to.

You also need to embed fonts if you're displaying rotated text anywhere in your application. If you set the `rotation` property of a Button control or use rotated labels on a charting control, you must embed the font. If you don't embed the font, then any rotated text disappears.

You embed fonts in your Flex application by using the `@font-face` CSS selector. You can tell Flex where to find the font that you're embedding in one of two ways:

- **Reference a TrueType Font file (`.ttf`).** Here's an example of how to embed the Impact font by referencing a TrueType Font file:

```
<mx:Style>
    @font-face
    {
        font-family: myImpact;
        font-weight: normal;
        src: url("impact.ttf");
    }
</mx:Style>
```

- **Reference a local system font by name.** Here's an example of embedding the Verdana local system font in bold typeface:

```
<mx:Style>
    @font-face
    {
        font-family: myBoldVerdana;
        font-weight: bold;
        src: local("Verdana");
    }
</mx:Style>
```

You can specify the `src` of the embedded font in two different ways. The first example in the preceding list uses `src: url("fontFile.ttf")`, and the second example uses `src: local("FontName")`. You can use any name that you like following `font-family:`. You use this name in other CSS styles to reference the embedded font. For example, after you embed those fonts, you can use the custom font names (`myBoldVerdana` and `myImpact`) in your CSS style definitions, like this:

```
Button {
    font-family: myBoldVerdana;
}

Label {
    font-family: myImpact;
}
```

The preceding code uses the `myBoldVerdana` font for all Button controls in your application and the `myImpact` font for all Label controls.

When you embed the fonts, you must specify the `font-weight`. In the preceding example, you embed the bold typeface for the `myBoldVerdana` font and the normal typeface for the `myImpact` font. When you embed a font, only a certain subset of the complete font is included. If you specify the bold typeface when you embed a font, then the normal typeface isn't embedded. This selective embedding also applies to the `font-style`, which can be `italic`, `normal`, or `oblique`. Make sure you embed the right combination of `font-weight` and `font-style` that your application uses.

Also, some of the Flex framework controls have default settings for `font-weight` or `font-style`. For example, the default Flex Button style uses a bold font, so if you embed a font that you plan to use on a Button control, you want to embed the bold typeface.

Before you go crazy with custom fonts and embed a ton of them, you should be aware of the downsides to font embedding:

- ✔ **Embedded fonts are huge.** Each font that you embed bloats the size of your compiled SWF file. Make sure you keep an eye on the size of your SWF file and the effect of embedded fonts.

- ✔ **You might not be allowed.** The fonts that you want to use might have licensing restrictions that prohibit you from embedding them in your application. Be sure you understand the licensing implications of any custom fonts that you embed.

Understanding the limitations of styling

You can do a lot to give your Flex application a unique look and feel by using some simple CSS styling. But even if you change every possible style of a component, such as a Panel container, you're still confined to working with the underlying skin. In the case of the Panel container, the skin defines the general layout of the title bar, background, and borders around the content. You can change all sorts of styles that change the colors, padding, and so on that the skin uses when it draws itself, but you're limited in what's possible. As long as you're using the default skin, you have to work within the boundaries of what the skin lets you do; and different skins support different styles. For example, the default Canvas skin supports custom values for `border-thickness`, `border-alpha`, and `border-color`. But the default Button skin supports only `border-color`; if you want to change the thickness or alpha of a Button control's border, you're out of luck.

The only way to break out of the constraints of the default Flex skins is to create your own skins. The following section explains how to use custom graphics assets as skins to give you more complete control over the look and feel of your components.

Skinning

If you reach the limits of customizing the Flex components' appearance by using CSS styling, then you might want to take full control and start skinning the components. The following sections cover how you can use graphical assets to completely change the visual display of your Flex components.

Using the Adobe CS3 skin extensions

In this chapter, we cover the basics of skinning Flex components with graphical skins. For more advanced skinning, Adobe has released a set of extensions for the different products in the CS3 product line that help with Flex skinning. These extensions work with the other CS3 products and make it much easier to export complete skins for various Flex components. For simple examples like the ones we present in this chapter, you don't need the extensions; however, if you start doing more advanced skinning, they can be very useful. Extensions are available for Fireworks, Flash, Illustrator, and Photoshop. You can download these extensions for free by visiting `www.adobe.com/go/flex3_skinning`. You can also find a number of tutorials about using these extensions at the Flex Developer Center at `www.adobe.com/devnet/flex/workflow.html`.

Using graphical skins

Graphical skinning involves creating images for each skin-able part of a Flex component. These image assets are embedded in your application, and Flex uses them rather than the default skins. Skinning a Button control, for instance, might involve creating different images for each state of the button, such as up, over, down, and so on. Skinning a TitleWindow component involves creating assets for the background and border, as well as the close button. You can create these image assets in whatever image editing or illustration software you like, as long as you can export one of the following image formats: SWF, PNG, GIF, JPEG, or SVG.

Simple example: Skinning a Button control

To understand how to apply a graphical skin, this section gives you a simple example that involves using image assets to re-skin a Button control. Instead of using the normal look of a Button control, you create a button that displays a selectable star icon. For the unselected state, the Button control displays an unfilled star; when the button's selected, it displays an orange-filled star. You apply these images to a toggle button, which switches between the different images.

To start creating graphical skins, you have to create graphical assets in an image editor. Figure 18-2 shows the individual images that you can use for this example. You use each of these images for a specific Button control's state.

Figure 18-2:
Use these individual image assets for your custom Button skin.

After you have your graphical assets ready, you can start bringing them into Flex Builder to skin the Flex Button control. The following steps guide you through this process:

1. **Create a new CSS file.**

   Choose File↪New↪CSS File. Name the CSS file **style.css**. This new file is created in your Flex project and opens in Flex Builder.

2. Create an empty style selector.

Start with a CSS file that creates a Button style called `starButton`. Your CSS file should start out like this:

```
Button.starButton {

}
```

This code creates a set of CSS styles that apply to any Button component that has `styleName` set to `starButton`.

3. Switch to CSS Design view.

CSS Design view loads the default styles for the Button control. Figure 18-3 shows a few of these default styles as they appear in Flex Builder. For an overview of CSS Design view, refer to Chapter 6.

Figure 18-3:
The default
Button
skin in CSS
Design
view.

4. Select Skin in the Flex Properties Panel.

CSS Design view presents two views for working with the visual CSS editor: Style or Skin. In this example, you want to skin the Button control with graphical assets, so switch to the Skin view.

5. Select Image Files from the Skin drop-down list.

The drop-down list, shown in Figure 18-4, lets you assign graphical assets from either images or Flash SWF files. In this example, you're using individual image files for your skin assets.

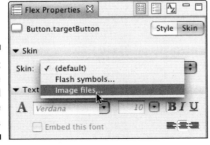

Figure 18-4:
Select the
graphical
assets type
for skinning.

6. Specify each image asset for each button state.

In this example, you're using five different images for the different button states. You can see these different images in Figure 18-5.

After you add all the images, Design view refreshes, and the buttons states appear with the images you specified, shown in Figure 18-6.

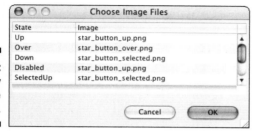

Figure 18-5: Specify the image assets.

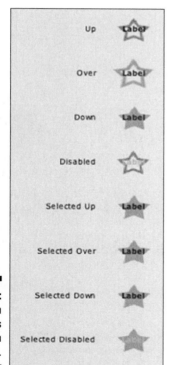

Figure 18-6: CSS Design view shows your custom skin.

You can switch back to the Source view of the CSS file and see the code that was generated:

```
Button.starButton {
    upSkin: Embed(source="star_button_up.png");
    overSkin: Embed(source="star_button_over.png");
    downSkin: Embed(source="star_button_down.png");
    disabledSkin: Embed(source="star_button_disabled.png");
    selectedUpSkin: Embed(source="star_button_selected.png");
    selectedOverSkin: Embed(source="star_button_selected.png");
    selectedDownSkin: Embed(source="star_button_selected.png");
    selectedDisabledSkin: Embed(source="star_button_selected.png");
}
```

7. **Apply the skin.**

   In your Flex application MXML file, create a `<mx:Button>` component tag and set the `styleName` property to `starButton` so that it matches the CSS declaration. Make sure to include a reference to the external CSS file that you created. Here's the code to use:

```
<?xml version="1.0" encoding="utf-8"?>
<mx:Application xmlns:mx="http://www.adobe.com/2006/
        mxml">
    <mx:Style source="style.css" />
    <mx:Button styleName="starButton" toggle="true" />
</mx:Application>
```

Extended example: Skinning a Panel container

The example in the preceding section uses multiple image assets to skin the different states of a Button control. In the example in this section, you skin a Panel container by creating a single image that you use as the background (including the title bar and border) of the Panel container. The default Panel skin, shown in Figure 18-7, shows the different elements of a Panel container: a title bar that has a title field, a border around the Panel contents, and a background behind the contents.

The custom Panel skin created in this example includes the same elements, but you create them outside of Flex, using a graphic editing program just like for the Button skinning example in the preceding section. The image asset that you'll use is shown in Figure 18-8.

The skin shown in Figure 18-8 has some elements that you can easily create by styling the default Panel skin. For example, you can set the `border-color`, `header-colors`, `header-height`, and other CSS styles to create a Panel container that has the same general color scheme, as shown in Figure 18-8. But you simply can't create the clouds in the title bar and the leaves in the bottom-left corner with styling alone.

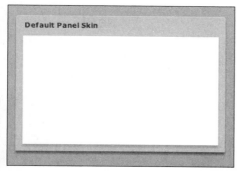

Figure 18-7:
The default
Panel skin.

Figure 18-8:
A custom
graphical
Panel skin.

To take the image shown in Figure 18-8 and turn it into a Panel skin, you follow the same process that we outline in the preceding section: Create a new CSS file, start with a CSS style for the Panel class, and then switch over to CSS Design view to visually edit the CSS skin. You can apply an image asset to the skin of a Panel container just like you can for the various skin states of a Button control.

When you specify an image asset as the skin for a Flex component like a Panel container, the default behavior stretches the image to fit the component's width and height, which often distorts the image. For example, imagine if you tried to take the image created in Figure 18-8 and apply it to a Panel container that was 400 pixels wide by 100 pixels high. The resulting Panel container would look like Figure 18-9, which probably isn't what you want.

You can overcome these distortion problems by using a scale-nine grid (also referred to as scale-9 or 9-slice scaling). A *scale-nine grid* defines four grid lines, which divide the image up into nine distinct parts, as shown in Figure 18-10.

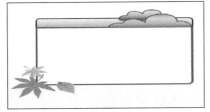

Figure 18-9:
This graphi-
cal skin is
incorrectly
scaled.

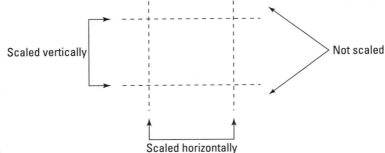

Scaled vertically

Not scaled

Figure 18-10:
A scale-nine
grid.

Scaled horizontally

These nine different parts of the image are scaled differently. The four corners aren't scaled at all; they always remain the same dimensions. The middle areas along the top and bottom edges scale horizontally, but not vertically. The two areas on the left and right edges scale vertically, but not horizontally. You may find scale-nine scaling especially useful when you work with rounded corners, as shown in Figure 18-11.

For this example, you don't want the clouds that appear in the top-left of the skin to scale at all, either vertically or horizontally. Similarly, you also don't want to scale the leaves in the bottom-left corner. The portions of the border on the left and the right of the skin should scale vertically, but not horizontally. The top portion (the title bar) and the bottom border should scale horizontally, but not vertically.

CSS Design view has a built-in scale-nine grid editor that you can access by clicking the Edit Scale Grid button, shown in Figure 18-12.The scale-nine editor lets you drag the four grid lines to create your custom scale-nine grid. By defining a custom scale-nine grid for this skin, as shown in Figure 18-13, you can control exactly how this image will scale, so you can make sure that the various elements aren't distorted.

This scale-nine grid lets you scale the Panel container to any dimensions while still retaining the correct proportions.

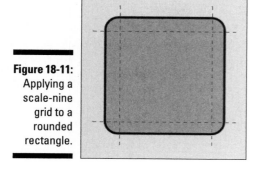

Figure 18-11:
Applying a scale-nine grid to a rounded rectangle.

Figure 18-12:
Accessing the scale-nine editor.

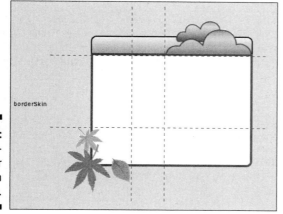

Figure 18-13:
The scale-nine grid for the custom Panel skin.

In addition to using the image asset as the skin for this Panel container, you also need to use additional CSS styles to complete the visual customization. Using a custom image skin doesn't change the font size or color of the title text, so for that, you still use the `font-size` and `color` CSS styles. In the end, your Panel CSS style includes the image skin that has the scale-nine grid defined, as well as all the other CSS styles that properly size and place the title text field and the Panel's contents. The full CSS listing for this skinned Panel is shown in Listing 18-6.

Listing 18-6: Defining a Custom Panel Skin in CSS

```
Panel {
    borderSkin: Embed(source="nature_panel.png",scaleGridLeft="130",scaleGridTop=
            "74",scaleGridRight="189",scaleGridBottom="205");
    titleStyleName: panelTitle;
    padding-top:85;
    header-height: 110;
    padding-left: 80;
    padding-right:20;
    padding-bottom:80;
    font-size:14;
    color: #282828;
    font-weight: bold;
}
.panelTitle
{
    color: #000000;
    font-weight: bold;
    font-family: Verdana;
    text-align: left;
    font-size: 24;
    font-style: italic;
    vertical-align:bottom;
    text-indent: 50;
}
```

Listing 18-6 produces a Panel that has a completely custom appearance, as shown in Figure 18-14.

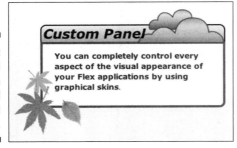

Figure 18-14:
This Panel has custom graphical skinning and CSS styling.

You can do this level of customization only through a combination of both styling and skinning. Styling alone can produce some great-looking results, but it can only get you so far when you want to radically alter the look of the Flex components. By utilizing both the CSS and graphical skinning capabilities of Flex, you can have full control over the visual appearance of your application.

Part VI
The Part of Tens

The 5th Wave   By Rich Tennant

"You ever get the feeling this project could just up and die at any moment?"

In this part . . .

We share ten open-source projects that you can download to enhance your Flex applications. The Flex open-source community is thriving, and new components and libraries are released every day. In Chapter 19, we pick ten projects that we think are especially worth checking out. You can also use many other resources to keep your Flex knowledge up-to-date after finishing this book. Chapter 20 lists ten helpful resources that you should bookmark as you continue using Flex.

Chapter 19

Ten Open-Source Flex Libraries

*T*here's nothing better than getting something for free. A strong open-source Flex community produces some fantastic code that you can freely use in your own applications. So why not grab a few open-source projects and drop them into your Flex application? If someone else has already done the work, there's no reason to reinvent the wheel.

In this chapter, we cover ten open-source projects that you can try using in your Flex applications. This list only scratches the surface of what's available in the Flex community. Use this list as a starting point, but keep in mind that new open-source projects are starting up all the time. (See Chapter 20 for some resources you can use to find more projects.)

FlexLib

```
http://code.google.com/p/flexlib
```

FlexLib is a popular collection of Flex user interface components that you can use in your own Flex applications. Many of the components in FlexLib extend the original controls in the Flex framework and add additional functionality. Here are a couple of examples:

✔ **The PromptingTextInput control:** A simple extension of the normal TextInput control in the Flex framework that adds a prompt message if the text area is empty, as shown in Figure 19-1

✔ **The SuperTabNavigator:** Adds closeable, re-orderable, scrollable tabs to the normal TabNavigator container, which you can see in Figure 19-2

FlexLib also contains a few subprojects, including the Flex Scheduling Framework (which we cover in the following section) and a Multiple Document Interface (MDI) framework. The MDI framework builds on the functionality of TitleWindow, adding features such as minimizing and resizing of windows and cascading and tiled window layouts to help you manage applications that work with multiple windows.

Figure 19-1:
The
Prompting
TextInput
control.

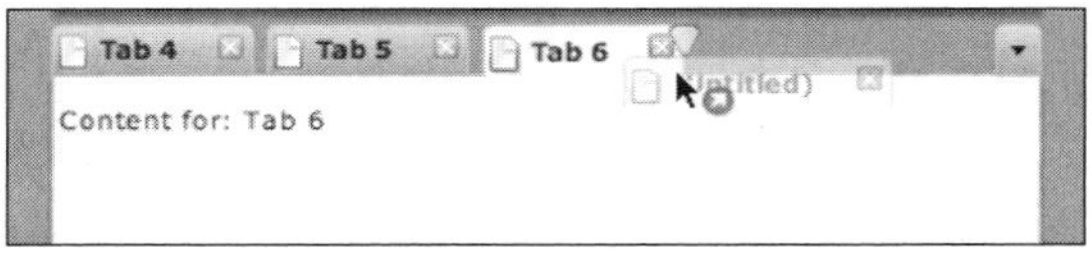

Figure 19-2:
Drag tabs
to reorder
them.

The Flex Scheduling Framework

http://code.google.com/p/flexlib

The *Flex Scheduling Framework* is a set of components that you can use to create calendar-like scheduling applications. For example, you can use the Scheduling Framework to create a reservation application that displays the available time slots for dinner at a restaurant. Figure 19-3 shows an example schedule created by using the framework.

Adobe Consulting created the Flex Scheduling framework and initially hosted it on the Adobe Labs Web site, but the Flex Scheduling framework has since merged with the FlexLib project, which community developers maintain.

Figure 19-3:
A sample
schedule
created
with the
Scheduling
Framework.

Flex Visual Graph Library

http://code.google.com/p/flexvizgraphlib

The *Flex Visual Graph Library* is a data visualization framework that you can use to create complex data diagrams. Fundamentally, you use the Visual Graph Library to draw connections (edges) between items (nodes). You can visualize the connections of a social networking Web site, a diagram of your office's network, or even an organization chart to show hierarchical data. The Library includes multiple layout algorithms that can produce various graph visualizations. Figure 19-4 shows a graph created by using the hierarchical renderer.

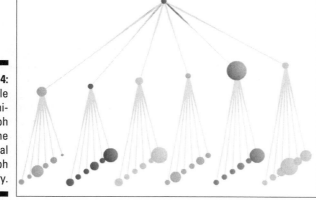

Figure 19-4:
A sample
hierarchi-
cal graph
from the
Flex Visual
Graph
Library.

Degrafa

```
http://degrafa.com
```

You can draw all kinds of complex graphics by using the low-level graphics API built into Flash Player. In fact, almost all the default skinning of the Flex SDK controls is drawn with ActionScript code that uses the graphics API (instead of using embedded image assets). But programmatically drawing complex compositions can be very complicated and burdensome. Degrafa, which stands for **De**clarative **Gra**phics **Fra**mework, solves this problem by letting you use MXML markup to draw graphics, instead of using the ActionScript APIs directly. For example, you can create complex shapes with layered gradient fills with a few lines of MXML code instead of the complex ActionScript code that you would need without the Degrafa library.

OpenFlux

```
http://code.google.com/p/openflux
```

OpenFlux is a Model View Controller (MVC) component framework for Flex UI components that applies the MVC design pattern on a component level (rather than on the application level, like Cairngorm does, which we cover in the section "Cairngorm," later in this chapter). The goal of the OpenFlux project is to define a new core set of Flex components that you can more easily extend and customize than the default Flex components in the Flex SDK. Each component follows the MVC pattern, which means that the view representation of a component is completely separate from the underlying data structure. You can swap out different views for the same component without changing the model or controller of the component.

FlexUnit

```
http://code.google.com/p/as3flexunitlib
```

FlexUnit is a unit-testing framework that helps you build unit tests for your ActionScript code. FlexUnit is modeled after JUnit, a unit-testing framework for Java. So, if you know how to unit test Java code, then you should be able to pick up the FlexUnit syntax fairly easily. If you're not familiar with the term *unit testing,* it is a fundamental principle of Test-Driven Development (TDD) that focuses on developing reliable test cases that ensure your code is working correctly while you develop your application.

Cairngorm

```
http://labs.adobe.com/wiki/index.php/Cairngorm
```

Cairngorm is a lightweight Model View Controller (MVC) *micro-architecture* framework that you can use for Flex application development. The MVC approach to development defines a set of design patterns that clearly separate your application into three main parts:

- ✔ **The model:** Holds all the underlying data in your application
- ✔ **The view:** The user interface that displays the data in the model
- ✔ **The controller:** The business logic that's used behind the scenes to populate the data in the model

Cairngorm provides a framework that specifically applies the MVC pattern to Flex application development. When you start designing larger and more complex Flex applications, you should look into Cairngorm or another MVC framework.

Cairngorm was originally developed by a company called iteration::two, which Adobe bought, creating Adobe Consulting. In case you're ever playing Flex trivia, you should know that Cairngorm is named after a mountain in Scotland (iteration::two was based in Scotland).

Flex-Spy

```
http://code.google.com/p/fxspy
```

Flex-Spy is a visual debugging tool that lets you inspect the properties and styles of any component in your application at runtime. When you include the Flex-Spy library in your application, you can launch the inspector with a keystroke. After the property inspector loads, select any UI component in your application, and a list of all the properties and styles of the component and the current values appears. You can see what the property inspector looks like in Figure 19-5. You can use this valuable tool to understand exactly what's happening while your application is running, without having to jump into the full-fledged Flex Debugger.

Figure 19-5:
The
Flex-Spy
property
inspector.

```
FlexSpy                                                    □ ×
▼ <> <dashboard id="dashboard">          Properties   Styles
     ⇕ <Spacer name="Spacer5">        Filter
   ▼ ⎕ <ApplicationControlBar id="appContro
     ▶ A <Label id="dashboardLabel">      Property        ▲   Value
     ▼ ⊡ <ComboBox id="revTimelineComb     alpha               1          ✎ ▲
        <> <HaloBorder name="HaloBorde      automationName                 ✎
     ▶ ☐ <Button name="Button12">          autoRepeat          false      ✎
     ▶ abc <TextInput name="TextInput1·     baselinePosition    13
     ⇕ <Spacer name="Spacer17">            blendMode           normal     ✎
```

PaperVision 3D, Away 3D, and Sandy 3D

```
http://code.google.com/p/papervision3d
www.away3d.com
www.flashsandy.org
```

This section and the following section cover 3D and physics engines written in ActionScript 3; however, none of the projects covered here are actually Flex projects. ActionScript-only projects don't use the Flex SDK framework. You can still use any ActionScript 3 project in your Flex applications, although you need a bit more technical ActionScript knowledge to figure out how to use these projects within your Flex applications. Even though the 3D and physics packages aren't Flex-specific projects, we include them in this chapter simply because they're amazingly cool and let you create experiences that push the boundaries of Web-based applications.

Some of the most cutting-edge Flex development has started to integrate 3D interfaces and effects, which produces some amazing visual results. Flash Player itself doesn't have any built-in 3D support (although some of that is coming in Flash Player 10), but developers in the Flash community have created a number of 3D engines. PaperVision 3D and Away 3D are related but separate projects. Both started from the same code-base and have since diverged into two distinct 3D engines. Sandy 3D has a longer history and started as an ActionScript 2 3D engine, which has since been ported to ActionScript 3 for continued development. All three of the main ActionScript 3 3D engines have similar capabilities and allow you to develop full 3D inter-active scenes.

An example of combining a 3D engine (in this case, PaperVision) and normal Flex components is shown in Figure 19-6.

Figure 19-6:
A 3D Flex
inter-
face that
uses the
PaperVision
3D engine.

APE and Box 2D

```
www.cove.org/ape
http://box2dflash.sourceforge.net
```

The other set of ActionScript 3 (not Flex-specific) libraries that we talk about in this chapter are physics engines. You can use these physics engines to add realistic physics simulations to your Flex applications. Game programmers often use these engines when they create games, but you don't have to limit the physics to gaming.

One of the earliest physics libraries was the ActionScript Physics Engine (APE), which lets you create a simulation of circular physics particles that can bounce off each other in a realistic manner. A few more recent physics engines add rigid bodies to the mix, so you can use polygons of any shape in the simulation. Box2D is a port of a physics engine of the same name originally written in C++.

We mention both physics and 3D libraries in this chapter to try to show that you can use all the fancy, cutting-edge ActionScript 3 libraries in your Flex applications, even if the original developers wrote the libraries primarily for Flash developers. You can use anything written in ActionScript 3 when you develop Flex applications, so if you think creatively, you can make some jaw-dropping applications.

Chapter 20

Ten Flex Resources

Now that you've begun your Flex development, you're part of the rich, robust, and active Flex community. As a Flex developer, you can take advantage of many Flex resources, both online and in the real world, that can sharpen your Flex skills and offer great tips and tricks for your application development. This chapter discusses those resources and how you can take advantage of them to better your Flex development experience.

flexcoders Yahoo! Group

When Flex 1.0 shipped, Adobe started a Yahoo! Groups mailing list dedicated to answering questions posed by the Flex community. At the time, the Flex community was small. Adobe engineers on the Flex team answered most of the posts themselves. This Yahoo! Group, called flexcoders, is still active, featuring hundreds of useful postings every day.

Anyone can submit a posting on flexcoders. Usually, you submit a question, and in time, other Flex developers reply to the message thread to answer the question. Flex domain experts, as well as engineers directly working on the Adobe Flex team, often answer questions posted on flexcoders. You usually get the highest-quality answers from this group of individuals. (We should know — we're both common posters to flexcoders, answering community questions!) Of course, anyone can answer a question on flexcoders, so dedicated Flex developers of any caliber answer questions. In addition to posting technical questions to flexcoders, people often post random Flex polls, commentary on the Flex community or the status of Flex, and calls to conferences and Flex community events.

Please be courteous when posting questions and answers to the flexcoders mailing list. Everyone who answers questions on the list is doing so voluntarily. Even the Adobe engineers who are active on the list are acting out of their own personal interest — it is not part of their job. If your question isn't answered right away, you might need to provide further clarification to explain your problem, or it might simply be that nobody knows the answer. Also, try searching the archives of the list before you post because many common questions have already been answered.

To subscribe to flexcoders visit `http://tech.groups.yahoo.com/group/flexcoders/`. After you have subscribed, you can post a question to the list by sending an e-mail to `flexcoders@yahoogroups.com`. To answer questions from other Flex developers posted to flexcoders, join the mailing list and reply to the e-mail threads to answer away!

Flex Developer Center

You can find a wealth of Flex knowledge at the Flex Developer Center (`www.adobe.com/devnet/flex/`). The Flex Developer Center is part of the Adobe Developer Connection and contains many technical articles and white papers about the Flex technology that you, as a Flex developer, may find very useful. Additionally, the Flex Developer Center hosts the Flex Cookbook, which contains easy-to-digest code snippets and tutorials that describe common Flex workflows, such as creating item renderers and custom ToolTips, and sorting a DataGrid in ActionScript. You can find the Flex Cookbook at `www.adobe.com/go/flex_cookbook`.

The Adobe Developer Connection has so much information that you might want to use the search utilities provided on the home page so that you can search the site for the information you need. You can use the keyword search to pull up information ranging from small code snippets all the way to large scale, multi-page whitepapers on various Flex topics. Adobe engineers, as well as non-Adobe third-party engineers and leading thinkers, write the Adobe Developer Connection content.

Flex User Groups

User Groups (UGs) allow like-minded developers working on common technologies to meet in person weekly or monthly to share ideas, tips, and tutorials; put faces to names; and, in general, empower and strengthen their respective development community. Flex User Groups exist in most metropolitan areas and meet, usually monthly, to share Flex development tips, conduct basic Flex training, and invite speakers from Flex or related technologies to speak to the group.

You can use two lists to find out if a Flex User Group exists in your vicinity and get the details on when and where it meets. First, try visiting http://flex.org/community/ to view a map of the user groups specifically devoted to Flex. Adobe also keeps an additional list of all user groups for all Adobe technology at www.adobe.com/cfusion/usergroups. Both of these resources provide the contact details and User Group home page, which should have more details about past meetings, dates for future meetings, and agendas.

We're both regulars at the Silicon Valley Flex User Group meeting and can attest to the breadth of knowledge and the feeling of community that permeate all Flex User Groups. We both encourage you to see if a user group meets in your area and try to attend a meeting so that you can become part of the Flex community. And if you're ever in San Francisco, see if our local user group is meeting (check www.silvafug.org) and come and say hello.

Flex Interface Guidelines

As most developers can attest, having a visual designer to help with the overall visual aesthetics of your Flex application can really improve the overall quality of the application. Many projects don't have designers, and Flex developers often have to wear both the developer hat and the designer hat. Adobe took a step toward helping developers in these situations by publishing a document titled The Flex Interface Guidelines (FIG), which highlights very common and useful design patterns that you can use in your application to improve the usability and general experience of navigating through the application. You can find the FIG document, as well as Flex components and code that highlight these design patterns, at the Flex Developer Center by visiting www.adobe.com/devnet/flex/ and clicking Flex Interface Guide.

The FIG highlights some common design patterns, such as how to add animation and movement to your application in a useful and not "busy" way. FIG also details similar patterns related to application navigation, ToolTip and callout management, and cursor management. It explains what Flex controls to use and how to configure them so that you can achieve the desired design pattern. Check out the FIG documents and code examples if you want to add some usable and clean visual design patterns to your Flex development.

Flex Blogs

With the number of Flex developers growing and the wealth of their knowledge increasing dramatically, many Flex developers (both internal and external to Adobe) have taken to sharing Flex information on their blogs. These blogs often contain critical information about workarounds on existing bugs in the Flex framework, workflow improvement tips, performance and memory management tips, and general thought-provoking questions about Flex, the future of Flex, and the Flex community.

A handy resource for finding valuable Flex blogs is Adobe's blog aggregator service (originally referred to as MXNA for Macromedia XML News Aggregator, but now known as AXNA after the Adobe acquisition). This service collects blogs related to any Adobe technology, such as Flex, and posts them to a central Web site. To query Adobe's blog aggregator service, go to `http://feeds.adobe.com`. On the aggregator site, you can browse and search blog entries on various Adobe topics, such as Flex, Air, or Photoshop, as well as use the keyword search on the right sidebar of the site to search for blog entries related to a particular topic. You can find a wealth of information stored in personal and professional Flex blogs, and this aggregator gives you a handy resource for accessing and viewing these blog entries.

While exploring the Adobe blog aggregator, you may notice that we both have our own Flex blogs in which we post tips and tricks, code snippets, Flex components, and general Flex commentary. The Flex community reads and respects both blogs, and you may want to check them out. Here are our blog site URLs:

- **Deepa Subramaniam:** `www.iamdeepa.com/blog`
- **Doug McCune:** `www.dougmccune.com/blog`

Open-Source Adobe Site

When Flex 3 shipped, Adobe Flex officially went open source. As part of this effort, Adobe created a Web site that held all the open-source information related to Flex, including nightly development builds of Flex, timelines and documents related to future releases of Flex, links to the Flex source code, and instructions on how to download and build Flex from the source code. When you advance in your Flex development, you may want to visit this site to find more information about Flex or submit your own code patches to the open-source Flex effort. You can find all the information you need about open-source Flex, as well as other open-source Adobe technologies, at `http://opensource.adobe.com`.

Flex Conferences

You can find many high-quality Flex conferences around the world where you can meet other Flex community members and find out more about the advanced technical aspects of Flex. Many of these conferences focus solely on Flex, but others incorporate information about Flash and other related Adobe (and non-Adobe) technologies. You may find Adobe's MAX conference and 360 | Flex conferences worth checking out because of their breadth and quality.

MAX

The yearly MAX conference is Adobe's user conference. This conference usually takes place in the fall in North America, Japan, and Europe. It's the largest conference that Adobe officially organizes. It involves talks and seminars about all Adobe technologies and often focuses heavily on Flex, as well as the Flash and AIR technologies. Speakers include many Adobe product-engineering team members (like Deepa!), as well as industry speakers who've proven their breadth of knowledge in their particular field. To find out more about MAX, when and where it's occurring, planned agendas, speaker lists, and details about past Adobe conferences, you can visit Adobe's MAX homepage at `http://max.adobe.com/`.

360\Flex

360 | Flex was the world's first conference to focus solely on Flex. These conferences happen all over the world, from San Jose to Milan. Speakers at the 360 | Flex conferences usually include some Adobe engineers and technical evangelists, as well as many leading Flex developers from the industry. The 360 | Flex conferences provide a great venue for Flex developers to meet face to face, exchange ideas and knowledge, and even get hired! Both of us have spoken extensively at 360 | Flex conferences, and we think they're some of the best Flex conferences out there. 360 | Flex conferences have abnormally low attendance fees when compared to other conferences because the event organizers strive to keep costs low and maintainable. To find out more about past and upcoming 360 | Flex conferences, visit `www.360flex.com`.

Flex.org

When Flex 2.0 released, Adobe decided to sponsor a Web site that consolidated various Flex-related information, such as technical articles, conference information, forum mailing lists, and third-party open-source works. This Web site became Flex.org (`www.flex.org`). The site has links to other Flex-related resources by both Adobe and community developers. Flex.org also serves as a great starting point for people new to the Flex technology family because it offers many small articles that describe what Flex is and how it relates to other technologies in the Rich Internet Application (RIA) development space, and it also includes a terminology guide. If you're new to Flex or helping someone on your team get up to speed, Flex.org is a great starting point to begin your exploration.

Public Flex Bugbase

Prior to the Flex 3 release, Adobe announced that the Flex SDK was going to be open-sourced (at this point, the Flex SDK was already free software). As part of this open-source movement, Adobe released an open bugbase for Flex in which anyone can file new bugs, check on the status of existing bugs, and vote on bugs as a way to indicate their priority when Adobe fixes bugs for the next release. You can access the public Flex bugbase at `http://bugs.adobe.com/flex`.

This bugbase is based on JIRA. (*JIRA* is a common technology used to host and serve bugbases.) Anyone can search the bugbase for all the filed bugs, although you get more functionality (such as being able to file new bugs or edit existing bugs to add comments) if you have a bugbase account. To create a bugbase account, follow the New User instructions at the site.

When you go forward with your Flex development, you'll probably want to report a bug or file an enhancement request for the technology at some point, and the public bugbase allows you to do this in an open and transparent manner that helps the entire Flex community.

flexjobs Yahoo! Group

Similar to the Group discussed in the section "flexcoders Yahoo! Group," earlier in this chapter, Adobe created a Yahoo! Group for job postings related to Flex and Flash. People looking for Flex contract work subscribe to this Group (`http://tech.groups.yahoo.com/group/flexjobs/`), as do people looking to hire Flex developers. If you're a Flex developer interested in finding contract or full-time work, or you want to hire Flex developers for a project, flexjobs is one of your best bets. Many talented Flex developers monitor the list looking for exciting and interesting possibilities, and you can get your work and talents in the public Flex eye.

Index